LIFE IN

non-sto

1960s

▪ News ▪ Football ▪ TV ▪ Cinema ▪ Pop Music
▪ Cars ▪ Beer ▪ Cigarettes

A Chronicle of Memories.

Ian Palmer

First edition published 2024

Gift Book For Dad
Rugeley
Staffordshire

ISBN 978-1-840-41037-2

The information in this book has been compiled from numerous sources over many years. The final text is arranged as a chronological review, designed to evoke memories of a time long past and to aid study of that era. This book describes events and popular culture from a particular time in history and reflects the values of those times. Readers might find some of the material offensive when judged by modern day standards.

All phrases, slogans and lyrics quoted are for study and review purposes.

The author and publisher cannot be held responsible for any errors or inaccuracies.

One or two fictional snippets may have been added for devilment.

Christmas 1959

The Age of the (M1) Motorway

Monarch:	Queen Elizabeth II (aged 33)
Prime-minister:	Harold Macmillan (aged 65)
Chancellor:	Derick Heathcoat-Amory (aged 60)
Home Secretary:	Rab Butler (aged 57)
Foreign Secretary:	Selwyn Lloyd (aged 55)
Football Manager:	Walter Winterbottom (aged 46)

▪ Families sit huddled together in small living rooms, on black, leatherette three-piece suites ▪ Bill Bruce presents the weather forecast on BBC television ▪ Storms batter Britain, leading to flash-floods and damaged buildings ▪ Temperatures remain mild ▪ 'You Roared at Carry On Sergeant! Howled at Carry On Nurse! You'll be Convulsed by -' *Carry On Teacher* goes on general release at picture houses, with 54-year-old Ted Ray playing the role of the headmaster and featuring 15-year-old Richard Sullivan as a schoolboy. Also appearing in the movie are: 41-year-old Kenneth Connor, 45-year-old Charles Hawtrey, 33-year-old Kenneth Williams, 35-year-old Leslie Phillips, 29-year-old Joan Sims and 37-year-old Hattie Jacques ▪ 44-year-old Norman Wisdom is pictured on the front cover of the latest edition of *TV Times* - available now at newsagents for fourpence ▪ "Happy talk, keep talking happy talk" - the LP soundtrack to Rodgers & Hammerstein's *South Pacific* (containing the song ***Happy Talk***) has been number one in the album chart for a year ▪ "Got no bags and baggage to slow me down" - ***Travellin' Light*** by 19-year-old Cliff Richard and the Shadows remains at number one in the singles chart ▪ 48-year-old Winifred Atwell from Trinidad reaches number ten with the popular medley ***Piano Party*** (comprising of the songs: *Baby Face, Comin' Thru' The Rye, Annie Laurie, Little Brown Jug, Let Him Go Let Him Tarry, Put Your Arms Around Me Honey, I'll Be With You In Apple Blossom Time, Sine On Harvest*

Moon, Blue Skies, I'll Never Say Never Again and *I'll See You In My Dreams*) ▪ The Quarrymen (a little-known skiffle group - comprising of: 19-year-old John Lennon, 18-year-old Paul McCartney and 16-year-old George Harrison) perform as Johnny and the Moondogs at a talent show in Liverpool ▪ 19-year-old Ringo Starr plays drums for Rory Storm and the Hurricanes ▪ 26-year-old army officer, businessman and parliamentary candidate Michael Hestletine enjoys an evening at the cinema ▪ *Tarzan's Greatest Adventure* (with 33-year-old Gordon Scott) is now showing ▪ Noisy schoolboys spend Saturday mornings in the stalls at the local *Odeon* ▪ 26-year-old Chelo Alonso (35-22-35) draws wolf-whistles and suggestive cheers from the young male audience as she stars alongside 40-year-old Lex Barker in *The Pirate and the Slave Girl* ▪ 13-year-old schoolboy David Suchet from London sits in his bedroom reading *Cat Among The Pigeons* - the latest 'whodunit' novel (featuring Belgian detective Hercule Poirot) from 69-year-old crime-writer Agatha Christie ▪ 'Good Boy' - *Love Hearts* (sweets) from Swizzels are enjoyed by many ▪ ***Put Your Head On My Shoulder*** ("... Hold me in your arms, baby") by 18-year-old Paul Anka is number seven on the hit parade ▪ "She comes on like a rose, but everybody knows, she'll get you in Dutch. You can look but you better not touch..." ***Poison Ivy*** by The Coasters is number fifteen ▪ The new three-lane M1 'national road' motorway is proving to be a great success ▪ 45-year-old Ernie Watkins from Towcester gets up to 73 mph in his new Triumph *Herald* ▪ The Midland Red company's supercharged express coach carries passengers between Birmingham and London in under three hours ▪ 33-year-old Jack Brabham pushes his Cooper-Climax racing car over the finish line at the USA Grand Prix to secure three points and pip British drivers Tony Brooks and Stirling Moss to the title of World Motor Racing Champion ▪ 25-year-old motorcycle racer John Surtees is BBC's 'Sports Personality of the Year' - after winning the

500cc world title for the third time in four years ▪ 22-year-old Manchester Utd footballer Bobby Charlton is runner-up ▪ ***What Do You Want*** ("... if you don't want money? What do you want if you don't want gold?") by 19-year-old Adam Faith from Acton climbs to number one on the hit parade ▪ ***Teen Beat*** (a drum based instrumental) by 21-year-old Sandy Nelson is number nine ▪ Conservative prime-minister Harold Macmillan considers the future of Commonwealth countries from within the African continent - many of which are now seeking independence from Britain ▪ MI6 boss Sir Dick White meets with his MI5 counterpart, Roger Hollis ▪ The security of the nation is in jeopardy ▪ Espionage is being conducted by the most unlikely people ▪ 54-year-old Harry Houghton and his lover, 45-year-old Ethel 'Bunty' Gee, steal 'top secret' military information from the Admiralty Underwater Weapons Establishment at Portland in Dorset ▪ Respectable married couple 46-year-old Lona Cohen and 49-year-old Morris Cohen pass on classified information to the USSR from a secret radio room in the basement of their bungalow at 45 Cranley Drive in Ruislip ▪ 37-year-old double-agent George Blake meets his KGB contact in Berlin and hands over 'top secret' Defence information ▪ Spy comedy *Our Man in Havana* (starring 45-year-old Alec Guinness, 60-year-old Noel Coward and 39-year-old Maureen O'Hara) goes on general release at cinemas ▪ 'There's music, laughter, colour and thrills in...' *Tommy the Toreador* is also now showing - with 23-year-old Tommy Steele, 25-year-old Janet Munro, 46-year-old Sid James and 30-year-old Bernard Cribbins ▪ "Once upon a time there was a little white bull. Very sad because he was a little white bull. (A little white bull)" - ***Little White Bull*** by Tommy Steele reaches number six in the pop chart ▪ ***Little Donkey*** ("... Little donkey, on the dusty road. Gotta keep on plodding onward with your precious load") by The Beverley Sisters is number fourteen ▪ Leo the Lion roars twice at the start of Metro

Goldwyn Mayer's latest Hollywood blockbuster, *Ben Hur* - with 36-year-old Charlton Heston and 49-year-old Jack Hawkins ▪ 'The master of suspense weaves his greatest tale!' - 55-year-old Cary Grant, 35-year-old Eva Marie Saint and 50-year-old James Mason star in Alfred Hitchcock's latest thriller, *North by Northwest* ▪ 'Johnny never had it so good - or lost it so fast!' - 31-year-old Laurence Harvey plays Johnny Jackson, alongside 19-year-old Cliff Richard as Bongo Herbert and 25-year-old Sylvia Sims as Maisie King, in *Expresso Bongo* - a new movie directed by 48-year-old Val Guest ▪ ***The Expresso Bongo EP*** by Cliff Richard and the Shadows reaches number fourteen in the pop chart ▪ ***Seven Little Girls Sitting In The Back Seat*** ("… huggin' and a-kissin' with Fred") by The Avons is number eight ▪ 'Cherr-cherr-cuff. Cherr-cherr-cuff' - children watch *Ivor the Engine* on television; a wonderful new animation from 34-year-old Oliver Postgate and 31-year-old Peter Firmin ▪ "Perhaps this year more of us could remember the true Christmas message, and also do some small thing for those who are less fortunate than ourselves" - 34-year-old MP for Finchley Margaret Thatcher delivers an inspirational, heart warming and selfless thought to her constituents ▪ Only 210 million tonnes of coal have been mined in Britain this year - down by 10 million compared to 1958 ▪ Men and boys hurry along to football matches and stand together on packed terraces ▪ 26-year-old striker Dennis Viollet bags a hat-trick for Matt Busby's Manchester Utd in a 5-1 win over Billy Walker's Nottingham Forest at Old Trafford ▪ 28-year-old striker Jimmy McIlroy scores twice for Harry Potts' Burnley in a 4-0 win over Bill Riddings' Bolton Wanderers at Turf Moor ▪ 22-year-old striker Les Allen leaves Chelsea and joins Bill Nicholson's top-of-the-table Tottenham Hotspur for a fee of £20,000 ▪ 24-year-old Sheffield Wednesday goalkeeper Ron Springett makes his debut for England - and saves a penalty in a 2-1 victory over Northern Ireland at Wembley. England's full line-up for the match is: R Springett, D Howe, A Allen, Clayton, Brown, Flowers, Connelly, Haynes, Baker, Parry and Holiday ▪ Schoolboys visit newsagents to buy *Tiger* - the 'sport and adventure picture story weekly' - for fourpence and keep up to date with the exciting adventures of footballer Roy Race and his Melchester Rovers team-mates ▪ "So..." ***What Do You Want To Make Those Eyes At Me For*** ("... if they don't mean what they say. They make me glad. They make me sad. They make me want a lot of things that I never had") by Emile Ford and the Checkmates is new at number one in the weekly pop chart ▪ ***Among My Souvenirs*** by 21-year-old Connie Francis reaches number eleven ▪ Families come together at Christmas ▪ Boys play with *Corgi* cars - and send them speeding over the lino ▪ Girls play with 'Little Beauty' dolls and dress them in colourful frocks ▪ The life story of 31-year-old Bruce Forsyth (host of *Sunday Night At The London Palladium*) features in the *TV Times* ▪ "Goodnight, all" - 64-year-old Jack Warner plays the title role in *Dixon of Dock Green* on BBC television on Saturday evenings ▪ Two-thirds of households in the UK now have a television set ▪ The latest Decca 17-inch model (with twin speakers, glide-away doors and a turntable stand) costs 78 guineas 'tax paid' ▪ "Oh Carol, I am but a fool. Darling I love you, though you treat me cruel" - ***Oh Carol*** by 20-year-old Neil Sedaka is new at number three on the hit parade ▪ "Jingle bell, jingle bell..." ***Jingle Bell Rock*** ("... Jingle bells swing and jingle bells ring") by 37-year-old Max Bygraves is number seven ▪ Adverts say, 'Have plenty of *Babycham* at home this Christmas - the genuine Champagne Perry' ▪ People in pubs all across the country raise a glass on New Year's Eve to toast in the 1960s ▪ A pint of Watney's *Red Barrel* costs 1s/10d.

New Year 1960

Wind of Change

Monarch:	Queen Elizabeth II (aged 33)
Prime-minister:	Harold Macmillan (aged 66)
Chancellor:	Derick Heathcoat-Amory (aged 60)
Home Secretary:	Rab Butler (aged 57)
Foreign Secretary:	Selwyn Lloyd (aged 55)
Football Manager:	Walter Winterbottom (aged 46)

▪ A swinging new decade begins ▪ 'The best of today's 'pop' entertainment' - 31-year-old Brian Matthew introduces *Saturday Club* on BBC radio's Light Programme ▪ ***What Do You Want To Make Those Eyes At Me For*** ("... if they don't mean what they say") by 22-year-old Emile Ford and the Checkmates remains at number one on the hit parade ▪ ***What Do You Want*** ("... if you don't want money") by 19-year-old Adam Faith is number two ▪ ***Seven Little Girls Sitting In The Back Seat*** ("... huggin' and a-kissin' with Fred") by The Avons moves up to number three ▪ 19-year-old bass player Stuart Sutcliffe joins 19-year-old John Lennon, 17-year-old Paul McCartney and 16-year-old George Harrison in The Quarrymen - a little-known skiffle group, based in Liverpool ▪ 29-year-old footballer Len White bags a hat-trick as Newcastle Utd thrash Manchester Utd 7-3 in front of 57,200 spectators at St. James' Park ▪ The weather is inclement ▪ 49-year-old Hugh Greene OBE takes up his new role as Director General of the BBC ▪ 49-year-old Mrs. E. R. Whitehouse enjoys a nice cup of tea at her home in rural Worcestershire ▪ Families gather together in living-rooms to watch the evening news (read by 35-year-old Kenneth Kendall) on rented *Rediffusion* television sets ▪ Prime-minister Harold Macmillan travels to Africa and makes a speech from Cape Town. The 65-year-old declares that a 'Wind of Change' is blowing across the great African continent and that British colonies could soon become independent ▪ England's cricketers are on tour in the West Indies. 28-year-old fast bowler 'fiery' Fred Trueman takes 5 wickets for just 35 runs in a Test Match victory in Port of Spain ▪ Back in England - racial discrimination in the workplace is commonplace ▪ The Bristol Omnibus Company operates a 'colour bar' policy - refusing to consider black people for job roles at the company. Only white staff are taken on as drivers or conductors ▪ Millions of television viewers enjoy BBC's *The Black and White Minstrel Show* (with 41-year-old Kenneth Connor as Master of Ceremonies) ▪ Rochdale Football Club's manager, 33-year-old Tony Collins, celebrates as his team beats Doncaster Rovers 2-0 in Division Four ▪ 17-year-old Billy Bremner makes his debut for Leeds Utd in a 1-3 victory over Chelsea in Division One ▪ "Why am I so starry eyed, starry eyed and mystified? Every time I look at you, falling stars come into view" - ***Starry Eyed*** by 35-year-old Michael Holliday moves up to number one on the hit parade ▪ "Oooo-oooh, oooo-oooo-oooh. Thought I was in love before, and then you moved in next-door. Pretty blue eyes..." ***Pretty Blue Eyes*** by 18-year-old Craig Douglas from the Isle of Wight climbs to number four ▪ ***Staccato's Theme*** by Elmer Bernstein also peaks at number four ▪ 34-year-old Peter Sellers is 'Dodger' and 56-year-old Wilfrid Hyde White is 'Soapy' in *Two Way Stretch* - a prison caper comedy now showing at cinemas ▪ 11-year-old Dennis Waterman features in *Night Train to Inverness* - a short B-movie ▪ Noisy schoolboys spend Saturday mornings in the stalls at the local *Gaumont* ▪ 'New Tarzan finds Forgotten Worlds of Adventure!' - 25-year-old Denny Miller stars as Tarzan, and 25-year-old Joanne Barnes is Jane, in *Tarzan the Ape Man* ▪ 'Excitement ... Danger ... Suspense' - 22-year-old James MacArthur stars as David Balfour in *Kidnapped* ▪ 'Well-to-do' families book their summer holidays abroad ▪ An eight day break on the Costa Brava (travelling by rail) costs 17 guineas ▪ A fifteen day break on Menorca (travelling by air) costs 36 guineas ▪ The Cold War between East and West continues ▪ Talks between Soviet leader Nikita Khrushchev and US president Dwight D. Eisenhower are not going well - and tensions between the two world powers look set to remain for some time ▪ ***Heartaches By The Number*** ("... troubles by the score. Everyday you love me less, each day I love you more") by 32-year-old Guy Mitchell is number five in the pop chart ▪ "Move 'em on, head 'em up. Head 'em up, move 'em on. Move 'em on, head 'em up..." ***Rawhide*** by 46-year-old Frankie Laine is number six ▪ The electric guitar / saxophone instrumental ***Beatnik Fly*** by Johnny and the Hurricanes is number fourteen ▪ 33-year-old Queen Elizabeth II gives birth to her third child - a son named Andrew Albert Christian Edward ▪ A *Rimmel* deodrant stick costs just 1s/3d at chemists - and masks the odours of perspiration ▪ The 'Margherita' pizza is a speciality at the *Olivelli* restaurant in Bloomsbury ▪ In the House of Commons, prime-minister Harold Macmillan proposes a motion of 'good wishes' to the Royal family on the birth of the new baby prince ▪ 53-year-old Labour leader Hugh Gaitskell and 46-year-old Liberal leader Jo Grimond also send their messages of congratulation to Buckingham Palace ▪ "My darling, forgive me, I yearn for your touch. Have pity, come back now, I need you so much" - ***A Voice In The Wilderness*** by Cliff Richard and the Shadows is number two on the hit parade ▪ "I'll never let you go. Why? Because I love you" - ***Why*** by 28-year-old Anthony Newley climbs to number one - and stays there for four weeks ▪ "Look, it's Count Moriarty giving chase in the tobacco powered ground Zeppelin. Full speed in all directions!" - Peter Sellers is Bloodnok, Harry Secombe is Seagoon and Spike Milligan is both Eccles and Moriarty in the final edition of the *Goon Show* - broadcast on BBC Home Service Radio ▪ 'The Hilarious 'Carry On' Shower in Another Riot of Laughter!' - 29-year-old Joan Sims and 46-year-old Sid James star at cinemas in new comedy film *Carry On Constable* ▪ 54-year-old Ted Ray, 35-year-old Leslie Phillips and

19-year-old Julia Lockwood star in *Please Turn Over* ▪ 44-year-old Norman Wisdom and 28-year-old June Laverick star in *Follow a Star* ▪ 22-year-old dancer Norma Arnould appears on the front cover of *Parade and Blighty* - a weekly paper on sale for sixpence every Monday ▪ "I don't know what to tell you…" ***When You Ask About Love*** by The Crickets is number twenty-seven in the pop chart ▪ The *J. Lyons & Co* teashop on Moorgate Street in London closes down ▪ 26-year-old gangster Reginald Kray is sentenced to eighteen months imprisonment for demanding money with menaces ▪ "All the people down the street, whoever you meet, say I'm a bad boy. Say I'm a bad boy, say I'm a..." ***Bad Boy*** by 20-year-old Marty Wilde reaches number seven in the pop chart ▪ "Oh, yeah, yeah, yeah. Ain't it wonderful..." ***We Got Love*** by 27-year-old Alma Cogan stalls at number twenty-six ▪ Officials from Clarence House in London announce the engagement of the Queen's sister, 29-year-old Princess Margaret, and 29-year-old commoner Antony Armstrong-Jones ▪ 25-year-old Elvis Presley is promoted to the rank of sergeant in the US Army - while serving in West Germany ▪ Back in England - men go to the pub on Friday nights and watch football matches on Saturday afternoons ▪ Graham's *Golden Lager* is now called *Skol* ▪ 22-year-old Bobby Charlton scores a hat-trick for Matt Busby's Manchester Utd in a 6-0 win over Blackpool ▪ 26-year-old Eddie Thomas scores a hat-trick for Johnny Carey's Everton in a 6-1 win over Nottingham Forest ▪ Harry Potts' Burnley are flying high in Division One ▪ 21-year-old John Connelly and 20-year-old Ian Lawson both score twice as Burnley thrash West Ham Utd 2-5 at Upton Park ▪ Two weeks later, 20-year-old Jimmy Robson scores twice as 'The Clarets' defeat Chelsea 2-1 at Turf Moor ▪ 46-year-old Bill Shankly is the new manager of Division Two side Liverpool ▪ Fifty-thousand people turn out at Vale Park to see an FA Cup tie between Third Division Port Vale and Second Division Aston Villa - the home team loses 1-2 ▪ ***Summer Set*** by Mr. Acker Bilk and his Paramount Jazz

Band is number five in the pop chart ▪ "Look at me, I'm as helpless as a kitten up a tree" - ***Misty*** by 24-year-old Johnny Mathis is number twelve ▪ BBC TV programmes on a Saturday night include: *Juke Box Jury* - with 33-year-old David Jacobs; *Dixon of Dock Green* - starring 64-year-old Jack Warner; *Laramie* - a 'Western' adventure; *The Billy Cotton Band Show*; and *Sports Special* - introduced by 39-year-old Kenneth Wolstenholme ▪ Twenty million people watch *Sunday Night At The London Palladium* on ATV when 19-year-old Cliff Richard is the headline star ▪ 'The Wackiest, Slap-Happiest, Rollicking Laughter Riot!' - 36-year-old Brian Rix and 52-year-old William Hartnell star at cinemas in *And the Same to You* - now showing on a double-bill, along with 39-year-old Jimmy Edwards in *Bottoms Up!* ▪ 46-year-old Peter Cushing and 40-year-old Donald Pleasance star in *The Flesh and the Fiends* - a horror movie based on the 19th century story of grave robbers Burke and Hare ▪ 11-year-old schoolboy John Cooper Clarke works as a bookie's runner in Salford ▪ Young American singers feature in the British pop charts ▪ ***On A Slow Boat To China*** by 22-year-old Emile Ford and the Checkmates climbs from number twenty-one to number six ▪ ***La Mer (Beyond The Sea)*** by 22-year-old Bobby Darin climbs from number fifteen to number eight ▪ "Well..." ***Way Down Yonder In New Orleans*** ("... in the land of the dreamy scenes, there's a garden of Eden. Ah! You know what I mean") by 19-year-old Freddy Cannon is new at number three ▪ Young American popstars travel to Britain to play rock 'n' roll shows in London ▪ 25-year-old Gene Vincent and 21-year-old Eddie Cochran perform to excited audiences at the Granada club in Woolwich ▪ Middle-class people throw dinner parties for their friends ▪ Small cubes of cheese and pineapple are 'speared' on wooden cocktail sticks ▪ Smirnoff Vodka is a popular tipple ▪ Adverts for ginger ale say, 'Canada Dry lets the spirit live'.

Spring 1960

My Old Man's a Dustman

Monarch:	Queen Elizabeth II (aged 34)
Prime-minister:	Harold Macmillan (aged 66)
Chancellor:	Derick Heathcoat-Amory (aged 60)
Home Secretary:	Rab Butler (aged 57)
Foreign Secretary:	Selwyn Lloyd (aged 55)
Football Manager:	Walter Winterbottom (aged 47)

▪ 'It's a fact! The working man has never before been offered a really comfortable boot - Dr. Marten's *AirWair* boots 'With Bouncing Soles' go on sale ▪ 'Rough, tough, deeply moving' - 36-year-old Richard 'Dicky' Attenborough stars at cinemas in *The Angry Silence* ▪ 26-year-old Sylvia Syms stars in *Conspiracy of Hearts* ▪ 35-year-old Tony Hancock and 46-year-old Sid James feature in a brand new series of *Hancock's Half Hour* on BBC television on Friday evenings ▪ 'Wakey! Wakey!' - *The Billy Cotton Band Show* (with 60-year-old band-leader Billy Cotton and 50-year-old singer Alan Breeze) is broadcast at 7.50 p.m. on Saturday evenings ▪ 'Hip' American pop stars, 23-year-old Bobby Darin and 21-year-old Duane Eddy, visit Britain for the first time, playing concerts at the Empire Theatre in Liverpool ▪ 25-year-old Gene Vincent and 21-year-old Eddie Cochran perform at the Manchester Hippodrome ▪ The Quarrymen (a little-known skiffle group from Liverpool) perform in front of a small audience at the Casbah Club on Hayman's Green, West Derby ▪ Elvis Presley is discharged from the US Army after completing two years of military service. The 25-year-old returns home to America from a base in West Germany ▪ 33-year-old Queen Elizabeth II welcomes 69-year-old president Charles de Gaulle of France on an official state visit to Britain ▪ 23-year-old footballer George Eastham goes on strike after his club, Newcastle Utd, refuse his request for a transfer ▪ "Poor me. Wa-a-ha-a-ho" - ***Poor Me*** by 19-year-old Adam Faith is new at number one on the hit parade ▪ "Fall in love, fall in love..." ***Fall In Love With You*** by Cliff Richard and the Shadows is number two ▪ 56-year-old Michael Brooke plays records 'Just For You' on BBC radio's Light Programme ▪ The soundtrack to Rodgers & Hammerstein's *South Pacific* is knocked off top spot in the LP chart (after holding the position for more than a year) by a new twelve-inch called *The Explosive Freddy Cannon* ▪ 41-year-old terrorist Nelson Mandela is leader of the armed wing of the African National Congress in South Africa ▪ Back in England - the first ever televised Grand National is won by thirteen to two favourite *Merryman II.* 22-year-old Gerry Scott is the winning jockey, riding to victory with a broken collar bone ▪ 19-year-old footballer Johnny Giles scores his first goal for Manchester Utd as Matt Busby's team defeats Fulham 0-5 in Division One. Alex Dawson, Mark Pearson and 26-year-old Dennis Viollet (2) are also on the score-sheet for Utd ▪ 18-year-old right-winger Ian Callaghan makes his debut for Liverpool as Bill Shankly's team beats Bristol Rovers 4-0 in Division Two. Jimmy Melia, Bobby Campbell, Roger Hunt and 25-year-old Alan A'Court score the goals for 'The Reds' ▪ The Quarrymen (a little-known skiffle group from Liverpool) change their name to The Silver Beetles and recruit 28-year-old Tommy Moore as drummer ▪ 8-year-old David Bartram listens to records in the front room of his parents' house in Leicester ▪ "You don't drive a big fast car. You don't look like a movie star, and on your money we won't get far, but baby..." ***You Got What It Takes*** by 21-year-old Marv Johnson peaks at number seven in the pop chart. Another version of the same song by Johnny Kidd and the Pirates stalls at number twenty-five ▪ 'Hip' American pop star Eddie Cochran completes a rock'n'roll show at the Hippodrome in Bristol, before taking a late night ride (along with his girlfriend Sharon Seeley, singer Gene Vincent and two others) in a Ford *Consul* back to London. The car crashes at Rowden Hill in Chippenham and

21-year-old Eddie Cochran dies in hospital the next day ▪ "On the bank of the river, stood Running Bear, young Indian brave" - ***Running Bear*** by 20-year-old Johnny Preston from Texas is number one in the pop chart ▪ "Oh what did Del-a-ware boy? What did Del-a-wear?" - ***Delaware*** by 47-year-old Perry Como from Pennsylvania is number three ▪ More than sixty-thousand boisterous 'Ban the Bomb' demonstrators gather in Trafalgar Square after a three-day march from Aldermaston by CND ▪ Communication technology moves on apace ▪ The radio telescope at Jodrell Bank makes contact with an American Space satellite over four-hundred thousand miles away ▪ The Lancaster bypass opens - eleven and a half miles of brand new motorway for car drivers to speed along ▪ The latest Austin *A55 Cambridge MKII* has a top speed of 75 mph and accelerates from 0-60 mph in 24.5 seconds ▪ The Ford *Zephyr MKII* has a top speed of 80 mph and accelerates from 0-60 mph in 23.2 seconds ▪ Times are changing ▪ 52-year-old Minister of Transport Ernest Marples is determined to modernise the country's railways ▪ A Standard Class 9F steam locomotive (named *Evening Star*) is the last ever steam engine to be manufactured for British Railways at the Swindon Works ▪ English Electric's Vulcan Foundry Works at Newton-le-Willows is now busy building Class 40 Diesel locomotives ▪ Class 45 Diesels are being manufactured by British Railways at Derby and Crewe ▪ New-fangled Class 84 electric engines are being produced by the North British Locomotive Company in Glasgow ▪ "They changed our local Palais into a bowling alley and..." ***Fings Ain't Wot They Used T'Be*** by 37-year-old Max Bygraves is number five in the pop chart ▪ "Come, come, come, come, come, come, I'm your..." ***Handy Man*** ("... Yeah, yeah, yeah") by 29-year-old Jimmy Jones is number three ▪ 38-year-old footballer Tom Finney (aka the 'Preston Plumber') plays his final match for Preston North End before retiring with a groin injury ▪ Manchester City sign Denis

Law from Huddersfield Town for £53,000. The blond haired 20-year-old striker scores on his debut for City in a 4-3 defeat against Leeds Utd ▪ 18-year-old goalkeeper Peter Bonetti makes his debut for Chelsea at Stamford Bridge ▪ 39-year-old football manager Harry Potts guides Burnley to five wins from their last eight league matches (with victories over Nottingham Forest, 1-0; Leicester City, 1-0; Luton Town, 3-0; Birmingham City, 1-0; and Manchester City, 2-1) - and 'The Clarets' are the new champions of Division One. Adam Blacklaw, Brian Miller, Bobby Seith, John Angus, Alex Elder, Jimmy McIlroy, Ray Pointer (with nineteen goals), Tommy Cummings, Brian Pilkington, Trevor Meredith, Ian Lawson, John Connelly (with twenty goals), Billy White, Jimmy Robson (with eighteen goals) and 31-year-old right-half Jimmy Adamson have all been outstanding ▪ 26-year-old centre-forward Dennis Viollet of Manchester Utd is the season's top scorer with thirty-two goals ▪ 20-year-old Jimmy Greaves of Chelsea has scored thirty ▪ Jack Taylor's Leeds Utd and Syd Owen's Luton Town are relegated to Division Two ▪ "I'm gonna stick like glue. Stick because, I'm..." ***Stuck On You*** by 25-year-old Elvis Presley reaches number three in the pop chart ▪ ***Wild One*** ("... I'll get you yet, you bet!") by 17-year-old Bobby Rydell peaks at number seven ▪ Football supporters converge on Wembley on Saturday the seventh of May for the FA Cup final ▪ 22-year-old Derek Dougan is on the losing side as Dally Duncan's Blackburn Rovers go down 3-0 to Stan Cullis' Wolverhampton Wanderers. Outside-right Norman Deeley scores twice for the Wolves. A ticket for the standing enclosure at the Empire Stadium costs 3s/6d ▪ "Now here's a little story, and to tell it is a must. About an unsung hero that moves away your dust" - ***My Old Man's A Dustman*** by 28-year-old Lonnie 'King of Skiffle' Donegan climbs to number one in the pop chart - and remains at the top for four weeks ▪ A dreamy instrumental called ***Theme From A Summer***

Place by 52-year-old Percy Faith and his Orchestra peaks at number two - and stays in the charts for thirty weeks ▪ 'Thrills. Adventure. Excitement. Laughter. What is the league ... Who are the gentlemen?' - *The League of Gentleman* (starring 49-year-old Jack Hawkins, 48-year-old Nigel Patrick, 53-year-old Roger Livesey and 36-year-old Richard 'Dicky' Attenborough) is now showing at picture houses ▪ 59-year-old Alastair Sim, 39-year-old Ian Carmichael and 48-year-old Terry-Thomas star in *School for Scoundrels* ▪ The Ritz cinema in Yiewsley, London closes down. *The Good Companions* (with Eric Portman) and *Last of the Badmen* (with George Montgomery) are the two movies screened on the final night ▪ 'Suitable Only For Adults' - Men flock to seedy 'pits' to see a naked Pamela Green (38-23-37) in the 'X' rated film *Peeping Tom* ▪ 'A Nightmare Manhunt for Maniac Prowler!' - Patrick Allen, Gwen Watford and 12-year-old Janina Faye star in the horror *Never Take Sweets from A Stranger* ▪ 33-year-old Jimmy Savile presents *Young at Heart* on Tyne Tees television ▪ ***He'll Have To Go*** by 35-year-old 'Gentleman' Jim Reeves is number twelve in the pop chart ▪ ***Collette*** by 19-year-old Billy Fury is number nine ▪ The nation rejoices as 29-year-old Princess Margaret marries 30-year-old commoner Antony Armstrong-Jones at Westminster Abbey. 34-year-old Queen Elizabeth II, the 38-year-old Duke of Edinburgh and the 11-year-old Prince of Wales are in attendance. 9-year-old Princess Anne is one of the bridesmaids. After the wedding, the happy couple travel to the Caribbean for a six-week honeymoon ▪ "If I say I love you..." ***Do You Mind*** by 28-year-old Anthony Newley spends a week at number one in the pop chart ▪ "Well, rock-a-bye baby in the treetop, when the wind blows the cradle will rock" - ***Cradle Of Love*** by 20-year-old Johnny Preston is number two ▪ 28-year-old Diana Dors is pictured on the front cover of *TV Times* - promoting 'The Innocent' a new Sunday night drama, part of the *Armchair Theatre* series

▪ 85-year-old Sir Winston Churchill spends a pleasant hour in the company of 69-year-old French president Charles de Gaulle at Hyde Park Gate in London ▪ 60-year-old bespectacled Chancellor of the Exchequer Derick Heathcoat-Amory presides over an economy that is slowing down - a brief period of deflation occurs in the month of March ▪ 'Murder Money marked his hands ... Blood Stained his soul!' - 33-year-old Stanley Baker stars in new movie *Hell is a City* ▪ 43-year-old Peter Finch stars in *The Trials of Oscar Wilde* ▪ "Don't want your love anymore. Don't want your kisses that's for sure" - ***Cathy's Clown*** by The Everly Brothers (23-year-old Don and 21-year-old Phil) reaches number one on the hit parade - and stays there for seven weeks! ▪ ***Someone Else's Baby*** ("... someone else's eyes are blue. Someone else's baby, someone else's five foot two") by 19-year-old Adam Faith is new at number two ▪ The Silver Beetles (a little-known rock'n'roll group from Liverpool, comprising of 19-year-old John Lennon, 17-year-old Paul McCartney, 17-year-old George Harrison, 19-year-old Stuart Sutcliffe and 28-year-old Tommy Moore) team up with 23-year-old pop singer Johnny Gentle on a tour of Scotland ▪ The 'Space Race' between the USA and the USSR intensifies ▪ Reports of recent progress in the Soviet's *Sputnik* programme causes dismay amongst NASA scientists ▪ Back in Britain - some retail prices begin to rise ▪ Critics of the government accuse 67-year-old prime-minister Harold Macmillan and 60-year-old Chancellor of the Exchequer Derick Heathcoat-Amory of failing to take action to control inflation ▪ Racial discrimination continues in the workplace ▪ The 'colour bar' operated by the Bristol Omnibus Company prevents black people for working on the buses. Only white people are considered for roles such as drivers or conductors ▪ All across the nation, hard working men pop into the chippy at the end of a long shift ▪ The average weekly wage is £14/2s ▪ Fish and chips wrapped in newspaper costs 1s/6d.

Summer 1960

Midland Red's Express Coach to London

Monarch:	Queen Elizabeth II (aged 34)
Prime-minister:	Harold Macmillan (aged 66)
Chancellor:	Selwyn Lloyd (aged 56)
Home Secretary:	Rab Butler (aged 57)
Foreign Secretary:	Alec Douglas-Home (aged 57)
Football Manager:	Walter Winterbottom (aged 47)

▪ Conservative prime-minister Harold Macmillan studies a worrying report from the Treasury ▪ The country is facing severe economic problems ▪ After the recent credit boom, there is now a risk of inflation ▪ Bespectacled Chancellor of the Exchequer Derick Heathcoat-Amory introduces retail credit restrictions ▪ The rules are tightened for hire-purchase transactions ▪ "Sweet nothin's, um, um..." ***Sweet Nothin's*** by 15-year-old Brenda Lee is number four in the pop chart ▪ "Lay that pistol down, babe. Lay that pistol down..." ***Pistol Packin' Mama*** ("... lay that pistol down") by 25-year-old Gene Vincent is number fifteen ▪ 27-year-old Jayne Mansfield (40-21-35) and 46-year-old Anthony Quayle star at cinemas in *The Challenge* - a crime thriller directed by 48-year-old John Gilling ▪ 'Never before revealed!' - 34-year-old Aldo Ray stars in *The Day They Robbed the Bank of England* ▪ 11-year-old schoolboy Jeremy Corbyn from Chippenham sits at home reading *The Amateur Gardener* - a fascinating book by A. G. L. Hellyer ▪ The sun shines ▪ A new *Butlin's* holiday camp opens at Bognor Regis ▪ 56-year-old entertainer George Formby appears in summer season at Blackpool ▪ 'It's a Scream - for Laughter!' - crowds flock to the cinema to see 32-year-old Bob Monkhouse in *Dentist in the Chair* ▪ 35-year-old Marcello Mastroianni and 28-year-old Anita Ekberg (40-24-36) star in *La Dolce Vita* - a suave new movie from 40-year-old director Federico Fellini ▪ Veteran footballer, publisher and radio presenter

Charles Buchan dies aged 68 in Monte Carlo ▪ Back in Britain - Triumph launches a convertible version of the popular *Herald* motor-car - the new model costs £766/2s/6d (including Purchase Tax), has a top speed of 78 mph and accelerates from 0-60 mph in 23 seconds ▪ ***Shazam!*** by Duane Eddy and the Rebels climbs to number four in the pop chart ▪ "I'll build a…" ***Stairway To Heaven*** ("… I'll climb to the highest star") by 21-year-old Neil Sedaka is number eight ▪ 26-year-old motorcycle racer John Surtees wins the 500cc Grand Prix on the Isle of Man riding an MV Agusta. Surtees then goes on to win three of the next five races (in Belgium, Germany and Italy) to become world champion for the fourth time in his career ▪ 24-year-old jockey Lester Piggott rides *St. Paddy* to victory in the Epsom Derby ▪ Fashionable young men wear dark, narrow fitting, single-breasted suits with a white shirt and slim tie ▪ Fashionable young women wear tight fitting dresses and shoes with high stiletto heels ▪ "Now there are…" ***Three Steps To Heaven*** ("… Just listen and you will plainly see. And as life travels on, and things do go wrong, just follow steps one, two and three") by the late Eddie Cochran moves to the top of the pop chart - and stays there for two weeks ▪ ***I'm Sorry*** ("... so sorry, that I was such a fool") by 15-year-old Brenda Lee is number twelve ▪ The new BBC Television Centre opens at Shepherd's Bush in London. The ultra-modern complex - with seven state-of-the-art television studios - has taken six years to build ▪ 34-year-old Nancy 'Nan' Winton from Portsmouth reads the weekend news bulletins ▪ 'The Wind of Change' blows as Harold Macmillan's Conservative government grants independence to Nigeria. 56-year-old Nnamdi Azikiwe becomes leader of the new republic - taking over from 57-year-old Governor-General Sir James Robertson ▪ Back in England - the economy remains sluggish and bespectacled Chancellor of the Exchequer Derick Heathcoat-Amory is under pressure ▪ In other news, the 'colour bar' operated by the Bristol Omnibus Company remains in place. Black people are not considered for employment. Only white people are taken on as drivers or conductors ▪ 'At last it can be told ... He Shocked the World!' - *Oscar Wilde* (with 52-year-old Robert Morley in the title role) is now showing at cinemas ▪ 'It's a smasher!' - 36-year-old Leslie Phillips stars in *No Kidding* ▪ *Today in Parliament* is broadcast, late, each evening on the BBC Home Service radio station ▪ Overall, the economy is weak and the deficit in the balance of payments is increasing ▪ Harold Macmillan shuffles his Cabinet ▪ One day before his 56th birthday, Selwyn Lloyd replaces bespectacled 60-year-old Derick Heathcoat-Amory as Chancellor of the Exchequer ▪ 48-year-old Enoch Powell replaces Derek Walker-Smith as Minister for Health ▪ 57-year-old Alec Douglas-Home (an Earl from the House of Lords) is appointed as Foreign Secretary ▪ 44-year-old Edward Heath is Lord Privy Seal - and will lead Britain's negotiations with representatives of countries from the European Common Market ▪ 45-year-old John Profumo is the new Secretary of State for War ▪ 18-year-old dancer Christine Keeler moves into a house owned by osteopath Stephen Ward at Wimpole Mews in Marylebone ▪ ***Love Is Like A Violin*** ("... with its strings around your heart") by 32-year-old Ken Dodd reaches number eight in the pop chart ▪ "Summertime and the living is easy" - 32-year-old Al Martino sings ***Summertime*** ▪ In an all Australian men's tennis singles final at Wimbledon, 26-year-old Neale Fraser defeats 21-year-old Rod Laver ▪ The sun shines ▪ Children paddle and splash in brooks and streams ▪ Teenage boys play football in the park ▪ 24-year-old centre-forward Bill Curry transfers from Brighton and Hove Albion to Derby County for £15,000 ▪ 38-year-old Anthony Brown reads the news on commercial television ▪ Thirty-eight miners lose their lives in an explosion at Monmouthshire ▪ Three brass bands play (and cup-cakes are served) as the new Lea Hall Colliery opens at Rugeley in Staffordshire ▪ 'A fabulous world below the world' - 50-year-old James Mason and 26-year-old Pat Boone star at cinemas in the Hollywood blockbuster *Journey to the Centre of the Earth* ▪ 40-year-old Richard Todd is desperate to retrieve his stolen Ford *Anglia* motorcar from gangster Peter Sellers in the movie *Never Let Go* ▪ 'The most evil Dracula of all!' - *The Brides of Dracula* (with 47-year-old Peter Cushing) premieres in London ▪ 24-year-old Donald Nappey from Bradford changes his name to Donald Nielson ▪ "I've been made blue. I've been lied to..." ***When Will I Be Loved*** by The Everly Brothers climbs to number four in the pop chart ▪ "I want a..." ***Robot Man*** ("... to hold me tight") by 22-year-old Connie Francis is number two. The disc is a double A side, with the track ***Mama*** on the reverse ▪ 30-year-old racing driver Stirling Moss wins the Monaco Grand Prix in a dark blue Lotus (number 28) ▪ 26-year-old John Surtees switches from motorbikes to racing cars - and finishes second in the British Grand Prix at Silverstone ▪ "All together now! Tie me kangaroo down, sport. Tie me kangaroo down" - ***Tie Me Kangaroo Down Sport*** by 30-year-old Rolf Harris from Australia reaches number nine on the hit parade ▪ "Two, three, four, tell the people what she wore!" - ***Itsy Bitsy Teeny Weeny Yellow Polka Dot Bikini*** by 16-year-old Brian Hyland reaches number eight ▪ The cricket Test series between England and South Africa is underway ▪ South African fast bowler Geoff Griffin takes a hat-trick at Lord's (with the wickets of Smith, Walker and Trueman) but a South African batting collapse ensures a victory for England ▪ In the third Test at Trent Bridge, England's batsman Ken Barrington scores 80 runs and fast bowler 'fiery' Fred Trueman takes 5 wickets for just 27. England are triumphant - taking an unassailable 3-0 lead in the series. Ted Dexter, Ray Illingworth, Colin Cowdrey, Brian Statham and 29-year-old 'fiery' Fred have all played their part in the splendid victory ▪ "Since you're g-o-o-o-on, I've got..." ***A Mess Of Blues*** by

25-year-old Elvis Presley reaches number two on the weekly hit parade ▪ The Silver Beetles (a little-known five-piece beat combo from Liverpool) change their name to The Beatles and head off to Hamburg to perform songs at a nightclub in the city's 'red-light' district ▪ Fans of Traditional Jazz music engage in a punch up with fans of Modern Jazz at a festival in Beaulieu, Hampshire ▪ London gangsters Reginald and Ronald Kray take over Esmeralda's Barn - a well known gambling club in Knightsbridge ▪ "You need timin'. A tick - a tick - a tick - a good timin'. A tock - a tock - a tock - a timin' is the th-i-ing, it's true..." ***Good Timin'*** ("... brought me to you") by 23-year-old Jimmy Jones is new at number one ▪ *Pencil and Paper* is a new quiz show on ITV - in the first programme, a team of beauty queens go 'head-to-head' with a team of char-women - the char-women are triumphant ▪ The 'Space Race' continues. NASA scientists look on enviously as the USSR launches *Sputnik 5* into space - with two dogs on-board ▪ "'Cause everybody's somebody's fool. Everybody's somebody's plaything. And there are no exceptions to the rule. Yes..." ***Everybody's Somebody's Fool*** by 21-year-old Connie Francis moves up to number five in the pop chart ▪ "Well, the..." ***Train Of Love*** ("... keeps moving on down the track") by 28-year-old Alma Cogan reaches number twenty-seven ▪ "You tell me that you love me baby, then you say you don't. You tell me that you'll come on over, then you say you won't" - ***Please Don't Tease*** by Cliff Richard and the Shadows spends three weeks at number one ▪ 'Movie wise, there has never been anything like The Apartment' - 35-year-old Jack Lemmon and 26-year-old Shirley MacLaine star at cinemas in *The Apartment* - a film directed by 54-year-old Billy Wilder ▪ 'You're all sinners ... You'll all burn in hell!' - 46-year-old Burt Lancaster and 31-year-old Jean Simmons star in *Elmer Gantry* ▪ The Olympic Games get underway in Rome ▪ 19-year-old swimmer Anita Lonsbrough and long-distance walker 27-year-old Don

Thompson win gold medals for Great Britain ▪ 20-year-old show jumper David Broome wins a bronze ▪ 18-year-old boxer Cassius Clay wins gold for the US in the light-heavyweight category ▪ Back in England - traffic jams form on the new M1 'national road' as motorists queue to visit the first large-scale service station at Newport Pagnell ▪ 46-year-old Ernie Watkins from Towcester gets up to 75 mph in his Triumph *Herald* on a stretch of motorway between Luton and Hemel Hempstead ▪ The Midland Red company's express coach reaches a speed of 78 mph on its journey into London ▪ The new Midland Pullman diesel train runs between Manchester Piccadilly and London St. Pancras at 80 mph ▪ People are outraged as *PG Tips* begin selling teabags - as an alternative to loose leaf tea ▪ 'The newest and funniest-' *Doctor in Love* (with 36-year-old Leslie Phillips, 32-year-old Michael Craig and 53-year-old James Robertson Justice) goes on general release at cinemas ▪ A film version of John Osborne's play *The Entertainer* (with 53-year-old Sir Laurence Olivier and 30-year-old Joan Plowright) is also now showing ▪ 66-year-old prime-minister Harold Macmillan meets his friend and ally US president Dwight D. Eisenhower to discuss the Polaris nuclear missile programme ▪ "When you move in right up close to me. That's when I get the shakes all over me. Quivers down the backbone!" - ***Shakin' All Over*** by 24-year-old Johnny Kidd and the Pirates climbs to number one on the hit parade ▪ ***Because They're Young*** (an electric guitar instrumental) by 22-year-old Duane Eddy and the Rebels reaches number two ▪ 38-year-old footballer Billy Liddell makes his final appearance for Liverpool before retiring ▪ 20-year-old Jimmy Greaves of Chelsea and England is pictured on the front cover of the latest *Charles Buchan Football Monthly* paper ▪ 18-year-old Geoff Hurst of West Ham Utd considers quitting football and playing cricket for Essex instead ▪ England is selected (ahead of Spain and West Germany) to host the 1966 FIFA World Cup football finals.

Autumn 1960

Don't Let the Bastards Grind You Down

Monarch:	Queen Elizabeth II (aged 34)
Prime-minister:	Harold Macmillan (aged 66)
Chancellor:	Selwyn Lloyd (aged 56)
Home Secretary:	Rab Butler (aged 57)
Foreign Secretary:	Alec Douglas-Home (aged 57)
Football Manager:	Walter Winterbottom (aged 47)

▪ *The News and the Weather* is broadcast on BBC television at 6 p.m. each evening ▪ Heavy rain leads to flooding across much of the country ▪ ***Paper Roses*** ("… paper roses, like your imitation love for me") by The Kaye Sisters is number seven in the pop chart ▪ ***If She Should Come To You*** by 28-year-old Anthony Newley is number four ▪ 52-year-old Ernest Marples is Secretary of State for Transport in Harold Macmillan's Conservative government ▪ Traffic wardens issue the first parking tickets to motorists ▪ Dr. Thomas Creighton receives a ticket (and a £2 fine) for leaving his Ford *Popular* outside a London hotel, while attending a heart attack victim ▪ 56-year-old Selwyn Lloyd is Chancellor of the Exchequer ▪ The economy is static and the value of the pound is under pressure ▪ 50-year-old Harold Watkinson is Secretary of State for Defence ▪ 34-year-old Queen Elizabeth II launches Britain's first nuclear powered submarine - HMS *Dreadnought* ▪ Prime-minister Harold Macmillan agrees for US Polaris missiles to be deployed in Britain ▪ More and more people join CND ▪ Hugh Gaitskell's Labour Party is in disarray over the issue of nuclear weapons - the 54-year-old leader urges Labour conference delegates to, "Fight and fight and fight again to save the party we love" ▪ Surveillance officers from the British intelligence service monitor the bungalow at 45 Cranley Drive in Ruislip where Lona and Morris Cohen are suspected of operating a spy network for the Soviets ▪ 18-year-old Hank Marvin of The Shadows plays a Fender *Stratocaster* electric guitar on ***Apache*** - the catchy tune climbs to number one on the hit parade and stays there for five weeks! ▪ ***Feel So Fine*** by 21-year-old Johnny Preston from Texas is number eighteen ▪ 11-year-old schoolboy Peter Shilton from Leicester plays football with his friends in the park ▪ 25-year-old Ron Springett wins his sixth international cap for England - as goalkeeper in Wing Commander Winterbottom's football team (R Springett, Armfield, McNeil, R Robson, Swan, Flowers, Douglas, Greaves, R Smith, Haynes, R Charlton) in a 2-5 victory over Northern Ireland in Belfast ▪ 'You Will Orbit into the Fantastic Future!' - 30-year-old Rod Taylor stars at cinemas in H. G. Wells' *The Time Machine* ▪ "Evening, all" - 64-year-old Jack Warner returns for a new series of *Dixon of Dock Green* on BBC television ▪ 42-year-old comedian Harry Worth stars in *Here's Harry* and popularises the 'trick' of standing at the corner of a shop window while raising one arm and leg in the air, to give the impression that *both* arms and legs are being raised ▪ A new series of *The Army Game*, starring 44-year-old Alfie Bass as Private 'Boots' Bisley, 52-year-old Bill Fraser as Sergeant Major Claude Snudge and with 45-year-old Dick Emery as Private 'Chubby' Catchpole, is on ITV ▪ 32-year-old Patrick McGoohan stars as secret agent John Drake in *Danger Man* ▪ The Beatles (a little-known beat combo from Liverpool), comprising of band members: 19-year-old John Lennon, 18-year-old Paul McCartney, 17-year-old George Harrison, 20-year-old Stuart Sutcliffe and drummer 18-year-old Pete Best, get up to all sorts of mischief as they play gigs in the 'red-light' district of Hamburg, Germany ▪ Back in England - 17-year-old student Mick Jagger attends lectures at the London School of Economics ▪ 16-year-old Keith Richards bunks off classes at Sidcup Art College ▪ "Some people like to rock. Some people like to roll" - ***Let's Have A Party*** by 22-year-old Wanda Jackson is number thirty-two in the pop chart ▪ ***Walking To New Orleans*** by 32-year-old Fats Domino is number nineteen ▪ 49-year-old executioner Harry Allen prepares the gallows at Wandsworth Prison ▪ 18-year-old convicted murderer Francis Forsyth is hanged by the neck until dead ▪ The brand new Cardinal Griffin Catholic School opens in Cannock ▪ 12-year-old Alan Sugar makes a profit by selling home-made fizzy pop drinks to his friends at Joseph Priestley Technical School ▪ "He saw a sign for a stock car race. A thousand dollar prize it read. He couldn't get Laura on the phone, so to her mother, Tommy said…" ***Tell Laura I Love Her*** by 21-year-old Ricky Valance spends three weeks at number one in the pop chart ▪ "Little girl..." ***Nine Times Out Of Ten*** ("... you have refused me") by 20-year-old Cliff Richard and the Shadows reaches number three ▪ Bill Nicholson's Tottenham Hotspur football team thrashes Aston Villa 6-2 in front of 61,356 spectators at White Hart Lane - it's Spurs' tenth straight victory and keeps them at the top of Division One ▪ Harry Potts' Burnley score twenty goals in just four games and gain convincing victories over Fulham, Blackburn Rovers, Manchester Utd and Chelsea ▪ 20-year-old Jimmy Greaves and 23-year-old Bobby Charlton both score hat-tricks as Wing Commander Winterbottom's England football team (R Springett, Armfield, McNeil, R Robson, Swan, Flowers, Douglas, Greaves, R Smith, Haynes, R Charlton) thrashes Luxembourg 9-0 ▪ The 'colour bar' operated by the Bristol Omnibus Company remains in place. Black people are not considered for employment. Only white people are taken on as drivers or conductors ▪ ***Only The Lonely*** ("... know the way I feel tonight") by 24-year-old Roy Orbison moves to the top of the weekly pop chart ▪ ***As Long As He Needs Me*** ("... I know where I must be") by 23-year-old Shirley Bassey is number two ▪ 23-year-old inside-forward Dennis Edwards scores a hat-trick for Charlton Athletic and 25-year-old centre-forward Brian Clough scores a hat-trick for Middlesbrough as the two teams draw 6-6 in a Division Two match at The Valley ▪ 15-year-old schoolboy footballer Rodney Marsh signs for Fulham FC ▪ After eight months on strike, 24-year-old inside-forward George Eastham finally reaches an agreement with Newcastle Utd and transfers to George Swindin's Arsenal for £47,500 ▪ 62-year-old Billy Walker steps down as Nottingham Forest manager and is succeeded by 47-year-old Andy Beattie (from Carlisle Utd) ▪ "I need love, Doctor!" - 26-year-old Sophia Loren (38-24-38) and 35-year-old Peter Sellers star at cinemas in the romantic comedy *The Millionairess*. The film is deemed 'not suitable for children' ▪ "Don't let the bastards grind you down" - 24-year-old Albert Finney stars in the 'kitchen-sink' drama, *Saturday Night and Sunday Morning* - a tough and realistic story of working class life for young men and women ▪ 17-year-old Carol White stars in *Linda* - the B-movie shown on the same bill as *Saturday Night and Sunday Morning* ▪ The paperback version of the sexually explicit novel *Lady Chatterley's Lover* by D H Lawrence 'sells out' in record time after its ban is lifted ▪ ***It's Now Or Never*** ("...come hold me tight. Kiss me my darling, be mine tonight") by 25-year-old Elvis Presley comes straight into the pop chart at number one - and stays there for eight weeks! ▪ "So, darling..." ***Save The Last Dance For Me*** by The Drifters climbs to number two ▪ "Somehow I can't dismiss, the memory of your kiss. Guess..." ***My Heart Has A Mind Of Its Own*** by 21-year-old Connie Francis also peaks at number two ▪ Under-18s lie about their age in order to gain access to 'X' rated films at their local picture house ▪ 'This could be your teenage daughter!' - 16-year-old Gillian Hills stars in gritty new movie *'Beat' Girl* ▪ 'The thrills - the chills of Witchcraft today' - 38-year-old Christopher Lee and 22-year-old Venetia Stevenson star in *The City of the Dead* ▪ 19-year-old David Lovell works as a bus conductor in Birmingham ▪ The Beatles (a little-known beat combo from Liverpool) return to the UK after performing to nightclub audiences in the 'red-light' district of Hamburg, Germany ▪ 17-year-old student Mick Jagger completes his homework ahead of his next lecture at the London School of Economics ▪ 20-year-old footballer Jimmy Greaves bags a hat-trick (and Ron Tindall scores twice) as Chelsea thrash Manchester City 6-3 at Stamford Bridge ▪ "My love for you is deep and endless as the sea, strong and mighty as a tree..." ***My Love For You*** by 25-year-old Johnny Mathis climbs to number nine in the pop chart ▪ "Oh..." ***Blue Angel*** ("... don't you cry, just because he said goodbye") by 24-year-old Roy Orbison is number eleven ▪ Presidential elections are underway in the USA to find a successor to 70-year-old Dwight D. Eisenhower ▪ Millions of Americans watch 'live' television debates between 43-year-old Democrat John F. Kennedy from Brookline in Massachusetts and 47-year-old Republican Richard Nixon from Yorba Linda in California ▪ Election day takes place on the eighth of November and Kennedy is triumphant - JFK becomes the thirty-fifth president of the USA ▪ British trawlers continue to fish in the disputed waters off Iceland ▪ An Icelandic gun boat opens fire on the trawlers *Kingston Emerald* and *Hackness* ▪ Royal Navy frigate HMS *Russell* is sent to the area to protect British ships ▪ Back in England - the Conservative government continues its road building programme, led by 52-year-old Ernest Marples, Minister for Transport in Harold Macmillan's Cabinet ▪ The recently opened M50 motorway enables car drivers to speed between Tewkesbury and Ross-on-Wye in just thirty minutes ▪ 'Cafeteria, Toilets, Pick-a-Platter' - a new large-scale service station (operated by Blue Boar) is now open on the M1 at Watford Gap ▪ A brand new Rolls-Royce *Phantom V* (ultra luxury) motorcar costs £10,700 - and has an in-built cocktail cabinet ▪ A brand new *Sunbeam Alpine* sports car costs £1,110 - and has independent front springs and disc brakes ▪ A brand new Ford *Anglia 105E De Luxe* costs £610 - and has front and rear ash-trays ▪ A packet of twenty cigarettes costs three shillings.

Christmas 1960

Coronation Street

Monarch:	Queen Elizabeth II (aged 34)
Prime-minister:	Harold Macmillan (aged 66)
Chancellor:	Selwyn Lloyd (aged 56)
Home Secretary:	Rab Butler (aged 58)
Foreign Secretary:	Alec Douglas-Home (aged 57)
Football Manager:	Walter Winterbottom (aged 47)

▪ 66-year-old prime-minister Harold Macmillan travels to Italy with his 57-year-old Foreign Secretay Lord Douglas-Home. The two men spend some time with 79-year-old Pope John XXIII and afterwards comment on the holy man's kindliness and courtesy ▪ 56-year-old Chancellor of the Exchequer Selwyn Lloyd and his team at the Treasury devise policies aimed at revitalising Britain's slow moving economy ▪ 44-year-old Edward Heath meets representatives from European countries - negotiating Britain's entry into the Common Market ▪ 46-year-old Kenneth More and 22-year-old Shirley Anne Field star at cinemas in *Man in the Moon* ▪ "As I was going to..." ***Strawberry Fair*** ("... Singing, singing, buttercups and daisies") by 29-year-old Antony Newley climbs to number three on the hit parade ▪ ***Man Of Mystery / The Stranger*** by The Shadows (led by 19-year-old guitarist Hank Marvin) is number five ▪ Elvis Presley, Bobby Darrin, The Everly Brothers and 44-year-old Frank Sinatra are featured on the front cover of the latest *New Musical Express* paper ▪ Star footballers, 34-year-old Danny Blanchflower (captain of Tottenham Hotspur) and 27-year-old Dennis Viollet (captain of Manchester Utd) are pictured on the front cover of *Charles Buchan's Football Monthly* ▪ 40-year-old Barbara Mandell announces the news on commercial television ▪ The USSR and the USA continue their tactical brinkmanship as the Cold War persists ▪ British prime-minister Harold Macmillan and US President Elect

John F. Kennedy discuss the Polaris missile programme ▪ 38-year-old double-agent George Blake meets his KGB contact and hands over 'top secret' Defence information ▪ 48-year-old osteopath Stephen Ward meets suspected Soviet spy Yevgeny Ivanov at Wimpole Mews in Marylebone. The two men are joined for drinks by 18-year-old Christine Keeler and 16-year-old Mandy Rice-Davis ▪ "It goes boom buddy-boom, buddy-boom, buddy-boom, buddy-boom, buddy-boom, buddy-boom-boom-boom" - ***Goodness Gracious Me*** by Peter Sellers and Sophia Loren (38-24-38) is number four in the pop chart ▪ ***Rocking Goose*** by Johnny and the Hurricanes is number three ▪ Men pay 2s/10d for a front row seat in the circle at the local cinema ▪ 27-year-old Jayne Mansfield (40-21-35) is Midnight Franklin in *Too Hot To Handle* ▪ 22-year-old Julie Alexander (41-21-32) is schoolgirl Rosalie Dawn in *The Pure Hell of St. Trinian's*. (35-year-old George Cole is Flash Harry) ▪ 20-year-old footballer Jimmy Greaves scores five goals as Chelsea thrash West Bromwich Albion 7-1 at Stamford Bridge ▪ 25-year-old 'would be' writer David Nobbs rushes along to support Tottenham Hotspur at White Hart Lane - and watches a thrilling 6-0 victory over Birmingham City. Spurs remain top of Division One, seven points ahead of Sheffield Wednesday in second place ▪ 24-year-old George Eastham scores twice on his debut for mid-table Arsenal in a 5-1 victory over Bolton Wanderers at Highbury ▪ ***It's Now Or Never*** by 25-year-old Elvis Presley remains at number one in the pop chart ▪ Output from industry has slowed and the country's balance of payments figure has moved into a £382 million deficit ▪ Coal production has fallen to 198 million tonnes ▪ The publicly owned British Railways network has lost £68 million ▪ 54-year-old Hugh Gaitskell (leader of the Labour opposition) is forthright in his criticism of Conservative prime-minister Harold Macmillan and Chancellor of the Exchequer Selwyn Lloyd ▪ After two years of rapid growth, the economy has now slowed and the value of the pound is coming under pressure ▪ 53-year-old radio and television star Gilbert Harding dies after an asthma attack in London ▪ 46-year-old Jack de Manio presents the *Today* radio programme on the BBC Home Service ▪ 19-year-old convicted murderer Anthony Miller is hanged by the neck until dead at Glasgow ▪ 43-year-old escaped convict Alfred 'Houdini' Hinds is caught after two years on the run and taken into custody ▪ Shops are busy ▪ Husbands purchase *Bri Nylon* nighties as Christmas gifts for their wives ▪ ***Lonely Pup (In A Christmas Shop)*** by 20-year-old Adam Faith is number four in the pop chart ▪ Parents take their young children to department stores to visit Father Christmas' grotto. Reluctant girls and boys sit on the knee of an elderly stranger (who's dressed in a red coat and wearing a false white beard) and claim to have "been good" - in the hope of getting the Christmas present they most desire ▪ A *Rosebud* doll is the perfect gift for schoolgirls ▪ A *Tri-ang Scalextric* miniature electric motor racing set (with two Jaguar racing cars) is the ideal gift for schoolboys ▪ Lesney Products introduce *King Size Matchbox* die-cast model cars ▪ The new Meccano *Set No 4* costs forty-eight shillings at toyshops ▪ A Bayko building set (of a house) is 23s/6d ▪ A small pack of thirteen (8 stud) basic *Lego* bricks is 2s/3d ▪ 'From the army's funniest private in The Square Peg to the navy's most riotous seaman!' - 45-year-old Norman Wisdom stars at cinemas in *The Bulldog Breed* - with 'unknowns' 22-year-old Oliver Reed and 27-year-old Michael Caine also making brief appearances ▪ "I'm Spartacus!" - 35-year-old Tony Curtis, 43-year-old Kirk Douglas, 53-year-old Sir Laurence Olivier, 39-year-old Peter Ustinov and 31-year-old Jean Simmons star in *Spartacus* ▪ 'A new and altogether different screen excitement!!!' - 33-year-old Janet Leigh and 28-year-old Anthony Perkins star in Alfred Hitchcock's latest thriller, *Psycho* ▪ 28-year-old Elizabeth Taylor plays the role of Gloria Wandrous (a glamorous

Manhattan call-girl) in *Butterfield 8* ▪ *Coronation Street* is a new soap-opera on ITV - the characters: Kenneth Barlow, Elsie Tanner, Minnie Caldwell, grumpy Albert Tatlock and miserable Ena Sharples (in a hairnet) will soon become household favourites ▪ 40-year-old Peter Dimmock presents *Sports Review of 1960* on BBC television ▪ 20-year-old show jumper David Broome wins the 'Sports Personality of the Year' award - and brings his horse, *Sunsalve*, into the TV studio ▪ Bill Nicholson's top-of-the-table Tottenham Hotspur football team beats Blackburn Rovers 5-2 with goals from Bobby Smith, Les Allen and 34-year-old Danny Blanchflower ▪ 25-year-old centre-forward Brian Clough scores twice for Middlesbrough in a 3-4 victory over Bill Shankly's Liverpool in Division Two ▪ Beryl Formby (wife and business manager of entertainer George Formby) dies aged 59 in Blackpool ▪ The Beatles (a little-known beat combo from Liverpool) perform in front of a small audience at the Casbah Club on Hayman's Green, West Derby ▪ ***Ol' MacDonald*** ("... had a farm. E-I-E-I-O") by 45-year-old Frank Sinatra reaches number eleven in the pop chart ▪ ***When You Come To The End Of A Lollipop*** ("… plop goes your heart!") by 38-year-old Max Bygraves fails to break into the Top Fifty ▪ "Kiss me my darling, be mine tonight" - ***It's Now Or Never*** by 25-year-old Elvis Presley is still at number one ▪ Courting couples enjoy passionate embraces on the back seats of motorcars ▪ A second-hand (1955) Ford *Zephyr* in two-tone fawn, with a heater and new white wall tyres is advertised for £575 ▪ A brand new Ford *Zephyr* costs £899/17s/6- ▪ A brand new Morris *Minor* two-door saloon is £599/9s/- ▪ Newly married couples move into their own homes and settle down to family life ▪ The average price of a house in the UK is £2,300 ▪ Adverts say, '*Omo* washing powder - adds brightness to cleanness and whiteness'

New Year 1961

The Beatles at the Cavern

Monarch:	Queen Elizabeth II (aged 34)
Prime-minister:	Harold Macmillan (aged 67)
Chancellor:	Selwyn Lloyd (aged 56)
Home Secretary:	Rab Butler (aged 58)
Foreign Secretary:	Alec Douglas-Home (aged 57)
Football Manager:	Walter Winterbottom (aged 47)

▪ National Conscription comes to an end and most young men breathe a sigh of relief ▪ 25-year-old Elvis Presley stars at cinemas, playing the role of Tulsa McLean (a US Army serviceman with dreams of leaving the military and running a nightclub) in the hit movie *G. I. Blues* ▪ "I've got those hup, two, three, four. Occupation G.I. blues" - The soundtrack album, *GI Blues*, by Elvis is number one in the LP chart ▪ "Your love means more to me than all the apples hanging on a tree. And like those apples, our love will grow, because..." ***I Love You*** by 20-year-old Cliff Richard and the Shadows replaces Elvis at the top of the singles chart ▪ The Beatles (a little-known beat combo) appear for the first time at the Cavern club in Liverpool. 19-year-old Pete Best is on drums. 20-year-old bass player Stuart Sutcliffe leaves the band to study at art college ▪ 'Shattering flight into flaming violence!' - *Passport to China* is at cinemas - with 46-year-old Richard Baseheart and 25-year-old Lisa Gastoni in the lead roles ▪ 20-year-old footballer Denis Law scores six goals in the pouring rain as Manchester City take a 2-6 lead over Luton Town in the fourth round of the FA Cup. The referee is forced to abandon the game in the 69th minute (due to a water-logged pitch). Luton go on to win the re-arranged match 3-1 and City are out of the cup - in the cruelest fashion ▪ Ted Drake's Chelsea (with Peter 'the cat' Bonetti, Ron Tindall, Bobby Tambling, Jimmy Greaves and 17-year-old Terry Venables) also suffer a shock defeat, losing 1-2 to Fourth Division Crewe Alexandra ▪ Matt Gillies' Leicester City (with Gordon Banks, Frank McLintock, Ken Leek and Jimmy Walsh) defeat Oxford Utd 3-1 at Filbert Street ▪ "When I see my baby, what do I see? Poetry..." ***Poetry In Motion*** by 22-year-old Johnny Tillotson is new at number one on the hit parade ▪ "Ooh, you come on like a dream, peaches and cream, lips like strawberry wine..." ***You're Sixteen*** ("... you're beautiful, and you're mine") by 26-year-old Johnny Burnette climbs from number twenty to number ten ▪ 43-year-old John F. Kennedy is inaugurated as US president in Washington ▪ 66-year-old prime-minister Harold Macmillan sends his congratulations to JFK from London ▪ MI5 boss Roger Hollis meets with his MI6 counterpart, Sir Dick White. The two men discuss recent 'top secret' security leaks ▪ 48-year-old Lona Cohen and 50-year-old Morris Cohen are arrested at 45 Cranley Drive in Ruislip and charged with spying for the Soviets ▪ 55-year-old Harry Houghton and his lover, 46-year-old Ethel 'Bunty' Gee, are also detained on charges of espionage ▪ 'Wash YOUR blues away with the 'Wide-Scream' Comedy of the Year!' - 49-year-old Terry-Thomas, 22-year-old Janette Scott and 57-year-old Wilfrid Hyde White star at cinemas in *His and Hers* - a bright new film from director Brian Desmond Hurst ▪ *The Singer Not the Song* is also now showing - with 39-year-old Dirk Bogarde, 52-year-old John Mills and 25-year-old Mylene Demongeot (36-21-36) ▪ "Anyone who sees her, soon forgets the Mona Lisa. It would take I know, a Michaelangelo, and he would need the glow of dawn that paints the sky above, to try and paint a..." ***Portrait Of My Love*** by 30-year-old Matt Monro climbs to number three in the pop chart ▪ ***Sway*** by 19-year-old Bobby Rydell is number twelve ▪ Matt Gillies' Leicester City thrash Fred Ford's Bristol City 5-1 at Filbert Street in the fourth round of the FA Cup ▪ High-flying Tottenham Hotspur thrash Jimmy McGuigan's Crewe Alexandra 5-1, with goals from

Mackay, Jones, Smith, Allen and Dyson ▪ Bedford Jezzard's Fulham team loses six consecutive league matches and slides down the Division One league table. 'The Cottagers' are now just four points above the bottom team ▪ 11-year-old Malcolm MacDonald from Fulham plays football with his friends in the park ▪ 38-year-old retired footballer Tom Finney (aka the 'Preston Plumber') is awarded an OBE ▪ 26-year-old centre-forward Gerry Hitchens scores his sixth goal in three games as Aston Villa draw 2-2 at home to Blackburn Rovers in Division One ▪ ***Are You Lonesome Tonight*** ("… do you miss me tonight? Are you sorry we drifted apart?") by 26-year-old Elvis Presley is number one on the hit parade for four weeks ▪ ***Pepe*** (an electric guitar / saxophone instrumental) by 22-year-old Duane Eddy and the Rebels is number two ▪ ***Calendar Girl*** by 21-year-old Neil Sedaka is number eight ▪ A campaign is under way to save the Doric arch at Euston Railway Station - 37-year-old journalist Charles Wheeler and 53-year-old architect James Maude Richards lead the calls for the monument to be preserved for posterity, but Minister of Transport Ernest Marples says the imposing relic must be demolished as part of Euston's modernisation plans ▪ An agreement over fishing rights is reached between Iceland and the UK. A zone of twelve nautical miles from the coastline of Iceland is established, with British trawlers being granted limited rights to fish within the outer six nautical miles ▪ Back in England - the 'colour bar' operated by the Bristol Omnibus Company remains in place. Black people are not considered for employment. Only white people are taken on as drivers or conductors ▪ BBC television's *The Black and White Minstrel Show* (with 35-year-old Stan Stennett and 27-year-old Leslie Crowther) is enjoyed by hundreds of thousands of families all across the country on a Saturday evening ▪ "'Cos I've been…" ***Counting Teardrops*** ("… instead of sheep. Honey, honey, I just can't sleep") by Emile Ford and the Checkmates climbs to number four on the hit parade chart ▪ "Well! Come a little baby..." ***Let's Jump The Broomstick*** ("... come on let's tie a knot") by 16-year-old Brenda Lee is number twelve ▪ 49-year-old Bill Hartley introduces *Motoring and the Motorist* on BBC radio's Home Service on Friday evenings. (The programme is repeated on Saturday afternoons) ▪ More than one million Morris *Minors* have been sold since the motorcar was launched twelve years ago ▪ The new Humber *Super Snipe* looks stunning - it's the first British car to come with a pair of twin headlights! ▪ 'They fought like seven-hundred!' - 40-year-old Yul Brynner, 30-year-old Steve McQueen, 28-year-old Robert Vaughn, 32-year-old James Coburn and 39-year-old Charles Bronson star at cinemas (along with two others) in *The Magnificent Seven* ▪ 'Wizard of Laughs!' - 45-year-old Norman Wisdom stars in *Girl on the Boat* ▪ "Sailor stop your roaming. Sailor leave the sea" - ***Sailor*** by 28-year-old Petula Clark is top of the pop chart ▪ "Like a rubber ball you come bouncin' back to me" - ***Rubber Ball*** by 17-year-old Bobby Vee is number four ▪ Bill Nicholson's high-flying Tottenham Hotspur are runaway leaders in Division One ▪ 65,251 turn out at White Hart Lane to see 23-year-old Les Allen score twice in a 4-2 victory over rivals Arsenal ▪ Spurs' 35-year-old captain Danny Blanchflower refuses to go on *This is Your Life* when Eamonn Andrews presents him with the big red book ▪ The £20-a-week maximum wage for footballers is scrapped ▪ 26-year-old Johnny Haynes (captain of Fulham) is the first English player to receive a wage of £100 a week - after turning down a lucrative move to Italy. 51-year-old Tommy Trinder (chaiman of Fulham) agrees to the deal in order to keep his highly rated player at Craven Cottage ▪ 24-year-old goalkeeper Chic Brodie transfers from Dave Smith's Fourth Division Aldershot to Stan Cullis' First Division Wolverhampton Wanderers for a fee of £9,000 ▪ Overall, the number of cinemas goers is declining but scores of people still enjoy a special night out at the pictures ▪ 'A body was the membership card' - 34-year-old Keith Michell stars in *The Hellfire Club* ▪ 44-year-old Peter Finch stars in *No Love for Johnny* ▪ Millions choose to stay at home and enjoy an evening in front of the TV ▪ 30-year-old Ian Hendry stars as Dr. David Keel in *The Avengers* - with 39-year-old Patrick Macnee playing the role of John Steed ▪ ***Walk Right Back*** ("... to me this minute. Bring your love to me, don't send it. I'm so lonesome every day") by The Everly Brothers (24-year-old Don and 22-year-old Phil) spends three weeks at the top of the hit parade ▪ ***A Thousand Stars*** ("... in the skies make me realise, you are the one love that I'll adore") by 20-year-old Billy Fury reaches number fourteen ▪ Prime-minister Harold Macmillan and his Chancellor of the Exchequer, Selwyn Lloyd, meet regularly to discuss the state of the economy and the growing deficit in the country's balance of payments ▪ The value of the pound is falling ▪ Trade union officials are becoming anxious - fearing that the government may seek to impose a freeze on wages ▪ 34-year-old disc jockey Jimmy Savile plays the latest pop hits on Radio Luxembourg ▪ "The farmer called on Lucy one dark and stormy night. She said, 'You are too old for me because your hair is white'" - ***Gather In The Mushrooms*** by 37-year-old Benny Hill reaches number twelve in the pop chart ▪ ***Shine*** by 19-year-old Joe Brown and his Bruvvers stalls at number thirty-three ▪ People attend matinee screenings at the local *Gaumont* picture house ▪ 'The Greatest Adventure Story of Them All!' - *The Swiss Family Robinson* is now showing ▪ Rosetted men and boys wearing hand knitted scarves (made of wool matching their team's colours) attend football matches and twirl wooden rattles ▪ A ball of blue knitting wool costs one-shilling ▪ A ball of white knitting wool is also one-shilling ▪ 23-year-old goalkeeper Gordon Banks is in fine form as Leicester City defeat Birmingham City 3-1 in front of 41,916 spectators at Filbert Street in an FA Cup fifth round replay.

Spring 1961

A Double for the Spurs!

Monarch:	Queen Elizabeth II (aged 35)
Prime-minister:	Harold Macmillan (aged 67)
Chancellor:	Selwyn Lloyd (aged 56)
Home Secretary:	Rab Butler (aged 58)
Foreign Secretary:	Alec Douglas-Home (aged 57)
Football Manager:	Walter Winterbottom (aged 48)

▪ "You are my theme for a dream. Yes, you are, a rare and lovely theme / You're a..." ***Theme For A Dream*** by Cliff Richard and the Shadows climbs to number three on the hit parade ▪ "Tonight the light of love is in your eyes, but…" ***Will You Love Me Tomorrow*** by The Shirelles peaks at number four ▪ The Beatles (a little-known beat combo from Liverpool), comprising of band members: 20-year-old John Lennon, 18-year-old Paul McCartney, 18-year-old George Harrison and 19-year-old Pete Best, travel to Germany for a second time and perform shows at the Top Ten Club in Hamburg ▪ Back in England - "Ancock's drawing London's biggest queues!' - 36-year-old comedian Tony Hancock is on the big screen - starring in *The Rebel* ▪ 'Belly Laughs all over La Belle France!' - 32-year-old Bob Monkhouse, 37-year-old Leslie Phillips, 59-year-old Irene Handl and 24-year-old Shirley Eaton star in *A Weekend with Lulu* ▪ 28-year-old Peter Walker is elected as a Conservative MP at a by-election in Worcester ▪ 39-year-old Francis Pym is elected as a Conservative MP at a by-election in Cambridgeshire ▪ 37-year-old Denis Howell is elected as a Labour MP at a by-election in Birmingham Small Heath ▪ The old white 'fiver' is withdrawn from circulation ▪ Harold Macmillan's Conservative government is criticised for its handling of the country's finances ▪ 56-year-old Chancellor of the Exchequer Selwyn Lloyd has, so far, been unable to re-start the stagnant economy and cuts in government spending now seem likely ▪ 54-year-old Hugh Gaitskell (leader of the Labour opposition) says he will oppose any cuts ▪ "Treat me nice, treat me good, treat me like you really should, 'cause I'm not made of wood and I don't have a..." ***Wooden Heart*** by 26-year-old Elvis Presley spends six weeks at number one on the hit parade ▪ "Up a lazy river, how happy we'll be. Up a..." ***Lazy River*** ("... with me") by 24-year-old Bobby Darin reaches number two ▪ ***Where The Boys Are*** ("... my true love will be") by 22-year-old Connie Francis is number five ▪ 26-year-old boxer Henry Cooper retains his British and Commonwealth Heavyweight title, defeating Joe Erskine in five rounds at the Empire Pool in Wembley ▪ Matt Gillies' Leicester City (with Gordon Banks, Frank McLintock, Ken Leek and Jimmy Walsh) gain a 1-2 victory over Barnsley at Oakwell in a quarter-final replay in the FA Cup ▪ Soviet spy Lona Cohen of 45 Cranley Drive, Ruislip is sentenced to twenty years imprisonment. Cohen's husband, Morris, gets twenty-five years ▪ Harry Houghton and his lover, Ethel 'Bunty' Gee, both receive fifteen year sentences ▪ 38-year-old MI6 operative George Blake is interrogated by senior security officers and confesses to being a double-agent working for the KGB ▪ 19-year-old dancer Christine Keeler entertains her landlord Stephen Ward and his friend Yevgeny Ivanov at Wimpole Mews in Marylebone ▪ 'A young girl's awakening in a summer of evil!' - *The Greengage Summer* (with 22-year-old Susannah York and 46-year-old Kenneth More) is now showing at cinemas ▪ 27-year-old Ann Lynn and 39-year-old John Hewer star in *Strip Tease Murder* ▪ 20-year-old Edwin Bush stabs Elsie Batten to death at an antique shop on Cecil Court in Covent Garden. Police issue an identikit image of the murderer - and Bush is caught and arrested five days later ▪ 29-year-old Elizabeth Taylor wins an Oscar for her performance as Gloria Wandrous (a glamorous Manhattan call-girl) in *Butterfield 8* - a film from MGM ▪ ***Buona Sera*** by 32-year-old Mr. Acker Bilk climbs to number seven in the pop chart ▪ ***African Waltz*** by 33-year-old Johnny Dankworth and his Orchestra reaches number nine ▪ 21-year-old striker

Jimmy Greaves bags a hat-trick as Wing Commander Winterbottom's England football team (R Springett, Armfield, McNeil, R Robson, Swan, Flowers, Douglas, Greaves, R Smith, Haynes, R Charlton) thrashes Scotland 9-3 at Wembley. Bryan Douglas, Bobby Smith (2) Johnny Haynes (2) and 28-year-old Bobby Robson are also on the score-sheet for England ▪ 33-year-old Don Revie is the new manager of Second Division Leeds Utd ▪ ***FBI*** by The Shadows (led by 19-year-old guitarist Hank Marvin) is number six on the hit parade ▪ ***And The Heavens Cried*** by 29-year-old Anthony Newley is number seven ▪ 'The most beautiful car in the world' - Jaguar launches the fabulous *E-Type* sports car at an international automobile exposition in Switzerland. With its sweeping lines, elongated bonnet and perfect poise, the new model steals the show at Geneva. The *E-Type 'Roadster'* costs £2,097. The *E-Type 'Coupe'* costs £2,196. Top speed is a 'rip-roaring' 150 mph and 0-60 mph takes just 7.4 seconds ▪ Back in England - the Maidenhead road bypass opens ▪ The new Triumph *Herald 1200* motorcar has a wood veneer dashboard and speeds along at 80 mph ▪ "Gee whiz it's you, you're the one that's makin' me blue. Gee whiz it's you, you're the one who can't be true" - ***Gee Whiz It's You*** by 20-year-old Cliff Richard and the Shadows peaks at number five in the pop chart ▪ ***Who Am I?*** by 20-year-old Adam Faith also reaches number five ▪ 60-year-old Gary Cooper and 39-year-old Deborah Kerr star at cinemas in *The Naked Edge* ▪ 33-year-old Michael Craig and 28-year-old Billie Whitelaw star in *Payroll* - a gritty crime thriller from 39-year-old director Sidney Havers ▪ High street bookmakers are legalised, and hopeful men queue at the counter to place their bets ▪ *Rockavon* wins the 2000 Guineas at Newmarket at odds of sixty-six to one. The seven to four favourite, *Pinturischio*, finishes in fourth place ▪ Crowds flock to football matches ▪ 37,190 spectators pack into St. Andrew's as Matt Gillies' Leicester City (with Gordon Banks, Frank McLintock, Ken Leek and Jimmy Walsh) beat Sheffield Utd 2-0 (after extra-time) in a second semi-final replay in the FA Cup. (The two previous ties had both ended in 0-0 draws) ▪ In the other semi-final, high-flying Tottenham Hotspur beat Burnley 3-0 in front of 69,968 at Villa Park - with goals from Bobby Smith (2) and Cliff Jones ▪ National treasure George Formby suffers a heart attack and dies in hospital aged 56. More than 100,000 people line the funeral route as the cortege of the popular entertainer passes through the streets of Warrington ▪ 'Funniest Carry On Ever!' - 30-year-old Joan Sims, 42-year-old Kenneth Connor, 46-year-old Charles Hawtrey and 47-year-old Sid 'Ha-ak-ak' James star at cinemas in *Carry On Regardless* ▪ 35-year-old Peter Sellers stars in *Mr. Topaze* ▪ *Panorama* is on BBC television - presented by 47-year-old Richard Dimbleby ▪ Double-agent George Blake is convicted of spying for the KGB and sentenced to forty-two years in prison ▪ "Goodbye, (goodbye). Farewell, (farewell). I'm not sure what to do. So long, (so long). Au-revoir, (au-revoir). It's hard but I'll pull through..." ***Are You Sure?*** ("... you won't be sorry. Comes tomorrow, you won't want me back again, to hold you tightly?") by The Allisons (a pop duo, comprising of 20-year-old Bob Day and 21-year-old John Alford) comes second at the Eurovision Song Contest - behind Luxembourg's Jean-Claude Pascal singing ***Nous Les Amoureux*** ▪ 44-year-old Edward Heath meets representatives from European countries to continue the negotiations for Britain's entry into the Common Market ▪ 31-year-old racing driver Stirling Moss (driving a dark blue Lotus, number 20) wins at Monaco for the second year running. 29-year-old Tony Brooks from Dukinfield finishes last (in a racing green BRM, number 16) ▪ *Nearly a Nasty Accident* - a funny new movie starring 41-year-old Jimmy Edwards, 42-year-old Kenneth Connor and 24-year-old Shirley Eaton is at cinemas ▪ Bill Nicholson's Tottenham Hotspur football team are the new champions of Division One. Bill Brown, Maurice Norman, Peter Baker, Ron Henry, Dave Mackay, Cliff Jones, John White, Danny Blanchflower (captain) and 23-year-old striker Les Allen have all been outstanding. Spurs then go on to complete a wonderful league and cup 'double' by beating Leicester City 2-0 in the FA Cup final with goals from 28-year-old Bobby Smith and 26-year-old Terry Dyson. A ticket for the standing enclosure at Wembley costs 3s/6d ▪ Everton finish the season in fifth position in Division One and manager Johnny Carey is sacked (in the back of a taxi) by John Moores ▪ 41-year-old Harry Catterick is installed as Carey's replacement at Goodison Park ▪ 51-year-old Cliff Britton resigns as manager of Preston North End after 'The Lilywhites' are relegated to Division Two ▪ Alf Ramsey's Ipswich Town gain promotion to Division One along with John Harris' Sheffield Utd ▪ ***Frightened City*** by The Shadows (led by 19-year-old guitarist Hank Marvin) climbs to number three in the pop chart ▪ The double A sided single ***More Than I Can Say / Staying In*** by 18-year-old Bobby Vee reaches number four ▪ Chelsea's 21-year-old prolific goal scoring striker Jimmy Greaves transfers to AC Milan for a fee of £80,000 - after netting forty-three goals this season ▪ Manchester City's 21-year-old striker Denis Law also attracts attention from foreign clubs - after scoring twenty-three goals ▪ "Bom ba-ba bom, ba bom, ba bom-ba-bom" - ***Blue Moon*** by The Marcels climbs to number one in the pop chart ▪ "War paint, war paint. You don't need-a war paint..." ***War Paint*** by the Brook Brothers is number five ▪ 'Half-Man ... Half-Wolf' - 23-year-old Oliver Reed stars at cinemas in *The Curse of the Werewolf* ▪ 'A dead hero - or a live coward?' - 29-year-old Virginia McKenna, 39-year-old Bill Travers and 33-year-old Patrick McGoohan star in *Two Living, One Dead* ▪ 48-year-old Percy Thrower appears on television in BBC's *Gardening Club* programme ▪ 35-year-old Richard Baker reads the news ▪ 35-year-old Labour MP Anthony Wedgwood Benn automatically inherits a peerage (on the death of his father) and can no longer take his seat in the House of Commons ▪ 53-year-old Minister of Transport Ernest Marples appoints 47-year-old Dr. Beeching as Chairman of the British Transport Commission ▪ 58-year-old Mr. Justice Stevenson dons a black cap and issues a death sentence to murderer Edwin Bush at the Old Bailey ▪ "De, de-de-d-d, de-de-de-de, der-d-d" - ***On The Rebound*** by Floyd Cramer spends a week at number one on the hit parade ▪ "I want to be your lover, but your friend is all I've stayed" - ***Halfway To Paradise*** by 21-year-old Billy Fury peaks at number three ▪ 26-year-old Elvis Presley stars at cinemas as Pacer Burton, a cowboy of mixed-blood, in *Flaming Star* - a gripping 'Western' adventure from 20th Century Fox ▪ The 'Space Race' continues ▪ NASA scientists look on enviously as 27-year-old Soviet cosmonaut Major Yuri Gagarin is the first man to orbit the Earth - travelling in the *Vostok 1* spacecraft ▪ Back in England - 67-year-old Conservative prime-minister Harold Macmillan and his Chancellor of the Exchequer, Selwyn Lloyd, meet to discuss ways of controlling inflation ▪ 54-year-old leader of the Labour opposition Hugh Gaitskell is ill in bed, suffering from laryngitis ▪ 47-year-old Liberal leader Jo Grimond addresses a rally at Manchester's Free Trade Hall and urges the government to take action on rising prices ▪ Housewives go shopping ▪ A loaf of bread is 10½d ▪ A pint of milk is 7d ▪ McDonald's new *Penguin* chocolate covered biscuits cost thruppence ▪ TV adverts say, 'Don't forget the *Fruit Gums*, Mum' ▪ Families attend matinee screenings at the local *Odeon* picture house ▪ 'Walt Disney's New All-Cartoon Feature' - *One Hundred and One Dalmations* is now showing ▪ Young men ride motorbikes ▪ A James *L1 Comet* has a 98cc engine and costs £102/15s/- (including Purchase Tax) ▪ A James *L24 Commodore* has a 250cc engine and costs £173 (including Purchase Tax) ▪ Middle aged men enjoy an evening in the pub ▪ ***You're Driving Me Crazy*** by The Temperance Seven moves to the top of the pop chart ▪ "Have a drink, have a drink, have a drink on me. Everybody..." ***Have A Drink On Me*** by 30-year-old Lonnie 'King of Skiffle' Donegan is number eight ▪ A pint of bitter costs 1s/5d.

Summer 1961

Fiery Fred Trueman

Monarch:	Queen Elizabeth II (aged 35)
Prime-minister:	Harold Macmillan (aged 67)
Chancellor:	Selwyn Lloyd (aged 57)
Home Secretary:	Rab Butler (aged 58)
Foreign Secretary:	Alec Douglas-Home (aged 58)
Football Manager:	Walter Winterbottom (aged 48)

▪ Cold, wet weather gives way to warm sunshine in late June ▪ 'Well-to-do' young men zip along English trunk roads in open-top sports cars ▪ The brand new MG *Midget* has a top speed of 86 mph and accelerates from 0-60 mph in 19 seconds ▪ The latest *Sunbeam Alpine* has a top speed of 99 mph and accelerates to 60 mph in 13.6 seconds ▪ The new Triumph *TR4* has a top speed of 110 mph and can hit 60 mph in 10.9 seconds ▪ The Doncaster bypass opens ▪ New-fangled push-button 'Panda' pedestrian crossing systems are tested on busy roads ▪ Men form queues at the new high-street bookies, eager to place their bets ▪ *Psidium* wins the Epsom Derby, at odds of sixty-six to one ▪ Retail prices are beginning to rise, putting pressure on hard working families ▪ Housewives in Leicester embrace the modern concept of 'self-service' shopping - and head for the bright new *Tesco* supermarket ▪ *Fairy* is a new type of washing-up liquid ▪ *Galaxy* is a new type of milk chocolate ▪ "So my darling please surrender, all your love so warm and tender" - ***Surrender*** by 26-year-old Elvis Presley is a number one smash hit on both sides of the Atlantic ▪ ***Little Devil*** by 22-year-old Neil Sedaka is number nine ▪ The Beatles (a little-known beat combo) perform lunch time shows at the Cavern Club in Liverpool - and go down a storm with the young audiences packed into the small, cramped venue ▪ 'A city terrorised by its own evil!' - 30-year-old Sean Connery stars as burglar Paddy Damion in new movie *The Frightened City* ▪ 38-year-old Max Bygraves stars as school teacher Mr. Saunders in *Spare the Rod* ▪ 49-year-old executioner Harry Allen prepares the gallows at Pentonville ▪ 21-year-old convicted murderer Edwin Bush is hanged by the neck until dead ▪ Construction work begins on a new 'sky scraper' building in London. When completed, the tower (commissioned by the General Post Office) will be the tallest building in Britain ▪ Noisy schoolboys spend Saturday mornings in the stalls at the local *Odeon* cinema ▪ 'Stupendous New Excitement!' - 34-year-old Gordon Scott is King of the Jungle in *Tarzan the Magnificent* ▪ 'The Wind of Change' continues to blow as Harold Macmillan's Conservative government grants independence to Sierra Leone and Tanganyika ▪ South Africa gives notice that it too wants to leave the Commonwealth ▪ Back in England - the 'colour bar' operated by the Bristol Omnibus Company remains in place. Black people are not considered for employment. Only white people are taken on as drivers or conductors ▪ 'Not suitable for children' - *Wind of Change* is at cinemas, starring 27-year-old Ann Lynn, 41-year-old Donald Pleasence and with 25-year-old Johnny Briggs as Frank Marley - an unemployed, discontented thug with an unfettered hatred of black people ▪ Families watch television ▪ A one-off TV 'special' of BBC's *The Black and White Minstrel Show* is broadcast from the Futurist Theatre in Scarborough ▪ 11-year-old schoolboy Jeremy Paxman from Leeds listens to a transistor radio at home and keeps up to date with the latest news and politics ▪ In a desperate attempt to bolster the value of the pound, 56-year-old Chancellor of the Exchequer Selwyn Lloyd raises the bank rate to seven percent ▪ After consulting with Cabinet colleagues, the Chancellor also announces a 'pay pause' in public sector wages ▪ Trade union leaders protest against the measures - but the Chancellor stands firm ▪ 67-year-old prime-minister Harold Macmillan and his 61-year-old wife Lady Dorothy Cavendish welcome 44-year-old US president John F. Kennedy and his 31-year-old wife Jackie at the start of their short visit to London ▪ ***A Girl Like You*** by Cliff Richard and the Shadows reaches number three in the pop chart ▪ Over in Berlin, thousands of

East German immigrants cross the border to begin a new life in the West ▪ "Protect me. Protect me" - 23-year-old Soviet born dancer Rudolf Nureyev escapes from his KGB minders and defects to Paris ▪ 'The Greatest High Adventure Ever Filmed!' - *The Guns of Navarone*, starring 45-year-old Gregory Peck, 46-year-old Anthony Quinn and 51-year-old David Niven, goes on general release at cinemas ▪ *Dentist on the Job* (with 33-year-old Bob Monkhouse and 24-year-old Shirley Eaton) is also now showing ▪ 22-year-old Susannah York and 29-year-old Alan Bates are pictured together on the front cover of *TV Times* - promoting 'Duel for Love' a new Sunday night drama, part of the *Armchair Theatre* series ▪ 39-year-old Anthony Brown reads the news on commercial television ▪ The blood stained body of Michael Gregsten (shot dead) and his severely injured girlfriend are discovered in a lay-by on the A6 road in Bedfordshire - a nationwide manhunt gets underway to find the murderer ▪ "My little..." ***Runaway*** ("... a run, run, run, run, a runaway") by 26-year-old Del Shannon climbs to number one in the pop chart ▪ ***She She Little Sheila*** by 26-year-old Gene Vincent is number twenty-two ▪ "A pint? That's very nearly an armful" - 37-year-old comedian Tony Hancock performs the blood donor sketch on BBC television ▪ Proven goal-scoring centre-forwards are in demand on football's transfer market ▪ 21-year-old Denis Law leaves Manchester City and joins Torino in Italy for £100,000 ▪ 26-year-old Gerry Hitchens leaves Aston Villa and joins Inter Milan for £85,000. (Villa sign 23-year-old Derek Dougan from Blackburn Rovers for £15,000 as a replacement) ▪ 26-year-old Brian Clough leaves Middlesbrough and joins Alan Brown's Sunderland for £55,000 ▪ "Yeah, yeah, yeah, yah! Yeah, yeah, yeah, yah! Yeah, yeah, yeah, yah!" - ***Temptation*** by The Everly Brothers climbs to number one in the pop chart ▪ 'Emotional Dynamite!' - 53-year-old John Mills and 27-year-old Sylvia Syms star at cinemas in *Flame in the Streets* ▪ 41-year-old Richard Todd stars in *Don't Bother to Knock!* ▪ 30-year-old Liz

Fraser stars in *Watch It, Sailor!* ▪ 12-year-old Prince Charles attends prep school at Cheam ▪ Vicount and Vicountess Althorp are proud parents of newborn baby girl, Diana Frances Spencer ▪ ***Hello Mary Lou*** ("… goodbye heart. Sweet Mary Lou, I'm so in love with you") by 21-year-old Ricky Nelson is number two in the pop chart ▪ Peter West, David Coleman and 53-year-old Dan Maskell commentate on tennis for BBC television ▪ An all-England ladies' final at Wimbledon sees 29-year-old Angela Mortimer from Plymouth defeat 20-year-old Christine Truman from Woodford Green, 4-6, 6-4, 7-5 ▪ 22-year-old Rod Laver wins the men's final ▪ E.W. Swanton, Denis Compton and 49-year-old Brian 'Johnners' Johnston commentate on cricket for BBC television ▪ Batsmen, 25-year-old Geoffrey Pullar and 29-year-old Raman Subba Row stride out together to open the innings for England against Australia at Edgbaston in the first Test Match of the summer. Pullar scores 17. Subba Row hits 59. The match ends in a draw (with Ted Dexter scoring 180 in England's second innings). 30-year-old fast bowler 'fiery' Fred Trueman takes eleven wickets as Peter May's England gain a victory in the third Test at Headingley, but Richie Benaud's Aussies win matches at Lord's and Old Trafford to take the series, 2-1, and retain the Ashes. England players - G Pullar, R Subba Row, E R Dexter, M C Cowdrey (cpt for first two Tests), D B Close, K F Barrington, P B H May (cpt from third Test onwards), M J K Smith, R Illingworth, J T Murray (wkt), D A Allen, G A R Lock, F S Trueman, J B Statham, H L Jackson and J A Flavell are all downcast by another Ashes defeat ▪ ***Well I Ask You*** ("…what a way to treat a guy. What a way to cheat and lie, because I wanted you") by 21-year-old Eden Kane is the new number one hit song ▪ ***Don't You Know It*** by 21-year-old Adam Faith is number twelve ▪ 57-year-old John Snagge reads the news on the wireless for the BBC ▪ The Cold War intensifies between East and West ▪ East Germans cross the border to the West ▪ The Soviets take action by erecting a barbed-wire and concrete wall - effectively partitioning the city of Berlin and stopping the flow of people. The rest of the world looks on, fearing what might develop ▪ Back in England - Trade union leaders continue to protest against the government imposed 'pay pause' and urge their members to strike or 'go slow' ▪ ***You Always Hurt The One You Love*** ("... the one you shouldn't hurt at all") by 24-year-old Clarence 'Frogman' Henry is number six in the pop chart ▪ ***Time*** by 20-year-old Craig Douglas from the Isle of Wight is number nine ▪ 19-year-old Christine Keeler swims naked in the pool during a party at Lord Astor's country residence in Berkshire. 46-year-old Secretary of State for War John Profumo is on hand with a towel to help her dry off ▪ ***Cupid*** ("... draw back you bow, and let your arrow go") by Sam Cooke climbs to number seven on the hit parade ▪ 'Exposure of Spy Activities in the Heart of London!' - thrilling new movie *Highway to Battle* (with 57-year-old Gerard Heinz and 29-year-old Margaret Tyzack) is at cinemas ▪ 48-year-old osteopath Stephen Ward (Christine Keeler's landlord) meets Soviet spy Yevgeny Ivanov for drinks ▪ A bottle of Carling's *Black Label* lager is available in pubs for 1s/6d ▪ A bottle of Ind Coope's *Skol* is 1s/8d ▪ ***That's My Home*** by Mr. Acker Bilk and his Paramount Jazz Band reaches number seven in the pop chart ▪ The 1961-1962 football season gets underway ▪ Aston Villa's new striker Derek Dougan (with shaven head) scores twice in a 2-2 draw against Wolverhampton Wanderers at Villa Park ▪ 25-year-old striker Ray Crawford scores twice as Alf Ramsey's newly promoted Ipswich Town thrash Burnley 6-2 at Portman Road ▪ With the economy faltering and a public sector pay freeze in place, prime-minister Harold Macmillan confirms that Britain has formally applied to join the European Community ▪ "Wo-wo-wo. Oh, yeah, yeah, yeah. Oh, yeah, yeah, yeah" - ***You Don't Know*** by 14-year-old Helen Shapiro from East London climbs to number one on the hit parade ▪ ***Don't Jump Off The Roof Dad*** ("... you might make a hole in the yard") by 40-year-old comedian Tommy Cooper is number forty.

Autumn 1961

The Milky Bars are on Me

Monarch:	Queen Elizabeth II (aged 35)
Prime-minister:	Harold Macmillan (aged 67)
Chancellor:	Selwyn Lloyd (aged 57)
Home Secretary:	Rab Butler (aged 58)
Foreign Secretary:	Alec Douglas-Home (aged 58)
Football Manager:	Walter Winterbottom (aged 48)

▪ "Evening, all" - 65-year-old Jack Warner returns for a new series of *Dixon of Dock Green* on BBC television ▪ Police arrest hundreds of CND protesters in London - including 24-year-old Vanessa Redgrave ▪ "When the mist's-a-rising and the rain is falling, and the wind is blowing cold across the moor"- ***Johnny Remember Me*** by 25-year-old John Leyton is number one in the pop chart ▪ ***Who Put The Bomp*** ("… in the bomp, a-bomp, a-bomp? Who put the ram in the ram-a-lam-a-ding-dong?") by The Viscounts is number twenty-one ▪ The pound remains weak against the dollar ▪ 67-year-old Conservative prime-minister Harold Macmillan meets president Charles de Gaulle to discuss Britain's application to join the European Common Market. De Gaulle expresses his concern; doubtful of the fact that Britain is truly committed to establishing greater unity between European countries ▪ "Spend, spend, spend" - 25-year-old Viv Nicholson and her husband Keith win £150,000 on the football pools and embark on a frenzied spending spree which sees the couple buy two houses, four cars (including a pink Cadillac) and a gold watch worth 80 guineas from *Harrods* ▪ 'Hide your whiskey and lock up your women!' - 42-year-old Richard Todd stars at picture houses in *The Hellions* ▪ 53-year-old Michael Redgrave and 19-year-old Juliet Mills star in *No, My Darling Daughter!* ▪ The double A sided pop single ***Reach For The Stars/ Climb Ev'ry Mountain*** by 24-year-old Shirley Bassey spends a week at number one on the hit parade ▪ "The wind blows…" ***Wild In The Country***

("… and part of the wild, wild country am I") by 26-year-old Elvis Presley is number four ▪ ***Michael Row The Boat*** ("... ashore. Hallelujah") by 30-year-old Lonnie 'King of Skiffle' Donegan is number six ▪ 11-year-old schoolboy Richard Branson from Blackheath enjoys an evening at the cinema ▪ 'Never have so few fiddled so many!' - *On The Fiddle* - a new comedy film, starring 30-year-old Alfred Lynch and 31-year-old Sean Connery (as two RAF pilots looking to make a bit of money on the side), is now showing ▪ 'It's the homicide-splitting comedy of the year' - 48-year-old Sid 'Ha-ak-ak' James, 43-year-old Kenneth Connor and 24-year-old Shirley Eaton star in *What a Carve Up* ▪ Elvis Presley stars as Glenn Tyler, a rowdy, young trouble-maker, in *Wild in the Country* ▪ "Was all over my jealousy, my crime was blind…" ***Jealousy*** by 21-year-old Billy Fury climbs to number two in the pop chart ▪ ***When The Girl In Your Arms Is The Girl In Your Heart*** by 21-year-old Cliff Richard reaches number three ▪ Groovy young people drive hip new motorcars ▪ The sporty Austin *Seven* (aka 'Mini') *Cooper* with 997cc engine is launched. It comes with a painted black roof, a top speed of 88 mph and accelerates from 0-60 mph in 13.5 seconds ▪ Motorists in Plymouth take a spin over the brand new Tamar Road Bridge ▪ Campaigners in London continue to lobby the government to save the Doric arch at Euston Railway Station ▪ Economics student Mick Jagger (aged 18) bumps into his old mate Keith Richards (aged 17) at Dartford Railway Station ▪ "Once…" ***Once in Every Lifetime*** ("… Once, someone will appear") by 33-year-old Ken Dodd reaches number twenty-eight in the pop chart ▪ ***You'll Answer To Me*** by 33-year-old Cleo Laine peaks at number five ▪ 46-year-old Secretary of State for War John Profumo meets up with 19-year-old dancer Christine Keeler for a romantic dinner followed by a night of hot passion in London ▪ The first edition of the satirical paper *Private Eye* is published - 24-year-old Willie Rushton is the designer. 24-year-old Christopher Booker is the editor ▪ The ITA (Initial

Teaching Alphabet) is introduced in some schools - and children now have to learn an extended alphabet consisting of forty-three characters ▪ "All right. Stay bright!" - 34-year-old DJ Alan 'Fluff' Freeman takes over from 35-year-old David Jacobs as presenter of BBC radio's *Pick of the Pops* ▪ ***Kon-Tiki*** by The Shadows (led by 19-year-old guitarist Hank Marvin) is new at number one on the hit parade ▪ ***Hats Off To Larry*** ("... He broke your heart, just like you broke mine") by 26-year-old Del Shannon is number four ▪ "I'm a big disgrace to the Aborigine race..." ***My Boomerang Won't Come Back*** by 36-year-old comedian Charlie Drake is number fourteen ▪ 27-year-old footballer Peter McParland scores the winning goal as Joe Mercer's Aston Villa defeat Danny Williams' Rotherham Utd 3-2 over two legs in the first ever League Cup final ▪ 24-year-old goalkeeper Chic Brodie leaves First Division Wolverhampton Wanderers (after making just one appearance) and signs for Northampton Town of Division Three for £4,000 ▪ Charlton Athletic install floodlights at The Valley football ground ▪ Men in grubby raincoats flock to seedy cinemas to see Pamela Green (38-23-37) in *Naked as Nature Intended* ▪ "The Milky Bars are on me!" - The Milky Bar Kid (played by 10-year-old Terry Brooks) makes his first appearance on television ▪ Ida Barlow (played by 44-year-old Noel Dyson) is knocked down and killed by a bus in *Coronation Street* ▪ "Everybody Out!" - 35-year-old Miriam Karlin and 44-year-old Reg Varney star in *The Rag Trade* ▪ Laughter, snorts and groans are heard - coming from the stalls at the local cinema ▪ 43-year-old Spike Milligan and 49-year-old John Le Mesurier star on the big-screen in the comedy *Invasion Quartet* ▪ 50-year-old Terry-Thomas stars in *A Matter of WHO* ▪ ***Michael*** ("... row the boat ashore. Hallelujah") by The Highwaymen spends a week at number one in the pop chart ▪ "We strolled the lane, together. Laughed at the rain..." ***Together*** by 22-year-old Connie Francis is number six ▪ ***Ain't Gonna Wash For A Week*** by the Brook Brothers is number thirteen ▪ Men with high aspirations visit car showrooms, coveting the latest models ▪ 'For business or pleasure, dual purpose perfection' - the Austin *Seven Countryman* and the Morris *Minor Traveller* (estate versions of BMC's popular 'Mini' cars) are launched ▪ Leather jacket clad 'Rockers' meet up at the *Ace Café* on the North Circular Road near Brent ▪ A Triton 650cc motorbike (a 'hybrid' bike comprising of a Norton frame and a Triumph engine) has a top speed of 125 mph ▪ A BSA *Gold Star* has a top speed of 110 mph ▪ "I'm going well. I'm going Shell. You can be sure of Shell!" - Shell advertise petrol on commercial TV ▪ ***Hit the Road Jack*** ("... and don't you come back no more, no more, no more, no more") by 31-year-old Ray Charles (from Georgia, USA) is number six on the weekly hit parade ▪ "A-hey there..." ***Wild Wind*** ("... A-blow away-a my blues") by 25-year-old John Leyton (from Frinton-on-Sea) is number two ▪ 18-year-old Rosemarie Frankland (36-22-36) is crowned Miss World at the Lyceum theatre ▪ ***You Must Have Been A Beautiful Baby*** ("... You must have been a beautiful child") by 25-year-old Bobby Darin is number ten in the pop chart ▪ "Funny but it's true, what loneliness can do. Since I've been away, I have loved you more each day" - 15-year-old singing sensation Helen Shapiro (from East London) achieves a second number one hit, with ***Walkin' Back To Happiness*** ("... Wo-pa-oh-yeah-yeah!) ▪ 67-year-old prime-minister Harold Macmillan is guest of honour at a dinner held by Fleet Street journalists at the London Press Club ▪ 46-year-old football legend Stanley Matthews (aka the 'Wizard of Dribble') plays his final game for Blackpool before returning to Stoke City. (Matthews' last match for 'The Seasiders' is a 3-0 defeat against Arsenal in front of 41,166 at Highbury) ▪ 16-year-old schoolboy footballer Alan Ball joins Blackpool as an apprentice ▪ 33-year-old Tommy Docherty takes over from 49-year-old Ted Drake as manager of Chelsea ▪ "Every mornin' at the mine you could see him arrive, he stood six foot six and weighed two forty-five. Kinda broad at the shoulder and narrow at the hip, and everybody knew you didn't give no lip to Big John. (Big John, Big J-o-ohn)..." ***Big Bad John*** by 32-year-old Jimmy Dean is number two in the pop chart ▪ ***Runaround Sue*** by 22-year-old Dion is number eleven ▪ 23-year-old Bobby Charlton scores twice as Wing Commander Winterbottom's England football team (R Springett, Armfield, McNeil, R Robson, Swan, Flowers, Douglas, Fantham, Pointer, Viollet, R Charlton) beats Luxembourg 4-1 at Highbury ▪ 'The Incredible Becomes Real!' - 41-year-old Leo McKern and 27-year-old Janet Munro star at cinemas in *The Day the Earth Caught Fire* ▪ 'A Strange New Experience in Shock' - 40-year-old Deborah Kerr and 53-year-old Michael Redgrave star in *The Innocents* ▪ 46-year-old Secretary of State for War John Profumo meets up with 19-year-old dancer Christine Keeler for a night of hot passion in London ▪ "A very old friend came by today, 'cause he was telling everyone in town about the love that he just found, and Marie's the name of..." ***His Latest Flame*** by Elvis Presley climbs to number one in the pop chart - and stays there for four weeks ▪ ***The Savage*** by The Shadows (led by 20-year-old guitarist Hank Marvin) reaches number ten ▪ 27-year-old businessman Brian Epstein stands in the audience at a lunch time show at the Cavern Club in Liverpool - watching a little-known beat combo called The Beatles (21-year-old John Lennon, 19-year-old Paul McCartney, 18-year-old George Harrison and 19-year-old Pete Best) performing rock'n'roll songs ▪ 25-year-old James Hanratty is arrested and charged with the murder of Michael Gregsten who was found shot dead on the A6 road in Bedfordshire ▪ Schoolboys play conkers ▪ Men sit in pubs, complaining about the government imposed 'pay pause' and rising prices ▪ A pint of Watney's *Red Barrel* costs 1s/11d ▪ Housewives seek value for money when they go shopping ▪ 'You get so much out of it, because so much goes into it' - tins of *Heinz* Spaghetti Bolognese are popular ▪ Children munch sweets ▪ Adverts say, '*Smarties Wotalot-Igot!*'

Christmas 1961

On the Pill

Monarch:	Queen Elizabeth II (aged 35)
Prime-minister:	Harold Macmillan (aged 67)
Chancellor:	Selwyn Lloyd (aged 57)
Home Secretary:	Rab Butler (aged 59)
Foreign Secretary:	Alec Douglas-Home (aged 58)
Football Manager:	Walter Winterbottom (aged 48)

▪ 45-year-old Cabinet minister Edward Heath meets representatives from European countries - and continues negotiations for Britain's entry into the Common Market ▪ *Pit of Darkness* (starring 36-year-old William Franklin and 33-year-old Moira Redmond) is now showing at cinemas ▪ 36-year-old Margaret Thatcher MP is the new parliamentary undersecretary in the Ministry of Pensions and National Insurance ▪ *So Evil, So Young* (starring 25-year-old Jill Ireland and 59-year-old Ellen Pollack) is at picture houses ▪ 46-year-old Secretary of State for War John Profumo meets up with 19-year-old dancer Christine Keeler for a night of hot passion in London ▪ Birth control pills are now available on the NHS ▪ "Tra la-la-la, la-la, la-la..." ***Happy Birthday Sweet Sixteen*** by 22-year-old Neil Sedaka from New York is number three on the hit parade ▪ "You'd be down on your knees, you'd be calling to me, but a..." ***Tower Of Strength*** ("... is a-something I'll never be") by 33-year-old Frankie Vaughan from Liverpool is new at number one ▪ 23-year-old Connie Francis from New Jersey features on the front cover of the latest *New Musical Express* paper ▪ 35-year-old David Jacobs presents *Wednesday Magazine* on BBC daytime television. 60-year-old Dilys Powell comments on the latest movie releases ▪ Film studios continue to produce dozens of high-quality pictures each month, in an effort to stem the falling number of people visiting cinemas ▪ 32-year-old Audrey Hepburn stars as Holly Golightly in

Breakfast at Tiffany's. 33-year-old George Peppard and 41-year-old Mickey Rooney also feature ▪ 23-year-old Natalie Wood stars as Maria in *West Side Story*. 23-year-old Richard Beymer and 29-year-old Rita Moreno also feature ▪ "Jesus Christ!" - 27-year-old Alan Bates appears alongside 15-year-old Hayley Mills in *Whistle Down the Wind* ▪ ***Let's Get Together*** by Hayley Mills is number seventeen in the pop chart ▪ ***I'll Get By*** ("... as long as I have you") by 24-year-old Shirley Bassey is number ten ▪ The concept of international travel is glamorous and exciting ▪ The number of trips made abroad each year is increasing ▪ More and more people are using London Airport ▪ The new Oceanic terminal building (for passengers on long-haul flights) is now open ▪ 23-year-old Ian McCaskill leaves the RAF to begin a new career with the Met Office ▪ Temperatures drop to below freezing and it's exceptionally cold during late December ▪ Trade union leaders are angry - Harold Macmillan's Conservative government maintains its 'pay pause' ▪ The cost of living is increasing ▪ A loaf of bread goes up in price, from 10½d to 11½d ▪ A new Ford *Anglia 105E* motorcar goes up from £606/8s/11d to £621/0s/7d ▪ 43-year-old Mrs. Mills performs a medley of pop songs on her piano and the recorded version enters the pop chart at number thirty-five ▪ People buy the latest 7-inch singles at *W. H. Smith & Son* for 6s/4d ▪ ***Stranger On The Shore*** by 32-year-old clarinetist Mr. Acker Bilk is a smash hit - the popular tune reaches number two in the pop chart ▪ ***Take Good Care Of My Baby*** ("... Please don't ever make her blue") by 18-year-old Bobby Vee is number three ▪ Boys and girls enjoy reading books ▪ *Five Go To Demon's Rock* is a smashing new *Famous Five* adventure story from 64-year-old author Enid Blyton ▪ 32-year-old racing driver Stirling Moss is BBC's 'Sports Personality of the Year' ▪ 21-year-old footballer Jimmy Greaves returns from Italy after just six months and signs for Tottenham Hotspur for £99,999 - Greavsie makes an immediate impact by scoring a hat-trick on his debut in a 5-2 win against Blackpool in front of 42,734 spectators at White Hart Lane ▪ Harry Potts' Burnley lead the way in Division One ▪ Bill Nicholson's Spurs and Harry Catterick's Everton are close behind ▪ Bill Shankly's Liverpool are top of Division Two with 23-year-old Roger Hunt, 23-year-old Ian St. John and 27-year-old Alan A'Court in tremendous form ▪ Norman Smith's Newcastle Utd draw 2-2 with Alan Brown's Sunderland in front of 53,991 spectators at St. James' Park ▪ 33-year-old Jimmy Hill takes over as manager of Third Division Coventry City ▪ 67-year-old prime-minister Harold Macmillan and 58-year-old Foreign Secretary Lord Douglas-Home travel to Bermuda for talks with US president J.F. Kennedy. Discussion on the nuclear capability of world powers, especially the Soviets, is high on the agenda ▪ Back in Britain - shops are busy before Christmas ▪ 'Bri-Lon, for the look of it' - Husbands purchase *Bri Nylon* nighties for their wives ▪ Christmas is a time for good cheer and happy tidings ▪ A bottle of *Downs'* Special Port costs 10s/6d ▪ A bottle of *Oloroso* Sherry is 11s/6d ▪ Affluent couples park their Morris *Minors* and Triumph *Heralds* in side-streets and file into *Regent* and *Odeon* cinemas for an evening of entertainment ▪ 'See the strange case of the strangler-killer on the night express!' - 69-year-old Margaret Rutherford is Miss Marple in *Murder, She Said* ▪ 'The story of an American airman in search of love and oblivion!' - 24-year-old Susan Hampshire is Jean, the daughter of a pub landlady, who falls in love with a USAF pilot in wartime Britain in *During One Night* ▪ "Oh, that Johnny, that no-good Johnny. He's been tryin' to steal my lovin' baby away-a" - ***Johnny Will*** by 27-year-old Pat Boone is number four on the hit parade ▪ ***My Friend The Sea*** ("... be true to me. My love, one day, sailed far away") by 29-year-old Petula Clark is number seven ▪ Christmas Day arrives ▪ Small children are excitable ▪ Grandparents come to visit ▪ "To both young and old I send my very best wishes and, as the carol says, may we all hear the angels sing in the coming year" - 35-year-old Queen Elizabeth II addresses the nation via the medium of television ▪ BBC's evening schedule on Christmas Day includes: *The World of Walt Disney* - presented by 35-year-old David Jacobs; *Just William's Luck* - starring William Grahame as William; *This Is Your Life* - where presenter Eamonn Andrews surprises veteran World War I nurse 88-year-old Isabella Woodford; *The Black and White Minstrel Show* - with The Mitchell Minstrels and featuring 28-year-old Leslie Crowther as guest star; and *Rebecca* - a 1940 film based on Daphne du Maurier's novel, starring Sir Laurence Olivier and Joan Fontaine ▪ ITV's evening television schedule on Christmas Day includes *Cartoon Time* - featuring Huckleberry Hound, The Flintstones and Popeye; *People and Places* - with 38-year-old Bill Grundy and 27-year-old Gay Byrne; *All Our Yesterdays* - with Brian Inglis; *Coronation Street* - with characters: Kenneth Barlow, Leonard Swindley, Annie Walker, Len Fairclough, Elsie Tanner, Minnie Caldwell, grumpy Albert Tatlock and miserable Ena Sharples; *Bonanza* - starring Lorne Greene and Michael Landon; and *A Merry Max* - with 39-year-old Max Bygraves ▪ "Moon river, wider than a mile. I'm crossing you in style, some day" - ***Moon River*** by 19-year-old Danny Williams from South Africa is the number one record at Christmas ▪ "'Cause if I searched my whole life through, I know there'll only be a second best for me..." ***I'd Never Find Another You*** by 21-year-old Billy Fury from Liverpool is number five ▪ 26-year-old Ted Dexter is England's cricket captain for a tour of India and Pakistan ▪ England lose the series against India but manage to beat Pakistan. 31-year-old Ken Barrington is England's top run scorer. 32-year-old Tony Lock is the top wicket taker ▪ Housewives hold *Tupperware* parties and purchase modern plastic sandwich boxes and drinks beakers with self-sealing lids for their families ▪ 'Sunfresh is Best' - *Sun-*

fresh orange squash is gulped down by thirsty children ▪ Working men aspire for better things ▪ 21-year-old David Lovell is training to be a bus driver in Birmingham, hoping to progress from his current role of conductor ▪ Motoring technology moves on apace ▪ The new Austin *A40 MkII* comes with fully hydraulic brakes and self-cancelling 'trafficators' as standard. Top speed is 75 mph ▪ 37-year-old Kenneth Kendall reads the news on BBC television ▪ 51-year-old Alf Robens is the new chairman of the National Coal Board ▪ Coal production is at its lowest level for fourteen years - just 195 million tonnes have been mined this year ▪ British Railways has lost £87 million in 1961 - and the losses are growing year-on-year ▪ The Doric arch at Euston Railway Station is demolished despite widespread protests ▪ The economy remains sluggish ▪ Postmen, railwaymen and miners are on a 'go slow' ▪ The government's 'pay pause' policy is criticsed by MPs on the opposition Labour benches 49-year-old Jim Callaghan (Labour, Cardiff South-East) moves a motion in the House of Commons deploring the handling of the economy and "regretting the failure of the Government to propose measures that will increase productivity and remove the underlying weakness in the national economy" ▪ 57-year-old Chancellor of the Exchequer Selwyn Lloyd holds firm, insisting that the Conservative government 'pay-pause' has contributed to increasing the feeling that Britain was again becoming able to beat competition overseas ▪ *Songs of Praise* is new on television - presented by 37-year-old Alan Gibson ▪ 52-year-old Col. Tom Parker (business manager of Elvis Presley) turns down a lucrative deal for his 26-year-old pop superstar to perform a number of shows in Britain ▪ The Beatles (a little-known beat combo from Liverpool) appear at the Tower Ballroom in New Brighton ▪ Inquisitive schoolboys peruse the shelves at newsagents ▪ 28-year-old Sonya Cordeau appears on the front cover of *Parade* - a weekly paper on sale every Friday.

New Year 1962

Z Cars and Steptoe and Son

Monarch:	Queen Elizabeth II (aged 35)
Prime-minister:	Harold Macmillan (aged 68)
Chancellor:	Selwyn Lloyd (aged 57)
Home Secretary:	Rab Butler (aged 59)
Foreign Secretary:	Alec Douglas-Home (aged 58)
Football Manager:	Walter Winterbottom (aged 48)

▪ 67-year-old prime-minister Harold Macmillan travels to Bonn for a meeting with West German Chancellor 85-year-old Dr. Konrad Adenauer ▪ Back in Britain - 35-year-old disc jockey Jimmy Savile presents the *Teen and Twenty Disc Club* on Radio Luxembourg ▪ "I'm rather worried about Jim" - popular BBC radio programme *Mrs. Dale's Diary* is now known simply as *The Dales*. The show has been running for fourteen years ▪ Families in Britain are feeling the squeeze with a national 'pay pause' in place and rising prices ▪ 'Home Help for Every Housewife!' - a *SewMaid* electric sewing machine is available at *Universal* stores for £11/19s/6d ▪ Labour leader Hugh Gaitskell heaps the pressure on Harold Macmillan - calling for the prime-minister to end the freeze on wages ▪ ***Multiplication*** ("... that's the name of the game. And each generation, they play the same") by 25-year-old Bobby Darin is number five on the hit parade ▪ ***Midnight In Moscow*** by 31-year-old Kenny Ball and his Jazzmen is number two ▪ 30-year-old Anne Heywood and 36-year-old Charlie Drake star at cinemas in *Petticoat Pirates* ▪ 21-year-old Jill St. John, 24-year-old Warren Beatty, 63-year-old Lotte Lenya and 48-year-old Vivien Leigh star in *The Roman Spring of Mrs. Stone* - 'the story of an American woman and her abandonment in Rome' ▪ 25-year-old James Hanratty stands trial for the murder of Michael Gregsten (whose body was found on the A6 road in Bedfordshire) ▪ Footballers, 24-year-old Jimmy Melia and 23-year-old Roger Hunt both score twice as Bill Shankly's Liverpool beat Willie Reid's Norwich City 5-4 in a Division Two match ▪ 11-year-old schoolboy Kevin Keegan from Doncaster plays football with his friends in the park ▪ 27-year-old businessman Brian Epstein is the new manager of The Beatles - a little-known beat combo from Liverpool ▪ Teenagers play the latest pop tunes on Columbia portable 4-speed record players ▪ "The young ones, darling we're..." ***The Young Ones*** by Cliff Richard and the Shadows enters the hit parade at number one - and stays there for six weeks! ▪ ***Let's Twist Again*** ("... like we did last summer") by 20-year-old Chubby Checker climbs to number two ▪ ***The Lion Sleeps Tonight (Wimoweh)*** by The Tokens is number eleven ▪ Millions of television viewers tune into BBC in early January to watch a brand new police drama called *Z Cars*. 36-year-old Stratford Johns is DCI Barlow, 34-year-old Frank Windsor is DS Watt, 31-year-old Jimmy Ellis is PC Lynch, 25-year-old Brian Blessed is PC 'Fancy' Smith and 44-year-old Leonard Williams is Desk Sergeant Twentyman ▪ Brian Epstein attempts to negotiate a record contract for his beat combo, The Beatles - but the bosses at Decca Records aren't interested; they turn Epstein down, saying there's no future for guitar bands ▪ Britain's largest car manufacturer makes a name change to one of its models. The Austin *Seven* moniker is dropped and the popular, small, two-door motorcar is now officially called the Austin *Mini* ▪ Triumph announces the new *Vitesse* (a six-cylinder version of the *Herald*) with a top speed of 90 mph and capable of accelerating from 0-60 mph in 17.1 seconds. A 'soft-top' version of the new car costs £893/7s/9d, including purchase tax ▪ Old people sit indoors, watching TV ▪ 36-year-old Harry H. Corbett and 49-year-old Wilfrid Brambell make the nation laugh as they star as rag-and-bone men in a brand new TV comedy called *Steptoe and Son* ▪ Young people enjoy an evening out at the dance hall ▪ 21-year-old rock'n'roll star Billy Fury appears on stage at the Gaumont in Derby. Seats are priced between 4s/6d and 8s/6d ▪ "Come on, baby, let's do..." ***The Twist*** ("... Take me by my little hand and go like this") by 20-year-old Chubby Checker is number fourteen in the pop chart ▪ "If somebody else can make you happier than I can make you..." ***Run To Him*** ("... my tears will dry") by 18-year-old Bobby Vee is number seven ▪ Footballers, 25-year-old Ray Crawford and 28-year-old Ted Phillips score the goals as Alf Ramsey's newly promoted Ipswich Town win three out of five matches to close the gap on Division One leaders Burnley to just four points ▪ 28-year-old striker Dennis Viollet leaves First Division Manchester Utd and joins Tony Waddington's Second Division Stoke City for £25,000 ▪ 31-year-old Roy Sproson is on the score-sheet for Third Division Port Vale in a 1-2 defeat against Bradford Park Avenue ▪ "So I leave you softly, long before you miss me, long before your arms can beg me stay for one more hour, or one more day" - ***Softly, As I Leave You*** by 31-year-old Matt Monro is number ten in the pop chart ▪ "If you keep tryin', you'll hear me sighin' ..." ***Forget Me Not*** by 21-year-old Eden Kane is number three ▪ The 'Space Race' continues. 40-year-old John Glenn is the first American in Space - Glenn orbits the Earth in *Friendship 7* ▪ Back in England - 'That Joyous, Jumping, Jubilant Musical!' - 21-year-old Cliff Richard and the Shadows star in *The Young Ones* at cinemas. Richard O'Sullivan, Melvyn Hayes, Carole Gray and 53-year-old Robert Morley also feature in the hit film ▪ 23-year-old Natalie Wood and 24-year-old Warren Beatty star as Deanie and Bud in *Splendor in the Grass* ▪ 27-year-old Elvis Presley stars in *Blue Hawaii* - playing the role of Chad Gates, a former G. I. in the US Army, now back at home on the exotic Pacific island, and caught up in a love triangle with two beautiful girls, ▪ "Rock-a-hula, rock-rock-a-hula" - ***Rock-A-Hula Baby*** by Elvis is new at number one ▪ "Don't dig there, dig it elsewhere. You're digging it round and it ought to be square" - ***The Hole In The Ground*** by 33-year-old

Bernard Cribbins is number nine ▪ Retail prices continue to rise ▪ Housewives in Bedford embrace the modern concept of 'self-service' shopping and head for the bright new *Safeway* supermarket - looking for a bargain ▪ TV adverts say, '*Daz* washes so white you can see the difference' ▪ Commercial television programmes on a Saturday night include: *Thank Your Lucky Stars* - introduced by Brian Matthews; *Our House* - starring 40-year-old Hattie Jacques and 28-year-old Bernard Bresslaw; *Cheyenne* - with 34-year-old Clint Walker as cowboy Cheyenne Bodie; and *Candid Camera* - 'The Hidden Eye of Television' featuring 34-year-old Jonathan Routh ▪ "They call me..." ***The Wanderer*** ("... Yeah, the wanderer. I roam around, around, around") by 22-year-old Dion enters the hit parade at number forty-three and climbs to number ten after six weeks ▪ ***Lonesome*** by Adam Faith peaks at number twelve ▪ The pay freeze continues ▪ Prime-minister Harold Macmillan and his Conservative government are under pressure ▪ 57-year-old Chancellor of the Exchequer Selwyn Lloyd introduces a white paper on Incomes Policy, linking any future public sector pay rise to increased productivity ▪ 55-year-old Hugh Gaitskell (leader of the Labour opposition) tells a conference in Harrogate that we are governed by "tired, stubborn men who know that all their cherished nostrums have failed, but have neither the courage nor the energy to change their course." ▪ People are forced to cut back on their spending ▪ The average price of a house in the UK is £2,400 ▪ A new Vauxhall *Velox* motorcar costs £956 ▪ A new Austin *A40 MkII* is £619/15s/3d ▪ A pint of bitter costs 1s/5d at the Red Lion ▪ A pint of mild is 1s/2d ▪ Those that can afford an evening out visit the local cinema ▪ 29-year-old Dorinda Stevens and 53-year-old Reginald Beckwith star in *Hair of the Dog* - the hilarious story of a commissionaire at a razor blade factory who decides to grow a beard ▪ 13-year-old Prince Charles undergoes an operation for appendicitis at Great Ormond Street Hospital.

Spring 1962

New-fangled 'Panda' road crossings

Monarch:	Queen Elizabeth II (aged 36)
Prime-minister:	Harold Macmillan (aged 68)
Chancellor:	Selwyn Lloyd (aged 57)
Home Secretary:	Rab Butler (aged 59)
Foreign Secretary:	Alec Douglas-Home (aged 58)
Football Manager:	Walter Winterbottom (aged 49)

▪ Inflation is rising and millions of people are finding life hard with the nationwide pay freeze still in place ▪ A loaf of bread goes up in price, from 11½d to 12d ▪ Questions are asked in the House of Commons about the ever increasing cost of living ▪ Pressure builds on Harold Macmillan and his 57-year-old Chancellor of the Exchequer Selwyn Lloyd ▪ The 68-year-old prime-minister stands firm and maintains his government's position on restricting wages - the long running 'pay pause' will remain ▪ 48-year-old Liberal leader Jo Grimond attacks the government's economic plans saying they show no proposals for sustained growth ▪ 19-year-old economics student Vince Cable listens to news reports on the radio ▪ The popularity of the Conservative government has plummeted ▪ The Tories lose a by-election to the Liberals at Orpington in Kent ▪ 'A Special Delivery of Laughs!' - *Postman's Knock* (with 44-year-old Spike Milligan and 30-year-old Barbara Shelley) is now showing at cinemas ▪ *HMS Defiant* (with 48-year-old Alec Guinness, 41-year-old Dirk Bogarde and 48-year-old Anthony Quayle) is coming soon ▪ A report by the Royal College of Physicians is published - conclusively linking smoking to lung cancer and warning that smokers will have shorter lives than non-smokers ▪ Adverts say, '*Park Drive* - "I Like Them" Available in Plain or Tipped' ▪ 50-year-old executioner Harry Allen prepares the gallows at Bedford Prison ▪ James Hanratty (the A6 road murderer) is hanged by the neck until dead ▪ ***Wonderful Land*** (another 'catchy' electric guitar instrumental) by The Shadows climbs to number one in the pop chart - and stays there for eight weeks! ▪ "Let me tell you about a place, somewhere up New York way" - ***Twistin' The Night Away*** by Sam Cooke is number six ▪ Millions of TV viewers enjoy *The Black and White Minstrel Show* on BBC on Saturday evenings ▪ In the West Country, the 'colour bar' operated by the Bristol Omnibus Company remains in place. Black people are not considered for employment. Only white people are taken on as drivers or conductors ▪ The old electric powered trolley-buses in London are replaced by diesel vehicles ▪ New-fangled push-button 'Panda' crossing systems are introduced throughout the country - after being trialed on busy roads last year. Some pedestrians and drivers still find the complex sequence of flashing lights a little confusing ▪ The Stevenage bypass opens - eight miles of brand new dual carriageway for drivers to speed along ▪ The latest Hillman *Super Minx* family motorcar costs £856 and has a top speed of 83 mph ▪ People enjoy an evening at the cinema ▪ 58-year-old Bing Crosby, 58-year-old Bob Hope and 28-year-old Joan Collins (36-23-37) star in *The Road to Hong Kong* - with 47-year-old Dorothy Lamour making a cameo appearance ▪ 41-year-old Kenneth Wolstenholme presents a round-up of football results on BBC television ▪ Accrington Stanley (of the Fourth Division) lose 4-0 away against Crewe Alexandra. Mounting debts at the Peel Ground club have become unsustainable and directors of Accrington have no choice but to send a letter of resignation to the Football League ▪ Second Division Norwich City defeat Fourth Division Rochdale 4-0 over two legs to win the League Cup ▪ 16-year-old goalkeeper Gary Sprake makes his debut for Leeds Utd in Division Two ▪ Alf Ramsey's Ipswich Town beat Wolverhampton Wanderers 3-2 and move above Burnley at the top of Division One ▪ Millions of people complete a pools coupon each week in the hope of winning a fortune ▪ Charles Dormer from Woodford in Essex wins £38,462 on *Littlewoods* - and donates most of his dividend to charity ▪ "I've lost him but I don't know how. He's going with another now" - ***Tell Me What He Said*** by 15-year-old singing sensation Helen Shapiro (from East London) is number two in the pop chart ▪ 33-year-old Jeremy Thorpe MP enjoys a tryst with 22-year-old stable-boy Norman Josiffe at a secret location in London ▪ 20-year-old Brian Jones meets 18-year-old Mick Jagger and his friend Keith Richards at a club in Ealing. The three young men decide to form a rhythm and blues band together ▪ "Dream..." ***Dream Baby*** by 25-year-old Roy Orbison moves up to number two in the pop chart ▪ ***March Of The Siamese Children*** by 31-year-old Kenny Ball and his Jazzmen reaches number four ▪ ***Fanlight Fanny*** by 30-year-old Clinton Ford from Salford stalls at number twenty-two ▪ Men dream of owning a fast sports car ▪ The sleek new MG *B* has a top speed of 100 mph and is capable of 0-60 mph in 11 seconds ▪ 33-year-old racing driver Graham Hill wins his first Formula One race when he takes the chequered flag at the Dutch Grand Prix ▪ 38-year-old Leslie Phillips, 36-year-old Stanley Baxter and 59-year-old Wilfrid Hyde White star at cinemas in *Crooks Anonymous* ▪ 25-year-old footballer Roy Vernon bags a hat-trick as Everton thrash Cardiff City 8-3 in a Division One match at Goodison Park ▪ ***The Theme From Z Cars*** by Johnny Keating climbs to number eight in the pop chart ▪ ***The Theme from Dr. Kildare*** by Johnnie Spence reaches number fifteen ▪ 27-year-old Sophia Loren (38-24-38) wins an Oscar for her performance in *Two Women* ▪ *A Kind of Loving* (starring 28-year-old Alan Bates, 23-year-old June Ritchie and 51-year-old Thora Hird) is on general release at cinemas ▪ 'That 'Carry On' Crew in a Luxury Laughter Cruise' - 48-year-old Sid 'Ha-ak-ak' James and 29-year-old Lance Percival star in *Carry On Cruising* - the first Carry On film in colour ▪ 22-year-old Billy Fury sings ***Last Night Was Made For Love*** ("... but where were you?") ▪ 27-year-old Pat Boone sings "Tell me..." ***Quando Quando Quando*** ▪ ***Wonderful Land*** by The Shadows (led by 20-year-old guitarist Hank Marvin) remains at number one on the weekly hit parade ▪ ***Hey! Little Girl*** ("... let me fix your broken heart") by 27-year-old Del Shannon is number two ▪ 42-year-old Alf Ramsey's Ipswich Town beat Aston Villa 2-0 on Saturday the twenty-eighth of April to become the new champions of English football - it's Ipswich's first ever Division One title and they've used a revolutionary 4-3-3 system, playing without the traditional two 'wingers'. Roy Bailey, Andy Nelson, Billy Baxter, Larry Carberry, John Compton, Jimmy Leadbetter, John Elsworthy, Roy Stephenson, Dougie Moran, Ray Crawford (with thirty-three goals) and Ted Phillips (with twenty-eight goals) have all been outstanding for the 'Tractor Boys' ▪ "Hey..." ***Hey! Baby!*** ("... I want to know, if you'll be my girl") by 21-year-old Bruce Channel is number two on the hit parade ▪ ***Johnny Angel*** ("... Sha-dum-da-dum. How I love him") by 18-year-old Shelley Fabares is number forty-one ▪ 48-year-old Bill Shankly's Liverpool are champions of Division Two - 23-year-old centre-forward Roger Hunt has scored forty-one goals and 23-year-old Ian St. John has scored eighteen. Liverpool are promoted to Division One along with Johnny Carey's Orient (who've pipped Alan Brown's Sunderland to the runners-up spot) ▪ 'Come on You Spurs!' - 22-year-old Jimmy 'Greavsie' Greaves scores a goal after just three minutes of the FA Cup final and Bill Nicholson's Tottenham Hotspur go on to beat Harry Potts' Burnley 3-1 at Wembley. 36-year-old captain Danny Blanchflower lifts the cup for Spurs. 47-year-old Jim Finney from St. Helens is referee. A ticket for the standing enclosure at the Empire Stadium costs five shillings ▪ ***Nut Rocker*** by B Bumble and the Stingers spends a week at number one in the pop chart ▪ "Love letters straight from your heart. Keeps us so near while apart" - ***Love Letters*** by 27-year-old Ketty Lester is number four ▪ "I only wanna love you..." ***As You Like It*** by 21-year-old Adam Faith is number five ▪ Stuart Sutcliffe, former bass player in The Beatles (a little-known beat combo from Liverpool), dies of a brain haemorrhage aged 21 ▪ 13-year-old Prince Charles begins his first term at Gordonstoun, a public school near Elgin in Scotland ▪ 14-year-old Jeremy Beadle attends Orpington County Secondary Boys' School ▪ Walt Disney's *The Prince and the Pauper* is now showing at cinemas ▪ George Swindin steps down as Arsenal football manager and 38-year-old Billy Wright takes over as boss at Highbury ▪ 21-year-old Bobby Moore makes his debut for England in a 0-4 win against Peru. (22-year-old striker Jimmy 'Greavsie' Greaves bags a hat-trick in the same match) ▪ Thunderstorms sweep across the country in late Spring ▪ The cost of living continues to rise ▪ Prime-minister Harold Macmillan and his Chancellor of the Exchequer, Selwyn Lloyd, remain under pressure due to the failing economy and the low value of the pound ▪ 56-year-old leader of the Labour opposition Hugh Gaitskell addresses a Young Socialists' rally in Skegness and talks of nationalising key industries if Labour were to come to power ▪ 21-year-old newly qualified bus driver David Lovell (badge number DD44615) asks 19-year-old 'clippy' Maggie Gilhooly to meet him for a drink after work ▪ "Well..." ***Do You Want To Dance*** ("... and a-hold my hand") by 21-year-old Cliff Richard / The Shadows reaches number two in the pop chart ▪ ***Ginny Come Lately*** ("... my dream come true - ooh - ooh -ooh") by 18-year-old Brian Hyland is number five ▪ The Beatles (a little-known beat combo from Liverpool), comprising of band members: 21-year-old John Lennon, 19-year-old Paul McCartney, 19-year-old George Harrison and 20-year-old Pete Best, travel to Germany for a third time, and perform shows at the Star Club in Hamburg ▪ Back in England - Groovy young 'cats' wear tight fitting 'drainpipe' jeans and sit together in the park drinking alcohol ▪ 'What's better than Long Life? .. Sharing it!' - *Long Life* canned beer (from Ind Coope) is available from the 'off-license' shop. Adverts say: 'It's the only beer brewed exclusively for the can. Buy it in the 6-pack.'

Summer 1962

Pete Best out. Ringo Starr in.

Monarch:	Queen Elizabeth II (aged 36)
Prime-minister:	Harold Macmillan (aged 68)
Chancellor:	Reginald Maudling (aged 45)
Home Secretary:	Henry Brooke (aged 59)
Foreign Secretary:	Alec Douglas-Home (aged 59)
Football Manager:	Walter Winterbottom (aged 49)

▪ The weather in early June is sunny and dry, but rather cool ▪ 68-year-old Conservative prime-minister Harold Macmillan is under pressure ▪ The Tories lose a by-election to Labour at Middlesbrough West ▪ "Don't want a four leaf clover. Don't want an old horseshoe. Want your kiss 'cause I just can't miss, with a good luck charm like you" - ***Good Luck Charm*** by 27-year-old Elvis Presley enters the pop chart at number sixteen ▪ The UK's first legal casino opens in Brighton ▪ Disused churches and cinemas are converted into bingo halls ▪ *Butlin's* open a new holiday camp at Minehead in Somerset ▪ "By Jove, Missus!" - 34-year-old entertainer Ken Dodd is in summer season at Blackpool ▪ 'She's Wonderful, Our Glad' - 43-year-old Mrs. Mills appears in a Bank Holiday Spectacular at Clacton-on-Sea ▪ Communication technology moves on apace ▪ American satellite *Telstar* is launched into space from Cape Canaveral - enabling television pictures to be beamed 'live' across the Atlantic. The first broadcast is made on the twenty-third of July, and features Richard Dimbleby reporting from Brussels for the BBC and Walter Cronkite reporting from the United States for CBS ▪ "Come on and be my little…"***Good Luck Charm*** ("… Uh-huh-huh, you sweet delight") by Elvis Presley moves to the top of the hit parade and stays there for five weeks! ▪ "V-A-C-A-T-I-O-N in the summer sun!" - ***Vacation*** by 24-year-old Connie Francis is number ten ▪ The Beatles (a little-known beat combo from Liverpool) sign a record contract with EMI (Parlophone) - a business deal negotiated by their manager, 27-year-old Brian Epstein. Shortly afterwards, 20-year-old drummer Pete Best is sacked from the group and 22-year-old Ringo Starr is hired as a replacement ▪ 11-year-old schoolboy Phil Collins from Chiswick in London dreams of one day playing drums in a rock'n'roll band ▪ 49-year-old Richard Dimbleby presents *Panorama* on Monday evenings on BBC television ▪ The government imposed 'pay pause' appears not to have worked; the economy remains weak and recent losses at by-elections show that voters have taken against the Conservatives. Running short on options, 68-year-old prime-minister Harold Macmillan decides to 'sacrifice' seven members of his Cabinet in order to save himself - in 'The Night of the Long Knives.' Chancellor of the Exchequer Selwyn Lloyd is one of the senior ministers unceremoniously sacked; 45-year-old Reg Maudling takes over at the Treasury ▪ "In the night there are sights to be seen. Stars like jewels on the crown of a Queen. But the only sight I wanna view, is that wonderful picture of you" - ***A Picture Of You*** by 21-year-old Joe Brown and the Bruvvers reaches number two in the pop chart ▪ ***Sharing You*** by Bobby Vee is number ten ▪ 47-year-old Norman Wisdom brings cheer and laughter to the nation. In the character of Norman Pitkin, Wisdom plays an undercover policeman in his latest film, *On the Beat* ▪ 'Twelve minutes to live … or die!' - 28-year-old Ann Lynn stars in a thriller called *Strongroom* ▪ 43-year-old Howard Keel and 23-year-old Janette Scott star in *The Day of the Triffids* ▪ Rain clouds gather, and the weather turns wet and grey ▪ Millions of people rely on the railways ▪ Commuters take the train - on their way to work ▪ Families take the train - as they go on holiday ▪ Steam locomotives speed between towns and cities and seaside resorts ▪ A Class 5101 (no. 4142) engine brings a train of passengers into Chipping Norton Railway Station ▪ The Transport Act 1962 is passed by Parliament ▪ Ernest Marples (Minister of Transport) instructs Dr. Beeching (Chairman of the British Transport Commission) to find ways of achieving greater efficiencies in the railway network ▪ Meanwhile, the national road network continues to develop and grow ▪ The first section of M5 motorway (running for twenty miles between Bromsgrove and Strensham) is now open to motorists ▪ More and more people purchase motorcars ▪ 'Every Road is Motorway Smooth!' - The brand new Morris *1100* comes with state-of-the-art hydrolastic suspension and front wheel drive; top speed is 78 mph and 0-60 mph acceleration time is 22.2 seconds ▪ Hollywood sex-siren Marilyn Monroe (36-23-36) dies from a drugs overdose aged 36 ▪ ***Jezebel*** ("... if ever the devil was born without a pair of horns, it was you, Jezebel, it was you") by 23-year-old Marty Wilde is number nineteen in the pop chart ▪ ***Right Said Fred*** ("... both of us together, one each end and steady as we go") by 33-year-old Bernard Cribbins is number ten ▪ 44-year-old terrorist Nelson Mandela is captured by police in South Africa and taken into in custody ▪ Back in England - the weather is inclement ▪ Cricketers, Geoff Pullar and Colin Cowdrey stride out together to open the batting for England against Pakistan at Edgbaston. Pullar makes 22 runs. Cowdrey scores an impressive 159 and England win the match. 31-year-old fast bowler 'fiery' Fred Trueman takes 6 wickets for just 31 runs in the second Test at Lord's. 35-year-old batsman Tom Graveney scores 114 in the fourth Test at Trent Bridge and Ted Dexter's team wins the summer Test series, 4-0 ▪ "How many kinds of sweet flowers grow in an..." ***English Country Garden*** by 28-year-old Jimmie Rodgers is number five on the hit parade ▪ ***The Green Leaves Of Summer*** by 32-year-old Kenny Ball and his Jazzmen is number seven ▪ 26-year-old racing driver Jim Clark wins the British Grand Prix at Aintree in a dark green Lotus (number 20). Clark's team mate John Surtees (the former motorbike racing world champion) is second and Graham Hill is fourth - in a dark green/blue BRM (number 12) ▪ 11-year-old schoolboy Barry Sheene from Holborn in London wins a pushbike race against his friends in the street ▪ Families gather around the television set ▪ 37-year-old Harry H. Corbett and 50-year-old Wilfrid Brambell star in the first full series of *Steptoe and Son* ▪ 35-year-old Terry Scott and 39-year-old Hugh Lloyd star in *Hugh and I* ▪ Soap-opera characters Ken Barlow (played by 30-year-old Bill Roache) and Valerie Tatlock (played by 27-year-old Anne Reid) are married in *Coronation Street* ▪ "Come outside / What for? / Come outside / What's the rush?" - ***Come Outside*** by Mike Sarne with Wendy Richard is number one for two weeks ▪ ***Don't Ever Change*** by The Crickets is number five ▪ England's footballers travel to Chile for the FIFA world cup tournament. Ron Flowers, Bobby Charlton and Jimmy 'Greavsie' Greaves score in a 3-1 victory over Argentina, but England are knocked out in the quarter finals - losing 3-1 to (eventual tournament winners) Brazil. Ron Springett, Ray Wilson, Jimmy Armfield, Bobby Moore, Maurice Norman, Johnny Haynes (captain), Ron Flowers, Alan Peacock, Bryan Douglas, Bobby Charlton, Jimmy 'Greavsie' Greaves and 27-year-old Gerry Hitchens all return home disappointed ▪ 49-year-old Wing Commander Walter Winterbottom announces that he is to step down as England's football manger after being in charge for sixteen years ▪ Building work begins on a new translucent roof for the Empire Stadium in Wembley; it's part of a modernisation plan ahead of the next world cup finals which are scheduled to be held in England in four years' time ▪ "Comma-comma, down-dooby-doo, down down. Comma-comma, down-dooby-doo, down down…" ***Breaking Up Is Hard To Do*** by 23-year-old Neil Sedaka reaches number seven in the pop chart ▪ "I've made up my mind to live in memory of the lonesome times" - ***I Can't Stop Loving You*** by 31-year-old Ray Charles is number one ▪ The Rolling Stones (with band members: Mick Jagger, Keith Richards, Brian Jones - aka Elmo Lewis, Dick Taylor, Ian Stewart and Mick Avory) play their first gig at the Marquee Club on Oxford Street in London ▪ 23-year-old footballer David Layne transfers from Bradford City to Sheffield Wednesday for

£22,000 ▪ 22-year-old Denis Law transfers from Torino in Italy to Manchester Utd for £115,000. Law scores a goal on his debut for Matt Busby's team in a 2-2 draw against West Bromwich Albion ▪ 22-year-old Joe Baker transfers from Torino in Italy to Arsenal for £70,000. Baker scores a goal on his debut for Billy Wright's team in a 1-2 victory over Orient ▪ 44-year-old Joe Harvey is the new manager of Second Division Newcastle Utd ▪ 44-year-old Tim Ward is the new manager of Second Division Derby County ▪ ***I Remember You*** ("…ooh") by 24-year-old Frank Ifield from Coventry reaches number one on the hit parade - and stays there for seven weeks! ▪ "You better come home..." ***Speedy Gonzales*** by 28-year-old Pat Boone is number two ▪ ***Once Upon A Dream*** by 22-year-old Billy Fury is number seven ▪ A major international 'situation' is developing in the Caribbean ▪ US Intelligence reports show that Cuban leader Fidel Castro has given the go-ahead for Soviet Union missiles to be installed on Cuba - within striking range of America ▪ 28-year-old Chris Bonnington and 25-year-old Ian Clough are the first British mountaineers to conquer the north face of the Eiger ▪ Back in England - violence breaks out in London at a street rally organised by 65-year-old Oswald Mosley's Union Movement. Police make fifty-four arrests including that of Mosley's son, 22-year-old Max ▪ 56-year-old Labour leader Hugh Gaitskell is given a civic reception by dignatries in Wolverhampton ▪ ***Guitar Tango*** by The Shadows (led by 20-year-old guitarist Hank Marvin) reaches number four in the pop chart ▪ ***Dancin' Party*** by 20-year-old Chubby Checker stalls at number nineteen ▪ 'Pete Forever! Ringo Never!' - fans of The Beatles protest outside the Cavern Club in Liverpool, upset over the recent change of drummer ▪ 21-year-old John Lennon (of The Beatles) marries 22-year-old Cynthia Powell ▪ 30-year-old (married) Elizabeth Taylor and 36-year-old (married) Richard Burton conduct an adulterous affair as they're filming the movie *Cleopatra* ▪ Adverts say, 'Schweppes Schhh… You Know who.'

Autumn 1962

Sean Connery is 007 in Dr. No

Monarch:	Queen Elizabeth II (aged 36)
Prime-minister:	Harold Macmillan (aged 68)
Chancellor:	Reginald Maudling (aged 45)
Home Secretary:	Henry Brooke (aged 59)
Foreign Secretary:	Alec Douglas-Home (aged 59)
Football Manager:	Walter Winterbottom (aged 49)

▪ US military leaders confirm to President Kennedy that the Soviets have missile bases established on the island of Cuba. (A distance of just 103 miles from the state of Florida) ▪ "What are you doing here? Looking for shells? / No, I'm just looking" - 32-year-old Sean Connery stars at cinemas as James Bond (aka 007) in *Dr. No*. 26-year-old Ursula Andress (38-25-35) also features - and, in one memorable scene, the beautiful actress emerges from the sea, onto a tropical beach, in a white bikini ▪ "Her hair is soft and her eyes are, oh, so blue. (Wah-doo-wap). She's all the things a girl should be, but..." ***She's Not You*** by 27-year-old Elvis Presley is number one in the pop chart ▪ ***It'll Be Me*** ("... and I'll be looking for you") by 22-year-old Cliff Richard and the Shadows is number two ▪ 20-year-old dancer Christine Keeler from London meets her friend 17-year-old Mandy Rice-Davies for drinks ▪ 49-year-old osteopath Stephen Ward meets his friend Yevgeny Ivanov (a Soviet spy) for drinks ▪ The Cuban missile crisis escalates ▪ The Soviet Foreign Minister warns that an American attack on Cuba could lead to full-scale war ▪ Millions look on anxiously as the two world super powers square up to each other ▪ British prime-minister Harold Macmillan pledges his support to America and speaks daily on the telephone with his friend President Kennedy ▪ Meanwhile, in Britain, television viewers tune in for a new series of *Z Cars* on BBC ▪ "Evening, all" - 66-year-old Jack Warner stars in a new series of *Dixon of Dock Green* ▪ 32-year-old footballer John Dick transfers from First Division West Ham Utd to Fourth Division Brentford for £17,500 ▪ "Thinking of things. Like a walk in the park. Things. Like a kiss in the dark..." ***Things*** by 26-year-old Bobby Darin climbs to number two in the pop chart ▪ 62-year-old Lady Dorothy Macmillan (wife of the prime-minister) visits the constituency of North Cornwall to see the new town hall and community centre building at Wadebridge. Lady Macmillan partakes in a coffee morning organized by the women members of North Cornwall Conservative Association, and later pays a brief visit to the seaside town of Looe ▪ 10-year-old schoolboy Douglas Adams from Brentwood finishes his homework and then drifts off into a pleasant daydream ▪ "I wish I was a spaceman, the fastest guy alive. I'd fly you round the universe in..." *Fireball XL5* (filmed in 'SUPERMARIONATION') is a wonderful new programme for children ▪ People enjoy an evening at the cinema ▪ 25-year-old Tom Courtenay and 54-year-old Michael Redgrave star in *The Loneliness of a Long Distance Runner* ▪ 41-year-old Peter Ustinov directs, produces and stars in *Billy Budd* - an epic adventure on the high seas ▪ "One time, a long time ago, on a mountain in Switzerland, yo-lo-lo-lo. There lived a fair young maiden, lovely, but lonely, yo-oh-oh-oh" - ***Swiss Made*** by 27-year-old Del Shannon is number two on the hit parade ▪ "Oh, Lordy..." ***Pick A Bale Of Cotton*** by 31-year-old Lonnie 'King of Skiffle' Donegan slides down the chart after peaking at number eleven ▪ Construction work begins beneath the streets of London on a brand new tube railway - the Victoria line ▪ 32-year-old Gerald Sinstadt presents *Sports Session* on BBC radio's Home Service on Saturday evenings ▪ 29-year-old American Sonny Liston is the new heavy-weight boxing champion of the world ▪ It's announced that Alf Ramsey (currently at Ipswich Town) is to be the next manager of the England football team. The 42-year-old will take over as boss of the national side at the end of the season ▪ The previous manager, Wing Commander Winterbottom, takes up a new post as secretary of the Central Council for Physical Recreation ▪ 22-year-old centre-forward Joe Baker bags a hat-trick as Arsenal defeat Wolverhampton Wanderers 5-4 in Division One at Highbury ▪ 24-year-old centre-forward Derek Dougan also bags a hat-trick as Aston Villa thrash Peterborough Utd 6-1 in the first round of the new League Cup competition - and 7-year-old schoolboy Jimmy Grant looks on from the Trinity Road Grand Stand at Villa Park ▪ ***The James Bond Theme*** by The John Barry Orchestra is number thirteen on the hit parade ▪ 34-year-old Roger Moore plays Simon Templar in a brand new TV series called *The Saint* - broadcast weekly on Thursday evenings ▪ 23-year-old David Frost and 28-year-old Millicent Martin present a satirical programme called *That Was The Week That Was* on BBC. This controversial new show contains songs and sketches designed to poke fun at 'the establishment'. (27-year-old 'would be' writer David Nobbs feels compelled to write a script and submit it) ▪ "Here's a starter for ten" - 27-year-old Bamber Gascoigne hosts *University Challenge* ▪ "What now my love, now that you left me? How can I live through another day?" - ***What Now My Love*** by 25-year-old Shirley Bassey from Cardiff reaches number five in the pop chart ▪ ***It Might As Well Rain Until September*** by 20-year-old Carole King from New York is number three ▪ The situation in Cuba has reached a dangerous and critical stage ▪ Millions of people around the world fear the worst. The outcome of this crisis could be a full-scale nuclear war ▪ President Kennedy considers making air-strikes on Soviet missile bases in Cuba ▪ US military forces go to DEFCON 3 ▪ The anxiety for most people is too much to bear. Then, suddenly, there's a glimmer of hope. First Secretary Khrushchev agrees to remove USSR missiles - in return for an American commitment not to invade Cuba. There could yet be a peaceful solution to the crisis ▪ ***Telstar*** by The Tornados climbs to number one in the pop chart - and stays there for five weeks! ▪ "Everybody's doing a brand new dance now" - ***The Loco-Motion*** by 19-year-old Little Eva is number two ▪ 15-year-old

Pete Waterman finishes a shift working on the railways in Wolverhampton and returns home to watch TV ▪ 35-year-old Huw Thomas reads the news for ITN ▪ 44-year-old terrorist Nelson Mandela is sentenced to five years imprisonment in South Africa - for inciting workers to go on strike ▪ The Americans and Soviets continue to negotiate over the grave situation in Cuba ▪ Back in England - 36-year-old Queen Elizabeth II bestows a knighthood on 59-year-old Foreign Secretary Alec Douglas-Home ▪ Ford launches the brand new *Consul Cortina* motorcar. It's 'the light car with a big difference.' The exciting new model is available as a two-door or a four-door saloon and comes with four-speed gearbox (with syncromesh on all four gears), a 1200cc engine and a top speed of 76 mph. There's a choice of separate front seats (with a central gear change) or a bench style front seat (with steering column gear change). A two-door *de lux* model costs £683/14s/- inc. Purchase Tax ▪ Triumph launches the *Spitfire* - a two seater, soft-top sports car with a top speed of 92 mph. Retail price is £729/15s/3d inc. Purchase Tax ▪ Construction work is underway on the new M6 motorway ▪ The Stafford bypass opens - five and a half miles of dual carriageway for car drivers to speed along ▪ The new football season is in full swing ▪ Johnny Carey's newly promoted Orient beat Matt Busby's Manchester Utd 1-0 in front of 24,901 at Brisbane Road ▪ Harry Catterick's Everton beat Ron Suart's Blackpool 5-0 in front of 39,517 at Goodison Park ▪ 28-year-old Dennis Viollet scores four goals as Tony Waddington's Stoke City beat Charlton Athletic 6-3 in Division Two ▪ 15-year-old Peter Lorimer makes his debut for Don Revie's hard-tackling Leeds Utd in a 1-1 draw against Southampton at Elland Road ▪ "I wanna be..." ***Bobby's Girl*** by 24-year-old Susan Maughan from Consett in County Durham is number three on the hit parade ▪ ***Sherry*** ("... Sherry, baby") by The Four Seasons is number eight ▪ 20-year-old convicted murderer Oswald Augustus Grey is hanged by the neck until dead at Winson Green Prison ▪ The fictional character Miss Marple features in *The Mirror Crack'd from Side to Side* - the latest 'whodunit' novel from 72-year-old crime-writer Agatha Christie ▪ Popular radio quiz *Top of the Form* is now being broadcast as a television programme - 32-year-old Geoffrey Wheeler is the question-master ▪ Schoolboys peruse the shelves at their local newsagents ▪ The *Valiant* comic is on-sale weekly and features exciting characters - 'The Steel Claw' and 'Captain Hurricane' ▪ Blue collar workers (on monthly salaries) visit car showrooms and dream of owning the latest sporty model ▪ The British Motor Corporation introduces a new *MG* version of the *1100* saloon. The two-door model costs £580 plus £218/10s/3d purchase tax ▪ A 'soft-top' *MGB* sports car (with wire wheels and 1,798 cc engine) is £690 plus £222/5s/3d purchase tax ▪ A 'soft-top' *MG Midget* (with steel wheels and 1,098 cc engine) is £495 plus £186/12s/9d purchase tax ▪ Conservative prime-minister Harold Macmillan remains unpopular with voters ▪ The Tories lose a by-election to Labour in South Dorset ▪ "Hey baby, won't you take a chance? Say that you'll let me have this dance. Well..." ***Let's Dance*** by 19-year-old Chris Montez from Los Angeles climbs to number two on the hit parade ▪ "My..." ***Venus In Blue Jeans*** ("... is the Cinderella I adore") by 19-year-old Mark Wynter from Woking reaches number four ▪ The Beatles (a little-known beat combo from Liverpool) perform their debut single, ***Love Me Do***, on Granada TV's *People and Places* programme. The song enters the pop chart at number forty-nine ▪ Men and boys flock to the cinema to see *The Longest Day* - an epic new war film telling the story of D Day. The all-star cast includes John Wayne, Henry Fonda, Robert Mitchum, Richard Burton, Kenneth More and 43-year-old Richard Todd ▪ First Secretary Khrushchev announces on Radio Moscow that he's agreed to remove Soviet missiles from Cuba ▪ People everywhere breathe a huge sigh of relief ▪ World War III has been averted - for now.

Christmas 1962

Dr. Beeching Sharpens his axe

Monarch:	Queen Elizabeth II (aged 36)
Prime-minister:	Harold Macmillan (aged 68)
Chancellor:	Reginald Maudling (aged 45)
Home Secretary:	Henry Brooke (aged 59)
Foreign Secretary:	Alec Douglas-Home (aged 59)
Football Manager:	Committee (Alf Ramsey to take over in May 1963)

▪ 11-year-old schoolboy Chris Rea from Middlesbrough writes pop songs in his bedroom ▪ Dads drive home for Christmas in their Ford *Anglias* and Vauxhall *Victors* ▪ Pollution from transport has become a major problem ▪ Pollution from industry in towns and cities is also a huge concern ▪ Thick, choking smog descends on London and claims more than one-thousand lives ▪ 203 million tonnes of coal have been mined in Britain this year - up by 8 million tonnes compared to last year ▪ British Railways has lost £104 million ▪ Dr. Beeching makes plans to axe over two-thousand railway stations and close around six-thousand miles of track ▪ The wider economy is in a poor shape ▪ The cost of living continues to rise ▪ 68-year-old prime-minister Harold Macmillan travels to Paris to meet with 72-year-old president Charles de Gaulle. With world politics currently focused on the on-going tensions between the United States and the Soviet Union, discussions of Britain's entry into the Common Market have moved into the background ▪ 56-year-old Hugh Gaitskell (leader of the Labour opposition) is against the idea of joining a European economic community ▪ ***He's A Rebel*** ("... and he'll never be any good") by The Crystals is number nineteen in the pop chart ▪ "I gotta feelin' called the bl-ooh-ooh-ooh, Lord, since my baby said goodbye" - ***Lovesick Blues*** by 25-year-old Frank Ifield from Coventry is new at number one ▪ 'Only one woman and five longing, desperate men!"- 31-year-old Carroll Baker (35-24-

35) stars at cinemas in *Station Six-Sahara* ▪ 27-year-old Elvis Presley stars in *Kid Galahad* - playing the role of a car mechanic turned boxer ▪ 58-year-old Cary Grant and 40-year-old Doris Day star in *That Touch of Mink* ▪ 'Bri-Lon, for the feel of it' - Husbands purchase *Bri Nylon* nighties as Christmas gifts for their wives ▪ Shop assistant Betty Hattersley helps out in Santa's grotto at the Beehive department store in Birmingham - handing out gifts to children ▪ 21-year-old Kathleen Conyon purchases a copy of P. D. James' debut novel, *Cover Her Face*, from Woodman's book-shop in Rugeley ▪ Paul Heaton from Hull is involved in a robbery. He keeps it to himself ▪ 42-year-old Kenneth Wolstenholme presents *Today's Sport* on BBC television on Saturday evenings, straight after *The News* ▪ Newcastle Utd beat Rotherham Utd 4-1 in a Division Two football match at St. James' Park, with 23-year-old Ken Hale scoring twice ▪ Ipswich Town beat Sheffield Wednesday 2-0 in Division One at Portman Road - and afterwards Wednesday players Peter Swan, David Layne and Tony Kay collect secret (and illegal) payments of £100 each for influencing the result ▪ Families spend the evening in, watching TV and eating snacks ▪ 21-year-old swimmer Anita Lonsbrough from York is BBC's 'Sports Personality of the Year' ▪ New 'cheese and onion' flavoured crisps from *Golden Wonder* taste great ▪ *Blue Peter* presenters - 29-year-old Christopher Trace and 25-year-old Valerie Singleton launch the program's first ever Christmas Appeal - Thousands of people donate toys for poor children otherwise unlikely to receive gifts on Christmas Day. The Appeal is a great success and hundreds of bags of toys are distributed to youngsters around the country ▪ ***Sun Arise*** ("... come every mornin', bringing back the warmth to the ground") by 32-year-old Rolf Harris from Australia is number three in the pop chart ▪ ***The Main Attraction*** by 28-year-old Pat Boone from America is number twelve ▪ Mariticidal serial killer Mary Elizabeth Wilson dies in her cell at Holloway pris-

on aged 73 ▪ 26-year-old convicted murderer James Smith is hanged by the neck until dead at Strangeways. (Smith had battered a 58-year-old female sweet-shop owner to death in Manchester in May) ▪ Small time crook Johnny Edgecombe is arrested for firing a gun outside a house at Wimpole Mews in Marylebone. 20-year-old Christine Keeler and 18-year-old Mandy Rice-Davies are inside the dwelling when the shots are fired ▪ 29-year-old gangster twins Reginald and Ronald Kray celebrate a record year of profit from their London gambling clubs, protection rackets and shady business deals ▪ Sheffield Wednesday's 25-year-old left-half Tony Kay transfers to Harry Catterick's high-flying Everton for £60,000 ▪ After his meeting with General de Gaulle in Paris, Britain's prime-minister Harold Macmillan flies across the Atlantic for a meeting in the Bahamas with 45-year-old US president J.F. Kennedy ▪ Labour leader Hugh Gaitskell is forced to cancel a trip to Moscow to meet Soviet leader Mr. Kruschev. The 56-year-old Mr. Gaitskell (widely expected to be the next prime-minister) is ill in hospital suffering with influenza ▪ "You are an Englishman. Are you not loyal to England? / To England, and to other things" - 30-year-old Peter O'Toole, 30-year-old Omar Sharif and 48-year-old Alec Guinness star at cinemas in *Lawrence of Arabia* ▪ 31-year-old Leslie Caron and 29-year-old Tom Bell star in *The L Shaped Room* ▪ Noisy schoolboys spend Saturday mornings in the stalls ▪ 'Newest Tarzan! Most Spectacular of them All!' - 43-year-old Jock Mahoney stars in *Tarzan Goes to India* ▪ 27-year-old entertainer Rod Hull plays the role of Constable Clot in *The Kaper Kops* on children's television in Australia ▪ "On the roof it's peaceful as can be, and there the world below can't bother me" - ***Up On The Roof*** by 24-year-old Kenny Lynch is number ten in the pop chart ▪ ***It Only Took A Minute*** by Joe Brown and the Bruvvers is number six ▪ Lucky schoolboys receive a *Matchbox* die-cast model of a Jaguar *MKII 3.4 Saloon* (with opening bonnet) on Christmas morning ▪ Lucky schoolgirls receive a copy of *Five Have A Mystery To Solve*, a smashing new *Famous Five* book from 65-year-old author Enid Blyton ▪ Families enjoy their turkey dinner before settling down in front of the television-set, with a box of Rowntree's *After Eight* mint chocolates - they're new this Christmas ▪ *The Black & White Minstrel* show is a favourite on BBC ▪ *Chipperfield's Circus* is popular on ITV ▪ The Boxing Day football programme is severely affected by snow and frost ▪ The scheduled match at Craven Cottage is one of the few fixtures that does go ahead - and 23,928 turn out to see Fulham lose 0-1 against Matt Busby's Manchester Utd, with a goal scored by 25-year-old Bobby Charlton ▪ 43-year-old Harry Catterick's high-flying Everton (with 25-year-old strike partners Alex Young and Roy Vernon scoring goals) continue to lead the way in Division One ▪ Harry Potts' Burnley, Bill Nicholson's Tottenham Hotspur and Matt Gillies' Leicester City are all close behind ▪ Johnny Carey's newly promoted Orient are bottom of the table ▪ Chelsea and Sunderland lead the way in Division Two ▪ Sunderland striker Brian Clough damages his right knee in a Boxing Day match against Bury. It's an injury that'll bring a premature end to the playing career of 27-year-old Clough ▪ 23-year-old Bert Lister scores six goals as Oldham Athletic thrash Southport 11-0 in Division Four ▪ Racing driver Jim Clark is forced to retire from the South African Grand Prix with an oil leak. 33-year-old Graham Hill wins the race in a dark green/blue BRM (number 3) and becomes the new world motor racing champion ▪ 27-year-old Ted Dexter is the captain of England's cricket team for an Ashes series tour of Australia. 31-year-old fast bowler 'fiery' Fred Trueman takes five wickets in the second Test at Melbourne and England take a 1-0 lead in the series ▪ "I gave a letter to the postman, he put it in his sack. Bright and early next morning, he brought my letter back. She wrote upon it..." ***Return To Sender*** by 27-year-old Elvis Presley from Memphis is number one at Christmas ▪ 18-year-old Brenda Lee from Atlanta sings ***Rockin' Around The Christmas Tree*** ("... at the Christmas party hop. A mistletoe hung where you can see, every couple tries to stop") ▪ Construction work continues on the M6 motorway - as the carriageway extends further North ▪ A new section between Stafford and Stoke-on-Trent is now open to motorists ▪ Dads take their new cars for a spin ▪ A Hillman *Minx de lux* has a 1600cc engine, a top speed of 80 mph and costs £616/16s/3d (including Purchase Tax) ▪ The ever-popular Morris *Minor 1000* has a 1098cc engine, a top speed of 76 mph and costs £573/0s/3d (including Purchase Tax) ▪ The weather turns cold ▪ A big freeze grips the country, with frost developing every night between now and March 1963 ▪ *The Woodentops* (with Spotty Dog - "the very biggest spotty dog you ever did see") feature on BBC television's *Watch With Mother* series ▪ "Love, love me do. You know I love you. I'll always be true, so please..." ***Love Me Do*** the debut single from The Beatles (22-year-old John Lennon, 22-year-old Ringo Starr, 20-year-old Paul McCartney and 19-year-old George Harrison) climbs to number seventeen on the hit parade ▪ 26-year-old bass player Bill Wyman joins the Rolling Stones ▪ A new look in fashion is developing ▪ Young male 'moderns' wear elastic-sided boots, narrow slacks and smart, single-breasted blazers ▪ Young female 'moderns' wear flat soled shoes, dogtooth check stretch trousers and skinny-rib sweaters with a polo neck ▪ Adverts for motor scooters declare - 'Vespa leads the way for cheaper, easier, handier travel' ▪ A new *Vespa* with 150cc engine, 4-speed gear, a dual-seat and parking light costs £139/19s/9d ▪ 22-year-old footballer Jimmy 'Greavsie' Greaves bags a hat-trick as Tottenham Hotspur thrash reigning champions Ipswich Town 5-0 at White Hart Lane ▪ 49-year-old Dr. Beeching sharpens his axe ▪ Chipping Norton Railway Station closes down.

New Year 1963

The big freeze

Monarch:	Queen Elizabeth II (aged 36)
Prime-minister:	Harold Macmillan (aged 69)
Chancellor:	Reginald Maudling (aged 45)
Home Secretary:	Henry Brooke (aged 59)
Foreign Secretary:	Alec Douglas-Home (aged 59)
Football Manager:	Committee (Alf Ramsey to take over in May)
New car reg. suffix:	'A'

▪ Freezing weather ▪ The country lies beneath a blanket of deep snow ▪ Roads are blocked ▪ Shops serving rural communities run short of essential supplies ▪ A Trojan 1-ton baker's van is stranded on the B1191 near Woodhall Spa ▪ An Atkinson rigid flatbed beer dray is stuck on the A444 at Swadlincote ▪ 11-year-old schoolboy John Kettley from Halifax listens to daily weather reports on the radio ▪ The big freeze continues into January and February ▪ Britain is at near standstill ▪ Arctic conditions see temperatures drop to almost minus three degrees Fahrenheit ▪ It's the coldest winter for eighty-two years ▪ Schools and factories are forced to close ▪ The sea freezes at Poole in Dorset ▪ Football matches are postponed ▪ The Pools Panel is set up ▪ Controversy ensues when Derby County versus Peterborough Utd (an FA Cup tie) is called as an 'away win' ▪ "When I was young my father said: Son, I've got something to say. And what he told me I'll never forget until my dying day. He said: Son, you are a…" ***Bachelor Boy*** by Cliff Richard and the Shadows is number one in the pop chart ▪ "'Cause..." ***The Night Has A Thousand Eyes*** ("… and a thousand eyes can't help to see if you are true to me") by 19-year-old Bobby Vee climbs to number three ▪ After months of negotiation, 72-year-old president Charles de Gaulle finally says "Non" to Britain's entry into the European Common Market. Prime-minister Harold Macmillan is despondent, but maintains a stiff upper lip ▪ Labour leader Hugh Gaitskell is taken to hospital, suffering with a viral infection ▪ The new Transport

Act comes into effect ▪ Dr. Beeching is installed as chairman of the newly formed British Railways Board ▪ The 24-mile long Truro and Newquay railway line (and its sixteen stations) in Cornwall closes down ▪ The *Flying Scotsman* (a class A3 Pacific) steam locomotive makes its final journey after serving on the railways for forty years ▪ 51-year-old Bill Hartley presents *Motoring and the Motorist* on BBC radio's Home Service on Friday evenings ▪ The first 'A' registration number plate is issued to a car in Middlesex ▪ Popular models on the road are: the Ford *Anglia 105E* (top speed 74 mph), the Austin *A40* (top speed 81 mph), the BMC *Mini* (top speed 72 mph), the Morris *Minor* (top speed 76 mph), the Morris *1100* (top speed 78 mph), the Riley *Elf* (top speed 76 mph) and the Triumph *Herald 1200* (top speed 80 mph) ▪ Ford introduces the *Cortina Super* - a 1500cc version of its new family car. Top speed is 82 mph and acceleration time from 0-60 mph is 20 seconds ▪ 'She's the fastest thing in town and oh, boy! What a CHASSIS!' - 55-year-old James Robertson Justice, 36-year-old Stanley Baxter, 38-year-old Leslie Phillips and 71-year-old Kathleen Harrison star at cinemas in *The Fast Lady* ▪ 'Never before has the screen exploded with such raw emotions!' - 32-year-old Richard Harris and 35-year-old Rachel Roberts star in *This Sporting Life* - a gritty drama set in Wakefield ▪ 56-year-old wide-eyed actress Jessie Matthews takes over from Ellis Powell as Mrs. Mary Dale on the ever popular radio show *The Dales*. (Powell had played the lead role for fifteen years before being unceremoniously sacked by the BBC) ▪ ***Big Girls Don't Cry*** ("... they don't cry-ie-ie") by The Four Seasons reaches number thirteen on the hit parade ▪ ***Dance On!*** by The Shadows (led by 21-year-old Hank Marvin) spends a week at number one ▪ Labour leader Hugh Gaitskell dies of an auto-immune disease aged 56 at the Middlesex Hospital in London. His wife Dora is at his side ▪ Tributes are paid and messages of condolences sent by prime-minister Mr. Macmillan, Sir Winston Churchill, Earl Attlee and the Queen ▪ 46-year-old

Harold Wilson (from Huddersfield) succeeds Gaitskell as Leader of the Opposition - seeing off challenges from 48-year-old George Brown and 50-year-old Jim Callaghan ▪ MI6 finally discover the truth after twelve years - former civil servant Kim Philby was indeed the 'third man' in the Burgess MacLean spy ring ▪ 51-year-old Philby evades arrest and flees to the Soviet Union. The whole sorry state is kept secret from the British public for the time being ▪ Other suspected communist spies are now under the surveillance of MI6 ▪ 37-year-old Yevgeny Ivanov (a friend of 50-year-old osteopath Stephen Ward) leaves London and returns to the USSR ▪ ***Diamonds*** (a catchy new electric guitar and drum instrumental) by Jet Harris and Tony Meehan is new at number one in the pop chart ▪ 16-year-old singing sensation Helen Shapiro appears at the Gaumont in Bradford on the opening night of her new tour - she's supported by up-coming group The Beatles ▪ "You *derty* old man!" - 37-year-old Harry H. Corbett and 50-year-old Wilfrid Brambell make the nation laugh as series two of *Steptoe and Son* begins ▪ BBC's popular *The Black and White Minstrel Show* moves from a Saturday night to a Sunday evening - and is broadcast straight after *Rejoice and Sing* ▪ *World in Action* (a news documentary) is new on Granada TV. 37-year-old Derek Cooper provides the narration ▪ 34-year-old Roy Hackett (a Jamaican now living in Bristol) and his friends set up the Commonwealth Co-ordinated Committee to challenge the local council to treat immigrants fairly ▪ ***What Now*** by 22-year-old Adam Faith is number thirty-one in the pop chart ▪ ***It's Up To You*** ("... because I've done everything I can") by 22-year-old Ricky Nelson peaks at number twenty-two ▪ Harry Catterick's Everton football team is one point ahead of Bill Nicholson's Tottenham Hotspur at the top of Division One ▪ Bill Shankly's Liverpool are fifth after a 4-0 victory over Aston Villa at Anfield (with 24-year-old strike partners Ian St. John and Roger Hunt both scoring twice for 'The Reds') ▪ "Come on, (come on). Come on, (come on). Come on, (come on). Come on, (come on)..." ***Please Please Me*** ("... Oh yeah, like I please you") - the second single from The Beatles climbs to number two on the hit parade ▪ "Oh, the..." ***Wayward Wind*** ("... is a restless wind") by Frank Ifield from Coventry reaches number one ▪ Schoolboys read comics ▪ *Buster* (with 'Buster' - son of Andy Capp) is 4½d, every Monday ▪ *The Dandy* (with 'Korky the Cat') is 3d, every Tuesday ▪ *The Beano* (with 'Dennis the Menace and Gnasher') is 3d, every Thursday ▪ Richie Benaud's Australian cricket team retains the Ashes after beating Ted Dexter's England in the third Test at Sydney and drawing the final two matches of the series. 32-year-old batsman Ken Barrington ends the series as England's top run scorer. 30-year-old bowler Fred Titmus is England's leading wicket taker. G Pullar, D S R Sheppard, E R Dexter (cpt), M C Cowdrey, T W Graveney, K F Barrington, A C Smith (wk), J T Murray (wk), P H Parfitt, F J Titmus, B R Knight, R Illingworth, F S Trueman, J B Statham, L J Coldwell and D A Allen are all downcast after failing to win the Ashes ▪ The long spell of cold weather continues ▪ Snow, ice and freezing temperatures prevail until March ▪ People brave the cold weather for an evening of entertainment and excitement at the cinema ▪ 28-year-old Elvis Presley stars in *Girls! Girls! Girls!* - playing the role of Ross Carpenter, a fisherman on the exotic island of Hawaii, caught up in a love triangle with two beautiful girls ▪ Groups of adolescent boys loiter inside the newagents ▪ 28-year-old Brigitte Bardot (36-20-35) is pictured on the front cover of *Parade* - on sale now for one shilling ▪ "Tell him that you're never gonna leave him. Tell him that you're always gonna love him. Tell him, tell him, tell him..." ***Tell Him*** ("... right now") by The Exciters enters the pop chart at number forty-six ▪ Another version of the same song by 17-year-old Billie Davis reaches number ten ▪ ***Sukiyaki*** by Kenny Ball and his Jazzmen also peaks at number ten ▪ 21-year-old drummer Charlie Watts joins the Rolling Stones ▪ A bottle of Haig's *Gold Label* whisky costs 41s/6d ▪ A miniature is 4s/3d.

Spring 1963

It's Beatlemania!

Monarch:	Queen Elizabeth II (aged 37)
Prime-minister:	Harold Macmillan (aged 69)
Chancellor:	Reginald Maudling (aged 46)
Home Secretary:	Henry Brooke (aged 60)
Foreign Secretary:	Alec Douglas-Home (aged 59)
Football Manager:	Committee (Alf Ramsey to take over in May)
New car reg. suffix:	'A'

▪ American satellite *Telstar 2* is launched into space from Cape Canaveral ▪ Back in England - there's widespread flooding as the big freeze comes to an end ▪ 17-year-old Guy Bailey applies for a job as a bus conductor with the Bristol Omnibus Company - but is turned down because he's black ▪ ***What Kind Of Fool Am I*** ("… who never fell in love") by 26-year-old Shirley Bassey is number forty-seven in the weekly pop chart ▪ "I'm all cried out over you, oh yeah" - ***The Alley Cat Song*** by David Thorne is number twenty-one ▪ Matt Busby's Manchester Utd play a third round FA Cup tie on the fourth of March and thrash Huddersfield Town 5-0. Denis Law bags a hat-trick and Albert Quixall and Johnny Giles are also on the score-sheet ▪ Dr. Beeching wields his axe - railway stations at Chesterfield Central and Nottingham Arkwright Street close down ▪ "We're going where the sun shines brightly. We're going where the sea is blue. We've seen it in the movies, now let's see if it's true" - ***Summer Holiday*** by 22-year-old Cliff Richard and the Shadows is top of the hit parade ▪ ***From A Jack To A King*** ("... From loneliness to a wedding ring") by 37-year-old Ned Miller is number two ▪ 21-year-old dancer Christine Keeler fails to appear as a witness at the trial of small time crook Johnny Edgecombe and media speculation is rife that Keeler is involved in a wider scandal - possibly involving a Soviet spy and a Cabinet minister in Harold Macmillan's Conservative government ▪ ***Foot Tapper*** by The Shadows (led by 21-year-old

Hank Marvin) spends a week at number one in the pop chart ▪ "Come sit by my side little darlin'. Come lay your cool hand on my brow, and promise me that you will never be..." ***Nobody's Darlin' But Mine*** by 25-year-old Frank Ifield from Coventry reaches number four ▪ 25-year-old Leicester City goalkeeper Gordon Banks makes his debut for England (G Banks, Armfield, R Byrne, Moore, Norman, Flowers, Douglas, Greaves, R Smith, Melia, R Charlton) in a 1-2 defeat against Scotland at Wembley ▪ 18-year-old Rodney Marsh scores on his debut for Fulham in a 1-0 victory over Aston Villa ▪ "Hey..." ***Hey Paula*** ("... I wanna marry you") by Paul and Paula (22-year-old Ray Hildebrand and 20-year-old Jill Jackson from Texas) is number eight in the pop chart ▪ "I wonder why you keep me wai-ai-aiting, Charmaine. My..." ***Charmaine*** by The Bachelors (with, lead singer, 27-year-old Con Cluskey from Dublin) is number six ▪ 'Meet the Mastermind who pulls the strings of the Underworld' - 37-year-old Peter Sellers stars at cinemas in *The Wrong Arm of the Law* ▪ 21-year-old Michael Crawford and 27-year-old Nyree Dawn Porter star in *My Two Left Feet* ▪ 32-year-old fast bowler 'fiery' Fred Trueman takes seven wickets in an English Test Match victory over New Zealand at Christchurch ▪ Back in Blighty - 46-year-old Chancellor of the Exchequer Reg Maudling delivers his first Budget for Macmillan's government and sets out a plan for economic expansion ▪ Income tax rates are cut in a desperate attempt to get the economy growing again ▪ Car workers in the Midlands go on strike for better pay ▪ "And then it will be..." ***Like I've Never Been Gone*** by 22-year-old Billy Fury is number three on the hit parade ▪ Crowds gather outside The Hippodrome in Birmingham to greet fab new band The Beatles (who are appearing as a support act for Chris Montez) ▪ The four lads from Liverpool disguise themselves as policemen to avoid being mobbed as they enter the building ▪ "Doo-lang, doo-lang, doo-lang" - ***He's So Fine*** by The Chiffons is number sixteen in the pop chart ▪ ***Walk Like A Man*** ("... talk like a man, walk like a man my son") by The Four Seasons is number twelve ▪ Fly-half Richard Sharp leads England's rugby team to victory in the Five Nations championship ▪ 47-year-old Gregory Peck wins an Oscar for his performance as Atticus Finch in *To Kill a Mockingbird* ▪ 34-year-old Roy Hackett and 25-year-old Paul Stephenson campaign for a public boycott against the Bristol Omnibus Company - protesting against the bus operator's 'colour bar' on employing black people ▪ The 51-year-old Duchess of Argyll is humiliated in divorce proceedings when evidence of her infidelity includes a photograph of her performing oral sex on an unnamed man ▪ "How do, you do what you do to me? I wish I knew. If I knew how you do it to me, I'd do it to you" - ***How Do You Do It?*** by Gerry and the Pacemakers (with, lead singer, 20-year-old Gerry Marsden) is new at number one in the hit parade ▪ "I wander the streets and gay crowded places trying to forget you" - ***Island Of Dreams*** by The Springfields (with, lead singer, 23-year-old Dusty Springfield) peaks at number five ▪ 18-year-old footballer Tommy Smith makes his debut for Bill Shankly's Liverpool in a 5-1 victory over Birmingham City in Division One. Roger Hunt (2), Ian St. John, Gordon Wallace and 21-year-old Ian Callaghan score the goals for 'The Reds' ▪ Robert Dougall reads the news on BBC television ▪ In response to growing speculation in the media, 48-year-old Secretary of State for War John Profumo makes a statement to the House of Commons confirming that he is acquainted with 21-year-old dancer Christine Keeler, but there is no impropriety in their relationship ▪ ***Little Town Flirt*** by 28-year-old Del Shannon reaches number four in the pop chart ▪ 'Sailor, sailor, home from the sea, whose little stranger can this one be?' - 25-year-old Barbara Windsor (36-23-34) and 35-year-old James Booth star at cinemas in *Sparrers Can't Sing* ▪ 31-year-old Anita Ekberg (40-24-36) and 59-year-old Bob Hope star in *Call Me Bwana* ▪ 'Ban the Bomb!' - Seventy-thousand CND activists march from Aldermaston to London ▪ 'An Inspiration in Light Car Design' - The all new Hillman *Imp* motorcar (with a rear mounted engine) is launched. Priced at £508/1s/3d, this stylish and groovy little car has a top speed of 80 mph, 'folding back' seats and a rear window that opens on a top hinge ▪ Ford introduces a *Super 123E* model to its *Anglia* range. Priced at £598/13/9d, the new car comes with a 1200cc engine, a synchromesh gearbox and a heater ▪ The country's first 'self-service' petrol station opens at Charles Church roundabout in Plymouth ▪ Pop stars, 21-year-old Joe Brown (from Plaistow), 24-year-old Marty Wilde (from Blackheath) and 24-year-old Susan Maughan (from Consett) star in new movie *What a Crazy World* ▪ "She fought and won herself a..." ***Brown-Eyed Handsome Man*** by the late Buddy Holly is number three in the pop chart ▪ "He let his hair grow long and he dressed in style..." ***The Folk Singer*** by 20-year-old Tommy Roe is number four ▪ "It's a grand old team to support!" - Harry Catterick's Everton beat Fulham 4-1 (with Roy Vernon bagging a hat-trick and Alex Scott also on the score-sheet) in front of 60,578 spectators at Goodison Park - to become champions of Division One. Gordon West, Alex Parker, Mick Meagan, George Thompson, Brian Harris, Jimmy Gabriel, Tony Kay, John Morrissey, Dennis Stevens, Roy Vernon (with twenty-four goals), Alex Young (with twenty-two goals), Alex Scott and 23-year-old centre-half Brian Labone have all been outstanding ▪ "If there's anything that you want. If there's anything I can do. Just call on me and I'll send it along, with love..." ***From Me To You*** is the first number one hit for The Beatles - and the record stays at the top of the singles chart for seven weeks! ▪ The 'Fab Four' play to packed venues at Liverpool (Empire), Mansfield (ABC), Exeter (ABC), Lewisham (Odeon), Portsmouth (Guildhall), Leicester (De Monfort Hall) and then continue onto Slough, Hanley, Southampton, Ipswich, Nottingham, Walthamstow, Sheffield, Liverpool, Worcester, York, Manchester and Southend ▪ Cool young kids embrace the new Mod 'look' ▪ Teenage boys grow their hair slightly longer and wear pastel coloured shirts and Chelsea boots ▪ Teenage girls, with sharp haircuts, wear flat soled shoes and tight white slacks ▪ 31-year-old Anthony Newley and 19-year-old Julia Foster star at cinemas in *The Small World of Sammy Lee* ▪ 'Wow!!! A real scooter for £26 down' - a new *Lambretta 125* costs £129/10s/-, or is available for a deposit of £26 followed by thirty-six monthly payments of £3/17s/4d ▪ 22-year-old John Lennon (of The Beatles) and 23-year-old wife, Cynthia, are proud parents of a newborn baby boy, Julian ▪ Millions of men spend Saturday afternoons in front of the television-set watching BBC's *Grandstand* ▪ '4.44 BRIGHTON 1 WATFORD 4 D3' - David Coleman reads the football results 'live', as they come in from the Teleprinter ▪ The season ends with Tottenham Hotspur finishing as runners-up to Everton in Division One ▪ Tony Waddington's Stoke City are promoted from Division Two along with Tommy Docherty's Chelsea, who pip Alan Brown's Sunderland to the runners-up spot by thrashing Portsmouth 7-0 in their final match ▪ 28-year-old David Herd scores twice as Matt Busby's Manchester Utd (with Noel Cantwell, Johnny Giles, Denis Law and Bobby Charlton) beat Matt Gillies' Leicester City (with Gordon Banks, Frank McLintock, Colin Appleton and Dave Gibson) 3-1 in the FA Cup final. A ticket for the newly covered standing enclosure at the Empire Stadium in Wembley costs 7s/6d ▪ 23-year-old Jimmy 'Greavsie' Greaves scores twice as Tottenham Hotspur beat Atletico Madrid 5-1 in the final of the European Cup Winners Cup in Rotterdam ▪ Back in England - Gill Merrick's Birmingham City defeat Joe Mercer's Aston Villa 3-1 over two legs to win the League Cup final ▪ 23-year-old centre-forward John Kaye transfers from Scunthorpe Utd to West Bromwich Albion for £45,000 ▪ 17-year-old goalkeeper

Pat Jennings leaves Newry Town in Northern Ireland and joins Third Division Watford ▪ ***Can't Get Used To Losing You*** ("... no matter what I try to do") by 35-year-old Andy Williams spends eighteen weeks in the pop chart, peaking at number two ▪ "Call the boys and tell them..." ***Say I Won't Be There*** by The Springfields reaches number five ▪ The sun comes out ▪ Children play in the park ▪ 'Stand by for launching. It's Zoom with three new flavours' - Lyons Maid introduces the *Zoom* ice-lolly ▪ Men flick through the pages of car magazines ▪ A brand new Austin *Mini Cooper S* with a sporty 1071cc engine is now in showrooms ▪ Motor industry magnate William Morris (now Lord Nuffield) dies aged 85 at his home in Oxfordshire ▪ BBC TV programmes on a Saturday night include: *Juke Box Jury* - with David Jacobs; *Bertram Mills Circus* - presented by brothers Cyril and Bernard Mills; *The Rag Trade* - starring Peter Jones, Reg Varney and Irene Handl; *The Saturday Film*; *The News and The Weather Man*; followed by *Saturday Sport* - introduced by 42-year-old Kenneth Wolstenholme ▪ Police begin an investigation into the murky affairs of 50-year-old osteopath Stephen Ward. Under questioning, Ward's friend (and lodger at his house in Wimpole Mews, Marylebone) 21-year-old Christine Keeler confirms that she did have a sexual relationship with 48-year-old Secretary of State for War John Profumo ▪ "Listen..." ***Do You Want To Know A Secret?*** ("... Do you promise not to tell. Woh-woh-woh!") by Billy J Kramer and the Dakotas reaches number two in the pop chart ▪ ***Lucky Lips*** ("... are always kissing. Lucky lips are never blue") by Cliff Richard and the Shadows is number four ▪ 69-year-old Conservative prime-minister Harold Macmillan clashes with 47-year-old leader of the opposition Harold Wilson in the House of Commons when Mr. Wilson accuses the premier of not giving straight answers at the twice weekly question time sessions. Mr. Macmillan responds to the Labour leader saying, "If anyone wished to learn how to give a straight answer, it would not be you." ▪ Life continues ▪ Housewives in Gateshead embrace the modern concept of 'self-service' shopping - and head for the bright new *Fine Fare* supermarket ▪ A loaf of bread costs 11d ▪ A pint of milk is 8½d ▪ Technological advances are made in household appliances ▪ Adverts say, 'When Mrs. West changed to a Hotpoint *Supermatic* she realised all she'd been missing' ▪ Washing powder companies battle for a greater share of the market ▪ *Daz* 'White Knights' call on households all around the country, giving out cash prizes ▪ *Omo* promotes the 'Blue Star' game in their special packs of powder - where towels, steam-irons and transistor radios can be won as prizes ▪ The concept of 'Do-It-Yourself' is becoming more and more popular ▪ Celebrity actor Jack Warner tells ITV viewers, "Formica Decorative Laminate is really easy to fit" ▪ Queues form on pavements outside record shops ▪ "One-two-three-farrgh!" - 20-year-old Paul McCartney counts in the opening track (***I Saw Her Standing There***) on The Beatles' first LP, *Please Please Me*. The new 12-inch disc from the group from Liverpool tops the album chart in early May and remains at number one for the entire summer season ▪ Courting couples spend an enjoyable evening at the cinema ▪ "We're going where the sun shines brightly. We're going where the sea is blue. We've seen it in the movies, now let's see if it's true" - 22-year-old Cliff Richard, 19-year-old Laurie Peters and a red double-decker London bus star in *Summer Holiday* ▪ 'Time is running out for the running man ... and his woman!' - 34-year-old Lawrence Harvey, 27-year-old Lee Remick and 29-year-old Alan Bates star in *The Running Man* ▪ "So, you see, Sir, my pack of cards serves me as a bible, an almanac and a prayer book. And friends, the story is true. I know, I was that soldier" - ***Deck Of Cards*** by 29-year-old Wink Martindale climbs to number five in the weekly pop chart.

Summer 1963

John Profumo MP and Christine Keeler

Monarch:	Queen Elizabeth II (aged 37)
Prime-minister:	Harold Macmillan (aged 69)
Chancellor:	Reginald Maudling (aged 46)
Home Secretary:	Henry Brooke (aged 60)
Foreign Secretary:	Alec Douglas-Home (aged 60)
Football Manager:	Alf Ramsey (aged 43)
New car reg. suffix:	'A'

▪ The sun shines in early June and temperatures are high ▪ The new open-air swimming pool at Pythingdean Club in Pulborough, in West Sussex, is full of excited bathers ▪ The new paddling pool at Fritwell Primary School, near Biscester, is full of excited young school children ▪ The old open-air pool at Valance School in Westerham, Kent is being converted to an in-door facility ▪ "I'm awrite. You awrite?"- 11-year-old schoolboy Michael Barrymore from Bermondsey hopes one day to have a swimming pool of his own ▪ "Ooh, you are awful… but I like you" - 48-year-old comedian Dick Emery stars on TV in *The Dick Emery Show* ▪ 33-year-old Bert Foord presents the weather forecast on BBC television ▪ After a few days of warm sunshine, temperatures drop and rain clouds gather ▪ The summer of '63 ends up being a wet washout ▪ Crowds of people endure deep mud on the banks of the River Thames at the Henley Royal Regatta ▪ Damp school children trudge around Twycross Zoo in Leicestershire, looking at the monkeys ▪ "All this world will be just like a dream come true..." ***When Will You Say I Love You*** ("... I love you, I love you") by 23-year-old Billy Fury is number three in the pop chart ▪ ***Take These Chains From My Heart*** ("... and set me free") by 32-year-old Ray Charles is number five ▪ Having served as leader of the Catholic church for four years, Pope John XXIII (aka the Good Pope John) dies aged 81 in the Vatican City in Rome. (He's succeeded by 65-year-old Pope Paul VI) ▪ Back in England - The Beatles remain at number one in the pop chart with their smash hit single, ***From Me To You*** ▪ The 'Fab Four' from Liverpool play in front of wild and hysterical audiences at 'sold-out' venues around the country - young girls scream and sob as The Beatles take in Tooting (Granada), Brighton (Hippodrome), Woolwich (Granada), Birmingham (Town Hall), Leeds (Odeon), Glasgow (Odeon), Newcastle (City Hall) and Blackburn (King George's Hall) ▪ 47-year-old leader of the opposition Labour party Harold Wilson travels to Moscow and Warsaw for high-level meetings with Russian leader Mr. Kruschev and Polish prime-minister Mr. Gromulka ▪ 69-year-old Conservative prime-minister Harold Macmillan visits Wolverhampton and addresses a meeting of two-thousand Conservative Party workers representing the sixty constituencies of the West Midlands ▪ Construction work continues on the M6 motorway ▪ A new twenty-eight mile stretch opens between Warrington and Preston - including the longest motorway bridge section in the country, carrying traffic over the Manchester Ship Canal ▪ Children watch TV for an hour or so in the evening ▪ A new *Blue Peter* badge is presented to anyone lucky enough to be invited onto the popular BBC programme ▪ 38-year-old Richard Baker reads the teatime news ▪ The sensational story of an affair between 48-year-old Secretary of State for War John Profumo and 21-year-old dancer Christine Keeler causes a nationwide scandal ▪ Profumo admits that he lied to the House of Commons and resigns immediately from the government and from Parliament ▪ 'I'll hold yer Two Plums Mister - You put the tanner in!' - saucy postcards continue to sell in high numbers ▪ *That Kind of Girl* - a hard hitting movie from 38-year-old Gerry O'Hara, exploring pre-marital sex and sexually transmitted diseases, is at cinemas. 18-year-old Margaret Rose Keil is the star ▪ *Tooty Frooty* sweets are new ▪ The Beatles are the biggest thing - *ever!* ▪ John, Paul, George and Ringo are mobbed by adoring fans, wherever they go ▪ The 7-inch disc of ***From Me to You*** sells out, fast, in record shops ▪ *Woolworths* begin stocking 45 rpm cover-versions of Beatles' hits (priced at 4s/3d) on its own *Embassy* record label ▪ Youngsters embrace the modern pop culture ▪ *Annabel's* nightclub opens in London ▪ *Atlantis* by The Shadows (led by 21-year-old guitarist Hank Marvin) climbs to number two on the hit parade ▪ ***Just Like Me*** by The Hollies reaches number twenty-five ▪ ***Shy Girl*** by 20-year-old Mark Wynter peaks at number twenty-eight ▪ US President Kennedy visits Germany and says, "Ich bin ein Berliner" ▪ Back in England - the boycott against the Bristol Omnibus Company gathers momentum. More and more people are happy to find alternative means of transport, in protest against the bus operator's refusal to employ black drivers and conductors ▪ 20-year-old tennis player Margaret Smith (from Australia) beats 20-year-old Billie Jean Moffitt (from America) 6-3, 6-4 in the women's singles final at Wimbledon ▪ 22-year-old Chuck McKinley (from America) beats 24-year-old Fred Stolle (from Australia) 9-7, 6-1, 6-4 in the men's final ▪ 28-year-old writer David Nobbs pens satirical scripts and one-line gags for the hit TV show *That Was The Week That Was* ▪ Frenzied newspaper, radio and television reports perpetuate the Profumo scandal ▪ The link between a former cabinet minister, his mistress and a Soviet spy is firmly established ▪ 47-year-old Leader of the Opposition Harold Wilson holds the Conservative government responsible for allowing such a serious breach in the nation's security ▪ The reputation of 69-year-old prime-minister Harold Macmillan sinks to an all time low ▪ ***If You Gotta Make A Fool Of Somebody*** ("... If you gotta make a fool of someone") by Freddie and the Dreamers is number three in the pop chart ▪ ***Scarlett O'Hara*** (an electric guitar and drum instrumental) by Jet Harris and Tony Meehan moves down to number four ▪ Beleaguered prime-minister Harold Macmillan asks 64-year-old Lord Denning (Master of the Rolls) to head an inquiry into the Profumo affair ▪ 31-year-old Ken Jones reports on football matters for the *Daily Mirror* newspaper ▪ 25-year-old centre-forward Derek Dougan leaves Joe Mercer's First Division Aston Villa and joins Jack Fairbrother's Third Division Peterborough Utd for £20,000 ▪ 28-year-old Albert 'Cheesy' Cheeseborough leaves Matt Gillies' First Division Leicester City and joins Freddie Steele's Third Division Port Vale for £15,000 ▪ 43-year-old Alf Ramsey commences his role as manager of England's football team. For the first time, the manager now has full authority to select players without going through an FA committee. Ramsey appoints 22-year-old Bobby Moore as captain and gets off to a winning start - when his eleven players (G Banks, Shellito, Wilson, Milne, Norman, Moore, Paine, Greaves. R Smith, Eastham, R Charlton) defeat Czechoslovakia 4-2 in Bratislava. Bobby Charlton, Bobby Smith and 23-year-old Jimmy 'Greavsie' Greaves (2) score the goals ▪ 49-year-old John Arlott and 56-year-old E. W. Swanton commentate on cricket for BBC radio's *Test Match Special* ▪ Micky Stewart and John Edrich stride out together at Old Trafford to open the batting for England against the West Indies in the first Test Match of the summer. Stewart makes 37 runs. Edrich hits 20. England lose the match by ten wickets. Throughout the series, 32-year-old fast bowler 'fiery' Fred Trueman is in tremendous form - taking eleven wickets at Lord's and seven wickets at Edgbaston, but Gary Sobers' West Indians go on to beat Ted Dexter's team by three Test Matches to one ▪ 34-year-old reigning world motor racing champion Graham Hill wins the Monaco Grand Prix driving a BRM ▪ Back in England - 'A Colossus of Adventure!' - Fathers take their sons to the cinema for the matinee screening of *Jason and the Argonauts*, starring 25-year-old Todd Armstrong as Jason and with Nigel Green as Hercules ▪ 'Laughs for everyone when the Parson practices what he preaches!' - 37-year-old Peter Sellers stars as the Reverend John Smallwood, a prison chaplain assigned to a conservative English town, in *Heaven's Above* ▪ Families enjoy a Sunday afternoon drive in the countryside in their motorcar ▪ 'Hydrolastic suspension smooths out ruts and ripples and bumps' - The wonderful new Morris *1100* (from BMC) is available in a choice of colours: Dove Grey, Smoke Grey, Tartan Red, Fiesta Yellow or Connaught Green. Black, is to special order ▪ 34-year-old reigning world champion racing driver Graham Hill finishes in third position at the British Grand Prix at Silverstone - completing a race podium that comprises of three Englishmen. 27-year-old Jim Clark (in a Lotus) is the winner. 29-year-old John Surtees (in a Ferrari) is second ▪ For one night only, 'Merseyside's Greatest' - The Beatles and Gerry and the Pacemakers are joint headline acts, playing to a packed house at New Brighton Tower on Friday the fourteenth of June. Tickets are 6s/- (or 7s/- on the door) ▪ "I like it, I like it. I like the way you run your fingers through my hair" - ***I Like It*** by Gerry and the Pacemakers moves to the top of the hit parade - replacing ***From Me To You*** by The Beatles which moves down to number two ▪ "Welcome to my world. Won't you come on in" - ***Welcome To My World*** by 39-year-old 'Gentleman' Jim Reeves is a new chart entry at number twenty-six ▪ 39-year-old Alan Weeks presents the sports news on BBC television ▪ 26-year-old footballer George Eastham (of Arsenal and England) wins a landmark case at the High Court - and football clubs will no longer be able to block transfers while holding players at a minimum wage ▪ 43-year-old Ludovic Kennedy reads the news for ITN ▪ Thieves steal £2.6 million in a daring train robbery at Ledburn in Buckinghamshire - the nation watches eagerly as police begin hunting down the culprits ▪ 69-year-old Harold Macmillan and his Conservative government suffer yet more embarrassment when it becomes public knowledge that Kim Philby *was* the 'third man' in the Burgess Maclean spy ring - and the 51-year-old traitor is now living in exile in Moscow ▪ 46-year-old US President John F. Kennedy visits beleaguered prime-minister Harold Macmillan at his country home in Sussex to offer kind words of support ▪ "I'm..." ***Confessin'*** ("... that I love you. Tell me, do you love me too - ooh?") by 25-year-old Frank Ifield from Coventry is new at number one in the pop chart ▪ Members of The Rolling Stones (19-year-old Mick Jagger, 19-year-old Keith Richards, 21-year-old Brian Jones, 26-year-old Bill Wyman and 22-year-old Charlie Watts) stop off at the Blue Boar Services on the M1 motorway at Watford Gap for a plate of egg and chips and a nice cup of tea ▪ ***Come On*** ("... since me and my baby parted. Come on. I can't get started") the debut single from 'The Stones' stalls at number twenty-one in the pop chart ▪ Business is brisk in record shops ▪ The Beatles' first LP, *Please Please Me*, remains at number one in the album chart for thirty weeks! Tracks include: ***I Saw Her Standing There***, ***Misery***, ***Love Me Do***, ***PS I Love You*** and ***Twist And Shout*** ▪ 'You won't believe him ... but you'll love him!' - 26-year-old Tom Courtenay and 22-year-old Julie Christie star at cinemas in *Billy Liar* ▪ Elsie Tanner (played by 39-year-old Pat Phoenix) turns down Len Fairclough's proposal of marriage in ITV's soap-opera *Coronation Street* ▪ 29-year-old boxer Henry Cooper unleashes 'Enry's 'Ammer at Wembley and puts 20-year-old Cassius Clay on his back-side ▪ 32-year-old veteran outside-right Billy Bingham transfers from Everton to Port Vale for £15,000 ▪ The new football season gets underway ▪ Bill Shankly's Liverpool beat Jack Marshall's Blackburn Rovers 2-1 at Anfield, with 29-year-old Ronnie Moran and 21-year-old Ian Callaghan on the score-sheet ▪ Matt Busby's Manchester Utd draw 3-3 against Vic Buckingham's Sheffield Wednesday, with 25-year-old Bobby Charlton scoring twice ▪ 22-year-old Johnny Giles transfers from Manchester Utd to Second Division Leeds Utd for £32,000 and makes his debut in a 3-0 win over Bury ▪ "You look like an angel, walk like an angel, talk like an angel, but I got wise..." ***(You're) The Devil In Disguise*** by Elvis Presley is number one on the hit parade for a week ▪ 'Now! For All the World to See! The Most Highly Acclaimed... Most Widely Discussed Entertainment in the History of the Screen!' - 31-year-old Elizabeth

Taylor and 37-year-old Richard Burton star at cinemas in *Cleopatra* ▪ A brand new TV pop music show called *Ready, Steady Go!* is a huge hit with viewers at home ▪ ***Sweets For My Sweet*** ("... Sugar for my honey. I'll never ever let you go") by The Searchers takes over from Elvis Presley at number one - and stays at the top of the pop chart for two weeks ▪ ***In Summer*** by 23-year-old Billy Fury is number eight ▪ ***Wipe Out*** by The Surfaris is number thirteen ▪ Construction work is underway to extend the new M6 motorway through Cheshire and Staffordshire ▪ Men purchase driving gloves (with chamois leather palms and net backs) for 16s/9d ▪ The sporty Ford Lotus *Cortina* motorcar has a top speed 104 mph and can reach 60 mph in 13.6 seconds ▪ 'Nothing you have ever witnessed before has prepared you for such sheer, stabbing shock!' - 63-year-old movie director Alfred Hitchcock's terrifying new film *The Birds* (starring Rod Taylor, Jessica Tandy and 33-year-old Tippi Hedren) is now showing at cinemas ▪ "I met him on a Monday and my heart stood still..." ***Da Doo Ron Ron*** ("...Ron. Da doo Ron Ron") by The Crystals climbs to number five on the hit parade ▪ ***You Don't Have To Be A Baby To Cry*** by The Caravelles is number six ▪ 49-year-old Jack de Manio presents the *Today* news programme on BBC radio's Home Service ▪ 37-year-old Queen Elizabeth II welcomes 74-year-old President Radhakrishnan of India on an official state visit to Britain ▪ Lord Denning questions 160 witnesses (including the prime-minister Harold Macmillan), gathering evidence for his inquiry into the Profumo affair ▪ 50-year-old Angus Maude holds the seat of Stratford-upon-Avon for the Conservatives at a by-election resulting from the resignation of shamed Minister for War John Profumo ▪ 38-year-old Anthony Wedgwood Benn is elected as a Labour MP, after a change in the law allows him to renounce his peerage ▪ 34-year-old Roy Hackett and 26-year-old Paul Stephenson (campaigners for equal rights) celebrate when the Bristol Omnibus Company finally agrees to end its 'colour bar' and begin employing black people. The four-month public boycott has been a success ▪ ***Take These Chains From My Heart*** ("... and set me free. You've grown cold and no longer care for me") by 32-year-old Ray Charles slides down the pop chart to number thirty-nine ▪ 16-year-old Pauline Reade goes missing on her way to a dance in Manchester ▪ 43-year-old Donald Pleasence stars at cinemas as the murderous *Dr. Crippen* - in a new film from 45-year-old director Robert Lynn ▪ Dr. Beeching wields his axe yet again - the railway station at Studley & Astwood Bank in Warwickshire closes down ▪ Construction work continues on the new Victoria underground train line in London ▪ 52-year-old traitor and former spy Guy Burgess dies of liver failure in exile in Moscow ▪ "If you ever leave me, I'll be sad and blue. Don't ever leave me, I'm so in love with you" - ***Bad To Me*** by Billy J Kramer and the Dakotas is new at number one ▪ ***I'm Telling You Now*** ("... I'm telling you right away") by Freddie and the Dreamers is number three ▪ Having now moved on to playing bigger venues, The Beatles perform for a final time at the Cavern Club in Liverpool. Tickets for the show are 9s/6d and they're available to Cavern Club members only ▪ Modelling a tiny, strapless bikini, 19-year-old Danish beauty Dorrit Von Haven appears on the front cover of *Parade* magazine ▪ After the Profumo affair, the reputation of many politicians has become tarnished ▪ "A well aimed tomato or a well matured egg should not be regarded as an entirely improper feature of the political scene. I speak as one who has been hit by an egg in my time. I do not have any objection to it" - 50-year-old Michael Foot MP (Labour Ebbw Vale) speaks at Westminster at the committee stage of a new Public Order Bill ▪ "Are you a Cadbury's fruit & nut case?" - Cadbury's *Fruit & Nut* bars are advertised on TV ▪ 'A hazelnut in every bite' - *Topic* bars are new ▪ Mackintosh's *Toffee Crisp* is new ▪ The term 'chocoholic' is also new.

Autumn 1963

Doctor Who

Monarch:	Queen Elizabeth II (aged 37)
Prime-minister:	Alec Douglas-Home (aged 60)
Chancellor:	Reginald Maudling (aged 46)
Home Secretary:	Henry Brooke (aged 60)
Foreign Secretary:	Rab Butler (aged 60)
Football Manager:	Alf Ramsey (aged 43)
New car reg. suffix:	'A'

▪ "Whenever I'm sad, whenever I'm blue, whenever my troubles are heavy. Beneath the stars, I play my guitar..." ***Just Like Eddie*** by 21-year-old Heinz reaches number five in the pop chart ▪ ***I'll Never Get Over You*** ("... No, I'll never get over you. I just can't keep it a secret anymore") by 27-year-old Johnny Kidd and the Pirates peaks at number four ▪ Obstreperous schoolboys spend Saturday mornings in the stalls at the local *Gaumont* cinema ▪ 'Three Times More Thrilling Than Any Tarzan Adventure You've Ever Seen!' - 44-year-old Jock Mahoney stars in *Tarzan's Three Challenges* ▪ 62-year-old Frank Phillips reads the news on BBC radio ▪ The Profumo Scandal and the Great Train Robbery continue to dominate the headlines ▪ Lord Denning's report into events surrounding the Profumo affair concludes that there was no security breach ▪ The credibility of the government has been damaged and beleaguered prime-minister Harold Macmillan is forced to consider his position ▪ 21-year-old dancer Christine Keeler is arrested on charges of perjury ▪ "She says 'she loves you', and you know that can't be bad. Yes, she loves you, and you know you should be glad. Ooooh" - ***She Loves You*** by The Beatles enters the pop chart at number twelve, climbs to number three the following week and then reaches top spot on the twelfth of September ▪ "Many a tear has to fall, but..." ***It's All In The Game*** ("... All in the wonderful game, that we know as love") by 22-year-old Cliff Richard is number two ▪ ***Applejack*** (an electric guitar and drum instrumental) by Jet Harris and Tony Meehan is new at number sixteen ▪ 'The whole world loves…' *Tom Jones* is a popular new movie. 27-year-old Albert Finney and 24-year-old Susannah York are the stars ▪ Rough! Ripping! Raw! - 45-year-old Mickey Spillane and 26-year-old Shirley Eaton star in *The Girl Hunters* - a gritty crime story featuring private detective Mike Hammer ▪ 23-year-old footballer Joe Baker bags a hat-trick as Billy Wright's Arsenal beat Joe Mercer's Aston Villa 3-0 in Division One ▪ 20-year-old Billy Bremner is on the score-sheet as Don Revie's Leeds Utd beat Portsmouth 3-1 in Division Two ▪ "Well, he walked up to me and he asked me if I wanted to dance. He looked kinda nice and so I said, I might take a chance. When he danced, he held me tight, and when he walked me home that night, all the stars were shining bright, and…" ***Then He Kissed Me*** by The Crystals is number two on the hit parade ▪ "So won't you, please, be my…" ***Be My Baby*** by The Ronettes climbs to number four ▪ 51-year-old Chief Superintendent Tommy Butler of Scotland Yard and his team of detectives (which includes 39-year-old Jack Slipper) begin rounding-up the train robbers. Ronnie Biggs, Charlie Wilson, Tommy Wisbey, Brian Field, Frank Munroe, Bob Welch and 33-year-old Gordon Goody are among the thieves caught. 31-year-old Bruce Reynolds and 32-year-old Buster Edwards remain at large ▪ Dr. Beeching wields his axe yet again - Market Drayton Railway Station closes down ▪ Millions of television viewers tune in for a new series of *Z Cars* on BBC (with 32-year-old Jimmy Ellis as PC Bert Lynch) ▪ "Evening, all" - 67-year-old Jack Warner stars in a new series of *Dixon of Dock Green* ▪ Satirical TV show *That Was The Week That Was* (with 24-year-old David Frost, 29-year-old Millicent Martin, 30-year-old Lance Percival and 26-year-old Willie Rushton) continues to shock 'the establishment' ▪ 69-year-old Harold Macmillan is rushed into hospital and undergoes tests for cancer ▪ Macmillan stands down as prime-minister and is succeeded by the former Foreign Secretary,

Sir Alec Douglas-Home ▪ As Sir Alec is transferring from the House of Lords to the House of Commons, the 60-year-old politician stands for the Conservatives at a by-election in Kinross and West Perth and wins the seat, taking almost sixty per-cent of the vote ▪ Sir Alec chairs a Cabinet meeting on Tuesday the twelfth of November ▪ 60-year-old Richard Austen 'Rab' Butler takes over at the Foreign Office ▪ 46-year-old Reg Maudling remains as Chancellor of the Exchequer ▪ 60-year-old Henry Brooke remains as Home Secretary ▪ 'Igniting the flames of rebellion in a land of blood and betrayal' - *The Scarlet Blade*, an adventure movie set at the time of the English Civil War (and starring 37-year-old Lionel Jeffries and 25-year-old Oliver Reed) is on general release at cinemas ▪ The *American Express* credit card is launched in Britain ▪ 'Dream kitchens come true with Credaplan build-in electrical equipment' - a *Credaplan* oven costs 59 guineas, a *Credaplan* 4-plate hob is 30 guineas and a *Credaplan* refrigerator is 58 guineas - and all appliances are designed to be fitted into modern, made-to-measure *Hygena* units and cupboards ▪ ***If I Had A Hammer*** ("... I'd hammer in the morning, I'd hammer in the evening, all over this land") by 26-year-old Trini Lopez is number four on the hit parade ▪ "How many roads must a man walk down before they call him a man?" - ***Blowing In The Wind*** by Peter, Paul and Mary (a trio from New York comprising of: 25-year-old Peter Yarrow, 25-year-old Paul Stookey and 26-year-old Mary Travers) is number fourteen ▪ 47-year-old Labour leader Harold Wilson makes a speech at Labour's party conference in Scarborough, urging people to embrace the 'White Heat' of technology ▪ Wilson's shadow Cabinet (which includes 51-year-old Jim Callaghan, 56-year-old Patrick Gordon-Walker, 61-year-old Frank Soskice and 53-year-old Barbara Castle) devises a plan to modernise Britain and end discrimination - if Labour is elected ▪ Construction work is underway on the Springfields housing estate in Rugeley, Staffordshire - a modern development of family houses ▪ *Five Are Together Again* is the latest *Famous Five* adventure story from 66-year-old author Enid Blyton ▪ Many children shun books, and prefer to watch TV instead ▪ *Fireball XL5* (with Steve Zodiac and Venus) is on ATV ▪ *Blue Peter* (with 30-year-old Christopher Trace and 26-year-old Valerie Singleton) is on BBC ▪ Men flick through the pages of car magazines ▪ Austin launches the *1100* - almost identical to the Morris *1100* ▪ Vauxhall launches the *Viva HA* to challenge the hugely popular Ford *Anglia 105E* ▪ A sleek new Jaguar *S Type* costs around £2,000 ▪ A luxurious Mercedes *600* is £8,000 ▪ 'Formality, timelessness and elegance' - The latest Rolls-Royce *Phantom V* is £9,000 ▪ 27-year-old racing driver Jim Clark wins the Italian Grand Prix in his Lotus and becomes the new Formula One world champion ▪ ***Shindig*** by The Shadows (led by 21-year-old guitarist Hank Marvin) climbs to number six in the pop chart ▪ ***She Loves You*** ("... yeah, yeah, yeah") by The Beatles spends a total of six weeks at number one ▪ The 'Fab Four' perform at the Odeon in Cheltenham and then embark on a thirty-three date nationwide tour - playing to venues packed with hysterical, screaming teenagers ▪ 15-year-old Cathy Jennings faints and has to be carried out of a show at the Pavilion Gardens Ballroom in Buxton ▪ "She's had her kicks" - 33-year-old Sean Connery stars as 007 in the second James Bond film, *From Russia With Love*. Lotte Lenya plays Rosa Klebb, an evil SPECTRE agent who tries to kill Bond with a poisoned spike in her shoe. 55-year-old Bernard Lee plays the role of M. 49-year-old Desmond Llewelyn is Major Boothroyd, head of Q branch ▪ Men form orderly queues outside picture houses ▪ "You read about her in Playboy magazine... Now See All of Jayne Mansfield!' - 30-year-old Jayne Mansfield (40-21-35) bares all in her new film, *Promises! Promises!* ▪ 'It's Beatlemania!' - The Beatles appear in front of the 63-year-old Queen mother at the Royal Variety Show - and millions of TV viewers watching at home get to see what all the fuss is about ▪ The 'Fab

Four' from Liverpool raise pandemonium whenever they perform ▪ John, Paul, George and Ringo are the most famous people in the country - and they're adored by almost everybody ▪ 29-year-old Brian Epstein makes plans to maximise the amount of money The Beatles can earn - there's talk of a lucrative tour of America ▪ The football season continues ▪ Malky McDonald's Brentford football team thrashes Ken Barnes' Wrexham 9-0 in Division Three ▪ 30-year-old striker Ambrose 'Amby' Fogarty transfers from Sunderland to Hartlepools Utd for £10,000 ▪ 17-year-old Georgie Best makes his debut for Matt Busby's Manchester Utd in a 1-0 victory over West Bromwich Albion at Old Trafford in Division One ▪ "Now..." ***Do You Love Me*** ("... do you love me, now that I can dance? Watch me, now. Work. Work. Ahh, work it out baby") by 21-year-old Brian Poole and the Tremeloes spends three weeks at number one in the pop chart ▪ "I'm going back someday, come what may on..." ***Blue Bayou*** by 27-year-old Roy Orbison is number three ▪ ***My Boyfriend's Back*** ("... and you're gonna be in trouble") by The Angels stalls at number fifty, despite being a smash hit in the US - making it to number one on the Billboard charts ▪ 23-year-old Jimmy 'Greavsie' Greaves scores four goals as Alf Ramsey's England football team (G Banks, Armfield, R Thomson, Milne, Norman, Moore, Paine, Greaves, R Smith, Eastham, R Charlton) beats Northern Ireland 8-3 at Wembley ▪ 22-year-old Harry Burrows bags a hat-trick as Joe Mercer's Aston Villa thrash Blackpool 0-4 at Bloomfield Road ▪ 6-year-old violinist Nigel Kennedy auditions for the Yehudi Menuhin School of Music ▪ 11-year-old Robin Friday from London bunks off school and spends the day kicking a football in Acton Park ▪ "I know these Earth people better than you. Their minds reject things they don't understand" - *Dr. Who* begins on BBC television, with 55-year-old William Hartnell in the title role and with 23-year-old Carole Ann Ford as Susan, the Doctor's time-travelling companion in the Tardis ▪ 13-year-old Susan George from Surbiton stars as Kitty in a six-part television serial version of *Swallows and Amazons* ▪ 'They're Here Again!' - Hattie Jacques, Kenneth Connor, Charles Hawtrey, Liz Fraser and 50-year-old Sid 'Ha-ak-ak' James star at cinemas in a new comedy film called *Carry On Cabby* ▪ 37-year-old David Coleman presents *Grandstand* on BBC One on Saturday afternoons ▪ Footballers, Ian St. John and Roger Hunt (both aged 25) score two late goals as Bill Shankly's Liverpool beat Bedford Jezzard's Fulham 2-0 in front of 38,478 spectators at Anfield ▪ "When you walk through a storm, hold your head up high and don't be afraid of the dark" - ***You'll Never Walk Alone*** by Gerry and the Pacemakers is top of the hit parade - it's the group's third number one hit in six months ▪ "Wait a minute, it's stopped raining. Guys are swimming, guys are sailing. Playing baseball, gee that's better. Mother, father kindly disregard this letter" - ***Hello Muddah Hello Faddah*** by 38-year-old Allan Sherman moves back down the singles' chart after peaking at number fourteen ▪ The Beatles' new LP, *With The Beatles*, replaces *Please Please Me* at the top of the album chart ▪ John and Francis Maher of Longsight in Manchester are proud parents of a newborn son, John Martin ▪ 12-year-old schoolboy John Kilbride goes missing while playing-out on a Saturday evening in Ashton-under-Lyme ▪ Dr. Beeching wields his axe yet again - the twenty-mile long Exe Valley railway line in Devon shuts down ▪ "Do anything that you want to, but darling, this I beg of you..." ***Don't Talk To Him*** by Cliff Richard and the Shadows is number two in the pop chart ▪ "Now I shout it from the highest hills, even told the golden daffodils, that once I had a secret love, that lived within the heart of me" - ***Secret Love*** by 24-year-old Kathy Kirby is number four ▪ There's world-wide shock and deep sadness when 46-year-old US president John F. Kennedy is assassinated in Dallas.

Christmas 1963

Young Georgie Best scores his first goal for Man Utd

Monarch:	Queen Elizabeth II (aged 37)
Prime-minister:	Alec Douglas-Home (aged 60)
Chancellor:	Reginald Maudling (aged 46)
Home Secretary:	Henry Brooke (aged 60)
Foreign Secretary:	Rab Butler (aged 61)
Football Manager:	Alf Ramsey (aged 43)
New car reg. suffix:	'A'

▪ 89-year-old Sir Winston Churchill (MP for Woodford) spends a couple of hours in the chamber at the House of Commons, listening to question time and other crucial debates taking place. After responding to questions at the dispatch box, 60-year-old prime-minister Sir Alec Douglas-Home moves off the front bench and sits beside the great war leader. The two men are seen smiling and exchanging warm words with one another during a debate on regional development ▪ "I wanna be your lover, baby…" ***I Wanna Be Your Man*** by The Rolling Stones (with, lead singer, 20-year-old Mick Jagger) reaches number twelve in the weekly pop chart ▪ ***She Loves You*** by The Beatles moves back to the top and stays at number one for a couple of weeks ▪ The weather turns chilly ▪ All around the country, children watch television ▪ *Blue Peter* presenters, 30-year-old Christopher Trace and 26-year-old Valerie Singleton, launch a new Christmas Appeal. For the second year running, thousands of people donate toys for poor children otherwise unlikely to receive gifts on Christmas Day ▪ Popular fictional detective Hercule Poirot features in *The Clocks* - the latest 'whodunit' novel from 73-year-old crime-writer Agatha Christie ▪ 50-year-old Mr. Paul Bryan (Conservative MP for Howden) accuses Labour leader Harold Wilson of being a one-man band. "At question time he is on his feet at every conceivable opportunity" [and] "In debates he must give twice as many speeches as anyone in the House. On television he will not let any other leading Socialist take a programme if he can help it." ▪

Sugar And Spice ("… and all things nice") by The Searchers (with, vocalist, 23-year-old Tony Jackson) is number two in the pop chart ▪ ***You Were Made For Me*** ("… everybody tells me so") by Freddie and the Dreamers (with, lead singer, 27-year-old Freddie Garrity) is number three ▪ There's snow in the air ▪ The Ronettes perform ***Frosty The Snowman*** ("… was a jolly, happy soul") ▪ 36-year-old Andy Williams sings ***It's The Most Wonderful Time Of The Year*** ▪ Mums, dads, boys and girls travel on steam trains to visit aunties and uncles for Christmas ▪ A total of 324 miles of railway track has been closed down this year as part of Dr. Beeching's cost saving plan ▪ People gather in living rooms to play games or watch television ▪ *Mousetrap* by Ideal is a fun new board game for all the family ▪ 54-year-old William Hartnell stars as *Dr. Who* on BBC - and terrified children, all around the country, peer from behind settees as the Daleks are seen for the first time ▪ 'You may not believe in Ghosts but you cannot deny Terror' - *The Haunting* is at cinemas, with 37-year-old Julie Harris and 32-year-old Claire Bloom in starring roles ▪ 'The Murder Mystery with a Difference … You Die Laughing!' - Tom Poston, Robert Morley, Janette Scott and 53-year-old Joyce Grenfell star in *The Old Dark House* ▪ Police mount a round-the-clock guard of Mr. Harold Wilson after an assassination threat is made on the Labour leader. The threat was made in two handwritten letters (sent to Scotland Yard and the *Daily Mirror*). A number of people are already being questioned in the Lancashire area ▪ Christmas arrives ▪ Lucky men receive a new-fangled electric razor as a gift ▪ A Ronson *21* costs £7/7s/- and comes with a money back guarantee ▪ 'Bri-Lon, for the sense of it' - Lucky wives receive a *Bri Nylon* nightie ▪ 'We Give Green Shield Stamps' - *Green Shield Stamps* are now available at *Tesco* ▪ ***I (Who Have Nothing)*** by 26-year-old Shirley Bassey is number six in the pop chart ▪ "I don't know what it is that makes me love you so" - ***I Only Want To Be With You*** by 24-year-old Dusty Springfield is number four ▪ 45-year-old terrorist Nelson Mandela appears in court in South Africa, facing new charges of sabotage and conspiracy to overthrow the government ▪ Back in England - 'Beatlemania' has taken a firm hold. The 'Fab Four' continue their tour of the country and thousands of awe-struck teenagers come to see them at Leicester, Portsmouth, Liverpool, Lewisham, Southend, Doncaster, Scarborough and Nottingham. The Beatles conclude their tour on the thirteenth of December at the Gaumont in Southampton - playing behind a steel barrier, which has been erected to protect them from the rowdy concert goers ▪ "Oh yeah, I-aah, tell you something, I think you'll understand. When I-aah, say that something, I wanna hold your hand' - ***I Want To Hold Your Hand*** by The Beatles enters the hit parade at number ten and climbs to number one the following week. The song is a smash hit - remaining top of the pop chart for five weeks! ▪ 11-year-old John Mellor (aka Joe Strummer) practices guitar at boarding school in Surrey ▪ 32-year-old Bruce Reynolds (suspected ring leader in the Great Train Robbery) is in hiding from the police, 'lying low' at a secret address in London ▪ 23-year-old footballer Denis Law scores four goals as Matt Busby's Manchester Utd beat Stoke City 5-2 at Old Trafford ▪ 26-year-old goalkeeper Chic Brodie transfers from Northampton Town to Brentford for £10,000 ▪ 50-year-old Robert Dougall reads the news on BBC television ▪ 200 million tonnes of coal have been mined in Britain this year. The number of mine workers has fallen to 520,000 ▪ The total number of unemployed people under Sir Alec Douglas-Home's Conservative government stands at 400,000 ▪ Labour leader Harold Wilson (from Huddersfield) points out that nobody from the prime-minister's privileged background could really understand the problems faced by ordinary families ▪ 21-year-old Christine Keeler is sentenced to nine months in prison for perjury ▪ ***Kiss Me Quick*** by 28-year-old Elvis Presley enters the pop chart at number twenty-five ▪ "Oh, I was only..." ***Twenty Four Hours From Tulsa*** by 23-year-old Gene Pitney is number nine ▪ TV show *That Was The Week That Was* (with 24-year-old David Frost) airs for the final time - after coming under pressure from the government ▪ 'The Great Adventure! The Great Entertainment!' - A new film called *The Great Escape* is now showing at cinemas, starring 33-year-old Steve McQueen, 35-year-old James Garner, 39-year-old Gordon Jackson, 40-year-old Richard 'Dicky' Attenborough and 44-year-old Donald Pleasence ▪ 'You'll Go Over Board For…' *Carry On Jack* (with 34-year-old Bernard Cribbins as Midshipman Albert Poop-Decker, 22-year-old Juliet Mills as Sally and 37-year-old Kenneth Williams as Captain Fearless) - is the second Carry On film to be made in colour ▪ 31-year-old Elizabeth Taylor stars alongside her lover, 38-year-old Richard Burton, in *The V.I.Ps* ▪ 30-year-old MJK Smith leads England's cricketers on a tour of India. The Test Match series will begin in the new year ▪ Back in England - the football season is now into its busy Christmas programme ▪ 46-year-old Jack Marshall's Blackburn Rovers beat West Ham Utd 8-2 on Boxing Day to go top of Division One ▪ On the same day, Tommy Docherty's Chelsea beat Ron Suart's Blackpool 1-5, Bill Shankly's Liverpool beat Tony Waddington's Stoke City 6-1 (with inside-forward Roger Hunt scoring four goals), Bedford Jezzard's Fulham thrash Jackie Milburn's Ipswich Town 10-1 (with outside-right Graham Leggat taking just three minutes to bag a hat-trick) and Manchester Utd lose 6-1 at Burnley (with centre-forward Andy Lochhead scoring four for 'The Clarets') ▪ Two days later, 17-year-old Georgie Best scores his first goal as Utd play Burnley again and, this time, gain a 5-1 victory ▪ "For goodness sake, I got the hippy hippy shakes" - ***Hippy Hippy Shake*** by the Swinging Blue Jeans (with, lead singer, 21-year-old Ray Ennis) enters the pop chart at number forty-one and climbs to number two a few weeks later ▪ 23-year-old Billy Fury from Liverpool features on the front cover of the latest *New Musical Express* paper ▪ School children run errands for their mothers ▪ A pint of milk costs 8d.

New Year 1964

Jimmy Savile introduces Top of the Pops

Monarch:	Queen Elizabeth II (aged 37)
Prime-minister:	Alec Douglas-Home (aged 60)
Chancellor:	Reginald Maudling (aged 46)
Home Secretary:	Henry Brooke (aged 60)
Foreign Secretary:	Rab Butler (aged 61)
Football Manager:	Alf Ramsey (aged 44)
New car reg. suffix:	'B'

▪ "Welcome to January the first, nineteen sixty-four. It's 6.34 p.m. and it's a programme that you've never heard of before - it's called Top of the Pops!" - 37-year-old Jimmy Savile presents the first edition of *Top of the Pops* on BBC television. The Rolling Stones, Dusty Springfield, The Dave Clark Five, The Hollies, The Swinging Blue Jeans and The Beatles are the featured artists ▪ ***I Want To Hold Your Hand*** by The Beatles remains at number one ▪ ***Dominique*** ("... nique, nique") by The Singing Nun (30-year-old Jeannine Deckers from Belgium) is number seven ▪ 'The frank look at today's pop world' - *Rave*, a monthly magazine (costing 2s/6d at newsagents) is launched for pop music fans. The Beatles (John, Paul, George and Ringo) are pictured on the front cover ▪ 'For go ahead teens' - *Jackie*, a weekly magazine (costing sixpence) is launched for teenage girls. 23-year-old Cliff Richard is pictured on the front cover ▪ 'When it comes to LOVE or MURDER ... there is no one as dangerous as the ...' *Paranoiac* - a chilling new movie, starring 25-year-old Janette Scott and 26-year-old Oliver Reed, goes on general release at cinemas ▪ 21-year-old Rita Tushingham, 27-year-old Colin Campbell and 30-year-old Dudley Sutton star in *Leather Boys* ▪ 'B' registration cars are newly available ▪ 'Rover 2000. Years ahead in every way' - The new Rover *P6* is a sensation. The four cylinder, 2000cc model costs £1,264 (including taxes) and has a top speed of 102 mph ▪ 'Viva!' - The new Vauxhall *Viva de Luxe* costs £566 (including taxes) and has a top speed of 78 mph ▪

'We were right to choose an Austin 1100' - The new Austin *1100* costs £592/12s/11d (including taxes) and has a top speed of 78 mph ▪ 30-year-old Paddy Hopkirk and 43-year-old Henry Liddon win the Monte Carlo Rally in a red *Mini Cooper S* with the registration 33 EJB ▪ 23-year-old footballer Jimmy 'Greavsie' Greaves bags a hat-trick as Bill Nicholson's Tottenham Hotspur beat Jack Marshall's Blackburn Rovers 4-1 at White Hart Lane ▪ 23-year-old West Ham Utd full-back John Lyall is forced to retire from the game with a long standing knee injury ▪ 47-year-old President of the Board of Trade Edward Heath proposes the abolition of Retail Price Maintenance and Sir Alec Douglas-Home's Cabinet approves the idea - hoping it will help lower the cost of living for the people of Britain ▪ 'Two books of vital importance to every thinking elector. No one should cast a vote in 1964 without having read and re-read them' - 47-year-old leader of the Labour opposition Harold Wilson promotes two new books which are to be published ahead of this year's general election: *Purpose in Politics* (30 shillings) and *The Relevance of British Socialism* (16 shillings) ▪ 10-year-old schoolboy Tony Blair from Durham is influenced by pop songs on the radio ▪ ***If I Ruled The World*** ("... every day would be the first day of Spring") by 42-year-old Harry Secombe is number twenty-one on the hit parade ▪ "Have I ever told you, how good it feels to hold you" - ***Baby I Love You*** by The Ronettes enters at number forty and climbs to number eleven a few weeks later ▪ 60-year-old Conservative prime-minister Sir Alec Douglas-Home and his Foreign Secretary 61-year-old Richard Austen 'Rab' Butler fly across the Atlantic in early February for high-level meetings ▪ After spending time in Ottawa with 66-year-old Lester Pearson (prime-minister of Canada), the two senior politicians move on to Washington for talks with 55-year-old Lyndon B. Johnson (president of the USA) ▪ Back in Britain - there's heavy snow over England and Wales - and traffic is disrupted ▪ A Ford *Consul MkII* (in Tuscan Yellow) is stranded on the A361 at Milverton ▪ A Morris *Cowley* (in Mineral Blue) is stuck on the B4293 near Monmouth ▪ The criminal trial of last year's train robbers begins at Aylesbury. 34-year-old Ronnie Biggs and 31-year-old Charlie Wilson are two of the men standing in the dock ▪ "At one-hundred yards, volley fire. Present! Aim! Fire!" - 30-year-old actor Michael Caine stars at cinemas in *Zulu* ▪ "There's only one way to figure it, and that is 'every man for himself'" - Buddy Hackett, Spencer Tracy, Mickey Rooney, Phil Silvers, Ethel Merman and 52-year-old Terry-Thomas star in *It's a Mad, Mad, Mad, Mad World* ▪ "Gentlemen, you can't fight in here! This is the War Room." - 38-year-old Peter Sellers and 36-year-old George C. Scott star in *Dr. Strangelove* - a dark comedy from 35-year-old director Stanley Kubrick ▪ 53-year-old Hugh Greene OBE (Director General of the British Broadcasting Corporation) is knighted in the New Year's Honour List ▪ A third series of *Steptoe and Son* is new on BBC television - starring 38-year-old Harry H. Corbett and 51-year-old Wilfrid Brambell. (37-year-old Leonard Rossiter makes an appearance in episode three - playing a crooked lead dealer) ▪ 38-year-old Pete Murray introduces an edition of *Top of the Pops* - with teenage kids in the studio, bopping and dancing to the latest groovy sounds ▪ 53-year-old Mrs. E. R. Whitehouse from rural Worcestershire decides enough is enough and begins a campaign to clean up television ▪ 21-year-old Paul McCartney, 23-year-old John Lennon, 20-year-old George Harrison and 23-year-old Ringo Starr take 'Beatlemania' to the USA - The 'Fab Four' appear on *The Ed Sullivan Show* in front of 70 million television viewers ▪ Pop music has become a worldwide phenomenon ▪ London based group The Detours (comprising of band members: 19-year-old John Entwistle, 18-year-old Pete Townshend and 19-year-old Roger Daltry) change their name to The Who ▪ "You say that you love me, all of the time. You say that you need me, you'll always be mine. And I'm feeling…" ***Glad All Over*** by The Dave Clark Five (with, singer / drummer, 24-year-old Dave Clark) moves to the top of the hit parade ▪ "Always onward, rode the six-hundred. (5-4-3-2-1). Down the valley on their horses they thundered..." ***5-4-3-2-1*** by Manfred Mann (with keyboard player, 23-year-old Manfred Mann and lead singer, 21-year-old Paul Jones) reaches number five ▪ 'You can expect the unexpected when they play …' *Charade* (starring 60-year-old Cary Grant, 34-year-old Audrey Hepburn, 43-year-old Walter Matthau and 35-year-old James Coburn) is on general release at picture houses ▪ The comedy *A Stitch in Time* (starring 48-year-old Norman Wisdom as Norman Pitkin and with 62-year-old Edward Chapman as Mr. Grimsdale) makes cinema audiences laugh ▪ 50-year-old Dr. Beeching wields his axe yet again - railway stations at Tadcaster, Towcester and Penda's Way in Yorkshire close down ▪ Meanwhile, beneath the streets of London, construction work continues on the new Victoria tube train line ▪ ***I'm The One*** ("… who cares about you. I'm the one who'll always be true") by Gerry and the Pacemakers (with, lead singer, 21-year-old Gerry Marsden) reaches number two on the hit parade ▪ "Don't blame me for falling in love with you. I'm under your spell, but how can I help it…" ***Don't Blame Me*** by 26-year-old Frank Ifield from Coventry is number eight ▪ 31-year-old cricketer Colin Cowdrey scores two centuries as England draw every one of the five Test Matches in India ▪ 22-year-old boxer Cassius Clay becomes heavy-weight champion of the world and changes his name to Muhammad Ali ▪ 38-year-old actor and comedian Peter Sellers from Southsea marries 21-year-old actress Britt Ekland from Stockholm ▪ "I saw her today, I saw her face, it was a face I loved, and I knew I had to run away, and get down on my knees and pray-ee-ay, that they'd go away" - ***Needles And Pins*** by The Searchers (with, vocalist, 22-year-old Mike Pender) spends three weeks at number one in the pop chart ▪ "Smile for me, my…" ***Diane*** by The Bachelors (with, vocalist, 28-year-old Con Cluskey) spends a week at the top ▪ ***I'm The Lonely One*** by 23-year-old Cliff Richard and the Shadows reaches number eight ▪ 38-year-old Detective Chief Inspector Leonard 'Nipper' Read investigates the shady business dealings of 30-year-old twins Reginald and Ronald Kray - hoping to gather sufficient evidence to make an arrest ▪ Families watch TV together ▪ BBC transmits a gritty court-room drama telling a tale of drug addiction, corruption and murder ▪ Mrs. R. Hallifax J.P. (President of the Mother's Union) writes to Mrs. E. R. Whitehouse to offer her support for the campaign to clean up television ▪ "She's pretty as a daisy, but look out man she's crazy"- ***Poison Ivy*** by The Paramounts (with, lead singer, 18-year-old Gary Brooker) is number thirty-five in the pop chart ▪ "When the night is cold and my arms want someone to hold..." ***I Think Of You*** by The Merseybeats (with, lead singer, 17-year-old Billy Kinsley) is number nine ▪ 60-year-old prime-minister Sir Alec Douglas-Home is the subject of a new book - *Modern Conservative* by Emrys Hughes, on sale now in bookshops for 12s/6d (or 5 shillings for a paperback copy) ▪ 25-year-old footballer Ian St. John scores a hat-trick as Bill Shankly's Liverpool thrash Sheffield Utd 6-1 to go second in Division One ▪ Bill Nicholson's Tottenham Hotspur beat Blackburn Rovers 4-1 and remain at the top of the table ▪ Fourth placed Manchester Utd beat West Bromwich Albion 4-1 - and the names 'Best, Charlton, Law' feature together on the score-sheet for the first time ▪ New movie star 30-year-old Michael Caine (from the hit film *Zulu*) is photographed in the newspapers along with his Mum, 63-year-old Mrs. Ellen Micklewhite of Brixton ▪ 29-year-old boxer Henry Cooper (aka Our 'Enry) is the new European Heavyweight Champion after defeating Brian London in Manchester ▪ Men spend a pleasant evening in the pub ▪ A pint of *Worthington E* in the Red Lion is 1s/6d ▪ A pack of twenty Player's *Weights* cigarettes is 3s/5d.

Spring 1964

Train Robbers sentenced to thirty years

Monarch:	Queen Elizabeth II (aged 38)
Prime-minister:	Alec Douglas-Home (aged 60)
Chancellor:	Reginald Maudling (aged 47)
Home Secretary:	Henry Brooke (aged 61)
Foreign Secretary:	Rab Butler (aged 61)
Football Manager:	Alf Ramsey (aged 44)
New car reg. suffix:	'B'

▪ Dr. Beeching wields his axe yet again - Penshaw Railway Station at Tyne and Wear closes down ▪ 10-year-old schoolboy Michael Portillo from Bushey spends an afternoon train-spotting ▪ 33-year-old Bert Foord presents the weather forecast on BBC television ▪ There's deep snow in the Midlands and Yorkshire ▪ Power cuts affect thousands of homes - and hardware shops run short of paraffin and candles ▪ 60-year-old prime-minister Sir Alec Douglas-Home travels to Belfast to address the Ulster Unionist Council. The meeting is followed by a pleasant luncheon with local dignitaries ▪ ***Anyone Who Had A Heart*** ("... would take me in his arms and love me, too. Oooh") by 20-year-old Cilla Black from Liverpool is new at number one on the hit parade ▪ ***Let Me Go Lover*** by 25-year-old Kathy Kirby from Ilford is number ten ▪ 37-year-old Queen Elizabeth II gives birth to her fourth child - a son: Edward Anthony Richard Louis ▪ 'It's so easy to set fire to a...' *Woman of Straw* (starring 36-year-old Gina Lollobrigida, 61-year-old Sir Ralph Richardson and 33-year-old Sean Connery) goes on general release at cinemas ▪ 32-year-old movie star Elizabeth Taylor divorces Eddie Fisher and marries her lover, 38-year-old Richard Burton, in Montreal - it's Taylor's fifth marriage ▪ Back in England - newspaper headlines announce, '307 Years' Jail' - as the trial of the train robbers ends with seven of the convicted men sentenced to thirty years in prison ▪ The world of football is thrown into turmoil when *The People* newspaper reports that a number of players (including Everton's Tony Kay) accepted bribes to 'throw' a match sixteen months ago. At the time, the accused players were with Sheffield Wednesday ▪ Gangs of young people head for the seaside ▪ Mods and rockers fight on the beach at Clacton ▪ Faberge introduces *Brut* cologne ▪ Mods and rockers fight on the beach at Margate ▪ 17-year-old drummer Keith Moon joins a little known band called The Who ▪ 'The weekend starts here' - ATV's Friday evening pop show *Ready, Steady Go!* features an interview with The Beatles ▪ Pirate radio station Caroline begins broadcasting pop music all day long, from a ship in the North Sea ▪ 'Discs - Stars - News from this week's Top Twenty' - *Top of the Pops* has become a hit television show for the BBC. On Wednesday the eighteenth of March, the programme is presented by 37-year-old Jimmy Savile ▪ "Little children, you better not tell on me. I'm tellin' you..." ***Little Children*** by Billy J Kramer and the Dakotas spends two weeks at the top of the pop chart ▪ ***Just One Look*** ("... is all it took") by The Hollies is number two ▪ BBC Two is a brand new television channel - serving viewers in London and the Home Counties ▪ 51-year-old Brian 'Johnners' Johnston presents *Off With A Bang* - a grand fireworks display to launch the new service on Monday the twentieth of April ▪ 74-year-old Athene Seylar reads stories for children, on an exciting new show called *Play School* ▪ 43-year-old Alan Tammadge presents *Mathematics '64* - a programme reflecting new trends in mathematics ▪ 38-year-old Maurice Shock presents *Power in British Politics* - a programme describing the development of the political system ▪ Conservative Prime-minister Sir Alec Douglas-Home meets with his Chancellor of the Exchequer, Reg Maudling, to discuss the problem of a growing deficit in the balance of payments ▪ The Labour opposition (led by 48-year-old Harold Wilson) is ahead in the polls ▪ People enjoy an evening at the cinema ▪ 'A spectacular story of conflict and conspiracy … murder and madness … revelry and revenge … love and hate that changed the course of human history!' - Richard Burton stars alongside 31-year-old Peter O'Toole in *Becket* ▪ 'Shock … Shock … Shock!!!' - 50-year-old Peter Cushing stars in *The Evil of Frankenstein* ▪ 29-year-old writer David Nobbs works on his first novel in a bedsit in London ▪ "If you want my love, won't you…" ***Tell Me When*** by The Applejacks reaches number seven on the hit parade ▪ ***Hubble Bubble (Toil and Trouble)*** by Manfred Mann peaks at number eleven ▪ 47,951 football supporters turn out on a Wednesday evening at Maine Road for the Testimonial of 40-year-old Manchester City goalkeeper Bert Trautmann. Star players: Denis Law, Bobby Charlton, Derek 'the tank' Kevan, Stanley Matthews (aka the 'Wizard of Dribble'), Tom Finney (aka the 'Preston Plumber') and Jimmy Armfield take part in the match ▪ 21-year-old footballer Bobby Hunt transfers from Neil Franklin's Third Division Colchester Utd to Dave Bowen's Second Division Northampton Town for £15,000 ▪ 28-year-old DJ Simon Dee spins discs for the exciting and new Radio Caroline - a pirate station, broadcasting from a ship anchored in the sea off the coast of Essex ▪ "I'm gonna tell you how it's gonna be, you're gonna give your love to me. I'm gonna love you night and day, well love is love and…" ***Not Fade Away*** by The Rolling Stones (with, lead singer, 20-year-old Mick Jagger) is number three in the pop chart ▪ ***Viva Las Vegas*** by 29-year-old Elvis Presley is number seventeen ▪ Families enjoy a Sunday evening in, watching TV ▪ BBC One's *Songs of Praise* is broadcast from Eastbrook Hall in Bradford ▪ *The Black and White Minstrel Show* comes from the Victoria Palace in London ▪ 'No blacks, no dogs, no Irish' - 26-year-old Paul Stephenson stages a peaceful sit-in at the Bay Horse pub in Bristol after being refused service due to the colour of his skin. Stephenson is arrested and spends a night in jail before being released on bail ▪ Cambridge win the Boat Race by six and a half lengths ▪ *Arkle* wins the Cheltenham Gold Cup by five lengths ▪ Matt Gillies' Leicester City football team (with Gordon Banks, Colin Appleton, Graham Cross and Ken Keyworth) defeats Tony Waddington's Stoke City (with Lawrie Leslie, Bill Asprey, Jimmy McIlroy and Dennis Viollet) 4-3 on aggregate over two legs to win the League Cup final ▪ In Division One, 29-year-old Cliff Jones scores a hat-trick for Tottenham Hotspur and 25-year-old Gerry Baker scores a hat-trick for Ipswich Town as Spurs win 6-3 at White Hart Lane ▪ Bill Shankly's Liverpool are the new champions of England - clinching the title with a 5-0 victory over Arsenal in front of 48,623 at Anfield. Tommy Lawrence, Gerry Byrne, Ronnie Moran, Ron Yeats, Ian Callaghan, Jimmy Melia, Gordon Milne, Peter Thompson, Alf Arrowsmith, Willie Stevenson, Ian St. John and 25-year-old top goal scorer Roger Hunt have all been outstanding for 'The Reds' ▪ "I'll buy you a diamond ring my friend if it makes you feel alright" - ***Can't Buy Me Love*** by The Beatles enters the pop chart at number eight and climbs to number one the following week ▪ ***I Believe*** ("... for every drop of rain that falls, a flower grows") by The Bachelors reaches number two ▪ The Rolling Stones feature in a special edition of *Ready, Steady, Go!* - as the popular programme is broadcast 'live' from the Empire Pool at Wembley ▪ On Thursday evenings at tea-time, the BBC transmits *Between the Lines* - a new satirical comedy presented by 41-year-old Fulton MacKay ▪ Around two-thousand people attend a meeting at Birmingham Town Hall - demonstrating against the falling moral standards in television. 54-year-old Mrs. Mary Whitehouse (from rural Worcestershire) addresses the audience and describes BBC One's *Between the Lines* as "the dirtiest programme that I have seen for a very long time." ▪ 43-year-old script writer Johnny Speight works on a new idea for a comedy show ▪ 38-year-old actor Warren Mitchell is currently 'resting' ▪ "When the night has come and the land is dark and the moon is the only light we see" - ***Stand By Me*** by 26-year-old Kenny Lynch stalls at number thirty-nine in the pop chart ▪ Leader of the Opposition Harold Wilson and shadow Chancellor Jim Callaghan persuade unions representing workers from the power industry not to call a strike - fearing that industrial action would lead to power cuts and affect Labour's chances of ousting the Tory government at the next general election ▪ 24-year-old 'goal machine' footballer Jimmy 'Greavsie' Greaves of Tottenham Hotspur is the top scorer in Division One - yet again! ▪ "Pick up the pieces..." ***Bits And Pieces*** by The Dave Clark Five peaks at number two in the pop chart ▪ "I don't care what they say, I won't stay in…" ***A World Without Love*** by Peter and Gordon is new at number one ▪ Hard-tackling Leeds Utd (with Gary Sprake, Paul Reaney, Willie Bell, Jack Charlton, Norman Hunter, Johnny Giles, Alan Peacock, Don Weston, Albert Johanneson, Bobby Collins, Terry Cooper and 21-year-old Billy Bremner) finish top of Division Two and 36-year-old manager Don Revie says, "We must get rid of this tag of 'dirty'" ▪ Alan Brown's Sunderland are runners-up and gain promotion to the First Division along with Leeds ▪ Jimmy Hill's Coventry City (with Bob Wesson, Brian Hill, Mick Kearns, John Sillett, Ron Farmer, Ernie Machin, Ronnie Rees, Billy Humphries, Ken Hale, Hugh Barr, George Hudson and 25-year-old George Curtis) are promoted from Division Three to Division Two ▪ 36-year-old Malcolm Allison takes over as manager of Plymouth Argyle ▪ ***Don't Throw Your Love Away*** ("… No, no, no, no") by The Searchers moves to the top of the hit parade ▪ "Our lips shouldn't touch..." ***Move Over Darling*** by 42-year-old Doris Day is number eight ▪ ***You're My World*** by 21-year-old Cilla Black is a new chart entry at number thirty ▪ London based group The Who change their name to The High Numbers ▪ Great excitement builds for the FA Cup final. 90,000 spectators converge on Wembley on a dry, overcast day in early May. 22-year-old Geoff

Hurst scores a goal as Ron Greenwood's West Ham Utd defeat Jimmy Milne's Preston North End by three goals to two. Hammers' captain, 23-year-old Bobby Moore, lifts the famous silver trophy. A ticket for the standing enclosure at the Empire Stadium in Wembley costs 7s/6d ▪ 22-year-old Rita Tushingham stars at cinemas in *Girl With Green Eyes* ▪ A documentary called *Seven Up!* is broadcast on commercial television - detailing the hopes and aspirations of a group of 7-year-old children ▪ HRH the Duke of Edinburgh, 42-year-old Prince Philip, opens the modern new Bull Ring centre in Birmingham - it's the first purpose-built indoor shopping area in Britain ▪ "I love you for a hundred thousand reasons, but most of all I love you 'cause you're you" - ***I Love You Because*** by 40-year-old 'Gentleman' Jim Reeves is number five in the pop chart ▪ ***Constantly*** by 23-year-old Cliff Richard reaches number four ▪ Families enjoy an evening in front of the TV ▪ Martha Longhurst (played by 49-year-old Lynne Carol) suffers a heart attack and dies in 'The Rovers Return' pub in ITV's *Coronation Street* ▪ 44-year-old Cliff Michelmore introduces *Tonight* on BBC One ▪ Keen motorists zip along Britain's ever growing network of motorways ▪ A Ford *Zephyr 6* reaches a speed of 92 mph on a stretch of the M1 in Bedfordshire ▪ A Humber *Super Snipe* 'tops out' at 96 mph on the M6 in Staffordshire ▪ An Austin *A40* overheats on the M5 in Worcestershire ▪ ***Juliet*** ("... don't forget") by The Four Pennies is new at number one in the pop chart ▪ "My boy lollipop, you make my heart go giddy-up" - ***My Boy Lollipop*** by 17-year-old Millie is number two ▪ Adolescent boys peruse the shelves at newspaper shops ▪ 21-year-old actress Susan Farmer is on the front cover of *Parade* ▪ 'Billy Whizz' makes his first appearance in *The Beano* comic ▪ 35-year-old Graham Hill (driving a racing green BRM - number 8) wins the Monaco Grand Prix for the second year running ▪ Adverts say, 'ESSO - Put A Tiger In Your Tank'.

Summer 1964

Geoffrey Boycott's first Test century

Monarch:	Queen Elizabeth II (aged 38)
Prime-minister:	Alec Douglas-Home (aged 61)
Chancellor:	Reginald Maudling (aged 47)
Home Secretary:	Henry Brooke (aged 61)
Foreign Secretary:	Rab Butler (aged 61)
Football Manager:	Alf Ramsey (aged 44)
New car reg. suffix:	'B'

▪ For the second year in a row, it's a wet washout of a summer ▪ "Can you dig it, man?" - Boys and girls on scooters head for the seaside ▪ Mods and rockers fight on the beaches of Hastings and Brighton ▪ "Don't you know that..." ***Everything's Alright*** by The Mojos slides down the pop chart after reaching number nine ▪ 'You can't beat Burton tailoring' - a hand-cut, made-to-measure suit from *Burtons* costs £10/19s/6d ▪ ***You're My World*** ("... you're every breath I take. You're my world, every move I make") by 21-year-old Cilla Black from Liverpool climbs to number one in the pop chart ▪ "You know you make me wanna shout! (Shout!) Look my hand's jumpin' (Shout!) Look my heart's thumpin' (Shout!) - ***Shout*** by 15-year-old Lulu and the Luvvers is number seven ▪ 21-year-old George Harrison (from The Beatles) is pictured on the front cover of the latest *Rave* magazine ▪ *Séance on a Wet Afternoon* is at cinemas - 41-year-old Richard 'Dicky' Attenborough and 39-year-old Kim Stanley are the stars ▪ 60-year-old Conservative prime-minister Sir Alec Douglas-Home and his 47-year-old Chancellor of the Exchequer Reg Maudling preside over a large deficit in the balance of payments - the value of imports is twice that of exports ▪ Harold Wilson's opposition Labour Party moves further ahead in the opinion polls ▪ There's a flurry of activity on football's transfer market ▪ 28-year-old Don Howe (a full-back) transfers from West Bromwich Albion to Arsenal for £42,000 ▪ 22-year-old Jeff Astle (a centre-forward) transfers from Notts County to West Bromwich Albion for

£25,000 ▪ 26-year-old Rodney Green (a centre-forward) transfers from Bradford City to Gillingham for £9,000 ▪ 19-year-old George Graham (a half-back) transfers from Aston Villa to Chelsea for £5,000 ▪ *The Beano Summer Special* (with a front cover depicting Biffo the Bear sunbathing on a beach) is now available at newsagents for 1s/6d ▪ *The Daily Sketch* newspaper goes up in price, from 3d to 4d ▪ 39-year-old Richard Baker reads the news on BBC television ▪ Dr. Beeching wields his axe yet again - Baptist End Railway Station near Dudley closes down ▪ 45-year-old terrorist Nelson Mandela is found guilty of conspiring to overthrow the government in South Africa - and is sentenced to life imprisonment. Mandela is taken to Robben Island where he spends his days breaking rocks and his nights sleeping on a straw mat in a damp prison cell ▪ Back in England - the front page of the *Sunday Mirror* informs the public that police from Scotland Yard are investigating an alleged homosexual relationship between a prominent peer and a London gangster ▪ 'A Little of What You Fancy Does You Good!' - saucy postcards are mailed to family and friends from holiday makers at the seaside ▪ Parliament passes the Resale Prices Act - a new law allowing retailers to set their own prices ▪ 'Pile it high. Sell it cheap' - *Tesco* expands its operation by buying ninety-seven *Charles Phillips* stores ▪ Traditional 'corner shops' in Hull, Nottingham, Worcester and Swindon are forced to close down ▪ 24-year-old disc jockey Chris Moore sits aboard a ship anchored in the sea off the coast of Essex and spins discs for pirate station Radio Caroline ▪ "Ridin' along in my automobile. My baby beside me at the wheel" - ***No Particular Place To Go*** by 37-year-old Chuck Berry is number three on the weekly hit parade ▪ ***Bama Lama Bama Loo*** by 31-year-old Little Richard is new at number twenty -nine ▪ A photograph in the *Daily Express* confirms that the 'prominent peer' mentioned in the *Sunday Mirror* article is 64-year-old Lord Boothby. The 'London gangster' is 30-year-old Ronald Kray ▪ The Beatles undertake a twenty-six date tour of the USA and Canada - including a show at the Hollywood Bowl ▪ The 'Fab Four' go down a storm across the Atlantic, as do The Dave Clark Five who are also touring in the States ▪ Back in Britain - ***Can't You See That She's Mine*** ("... We've been together for a long, long time, and yet they try so very hard to pull us apart") by The Dave Clark Five climbs to number ten in the pop chart ▪ "When someone really loves you (someone), that's when your life begins" - ***Someone Someone*** by Brian Poole and the Tremeloes is number two ▪ 25-year-old footballer Roger Hunt scores four goals and 23-year-old Fred Pickering bags a hat-trick as Alf Ramsey's England team (G Banks, Cohen, R Thomson, M Bailey, Norman, Flowers, Paine, Hunt, Pickering, Eastham, P Thompson and substitute, R Charlton) thrashes the USA 10-0 in New York ▪ Three days later, 23-year-old Pele scores a goal as Brazil beat England 5-1 ▪ Cricketers, 23-year-old Geoffrey Boycott and 31-year-old Fred Titmus stride out together to open the batting for England against Australia at Trent Bridge in the first Test Match of the summer series. Boycott makes 48 runs. Titmus hits 16. The match ends in a draw ▪ 11-year-old schoolboy cricketer Graham Gooch from Leytonstone listens to coverage on the radio ▪ Three of the next four Test Matches also end in draws before Bob Simpson's Australians win a match at Headingley - and this single victory means the Aussies retain the Ashes. Notable performances from England players come from 33-year-old fast bowler 'fiery' Fred Trueman who takes 5 wickets for just 48 runs at Lord's and batsman Boycott who makes his maiden Test Match century at the Oval. G Boycott, F J Titmus, J H Edrich, E R Dexter (cpt), M C Cowdrey, K F Barrington, R W Barber, P H Parfitt, K Taylor, P J Sharpe, J M Parks (wk), F S Trueman, D A Allen, N Gifford, J B Mortimore, L J Coldwell, J A Flavell, T W Cartwright, J S E Price and F E Rumsey are all downcast by another Ashes defeat - Australia have now held the trophy for five years ▪ "It's over, it's over..." ***It's Over*** by 28-year-old Roy Orbison from Tennessee spends two weeks at number one on the hit parade ▪ ***I Just Don't Know What To Do With Myself*** ("... Don't know just what to do with myself") by 25-year-old Dusty Springfield from London is number three ▪ 21-year-old tennis player Billie Jean Moffitt from Long Beach, California is knocked-out of the Wimbledon tennis championships in the semi-finals against Margaret Smith from Australia ▪ 27-year-old Roy Emerson (from Queensland) makes it an Aussie double by winning the men's singles final ▪ 12-year-old Keith Bennett goes missing on the way to his grandmother's house in Manchester ▪ Hilda and Stan Ogden (played by 37-year-old Jean Alexander and 49-year-old Bernard Youens) appear for the first time in *Coronation Street* on ITV ▪ 32-year-old Bill Simpson plays the title role in *Dr. Finlay's Casebook* on BBC One ▪ James Bond author Ian Fleming dies of a heart attack aged 56 in Canterbury ▪ 28-year-old reigning world champion racing driver Jim Clark wins the British Grand Prix at Brands Hatch. Graham Hill and John Surtees share the podium with Clark - as all three top positions go to British drivers for the second year running! ▪ Standard grade petrol has risen in price - to five shillings a gallon! ▪ The stylish 2000cc V4 Ford *Corsair* motorcar has a top speed of 106 mph and accelerates from 0-60 mph in 13 seconds ▪ The nippy MG version of the *1100* saloon has a top speed of 84 mph and accelerates from 0-60 mph in 17.9 seconds ▪ 43-year-old Donald Campbell sets a new water speed record of 403 mph in *Bluebird CN7* on Lake Eyre in Australia ▪ Construction work is underway to extend the M6 motorway through Lancashire ▪ Britain's economy is weak ▪ Conservative prime-minister Sir Alec Douglas-Home is coming under pressure to set a date for a general election ▪ Disgraced politician John Profumo helps out at a community centre in the East End of London - cleaning, sweeping-up and washing dishes ▪ "There is a house in New Orleans, they call 'The Rising Sun'. It's been the ruin of many a poor boy, and God, I know, I'm one" - ***House Of The Rising Son*** by The Animals spends a week at the top of the pop chart ▪ Alexander Boris de Pfeffel Johnson is born in Manhattan ▪ "Maybe there's a beast. Maybe it's only us." - Controversial film *Lord of the Flies*, starring James Aubrey as Ralph, Tom Chapin as Jack and 12-year-old Hugh Edwards as Piggy, is now showing at cinemas in London ▪ BBC Two television launches a new football programme called *Match of the Day*, presented by 44-year-old Kenneth Wolstenholme. The first show features highlights of a game between Liverpool and Arsenal at Anfield. The match ends in a 3-2 victory for Liverpool, with Roger Hunt and Gordon Wallace (2) scoring the goals for Liverpool. Geoff Strong and Joe Baker score the consolation goals for Arsenal ▪ 49-year-old Joe Mercer steps down as manager of Aston Villa and is replaced by his assistant, Dick Taylor ▪ "Because I used to love her, but…" ***It's All Over Now*** by The Rolling Stones (with, lead singer, 21-year-old Mick Jagger) climbs to the top of the pop chart - it's the group's first number one song ▪ "Round round, get around…" ***I Get Around*** by The Beach Boys (with, lead singer, 22-year-old Brian Wilson) is number seven ▪ Convicted murderer Peter Anthony Allen is hanged by the neck until dead at Liverpool ▪ Convicted murderer Gwynne Owen Evans is hanged by the neck until dead at Strangeways ▪ 19-year-old goalkeeper Pat Jennings leaves Bill McGarry's Watford and joins Bill Nicholson's Tottenham Hotspur for £27,000. (Jennings makes his debut for Spurs in a home game against Sheffield Utd and performs well in a 2-0 victory) ▪ 49-year-old Sunderland manager Alan Brown shocks the supporters at Roker Park by leaving to take over at Sheffield Wednesday ▪ More than one hundred-thousand screaming fans greet The Beatles at Liverpool airport as the 'Fab Four' return home from the USA ▪ "It's been…" ***A Hard Day's Night*** ("… and I've been working like a dog") moves to the top of the hit parade and stays there for three weeks ▪ 51-year-old Richard Dimbleby introduces *Panorama* on BBC One. 40-year-old Robin Day is a roving reporter for the programme ▪ The gap in the polls narrows between the governing Conservatives and Harold Wilson's opposition Labour Party ▪ Prime-minister Sir Alec Douglas-Home considers calling an election - but doesn't do so yet ▪ Sir Alec leaves Number 10 Downing Street to take a holiday in Scotland ▪ Mr. Wilson takes a break in the Isles of Scilly ▪ In other news - a leprechaun is spotted in a park in Liverpool and school children are encouraged to spend their days searching to find more ▪ 'You Only Live Once... So See The Pink Panther Twice!!' - 54-year-old David Niven and 38-year-old Peter Sellers star at cinemas in Blake Edwards' new film, *The Pink Panther* ▪ 'They're At It Again O-O-Oh!' - 26-year-old Barbara Windsor (36-23-34) plays bubbly secret agent Daphne Honeybutt (38-22-35) in *Carry On Spying* ▪ "There she was just a walkin' down the street, singing..." ***Do Wah Diddy Diddy*** ("...dum diddy doo") by Manfred Mann spends two weeks at number one in the pop chart ▪ "Only you know how I loathe this place called..." ***Tobacco Road*** by The Nashville Teens is number six ▪ 44-year-old Jimmy Edwards and 45-year-old Beryl Reid star in *Bold As Brass* on BBC television ▪ 44-year-old Hughie Green presents a new series of *Opportunity Knocks* on ITV ▪ 32-year-old train robber Charlie Wilson breaks out of Winson Green Prison and goes on the run ▪ 40-year-old 'Gentleman' Jim Reeves dies in a plane crash in Tennessee ▪ Back in England - there's a brief spell of warm weather at the end of August ▪ "All your troubles will be out of reach..." ***On The Beach*** by 23-year-old Cliff Richard and the Shadows is number seven in the pop chart ▪ "'C'est la vie', say the old folks, it goes to show..." ***You Never Can Tell*** by 37-year-old Chuck Berry enters the pop chart at number forty-five ▪ The Lennon-McCartney song ***I Should Have Known Better*** ("... with a girl like you, that I would love everything that you do, and I do, hey hey hey, and I do") by The Naturals is new at number thirty-nine ▪ 61-year-old prime-minister Sir Alec Douglas-Home cuts short his holiday in Scotland and returns to Downing Street to deal with an international crisis that is developing between Turkey and Greece ▪ 48-year-old Labour opposition leader Harold Wilson also ends his holiday (in the Scillies) and returns to London to meet with the prime-minister ▪ Racial tension is growing ▪ Across Britain, in areas with high levels of imigrant families, friction exists between deeply rooted white populations now living alongside people from the West Indies, India and Pakistan ▪ In Smethwick (a town of approximately 70,000 people, of which ten per-cent is made up of imigrants) white prejudices have led to imigrants being excluded from some pubs, cafes, shops and barbers ▪ "Mother told me always to follow the golden rule, and she said it's really a sin to be mean and cruel" - ***You'll Never Get To Heaven*** by 23-year-old Dionne Warwick is number twenty on the weekly hit parade ▪ Black people are abused verbally in the street and on public transport ▪ Racial discrimination prevents many for spending an evening at the pictures ▪ 34-year-old Ronald Fraser, 35-year-old Bernard Cribbins and 27-year-old Barbara Windsor (36-23-34) star on the big screen in *Crooks in Cloisters* ▪ 'Now - A Startling Expose!' - *The Beauty Jungle* - a film from 52-year-old director Val Guest, which shows the grim realities of the exploitative world of beauty queen competitions and fashion parades is on general release ▪ 32-year-old Terence Conran opens a groovy new shop on the Fulham Road - *Habitat* ▪ Highflying business executives drive to the office ▪ An upmarket Rover 3-litre saloon costs £1707/14s/7d and has a top speed of 100 mph ▪ Middle managers take the missus shopping ▪ An Austin *1800* costs £808/14s/7d and has a top speed of 90 mph ▪ Adverts say, 'Nuttall's *Mintoes* - the five minute mint' ▪ Families move into modern houses on the new Springfields estate in Rugeley, Staffordshire ▪ Housewives embrace the modern concept of frozen food - buying items from *Cordon Bleu* shops and storing them at home in a new-fangled fridge-freezer ▪ 'Delicious fish, the way everyone loves it!' - a pack of Birds Eye *Fish Fingers* costs 1s/8d.

Autumn 1964

Harold Wilson wins the General Election

Monarch:	Queen Elizabeth II (aged 38)
Prime-minister:	Harold Wilson (aged 48)
Chancellor:	James Callaghan (aged 52)
Home Secretary:	Frank Soskice (aged 62)
Foreign Secretary:	Patrick Gordon Walker (aged 57)
Football Manager:	Alf Ramsey (aged 44)
New car reg. suffix:	'B'

▪ The month of September is warm and sunny ▪ A Trinidadian steel band takes part in a colourful street carnival at Notting Hill ▪ 19-year-old Alexander Hughes listens to Jamaican ska and reggae records with his friends in Brixton ▪ 61-year-old prime-minister Sir Alec Douglas-Home sets a date for a general election and campaigning gets underway ▪ Activists pin posters on lamp-posts ▪ 'Let's GO with Labour and we'll get things done' - is a typical message from Labour activists ▪ 'If you desire a COLOURED for your neighbour, Vote Labour' - is a typical message from some Conservative activists ▪ A new series of popular police drama *Z Cars* begins on BBC One. 38-year-old Stratford Johns (Det. Chief Inspector Charlie Barlow) and 39-year-old Robert Keegan (Sgt. Blackitt) are pictured together on the front cover of the latest *Radio Times* ▪ *Emergency Ward 10* - with 27-year-old Joan Hooley (surgeon Louise Mahler) and 27-year-old John White (Doctor Giles Farmer) is on ITV ▪ 23-year-old bus driver David Lovell marries his sweetheart, 21-year-old Maggie Gilhooly, and the two newly-weds drive to Cornwall in a rented Austin *1100* for a week-long honeymoon at Praa Sands ▪ ***Have I The Right*** ("... to hold you? You know I've always told you, that we must never, ever part") by The Honeycombs climbs to number one in the pop chart ▪ "I'll forget many things in my lifetime, but my darling..." ***I Won't Forget You*** by the late Jim Reeves is number three ▪ Couples enjoy a romantic evening at the cinema ▪ 29-year-old Elvis Presley stars in the movie *Viva Las Vegas*, playing the role of Lucky Jackson - an impoverished racing driving forced to work as a waiter in a Vegas hotel, whilst being pursued by beautiful swimming instructor, Rusty Martin (played by 23-year-old Ann-Margret) ▪ 11-year-old schoolboy Nigel Mansell from Birmingham stays in, watching motor racing on television ▪ 30-year-old John Surtees wins the Italian Grand Prix at Monza in a Ferrari. Graham Hill is third in a BRM. Jim Clark is fourth in a Lotus ▪ 'Good Morning! Yes, it's time for a new newspaper' - *The Sun* newspaper is launched (replacing the *Daily Herald*) ▪ Schoolboys read comics ▪ *Buster* is 6d, every Monday ▪ *The Beano* is 3d, every Thursday ▪ Talented young footballer Georgie Best is on the score-sheet for Matt Busby's Manchester Utd in a 3-1 victory over Ron Greenwood's West Ham Utd at Old Trafford ▪ 24-year-old Jimmy 'Greavsie' Greaves scores the winning goal for Bill Nicholson's Tottenham Hotspur in a 1-0 victory over Jimmy Hagan's West Bromwich Albion at White Hart Lane ▪ 50-year-old Robert Dougall reads the news on BBC television ▪ Campaigning for the general election gathers momentum ▪ With just seven days to go before voting, the Tories move slightly ahead of Labour in the opinion polls ▪ Labour leader Harold Wilson reminds everyone that, "a week is a long time in politics" ▪ People cast their votes on Thursday the fifteenth of October ▪ With the slimmest of majorities, 48-year-old Wilson from Huddersfield defeats 61-year-old Sir Alec Douglas-Home from Mayfair - and Labour is in power for the first time in thirteen years. (Labour: 317 seats, Conservatives: 304 seats, Liberals: 9 seats) ▪ 52-year-old Jim Callaghan is the new Chancellor of the Exchequer ▪ 62-year-old Frank Soskice is Home Secretary ▪ 57-year-old Patrick Gordon-Walker is Foreign Secretary ▪ 47-year-old Denis Healey is Defence Secretary ▪ 54-year-old Barbara Castle is Minister for Overseas Development ▪ In Douglas-Home's opposition Conservative ranks, 39-year-old Margaret Thatcher MP is promoted to shadow for Pensions ▪ 37-year-old Geoffrey Howe is the new Tory MP for

Bebington ▪ "Baby, baby…" ***Where Did Our Love Go*** by The Supremes (featuring 20-year-old Diana Ross) is number four in the pop chart ▪ "Called her..." ***Rag Doll*** ("... Little rag doll, such a pretty face, should be dressed in lace") by The Four Seasons is number two ▪ Families in Nottinghamshire enjoy a brand new (American-style) shopping experience at the massive *GEM* superstore in West Bridgford; where all of the weekly shopping can be purchased in one go and loaded straight into the family car parked outside ▪ The latest 'Series Five' Humber *Super Snipe* motorcar has a top speed of 99 mph and power assisted steering is available as an optional extra ▪ British racing drivers, Jim Clark, Graham Hill and John Surtees continue to dominate the 1964 'World Championship of Drivers' ▪ In the final race, in Mexico, 30-year-old Surtees (in a Ferrari) pips his rivals to the title - finishing the season one point ahead of 35-year-old Hill (in a BRM) and eight points ahead of 28-year-old Clark (in a Lotus) ▪ 45-year-old disc jockey Jimmy Hanley invites you to start the day right on BBC radio's Light Programme ▪ 28-year-old disc jockey Tom Lodge sits aboard a ship anchored in the sea off the coast of Essex and spins discs for pirate station Radio Caroline ▪ ***I Wouldn't Trade You For The World*** ("… or the pearls in the sea") by The Bachelors is number four on the hit parade ▪ "But it's too late to say you're sorry. How would I know, why should I care? Please don't bother tryin' to find her …" ***She's Not There*** by The Zombies is number twelve ▪ London based group The High Numbers change their name back to The Who ▪ 22-year-old footballer Barrie Jones transfers from Second Division Swansea Town to Second Division Plymouth Argyle for a fee of £45,000 ▪ 24-year-old Frank McLintock transfers from First Division Leicester City to First Division Arsenal for a fee of £80,000 ▪ 44-year-old 'Gentleman' George Hardwick is appointed manager of Sunderland Football Club ▪ 20-year-old Ann Sydney from Poole is crowned Miss World at the Lyceum Theatre in London ▪ "Girl, you really got me goin'. You got me so I don't know what I'm doin' now. Yeah..." ***You Really Got Me*** ("... now. You got me so I can't sleep at night") by The Kinks (with, lead singer, 20-year-old Ray Davies) is top of the pop chart ▪ 'Standby for Action! We are about to launch Stingray!' - schoolboys watch, agog, as *Stingray* begins on TV ▪ The film *Goldfinger* goes on general release at cinemas, with 34-year-old Sean Connery as James Bond (aka 007), 51-year-old Gert Frobe as Goldfinger and 39-year-old Honor Blackman as Pussy Galore. In one scene, Bond asks Goldfinger, "Do you expect me to talk?" to which Goldfinger responds, "No Mr. Bond, I expect you to die" ▪ *Carry On Cleo* stars Kenneth Williams as Julius Caesar, Kenneth Connor as Hengist Pod, Sid 'Ha-ak-ak' James as Mark Anthony and 29-year-old Amanda Barrie as Cleopatra. In one scene, Caesar realises his friends have turned against him and so declares, "Infamy, infamy. They've all got it in for me" ▪ 27-year-old Shirley Bassey from Cardiff sings ***Goldfinger*** ("... he's the man, the man with the Midas touch") and the song reaches number twenty-one in the chart ▪ "Something tells me..." ***I'm Into Something Good*** by Herman's Hermitts is number one ▪ 42-year-old Judy Garland and her daughter, 18-year-old Liza Minnelli, appear together on stage at the London Palladium ▪ A new series of *The Saint* begins on ITV on Thursday evenings, with 36-year-old Roger Moore playing Simon Templar. In the opening episode, 30-year-old Nanette Newman features alongside Moore ▪ "Pretty woman, walking down the street" - ***Oh Pretty Woman*** by 28-year-old Roy Orbison climbs to the top of the singles chart ▪ *1a - Play with us, 1b - Look at this, 1c - Read and write* - Ladybird introduces the *Key Words* Reading Scheme for young school children ▪ Boys at secondary school play conkers at lunchtime ▪ The Tokyo Olympics get underway ▪ There are gold medals for 30-year-old Ken Matthews (20km walk), 22-year-old Lynn Davies (long jump), 22-year-old Ann Packer (800m) and 24-year-old Mary Rand (long jump) ▪ ***(There's) Always Something***

There To Remind Me by 17-year-old Sandie Shaw from Dagenham reaches number one - and stays at the top of the chart for three weeks ▪ ***Walk Away*** ("... Please go. Before you throw your life away") by 33-year-old Matt Monro climbs to number four ▪ "Who put salt in the sugar bowl? Who put fireworks in the coal? Who put a real live toad in the hole?" - ***My Brother*** by 37-year-old Terry Scott from Watford is a minor hit ▪ First Division Wolverhampton Wanderers cause a football sensation by sacking their manager, 48-year-old Stan Cullis ▪ Third Division Watford appoint 33-year-old Ken Furphy as player-manager ▪ 5-year-old Andy Burrell attends a match at Vicarage Road and becomes a fan of 'The Hornets' ▪ 22-year-old Geoff Hurst scores twice as Ron Greenwood's West Ham Utd draw 2-2 with Bill Shankly's Liverpool at Anfield ▪ 24-year-old Denis Law scores four as Matt Busby's Manchester Utd thrash Dick Taylor's Aston Villa 7-0 at Old Trafford ▪ "Baby love, my..." ***Baby Love*** ("... I need you, oh, how I need you") by The Supremes (featuring 20-year-old Diana Ross) climbs to number one in the pop chart ▪ "I'm not content to be with you in the daytime. Girl, I want to be with you all of the time" - ***All Day And All Of The Night*** by The Kinks is number two ▪ The Beatles undertake a twenty-six date tour of the UK - The 'Fab Four' open at the Gaumont in Bradford and finish at Colston Hall in Bristol on the tenth of November ▪ People buy the latest 7-inch singles at *Woolworths* for 6s/8d ▪ "I see the church, I see the people. Your folks and mine, happy and smiling. And I can hear sweet voices singing, Ave Maria" - ***The Wedding*** by 21-year-old Julie Rogers from Bermondsey climbs to number three in the pop chart ▪ "It is the evening of the day. I sit and watch the children play. Smiling faces I can see, but not for me, I sit and watch..." ***As Tears Go By*** by 17-year-old Marianne Faithfull from Hampstead is number nine ▪ Matt Busby's high-flying Manchester Utd follow up a 6-1 victory over Djurgardens of Stockholm in the Inter Cities Fairs Cup with a 6-1 win against Borussia Dortmund - and the names 'Best, Charlton, Law' feature together on the score-sheet for both matches ▪ The new Labour prime-minister Harold Wilson hosts a reception at Number 10 Downing Street for the athletes who represented Briatin in the recent Tokyo Olympics ▪ 52-year-old Chancellor of the Exchequer Jim Callaghan raises the basic rate of income tax to 8s/3d in the pound ▪ Working men put the 'world to right' down the pub ▪ A pint of Ansells bitter costs 1s/8d ▪ A pack of twenty Player's *Weights* cigarettes is 3s/9d ▪ 27-year-old Paul Stephenson is found not guilty and awarded £25 damages after being refused service, due to the colour of his skin, at the Bay Horse pub in Bristol ▪ Labour prime-minister Harold Wilson writes to Mr. Stephenson outlining his government's plans to bring in a new law to end racial discrimination ▪ Families gather together to watch TV ▪ John Boulter, Dai Francis and Tony Mercer blacken their faces and perform as the Mitchell Minstrels on BBC One's hugely popular *The Black and White Minstrel Show* ▪ ***Whatcha Gonna Do About It*** by 27-year-old Doris Troy from New York is number thirty-seven on the hit parade ▪ 44-year-old Cliff Michelmore presents a current affairs programme called *Tonight* ▪ Dr. Beeching wields his axe yet again - railway stations at Andover Town, Saffron Walden, Widnes Central, Marfleet, Mansfield, Barnard Castle, Kidlington, Churchdown and Wigan Central all close down ▪ 45-year-old motorist Bill Owens from Shilbottle in Northumderland collides with a van at a busy road junction when the sun gets in his eyes ▪ A birthday cake weighing 120lb is delivered to Sir Winston Churchill at his home in Hyde Park Gate, London to mark the great man's 90th birthday. Prime-minister Harold Wilson calls on Sir Winston to offer him birthday greetings from the government. Sir Alec Douglas-Home sends a telegram of congratulation on behalf of the opposition Conservative party ▪ "Crossroads Motel, good evening" - Jill Richardson (played by 21-year-old Jane Rossington) speaks the first words as a new television soap-opera called *Crossroads* begins on ATV.

Christmas 1964

Lesley Ann Downey is missing

Monarch:	Queen Elizabeth II (aged 38)
Prime-minister:	Harold Wilson (aged 48)
Chancellor:	James Callaghan (aged 52)
Home Secretary:	Frank Soskice (aged 62)
Foreign Secretary:	Patrick Gordon Walker (aged 57)
Football Manager:	Alf Ramsey (aged 44)
New car reg. suffix:	'B'

▪ It's a white Christmas for most parts of the UK ▪ The Beatles perform their new single, ***I Feel Fine***, on popular Friday evening show *Ready, Steady, Go!* ▪ 48-year-old Labour prime-minister Harold Wilson travels to America for talks with 56-year-old US president Lyndon B. Johnson ▪ 24-year-old footballer Jimmy 'Greavsie' Greaves scores twice for Tottenham Hotspur in a 3-2 victory over Sheffield Wednesday in front of 24,019 spectators at White Hart Lane ▪ Pirate radio station Caroline attracts millions of listeners ▪ Disc jockeys - 21-year-old Tony Blackburn, 24-year-old Tommy Vance and 29-year-old Simon Dee broadcast on the medium wave from a ship anchored in the sea off the coast of Essex ▪ "I am the ..." ***Little Red Rooster*** by The Rolling Stones (with, lead singer, 21-year-old Mick Jagger and, lead guitarist, 20-year-old Keith Richards) is number one for a week ▪ "When you're alone and life is making you lonely you can always go..." ***Downtown*** by 32-year-old Petula Clark peaks at number two ▪ *Blue Peter* presenters - 31-year-old Christopher Trace and 27-year-old Valerie Singleton launch a new Christmas Appeal ▪ Viewers are urged to send in silver foil and milk bottle tops to help raise money to fund guide dogs for blind people ▪ 24-year-old long-jumper Mary Rand from Wells is BBC's 'Sports Personality of the Year' ▪ 'Beatlemania' continues ▪ "Baby's good to me, you know. She's happy as can be, you know. She said so. I'm in love with her and I feel fine" - the 'Fab Four' climb to number one in the pop chart with ***I Feel Fine*** ▪ "I'll have a..." ***Blue Christmas*** ("...

without you") by 29-year-old Elvis Presley is new at number twenty-six ▪ "It's behind you!" - Middle-class families enjoy an evening at the Pantomime ▪ 38-year-old Eric Morecambe and his comedy partner, 39-year-old Ernie Wise, appear in *Sleeping Beauty* at the Bristol Hippodrome ▪ 48-year-old Reg Varney appears in *Robinson Crusoe* at the Theatre Royal in Nottingham ▪ Husbands and wives enjoy an evening at the pictures ▪ 34-year-old Sean Connery stars alongside 34-year-old Tippi Hedren in *Marnie* - Alfred Hitchcock's new film, which is described as a 'Suspenseful Sex Mystery' ▪ Children's book *Chitty Chitty Bang Bang* by the late Ian Fleming is on sale now in book shops ▪ The fictional character Miss Marple features in *A Caribbean Mystery* - the latest 'whodunit' novel from 74-year-old crime-writer Agatha Christie ▪ Christmas shoppers flock to the new Bull Ring Shopping Centre in Birmingham ▪ Excited schoolboys hope to receive a *Scalextric '50'* 'figure-of-eight' racing set for their main Christmas present ▪ A green and white *Matchbox* die-cast model of a BP petrol tanker lorry would be an acceptable stocking-filler ▪ ***I'm Gonna Be Strong*** ("... and stand as tall as I can") by 24-year-old Gene Pitney is number two on the hit parade ▪ "He rode into the night, accelerated his motorbike. I cried to him in fright, don't do it, don't do it, don't do it" - ***Terry*** by 16-year-old Twinkle from Surbiton climbs from number twenty-four to number fifteen ▪ 40-year-old Kenneth Kendall reads the news on television ▪ The country's balance of payments deficit has increased to £610 million - the worst trade figures since 1951 ▪ Coal production has fallen below 200 million tonnes and the number of working miners is at its lowest level this century - just 500,000 ▪ A total of 1,058 miles of railway track has closed down this year as part of Dr. Beeching's plan ▪ Labour prime-minister Harold Wilson and his Chancellor of the Exchequer Jim Callaghan set course for economic expansion by facilitating advances in scientific research and technology - with the aim of increasing exports ▪ Radical changes are also planned in social security and health and welfare services ▪ NHS prescriptions become free of charge ▪ "You have a date for half past eight tonight" - ***Girl Don't Come*** by 17-year-old Sandie Shaw climbs to number three in the pop chart ▪ "Somehow, someday..." ***Somewhere*** by 26-year-old PJ Proby reaches number six ▪ On the run from police, train robbers Bruce Reynolds (aged 33), Buster Edwards (aged 33) and Charlie Wilson (aged 32) spend Christmas together in Acapulco ▪ Families watch television together ▪ *The Likely Lads* (a new comedy drama written by 27-year-old Dick Clement and 27-year-old Ian La Frenais) is on BBC Two - with 29-year-old James Bolam as Terry Collier and 27-year-old Rodney Bewes as Bob Ferris ▪ Nine out of ten households now have a television set ▪ Adverts say, 'Yellow Pages - Let Your Fingers Do the Walking' ▪ ***I Understand*** by Freddie and the Dreamers (with, lead singer, 28-year-old Freddie Garrity) is number five in the pop chart ▪ ***No Arms Can Ever Hold You*** by The Bachelors (with, lead singer, 29-year-old Con Cluskey) is number seven ▪ ***Ringo*** by 49-year-old Lorne Greene is number thirty-seven ▪ 31-year-old MJK Smith is England's cricket captain for a tour of South Africa. 24-year-old Geoffrey Boycott makes 73 runs. 34-year-old Ken Barrington scores 148 and wicket keeper 33-year-old Jim Parks hits 108 not out as England win the first Test in Durban ▪ Back in England - there's sleet, rain and fierce winds ▪ Drivers of high sided vehicles take extra care on the roads ▪ A Pickford's removal lorry makes its way slowly along Sunnyfield in Barnet, London ▪ A Carney's double-decker bus picks its way steadily around the Pear Tree housing estate in Rugeley, Staffordshire ▪ Fathers and sons pack the terraces at football grounds all around the country ▪ Footballers, 27-year-old Bobby Charlton, 24-year-old Denis Law and 18-year-old Georgie Best are in tremendous form for Matt Busby's high-flying Manchester Utd. After winning eight matches on the trot, 'The

Red Devils' are top of the First Division ▪ Tommy Docherty's Chelsea and Don Revie's hard-tackling Leeds Utd are close behind ▪ "If you should tell me that I'll always be, the one you'll always love so true. Then I can tell you I could easily..." ***I Could Easily Fall*** ("... in love with you") by 24-year-old Cliff Richard and the Shadows climbs to number nine on the hit parade ▪ 27-year-old footballer Ron McGarry bags a hat-trick as Joe Harvey's Newcastle Utd beat Northampton Town 5-0 in Division Two ▪ 17-year-old Peter 'Ossie' Osgood scores twice on his debut as Chelsea beat Workington 2-0 in the fifth round of the League Cup ▪ 21-year-old Terry Venables wins his second (and final) cap for England in a 1-1 draw against Holland in Amsterdam. England's full line-up for the match is: Waiters, Cohen, R Thomson, Mullery, Norman, Flowers, P Thompson, Greaves, Wignall, Venables and R Charlton ▪ Footballing legend (and veteran of World War I) Major Frank Buckley dies aged 82 in Walsall ▪ ***Walk Tall*** ("... walk tall. Walk straight, and look the world right in the eye. That's what my mama told me when I was about knee high") by 37-year-old Val Doonican is number three in the pop chart ▪ ***Ferry Cross The Mersey*** ("... 'cause this land's the place I love, and here I'll stay") by Gerry and the Pacemakers is number eight ▪ The Beatles' new LP, *Beatles For Sale*, is number one in the album chart - tracks include: ***No Reply***, ***I'm A Loser***, ***Eight Days A Week*** and ***I Don't Want To Spoil The Party*** ▪ Families settle down in front of the TV on Christmas Day ▪ *Billy Smart's Circus* follows The Queen's speech on BBC One ▪ 28-year-old Tommy Steele stars as Dick Whittington in *Richard Whittington Esquire* on ATV ▪ "Ooh, you are awful... but I like you" - 49-year-old comedian Dick Emery makes the nation laugh ▪ 20-year-old Brenda Lee sings ***Jingle Bell Rock*** ▪ 34-year-old Rolf Harris sings ***The Court Of King Caractacus*** ▪ MPs vote for the abolition of the death penalty ▪ 10-year-old Lesley Ann Downey goes missing from a fairground in Manchester.

New Year 1965

Sir Winston Churchill is Dead

Monarch:	Queen Elizabeth II (aged 38)
Prime-minister:	Harold Wilson (aged 48)
Chancellor:	James Callaghan (aged 52)
Home Secretary:	Frank Soskice (aged 62)
Foreign Secretary:	Michael Stewart (aged 58)
Football Manager:	Alf Ramsey (aged 45)
New car reg. suffix:	'C'

▪ The new year brings widespread frost ▪ Harold Wilson's Labour government sets out its ambitious programme for house-building and also its plans for a new 'comprehensive' education system ▪ "My baby loves me, she gets a feeling so fine. And when she loves me, she makes me know that she's mine" - ***Yeh Yeh*** by 21-year-old Georgie Fame and the Blue Flames climbs to number one in the pop chart ▪ "Baby, please don't go down to New Orleans. You know I love you, so..." ***Baby Please Don't Go*** by Them (with, lead singer, 19-year-old Van Morrison) peaks at number ten ▪ Dr. Beeching wields his axe yet again - railway stations at Brownhills, Hednesford and Rugeley Town close down ▪ The national road network continues to develop and grow ▪ A new link section of the M6 opens between Preston and Lancaster and motorists can now travel uninterrupted along a stretch of motorway, covering one-hundred miles between Stafford and Carnforth in Lancashire ▪ At Alnwick magistrates court, 45-year-old coal-miner Bill Owens from Shilbottle pleads guilty to driving without due care and attention after colliding with a van at the junction of Selby Road and Farne Road. Mr. Owens is fined £5 and has his license is endorsed ▪ 'C' registration cars go on sale ▪ The latest Austin *1800* has a top speed of 90 mph and is capable of 29 miles to the gallon ▪ Ford's *Zephyr Four* has a bench seat in the front and a column gearshift ▪ Sharp dressed youngsters congregate at the Flamingo Club in Soho. Scooters and mopeds are parked outside on Wardour Street ▪ 49-year-old Stanley Matthews (aka the 'Wizard of Dribble') becomes a Sir in the New Year's Honours list - Sir Stan is the first footballer to be knighted ▪ 11-year-old schoolboy Matthew Harding from Haywards Heath stands on the terrace at Stamford Bridge football ground (amongst a crowd of 28,344 spectators) as Tommy Docherty's Chelsea defeat Matt Gillies' Leicester City 4-1. McCreadie, Graham, Bridges and Murray are on the score-sheet for Chelsea ▪ Dazzling young striker Georgie Best scores a goal for Manchester Utd in a 1-1 draw against Sunderland at Old Trafford ▪ 17-year-old John Radford bags a hat-trick for Arsenal in a 4-1 victory over Wolverhampton Wanderers at Highbury ▪ Bill Shankly's Liverpool (with Tommy Lawrence, Tommy Smith, Ian Callaghan, Roger Hunt and Ian St. John) beat West Bromwich Albion 1-2 at the Hawthorns in the third round of the FA Cup ▪ "Six guineas a day plus expenses" - 46-year-old Alfred Burke stars as Private Investigator Frank Marker in *Public Eye* on ATV ▪ 22-year-old disc jockey Dave Cash joins the pirate Radio London ship in the North Sea - and begins broadcasting on the station known as 'Big L' ▪ "Dizzy in the head and I'm feeling blue. Things you've said, well maybe they're true. Getting' funny dreams again and again. I know what it means, but can't explain" - ***I Can't Explain*** by The Who climbs to number eight on the hit parade ▪ Three members of The Beatles (John Lennon, George Harrison and Ringo Starr) begin experimenting with LSD ▪ Everything is 'like, crazy and far out, man' ▪ Somewhere, beside a river, yellow and green cellophane flowers grow incredibly high amongst tangerine trees, capped by marmalade skies ▪ 48-year-old prime-minister Harold Wilson flies across the Atlantic again and has an informal meeting with president Johnson. The following day, Mr. Wilson addresses delegates at the General Assembly of United Nations before travelling onto Ottawa for a meeting with 67-year-old Canadian prime-minister Lester Pearson ▪ Back in Britain - 38-year-old David Coleman presents

Grandstand on BBC One on Saturday afternoons ▪ Bill Shankly's Liverpool are held to a 1-1 draw by Fourth Division Stockport County at Anfield in the fourth round of the FA Cup, but 'The Reds' go on to win the replay 0-2 at Edgeley Park ▪ 18-year-old footballer Georgie Best passes his driving test and arrives at a training session for Manchester Utd in his 'B' reg Austin *1100* ▪ Construction work to extend the Chiswick flyover and form a new viaduct motorway (known as the M4) to the west of London is almost complete ▪ 31-year-old gangster twins Reginald and Ronald Kray are arrested in London and charged with demanding money with menaces from a nightclub owner in Soho ▪ "I'm just a soul whose intentions are good. Oh, Lord, please..." ***Don't Let Me Be Misunderstood*** by The Animals is number three in the pop chart ▪ "Go now, go now..." ***Go Now*** ("... ooh") by The Moody Blues spends a week at number one ▪ 37-year-old Allan Smethurst (aka the Singing Postman) performs ***Hev Yew Gotta Loight Boy*** ▪ 44-year-old Dirk Bogarde and 26-year-old Susan Strasberg star at cinemas in *The High Bright Sun* ▪ 32-year-old Peter O'Toole and 55-year-old James Mason star in *Lord Jim* ▪ *World of Sport* debuts on ITV on Saturday afternoons. 42-year-old Eamonn Andrews is the main presenter, supported by John Rickman (horse-racing) and Peter Lorenzo (football) ▪ 28-year-old motor racing driver Jim Clark wins the opening Formula One race of the season in South Africa in a Lotus ▪ 35-year-old Graham Hill is third in a BRM. 25-year-old Jackie Stewart makes his Grand Prix debut in the same race - also driving a BRM ▪ Sir Winston Churchill dies aged 90 and the whole of the United Kingdom mourns the passing of its greatest leader. A state funeral takes place at St. Paul's Cathedral on the thirtieth of January with the BBC broadcasting television pictures 'live' to the nation. Queen Elizabeth II and Prince Philip, the Duke of Edinburgh, are in attendance as well as members of the wider Royal Family, all keen to pay their final respects to the great wartime leader ▪ "Please wait at the gate for me…” ***Terry*** by 16-year-old Twinkle climbs to number four in the pop chart ▪ “That’s why I fell for the…” ***Leader Of The Pack*** by The Shangri-Las is number nine ▪ The world of football is rocked by scandal ▪ 26-year-old Tony Kay of Everton and nine other players are jailed after being found guilty of fixing match results ▪ 19-year-old defender Tommy Smith is in fine form as Bill Shankly’s Liverpool maintain their cup run with a 0-1 victory over Bolton Wanderers at Burnden Park ▪ Up to twelve inches of snow falls across the country and traffic is disrupted on roads and railways ▪ A Wolseley *6/110* motorcar is stranded on the B4214 at Munderfield Row ▪ A British Rail *Class 22* diesel locomotive is stuck on the West Coast Main Line between Stoke-on-Trent and Crewe ▪ *2a - We have fun, 2b - Have a go, 2c - I like to write* - school children improve their reading skills, using Ladybird’s *Key Words* range of books ▪ “You never close your eyes anymore when I kiss your lips. And there’s no tenderness like before in your finger tips. You’re trying hard not to show it, but baby, baby I know it” - ***You’ve Lost That Loving Feelin’*** by The Righteous Brothers (24-year-old Bill Medley and 24-year-old Bobby Hatfield) spends two weeks at the top of the pop chart. 25-year-old Phil Spector is the record’s producer ▪ 26-year-old Vincent Duggleby presents *Sports Session* on BBC radio, and announces the latest sports news and football results ▪ Don Revie’s hard-tackling Leeds Utd football team faces Tommy Docherty’s Chelsea in a top-of-the-table Division One clash at Elland Road. The match ends in a 2-2 draw with Jim Storrie and Johnny Giles scoring for Leeds and George Graham and Barry Bridges scoring for Chelsea ▪ Manchester Utd (currently in third place) are held to a 1-1 draw at Old Trafford by Stoke City ▪ Two weeks later, 50-year-old Sir Stanley Matthews of Stoke plays the final league match of his long career as ‘The Potters’ defeat Fulham 3-1 in front of 28,585 spectators at the Victoria Ground ▪ 25-year-old Jimmy ‘Greavsie’ Greaves and

23-year-old Alan Mullery are on the score-sheet for Tottenham Hotspur in a 4-1 victory over Blackpool ▪ "So tired, tired of waiting..." ***Tired Of Waiting For You*** by The Kinks (with, lead singer, 20-year-old Ray Davies) spends a week at number one on the hit parade ▪ "The purpose of a man is to love a woman, and the purpose of a woman is to love her man" - ***Game Of Love*** by 19-year-old Wayne Fontana and the Mindbenders is number five ▪ Families flock to the cinema ▪ "Supercalifragilisticexpialidocious, even though the sound of it is something quite atrocious" - 29-year-old Julie Andrews and 39-year-old Dick Van Dyke star in *Mary Poppins* ▪ The nation's economy is weak ▪ Prime-minister Harold Wilson and Chancellor of the Exchequer Jim Callaghan are at work in Downing Street - devising ways to increase productivity and reduce the deficit in the balance of payments ▪ Leader of the Opposition Sir Alec Douglas-Home promotes 48-year-old Edward Heath to Shadow Chancellor and 55-year-old Peter Thorneycroft to Shadow Home Secretary ▪ There's much consternation in Regents Park ▪ Goldie the eagle is missing after escaping from his cage at London Zoo ▪ "I could search the whole world over until my life is through, but I know..." ***I'll Never Find Another You*** by The Seekers (with, lead singer, 21-year-old Judith Durham) climbs to number one in the pop chart ▪ "There she goes with her nose in the air..." ***Funny How Love Can Be*** by The Ivy League (with 24-year-old John Carter, 24-year-old Ken Lewis and 31-year-old Perry Ford) is number eight ▪ 37-year-old Gwen Watford is pictured (in colour) on the front cover of *TV Times* - promoting 'The Rules of the Game' a new Monday night drama, part of the *Play of the Week* series ▪ 20-year-old Mia Farrow stars in *Peyton Place* on Saturday nights ▪ Friends meet up for a drink and a chat ▪ The new Watney's *Party Four* can costs 8s/1d ▪ A nice cup of tea at a *J. Lyons & Co* teashop is thruppence.

Spring 1965

The Beatles v The Stones

Monarch:	Queen Elizabeth II (aged 39)
Prime-minister:	Harold Wilson (aged 49)
Chancellor:	James Callaghan (aged 53)
Home Secretary:	Frank Soskice (aged 62)
Foreign Secretary:	Michael Stewart (aged 58)
Football Manager:	Alf Ramsey (aged 45)
New car reg. suffix:	'C'

▪ The weather is wet and windy ▪ US troops are sent to Vietnam ▪ The 'Space Race' continues. NASA scientists look on enviously as Soviet cosmonaut Alexei Leonov becomes the first man to walk in Space, as part of his country's *Voskhod 2* orbital mission ▪ In the House of Commons, 39-year-old Margaret Thatcher MP speaks with authority on matters relating to benefit payments to coal miners suffering work related injuries or diseases ▪ 'SHE who must be obeyed! SHE who must be loved! SHE who must be possessed!' - *She*, starring 29-year-old Ursula Andress (38-25-35), goes on general release at cinemas ▪ *The Truth About Spring*, starring 19-year-old Hayley Mills, 27-year-old James MacArthur and 57-year-old John Mills, is also now showing ▪ Goldie the eagle is recaptured after twelve days of freedom in Regent's Park, when a zoo keeper uses a dead rabbit to lure the bird of pray back to earth ▪ Crazy young pop 'cats' adore The Rolling Stones ▪ "Well I told you once and I told you twice, but you never listen to my advice" - ***The Last Time*** by The Rolling Stones (with, lead singer, 21-year-old Mick Jagger) is new at number one - the record is the group's third '45' single to reach the top of the weekly hit parade ▪ "Yes, I'll be as true as true can be, if you'll..." ***Come And Stay With Me*** by 18-year-old Marianne Faithfull is number four ▪ Bill Shankly's Liverpool football team (with goalkeeper Tommy Lawrence, defender Tommy Smith, midfielder Ian Callaghan and forwards - Roger Hunt and Ian St. John) gains a 1-0 victory over Leicester City at Anfield in a quarter-final replay in the FA Cup. (The initial tie had ended 0-0 at Filbert Street) ▪ In League Division One, Don Revie's hard-tackling Leeds Utd follow up a 5-1 thrashing of Burnley with a 4-1 victory over Everton to go level on points with Chelsea at the top-of-the-table - and well on course to become champions of England ▪ Matt Busby's Manchester Utd are in third place - just one point behind ▪ On Sundays, family men reverse the car out of the garage and spend a happy hour cleaning and polishing their cherished motor ▪ A Morris *Minor 1000* costs £516/6s/3d and has drum brakes all round ▪ A Triumph *Herald 1200* costs £608/18s/9d and has disc brakes on the front wheels ▪ Dr. Beeching wields his axe yet again - Armley Canal Road Railway Station in Leeds closes down ▪ The judge in the legal trial of the Kray twins throws out the charges, and the 31-year-old brothers walk free. 39-year-old Detective Chief Inspector Leonard 'Nipper' Read is invited to the celebration party - and is later photographed drinking Champagne with Ronald Kray ▪ *Penthouse* magazine is launched ▪ "Oooh, hello! I'm Julian and this is my friend Sandy" - *Round the Horne* is a new radio show, featuring 49-year-old Hugh Paddick as Julian and 39-year-old Kenneth Williams as Sandy ▪ ***Times They Are A-Changin'*** by 23-year-old Bob Dylan from Minnesota is a hit record - the song reaches number nine in the pop chart ▪ ***It's Not Unusual*** ("... to be loved by anyone") by 24-year-old Tom Jones from Pontypridd is also popular - the song spends a week at number one ▪ Adolescent boys hang around on the pavements outside picture houses, gawping at publicity posters of the latest films ▪ 19-year-old Francesca Annis, 23-year-old Anneke Wills and 19-year-old Suzanna Leigh star in *The Pleasure Girls* - a movie from 40-year-old director Gerry O'Hara ▪ People watch television ▪ Ken and Valerie Barlow (played by 33-year-old Bill Roache and 30-year-old Anne Reid) are proud parents of newborn twins, Peter and Susan, in ITV's popular soap-opera *Coronation Street* ▪ 39-year-old Richard Baker reads the news on BBC One ▪ 26-year-old David Steel is elected as a Liberal MP after winning a by-election in Scotland ▪ 53-year-old Chancellor of the Exchequer Jim Callaghan presents a controversial Budget on behalf of Harold Wilson's Labour government ▪ Aiming to reduce the pressure on national resources, Callaghan confirms there will be lower public expenditure and higher taxation ▪ A new Capital Gains Tax is introduced ▪ A new Corporation Tax is introduced ▪ An explosion at Cambrian Colliery in the Clydach Valley kills thirty-one people ▪ "All my dreams are uncovered. I belong. I belong..." ***I Belong*** by 26-year-old Kathy Kirby from Ilford finishes in second place (six points behind Luxembourg) at the Eurovision Song Contest in Naples ▪ Back in England - There's pandemonium in Essex, when The Rolling Stones appear 'for one night only' on stage at the ABC in Romford ▪ The first *Pizza Express* restaurant opens on Wardour Street in London ▪ 5-year-old Prince Andrew plays out on the lawns at Windsor Castle ▪ *Three Hats for Lisa* (starring 24-year-old Joe Brown and 28-year-old Una Stubbs) goes on general release at cinemas ▪ Tommy Docherty's Chelsea football team beats Matt Gillies' Leicester City 3-2 over two legs in the League Cup final - and 22-year-old Chelsea captain Terry Venables lifts the unique, three-handled silver trophy ▪ 27-year-old Bobby Charlton bags a hat-trick for Manchester Utd in a 5-0 victory over Jack Marshall's Blackburn Rovers in Division One ▪ 27-year-old Barrie Thomas scores five as Scunthorpe Utd thrash Luton Town 8-1 in Division Three ▪ Oxford win the Boat Race by four lengths ▪ Crowds flock to the cinema ▪ "The hills are alive with..." *The Sound of Music* - starring 29-year-old Julie Andrews and 35-year-old Christopher Plummer is now showing ▪ "Do you always wear your glasses? / Yes. Except in bed" - 32-year-old Michael Caine stars as Harry Palmer in the *Ipcress File* ▪ "Lord, forgive them, for they know not what they do" - 35-year-old Max von Sydow is Jesus, 48-year-old Dorothy McGuire is the Virgin

Mary and 42-year-old Charlton Heston is John the Baptist in *The Greatest Story Ever Told* ▪ "You dirty whore!" - 61-year-old Rita Webb, 30-year-old Finnuala O'Shannon and 27-year-old Tony Selby star in *Three Clear Sundays* - a controversial drama broadcast as part of BBC One's 'The Wednesday Play' series ▪ 54-year-old Mrs. Mary Whitehouse (from rural Worcestershire) addresses an audience at the Cathedral Hall in Nottingham and demands that the BBC stops showing programmes that endorse and promote promiscuity ▪ "See that boy who just walked by? Well, he's the one my heart's set on" - ***I'll Stop At Nothing*** by 18-year-old Sandie Shaw climbs to number four in the pop chart ▪ ***I Know A Place*** ("... where the music is fine and the lights are always low") by 32-year-old Petula Clark stalls at number seventeen ▪ "Say, 'cheese!'" - 27-year-old David Bailey photographs 31-year-old gangster Reginald Kray and his bride, 21-year-old Frances Shea, at the couples' wedding in London. Reggie's twin brother, Ronald, is best man ▪ David Griffiths presents *Newly Pressed* on BBC radio's Light Programme - and listeners hear about the very latest pop single releases ▪ "Vowed that you and I would be two silhouettes on the shade, all our days, two..." ***Silhouettes*** ("... on the shade") by Herman's Hermits (with, lead singer, 17-year-old Peter Noone) is number three on the hit parade ▪ ***Everybody's Gonna Be Happy*** by The Kinks (with, lead singer, 20-year-old Ray Davies) is number seventeen ▪ Bill Shankly's Liverpool defeat Tommy Docherty's Chelsea 2-0 in an FA Cup semi-final, played in front of 67,686 spectators at Villa Park. Peter Thompson and Willie Stevenson score the goals for 'The Reds' ▪ 23-year-old boxer Muhammad Ali defeats 33-year-old Sonny Liston to retain the world heavy-weight title ▪ After leading the way in Division One for much of the season, Don Revie's hard-tackling Leeds Utd football team (with Gary Sprake, Willie Bell, Jack Charlton, Johnny Giles, Norman Hunter and 22-year-old Billy Bremner) can only draw its final match of the season (3-3 against bottom-of-the-table Birmingham City) and Matt Busby's Manchester Utd are the new champions of Division One - by goal average only. Pat Dunne, Shay Brennan, Tony Dunne, Bill Foulkes, Nobby Styles, Paddy Crerand, Bobby Charlton, John Connelly, David Herd, Georgie Best and 25-year-old top scorer Denis Law have all been outstanding for Utd ▪ Leeds also lose out in the FA Cup final when Bill Shankly's Liverpool defeat them 2-1 at the Empire Stadium in Wembley. Roger Hunt and Ian St. John score the goals for Liverpool. (It's the first ever FA Cup victory for the Anfield club). A ticket to watch the final in the standing enclosure costs 7s/6d ▪ The songs, ***Concrete And Clay*** by Unit Four Plus Two and ***The Minute You're Gone*** by 24-year-old Cliff Richard, both spend a week at number one in the pop chart ▪ ***Stop In The Name Of Love*** ("... before you break my heart") by The Supremes (21-year-old Florence Ballard, 21-year-old Mary Wilson and 21-year-old Diana Ross) reaches number seven ▪ 11-year-old schoolboy Trevor Francis from Plymouth plays football with his friends in the park ▪ Joe Mallet's Birmingham City football team finishes bottom of Division One and is relegated to Division Two - along with Wolverhampton Wanderers ▪ 29-year-old Jack Charlton and his 27-year-old brother Bobby play together in England's national team for the first time - as manager Alf Ramsey assesses his best options for next year's World Cup tournament ▪ 19-year-old midfielder Alan Ball makes his international debut in a 1-1 draw against Yugoslavia ▪ West Ham Utd beat 1860 Munich 2-0 in the UEFA Cup Winners Cup final at Wembley - outside right Alan Sealey scores both goals and 24-year-old captain Bobby Moore lifts the trophy ▪ 27-year-old Peterborough Utd centre-forward Derek Dougan transfers to Matt Gillies' Leicester City for £25,000 ▪ Crazy young pop 'cats' adore The Beatles ▪ "She's got a..." ***Ticket To Ride*** ("... but she don't care") by the 'Fab Four' is new at number one on the hit parade - and stays there for three weeks. It's the group's seventh '45' single to hit top spot in the weekly chart ▪ "Ah, but I may as well try and..." ***Catch The Wind*** by 18-year-old Donovan is number four ▪ Cool beatniks in roll-neck jumpers and drainpipe jeans enjoy an evening out ▪ The Kinks appear 'for one night only' on stage at the Guildhall in Portsmouth. The Yardbirds are also on the bill ▪ 'What really happened to Melina that night at the wild party?' - 27-year-old Oliver Reed and 31-year-old Ann Lynn star at cinemas in *The Party's Over* ▪ 29-year-old Donald Sutherland, 34-year-old Philip Gilbert, 41-year-old Peter Vaughan, 63-year-old Tallulah Bankhead, 22-year-old Stefanie Powers and 36-year-old Yootha Joyce star in *Die! Die! My Darling!* - a Hammer horror film ▪ 35-year-old jockey Pat Taafe rides *Arkle* to victory in the Cheltenham Gold Cup for the second year running ▪ Enthusiastic motorcar drivers race along the M1 and M6 motorways in their Austin *1100s*, Morris *Minors*, Triumph *Heralds* and Ford *Anglias* ▪ A trial speed limit of 70 mph is introduced to slow down the speed merchants ▪ "Whoa, here it comes..." ***Here Comes The Night*** by Them (with, lead singer, 19-year-old Van Morrison) is number two in the pop chart ▪ "I'd give the moon if it were mine to give..." ***For Your Love*** by The Yardbirds (with guitarist 20-year-old Eric Clapton) peaks at number three ▪ Millions of listeners tune in to the exciting new *Kenny & Cash Show* on pirate radio station 'Big L' (Radio London). Disc jockeys - 19-year-old Kenny Everett and 22-year-old Dave Cash deliver quick fire, irreverent humour and play the latest pop singles ▪ "I could go anyway, the way I choose. I could live anyhow, win or lose" - ***Anyway Anyhow Anywhere*** by The Who reaches number ten on the hit parade ▪ ***Wonderful World*** by Herman's Hermits is number seven ▪ Families gather around the telly on Friday evenings at 8 p.m. ▪ 50-year-old Lorne Greene plays Ben and 28-year-old Michael Landon plays Little Joe in *Bonanza* - a hugely popular 'Western' show ▪ The hard hitting and highly controversial *For the West* (a drama describing a violent, ugly and explosive situation in the Congo, written by Michael Hastings) is transmitted as part of BBC One's 'The Wednesday Play' series ▪ 54-year-old Mrs. Mary Whitehouse (from rural Worcestershire) writes to prime-minister Harold Wilson asking if it's government policy to allow television screens to be used for the propagation of obscenity, violence and racial hatred ▪ "Well I told you twice and I told you once, this job won't last another two months" - the humorous song ***Pop Go The Workers*** by The Barron Knights (a group from Leighton Buzzard) is number five in the pop chart ▪ ***That's Why I'm Crying*** by The Ivy League (a trio featuring John Carter and Ken Lewis from Birmingham and Perry Ford from Lincoln) is number twenty-two ▪ The 'Space Race' continues ▪ NASA scientists look on enviously as the USSR's unmanned *Luna 5* spacecraft lands on the Moon ▪ Back in England - the Resale Prices Act is in full effect ▪ *Asda* is a new name on the high street ▪ *Tesco* opens a smart new store at Elephant & Castle ▪ 45-year-old 'Gentleman' George Hardwick is sacked as Sunderland manager ▪ The songs - ***King Of The Road*** by Roger Miller (from Texas) and ***Where Are You Now (My Love)*** by 24-year-old Jackie Trent (from Newcastle-under-Lyme) both spend a week at number one in the pop chart ▪ "Sometimes we'll sigh. Sometimes we'll cry and we'll know why, just you and I, know..." ***True Love Ways*** by Peter and Gordon reaches number two ▪ "Close the door, light the light. We're stayin' home tonight" - ***A World Of Our Own*** by The Seekers peaks at number three ▪ Gangs of children, boys in grey flannel shorts and girls in grey pinafore dresses, rush to the sweet shop after school ▪ 'Chewiest Sweets Hit the Streets!' *Chewits* (available in blackcurrant and orange flavours) go on sale costing thruppence a packet.

Summer 1965

Ronnie Biggs escapes

Monarch:	Queen Elizabeth II (aged 39)
Prime-minister:	Harold Wilson (aged 49)
Chancellor:	James Callaghan (aged 53)
Home Secretary:	Frank Soskice (aged 63)
Foreign Secretary:	Michael Stewart (aged 58)
Football Manager:	Alf Ramsey (aged 45)
New car reg. suffix:	'C'

▪ It's another cool, dull and wet summer ▪ Motorists speed along twisty country roads in sports cars ▪ The latest MG *Midget MKII* (two-seater, soft-top) costs £623/17s/1d and has a top speed of 90 mph ▪ Schools put on sports days and jamborees ▪ 6-year-old Andrew Drake from Stafford comes second from last in the bean-bag race ▪ 'Comedy has a new Freedom!' - 23-year-old Rita Tushingham stars at cinemas in *The Knack ... and How to Get It* ▪ "Johnny's in the basement mixing up the medicine. I'm on the pavement thinking about the government" - ***Subterranean Homesick Blues*** by 24-year-old Bob Dylan is number nine in the pop chart ▪ ***This Little Bird*** ("... who lives on the wind. This little bird that somebody sends") by 18-year-old Marianne Faithfull is number six ▪ ***All Over The World*** ("… others are sad tonight") by 21-year-old Francoise Hardy is number sixteen ▪ 10-year-old schoolboy Steve Wright from Greenwich sits alone in his bedroom listening to a transistor radio ▪ *Desert Island Discs* (presented by 51-year-old Roy Plomley) is transmitted on Monday afternoons ▪ *Pick of the Week* (presented by 53-year-old John Ellison) is transmitted on Fridays ▪ *Pick of the Pops* (presented by 37-year-old Alan 'Fluff' Freeman) is transmitted on Sundays ▪ "We meet every night at eight, and I don't get home till late. I say to myself each day, baby, oh long…" ***Long Live Love*** ("… mmm-mmm") by 18-year-old Sandie Shaw spends three weeks at number one on the hit parade ▪ ***Help Me Rhonda*** ("…help, help me Rhonda") by The Beach Boys reaches number twenty-seven ▪ United States astronaut Edward H. White II is the first American to walk in Space as part of his country's *Gemini 4* mission ▪ Back in England - the economy is in a poor shape ▪ The deficit in the balance of payments remains high ▪ Inflation has risen to four percent ▪ 49-year-old Labour prime-minister Harold Wilson and 53-year-old Chancellor of the Exchequer Jim Callaghan resist pressure to devalue the pound - they focus instead on improving the country's overall productivity ▪ Cranleigh Railway Station in Surrey closes down ▪ 52-year-old Dr. Beeching ends his tenure as chairman of the British Railways Board ▪ Schools break up and the summer holidays begin ▪ Boys play-out - enjoying army games (English versus Germans) 'down the field' ▪ "Are we nearly there yet?" - families drive off in Vauxhall *Vivas*, or Austin *1100s*, or Ford *Anglias*, or Morris *Minors* for a camping holiday at the seaside ▪ Young women relax on the beach ▪ A one-piece Slix swimsuit in *Bri Nylon* costs 63s/- ▪ A stick of rock costs tuppence ▪ 37-year-old jockey Pat Glennon from Australia rides *Sea-Bird* to victory in the Epsom Derby ▪ For the second year running, it's a double Aussie victory at the Wimbledon tennis championships with 28-year-old Roy Emerson taking the men's singles title and 22-year-old Margaret Smith taking the women's title ▪ 36-year-old racing driver Graham Hill wins the Monaco Grand Prix for the third year running ▪ 29-year-old Jim Clark wins the British Grand Prix for the fourth year running and goes on to be crowned world motor racing champion for the second time in his career ▪ Prime-minister Harold Wilson and 62-year-old Home Secretary Frank Soskice work on a new white paper - planning to make racial discrimination illegal in public places ▪ *Till Death Us Do Part* (written by Johnny Speight and starring Warren Mitchell as Alf Garnett) is broadcast on BBC One as part of the long running *Comedy Playhouse* series ▪ 55-year-old Mrs. Mary Whitehouse (from rural

Worcestershire) demands that Sir Hugh Greene stands down from his position as Director General of the British Broadcasting Corporation ▪ "Up the 'ammers!" - 16-year-old schoolboy footballer Trevor Brooking signs as an apprentice for Ron Greenwood's West Ham Utd ▪ 38-year-old Ian McColl succeeds 45-year-old 'Gentleman' George Hardwick as manager of Sunderland ▪ "You saw me crying in the chapel, the tears I shed were tears of joy. I know the meaning of contentment, now I am happy with the Lord" - ***Crying In The Chapel*** by 30-year-old Elvis Presley is new at number one in the pop chart ▪ "That's the price of love..." ***The Price Of Love*** by The Everly Brothers (28-year-old Don and 26-year-old Phil) is number two ▪ "By Jove, Missus!" - 37-year-old Ken Dodd is headline act at the London Palladium - Doddy's show is a roaring success and the popular entertainer from Liverpool plays to a packed house every night for forty-two weeks! ▪ 30-year-old James Bolam and 27-year-old Rodney Bewes star in a new series of *The Likely Lads* on BBC Two television ▪ The cool, damp summer weather continues ▪ At seaside resorts, families take shelter from the drizzle ▪ Children enjoy ice-lollies and ice-creams on the beach ▪ A Wall's *Orange Sparkle* costs 9d ▪ A Wall's *Sky Ray* is 6d ▪ A Wall's *Rasberry Splice* is 9d ▪ Middle-class, retired couples take a leisurly drive on Sunday afternoons ▪ A Riley *Elf MkII* motorcar has real-leather seats, wall-to-wall carpeting and costs £596/13s/4d ▪ ***You've Got Your Troubles*** ("... I've got mine") by The Fortunes is number two in the pop chart ▪ ***He's Got No Love*** by The Searchers is number twelve ▪ 53-year-old Brian 'Johnners' Johnston and 44-year-old Peter West commentate on Test Match cricket for BBC Two ▪ 24-year-old Geoffrey Boycott and 29-year-old Bob Barber stride out together to open the batting for England against New Zealand at Edgbaston. Boycott scores 23 runs. Barber makes 31. Further down the batting order, Ken Barrington scores 137 and Colin Cowdrey makes 85 and MJK

Smith's England team wins the match by nine wickets ▪ John Tidmarsh reads the news on BBC Two ▪ Chancellor of the Exchequer Jim Callaghan puts a brake on public spending - and government departments have their budgets cut ▪ The Labour government bans cigarette adverts from television ▪ Local authorities begin the process of adopting schools into a new 'fully comprehensive' education system ▪ 49-year-old Edward Heath takes over from 62-year-old Alec Douglas-Home as Leader of the Opposition Conservative Party - and the Tories now have a credible challenger to Harold 'man of the people' Wilson ▪ 35-year-old train robber Ronnie Biggs scales a wall and escapes from Wandsworth Prison ▪ ***We Gotta Get Out Of This Place*** ("... if it's the last thing we ever do") by The Animals climbs to number two in the pop chart ▪ ***Catch Us If You Can*** by The Dave Clark Five is number five ▪ 43-year-old Raymond Baxter presents the first edition of *Tomorrow's World* on BBC One - and viewers learn about Deep Space and how science is helping in the search for life on other worlds ▪ 45-year-old Hughie Green presents a new series of *Opportunity Knocks* on ITV ▪ "I'm alive, I'm alive, I'm alive, I'm alive..." ***I'm Alive*** by The Hollies is number one on the hit parade ▪ "Oh, I would never make her sad. I got a..." ***Heart Full Of Soul*** by The Yardbirds is number two ▪ ***Trains And Boats And Planes*** ("... are passing by") by 37-year-old Burt Bacharach slides down the chart after peaking at number four ▪ Families enjoy a night in front of the TV 'box' on Friday evenings ▪ Bill Simpson plays the title role in *Dr. Finlay's Casebook* ▪ Robert Robertson presents *Points of View* ▪ 34-year-old fast-bowler 'fiery' Fred Trueman bows out of international cricket - after taking a record breaking 307 Test wickets for England ▪ Former boxing champion Freddie Mills is found shot dead in his car ▪ "Hey..." ***Mr. Tambourine Man*** ("... play a song for me. I'm not sleepy and there is no place I'm going to") by The Byrds is new at number one ▪ "Turning and tossing..." ***Tossing And Turning*** ("... all night") by The Ivy League is number three ▪ John, Paul, George and Ringo of The Beatles receive MBEs from the Queen, then fly to the USA to perform to 56,000 people at Shea Stadium. The 'Fab Four' play ten more dates in the USA, including two consecutive nights at the Hollywood Bowl ▪ "When I was younger, so much younger than today, I never needed anybody's help in anyway" - ***Help!*** tops the pop chart for three weeks - and a new film of the same title featuring The Beatles is now showing in British cinemas ▪ The 1965-66 football season gets underway with a new rule permitting the use of substitutes ▪ 20-year-old half-back Keith Peacock of Charlton Athletic is the first substitute used - when he comes on after eleven minutes to replace an injured team-mate in a 4-2 defeat against Bolton Wanderers in Division Two ▪ Schoolboys rush to the newsagent to buy *Tiger and Hurricane* for sevenpence - and keep up to date with the weekly adventures of footballer 'Roy of the Rovers' and trouble-shooter 'Typhoon Tracey' ▪ *The Itinerant Lodger*, the debut novel from 30-year-old writer David Nobbs, is published ▪ ***What's New Pussycat*** ("... whoa, oh, oh") by 25-year-old Tom Jones from Pontypridd is number eleven in the pop chart ▪ "Don't let them say your hair's too long, 'cause I don't care, with you I can't go wrong" - ***I Got You Babe*** by Sonny and Cher climbs to number one ▪ 37-year-old Allan Smethurst (aka the Singing Postman) performs ***They're Orl Playin' Dommies In The Bar*** ▪ A new van sales company called *Music For Pleasure* is launched, distributing budget priced L.P. records (with a retail price of 12s/6d) to book shops, wallpaper shops and department stores ▪ Dads take their sons to the cinema for the matinee screening of *Those Magnificent Men In Their Flying Machines* (or 'How I Flew from London to Paris is 25 hours and 11 minutes'), starring Robert Morley, James Fox, Sarah Miles, Stuart Whitman and 54-year-old Terry-Thomas ▪ 36-year-old Bernard Cribbins stars in *Cup Fever* - a film telling the story of a boys football team ejected from their ground ▪ 19-year-old Georgie Best scores a goal for Manchester Utd in a 2-2 draw against Liverpool in the Charity Shield played at Old Trafford ▪ "Sun coming out in the middle of June..." ***Everyone's Gone To The Moon*** by 20-year-old Jonathan King is number four on the hit parade ▪ "How does it feel, how does it feel? To be on your own, with no direction home. Like a complete unknown ..." ***Like A Rolling Stone*** by 24-year-old Bob Dylan enters the chart at number forty-two ▪ "All that matters to me is that you are here, on..." ***Summer Nights*** by 18-year-old Marianne Faithfull peaks at number ten ▪ 32-year-old Kim Novak stars in *The Amorous Adventures of Moll Flanders* - now showing at cinemas all across the country ▪ 'A Movie That You Should Not Miss' - *Darling* (with 25-year-old Julie Christie) is coming soon ▪ The annual Summer Bank Holiday Monday is switched from the first week in August to the last week in August ▪ Morecambe & Wise appear twice nightly at the ABC in Blackpool ▪ Russ Conway entertains the crowds at the Winter Gardens in Bournemouth ▪ 49-year-old prime-minister Harold Wilson enjoys a summer holiday in the Scillies ▪ 54-year-old Transport Minister Tom Fraser reviews his five-year plan for road building following the recent cut in government spending ▪ A number of road improvement projects are already underway ▪ A new one-way road system opens in Wolverhampton ▪ A new two-mile section of bypass opens from Babingley to Rising Lodge near King's Lynn in Norfolk ▪ The wonderful Rover *P6 2000* motorcar has a top speed of 102 mph and accelerates from 0-60 mph in 15.1 seconds ▪ The luxurious Jaguar *MKII 2.4* has a top speed of 102 mph and accelerates from 0-60 mph in 14.5 seconds ▪ A pint of Watney's *Red Barrel* costs two shillings ▪ Plans for an alcohol drink driving limit are announced.

Autumn 1965

Mini Skirts are fab and groovy, baby.

Monarch:	Queen Elizabeth II (aged 39)
Prime-minister:	Harold Wilson (aged 49)
Chancellor:	James Callaghan (aged 53)
Home Secretary:	Frank Soskice (aged 63)
Foreign Secretary:	Michael Stewart (aged 59)
Football Manager:	Alf Ramsey (aged 45)
New car reg. suffix:	'C'

▪ The summer holidays come to an end and children return to school ▪ *3a - Things we like, 3b - Boys and girls, 3c - Let me write* - youngsters improve their reading skills, using Ladybird's *Key Words* range of books ▪ 22-year-old model Jean Shrimpton wears a strikingly short dress during a photographic session in Australia - and the concept of the 'mini-skirt' is born ▪ ***All I Really Want To Do*** ("... is, baby, be friends with you") by The Byrds is number four in the pop chart ▪ ***Zorba's Dance*** by Marcello Minerbi is number six ▪ 'How You Cats Will Laugh' - Crowds flock to the cinema to see comedy film *What's New Pussy Cat?*, starring 29-year-old Woody Allen, 40-year-old Peter Sellers, 33-year-old Peter O'Toole and 27-year-old Romy Schneider ▪ 33-year-old Elizabeth Taylor stars alongside her husband, 40-year-old Richard Burton, in *The Sandpiper* - 'an adult love story' with 41-year-old Eve Marie Saint and 43-year-old Charles Bronson also in the cast ▪ A new series of popular police drama *Z Cars* (with 40-year-old Stratford Johns as Chief Inspector Charlie Barlow and 34-year-old Jimmy Ellis as PC Bert Lynch) begins on BBC One television ▪ "Evening, all" - 69-year-old Jack Warner stars in a new series of *Dixon of Dock Green* ▪ More than a year after it was launched in the South East, BBC Two is now transmitting to viewers in the North ▪ 32-year-old Marla Landi and 32-year-old Brian Cant present children's programme *Play School* ▪ Over on ITV, Elsie Tanner (played by 41-year-old Pat Phoenix) meets a man in a pub in soap-opera *Coronation Street*. Later, in the same episode, the man dies in a car crash and Elsie is questioned by police ▪ Crazy young pop 'cats' continue to go wild for The Rolling Stones ▪ "When I'm watchin' my TV, and that man comes on to tell me how white my shirts can be. But he can't be a man 'cause he doesn't smoke the same cigarettes as me" - ***(I Can't Get No) Satisfaction*** by The Rolling Stones (with, lead singer, 22-year-old Mick Jagger) is top of the hit parade for two weeks ▪ ***A Walk In The Black Forest*** by 29-year-old pianist Horst Jankowski is number three ▪ ***Look Through Any Window*** by The Hollies (with, lead singer, 23-year-old Allan Clarke) peaks at number four ▪ Footballers, Alan Suddick and Bobby Cummings score the goals as Newcastle Utd beat Northampton Town 2-0 in Division One ▪ 27-year-old centre-forward Derek Dougan is on the score-sheet for Leicester City in a 4-1 victory over Sunderland ▪ The economy remains weak ▪ Harold Wilson's Labour government attempts to 'build' its way out of trouble ▪ A nationwide construction programme is underway ▪ The number of council homes is increasing ▪ Multi-storey concrete tower blocks are erected in towns and cities across Britain ▪ 57-year-old Dick Crossman is Labour's Minister for Housing and Land. Crossman's 'shadow' in the Tory opposition is 40-year-old Margaret Thatcher MP ▪ "But you tell me over and over and over again my friend, ahh, you don't believe we're on the..." ***Eve Of Destruction*** by 30-year-old Barry McGuire climbs to number three in the pop chart ▪ ***Make It Easy On Yourself*** ("... 'cause breaking up is so very hard to do") by the Walker Brothers is new at number one ▪ 27-year-old misfit Ian Brady is charged with the brutal murder of a 17-year-old youth. Brady's girlfriend, 23-year-old Myra Hindley, is arrested shortly afterwards as an accessory. Further investigations lead to a large scale search of Saddleworth Moor. Police find the bodies of 10-year-old Lesley Ann Downey and 12-year-old John Kilbride ▪ Capital punishment is suspended for murderers ▪ 45-year-old Tony

Randall, 57-year-old Robert Morley and 34-year-old Anita Ekberg star at cinemas in *The Alphabet Murders* - a film based on Agatha Christie's 1936 novel, *The A.B.C. Murders* ▪ "Tears for souvenirs are all you left me. Memories of a love you never meant" - ***Tears*** by 38-year-old Ken Dodd climbs to the top of the pop chart - and stays there for five weeks! ▪ "But..." ***If You Gotta Go, Go Now*** ("... or else you gotta stay all night") by Manfred Mann is number two ▪ 40-year-old Harry H. Corbett and 53-year-old Wilfrid Brambell return for a new series of *Steptoe and Son*. In episode six, working-class Harold is shocked into shame to discover that his dad is, in fact, a Tory ▪ 22-year-old footballer Ernie Hunt transfers from Swindon Town to Wolverhampton Wanderers for £40,000 ▪ 29-year-old Bobby Cummings transfers from Newcastle Utd to Darlington for £6,000 ▪ 21-year-old 'bottle blonde' Lesley Langley (34-24-36) from Weymouth wins £2,500 as she's crowned Miss World at the Lyceum Theatre in London ▪ ***Hang On Sloopy*** ("... Sloopy hang on") by The McCoys is number five in the pop chart ▪ ***Like A Rolling Stone*** by 24-year-old Bob Dylan climbs to number four ▪ The country's motorway network continues to develop and grow ▪ A new section of M1 opens between Rugby and Kegworth ▪ A new section of M5 opens between Quinton and Bromsgrove ▪ Torrential rain and flooding puts a temporary halt to construction of a new stretch of M6 near Bloxwich in the Midlands ▪ Prime-minister Harold Wilson opens the Post Office tower in London. Standing at 581 feet - the modern new building is the tallest in Britain ▪ The Labour government's Race Relations Bill gains royal assent in parliament and will soon become law ▪ ***Almost There*** by 37-year-old Andy Williams is number two in the pop chart ▪ ***Papa's Got A Brand New Bag*** by 32-year-old James Brown is number twenty-six ▪ 'How the West was Lost!' - *Carry On Cowboy* is at cinemas, with 30-year-old Jim Dale as Marshal P Knutt, 50-year-old Charles Hawtrey as Big Heap, 31-year-old Bernard Bresslaw as Little Heap and 52-year-old Sid 'Ha-ak-ak'

James as the Rumpo Kid ▪ 'It's that Way-Out Whopper of a Funny Western' - 27-year-old Jane Fonda and 41-year-old Lee Marvin star in *Cat Ballou* ▪ 26-year-old racing driver Jackie Stewart wins his first ever Grand Prix - when he takes the chequered flag at Monza in Italy in a racing green BRM (number 32) ▪ 25-year-old footballer Denis Law bags a hat-trick, and Bobby Charlton scores once, as Manchester Utd beat Chelsea 4-1 in Division One. (22-year-old Terry Venables scores Chelsea's goal) ▪ 25-year-old Jimmy 'Greavsie' Greaves is on the score-sheet for Tottenham Hotspur in a 3-0 victory over Sunderland ▪ 51-year-old Joe Mercer is the new manager of Second Division Manchester City ▪ 30-year-old Brian Clough is the new manager of Fourth Division Hartlepools Utd ▪ 23-year-old disc jockey Dave Cash is the new host of the breakfast show on pirate radio station 'Big L' (Radio London) ▪ "Then in flies a guy who's all dressed up just like a Union Jack. And says I've won five pounds if I have his kind of detergent pack. I said: Hey! (Hey). You! (You). Get off of my cloud" - ***Get Off My Cloud*** by The Rolling Stones (with 22-year-old Mick Jagger, 21-year-old Keith Richards, 23-year-old Brian Jones, 29-year-old Bill Wyman and 24-year-old Charlie Watts) spends three weeks at number one in the pop chart ▪ "People try to put us down, just because we get around. Things they do look awful cold, I hope I die before I get old. This is..." ***My Generation*** ("... My generation, baby") by The Who (with 21-year-old Roger Daltrey, 20-year-old Pete Townshend, 20-year-old John Entwistle and 19-year-old Keith Moon) reaches number two ▪ 18-year-old footballer Peter 'Ossie' Osgood scores his first league goal for Chelsea in a 1-2 away victory over Sheffield Utd ▪ 'Almost a love story' - 27-year-old Terrence Stamp and 26-year-old Samantha Eggar star at cinemas in *The Collector* ▪ 52-year-old Sid 'Ha-ak-ak' James, 31-year-old Sylvia Syms, 50-year-old Dick Emery and 30-year-old Jim Dale star in comedy film *The Big Job* ▪ Ford launches the *Tran-*

sit van as a replacement for the ageing *Thames 400E* ▪ The millionth *Mini* motorcar is on display at the Earls Court Motor Show ▪ The latest Vauxhall *Viva* now comes with disc brakes - available as an option at extra cost ▪ The Hillman *Super Minx* is now available as an estate car ▪ More American troops are sent to Vietnam prompting anti war demonstrations on the streets of Britain ▪ The BBC decides not to broadcast *The War Game* - a realistic drama from Peter Watkins, depicting the horrors of fall-out from a nuclear missile strike ▪ "I said 'Message understood'..." ***Message Understood*** by 18-year-old Sandie Shaw is number six in the pop chart ▪ 'Five! Four! Three! Two! One! Thunderbirds Are Go!' - schoolboys are enthralled as 36-year-old Gerry Anderson's *Thunderbirds* puppets, and fine array of space-age rescue craft, are seen for the first time on ATV ▪ 'Thunderbird 1' is piloted by Scott Tracy ▪ 'Thunderbird 2' is piloted by Virgil Tracy ▪ Gordon Tracy goes underwater in 'Thunderbird 4' ▪ *The Adventures of Robinson Crusoe* - a thirteen-part film series for children - is broadcast by the BBC on Tuesday evenings at 5.00 p.m. ▪ *The Magic Roundabout* is on at 5.50 p.m. ▪ BBC One programmes on a Saturday night include: *Juke Box Jury* - presented by 39-year-old David Jacobs; *The News and The Weather*; *Dr. Who* - starring 57-year-old William Hartnell; *The Dick Van Dyke Show* - with the popular 39-year-old American entertainer; and *The Wayne and Shuster Show* - featuring Canada's favourite comedians, Johnny Wayne and Frank Shuster ▪ 'The Wednesday Play' broadcast on the third of November is *Up the Junction* - a gritty 'kitchen-sink' drama directed by Ken Loach and based on a story from Nell Dunn. Millions watch the harrowing scene of Rube (played by Geraldine Sherman) undergoing a back street abortion ▪ 55-year-old Mrs. Mary Whitehouse (from rural Worcestershire) writes a letter to the BBC, complaining that the corporation is acting in an irresponsible manor and seems to regard promiscuity as normal ▪ "How gentle is the rain, that falls softly on the meadow?" - ***A Lover's Concerto*** by The Toys climbs to number fifteen on the weekly hit parade ▪ ***Evil Hearted You*** ("... You always try to put me down") by The Yardbirds (with, lead singer, 22-year-old Keith Relf) moves down to number nine ▪ The Labour government continues it's national house building programme ▪ A new council estate opens at Yeading Lane, Northolt ▪ A new council estate is planned for Great Bourton near Banbury ▪ In South Wales, the Midlands, Merseyside and the North East, housewives queue outside shops as a bakers' strike leads to a shortage of loaves ▪ Schoolboys stay home and read comics ▪ *The Beezer* (with 'Pop, Dick and Harry', 'Ginger', 'Little Mo' and 'The Numbskulls') is 5d, every Tuesday ▪ *The Beano* (with 'Biffo the Bear', 'Roger the Dodger', 'Dennis the Menace' and 'The Bash Street Kids') is 3d, every Thursday ▪ 21-year-old footballer Keith East scores five goals as Swindon Town thrash Mansfield Town 6-2 in front of 12,213 at the County Ground in Division Three ▪ 19-year-old 'super' Georgie Best scores twice as Manchester Utd defeat Sheffield Utd 3-1 in front of 38,216 at Old Trafford in Division One ▪ Bakers continue their industrial action in four areas of the country with the Bakers' Union demanding a pay increase of £3/10s a week and a reduction in overtime hours ▪ Many families are affected by a shortage of bread ▪ 53-year-old Chancellor of the Exchequer Jim Callaghan says "It is deplorable that families should go without bread, or have to queue for hours to get it." ▪ Elderly, conservative minded people are starting to worry that standards in society are slipping ▪ Rebellious youngsters challenge authority ▪ The Beatles smoke marijuana as they record a brand new album at EMI's Abbey Road Studios ▪ 38-year-old Kenneth Tynan says the word, "fuck" on BBC Two's late-night debate programme ▪ Mrs. Mary Whitehouse (from rural Worcestershire) is apoplectic.

Christmas 1965

The wonderful new GPO Trim-Phone

Monarch:	Queen Elizabeth II (aged 39)
Prime-minister:	Harold Wilson (aged 49)
Chancellor:	James Callaghan (aged 53)
Home Secretary:	Roy Jenkins (aged 45)
Foreign Secretary:	Michael Stewart (aged 59)
Football Manager:	Alf Ramsey (aged 45)
New car reg. suffix:	'C'

▪ There's heavy snow in the North of England and in Scotland ▪ The bakers' stike is on-going, and shortages of bread continue to affect families in four regions of the country ▪ Jim Callaghan (Chancellor of the Exchequer in Harold Wilson's Labour Cabinet) is angry and describes the strike as, "a classic example of the merry-go-round of higher prices and higher wages that the Government is trying urgently to halt" ▪ "High above, the dawn is waiting, and my tears are falling rain. For the carnival is over, we may never meet again" - ***The Carnival Is Over*** by The Seekers spends three weeks at number one in the pop chart ▪ ***Rescue Me*** ("… take me in your arms. Rescue me, I want your tender charm") by 25-year-old Fontella Bass reaches number eleven ▪ Men wrap-up in overcoats and venture out in the cold weather to endure a Saturday afternoon standing on the terraces at the football ▪ 20-year-old George Graham, 18-year-old Peter 'Ossie' Osgood and 24-year-old Bobby Tambling (2) score the goals as Chelsea beat Aston Villa 1-4 at Villa Park ▪ 27-year-old Roger Hunt, 28-year-old Geoff Strong, 23-year-old Peter Thompson and 27-year-old Ian St. John score the goals as top-of-the-table Liverpool beat Arsenal 4-2 at Anfield ▪ 49-year-old Labour prime-minister Harold Wilson flies across the Atlantic and meets 57-year-old US president Lyndon B. Johnson in Washington. The two men hold wide ranging talks including the subject of defence budgets and responsibilities on a world-wide scale. Mr. Wilson states: "we are carrying commitments beyond the economic capacity of Britain and they have got to be cut." ▪ Back in England - couples enjoy an evening at the cinema ▪ 57-year-old James Stewart stars in *Shenandoah* - a 'Western' from Universal Pictures ▪ 57-year-old Bette Davis and 31-year-old Wendy Craig star in *The Nanny* - a film directed by 42-year-old Seth Holt ▪ 31-year-old Sophia Loren, 40-year-old Paul Newman and 55-year-old David Niven star in *Lady L* - a film directed by 44-year-old Peter Ustinov ▪ "I got sunshine on a cloudy day" - ***My Girl*** by 24-year-old Otis Redding is number twenty-eight in the pop chart (and will climb to number eleven in the new year) ▪ Schoolboys ask Father Christmas for a die-cast model of James Bond's silver Aston Martin *DB5* - complete with opening roof and ejector seat ▪ Chocolate selection boxes are devoured by children on Christmas Day ▪ *Lego* sets are popular gifts ▪ Fathers spend time with their sons ▪ 'Reproducing all the thrills of real football by Finger Tip Control' - the latest *Subbuteo* set comes complete with self-balancing teams, goals, balls and a cloth playing pitch ▪ Great expectations are building for the football world cup tournament due to be held in England next summer ▪ 27-year-old striker Roger Hunt is on the score-sheet as Alf Ramsey's team (G Banks, Cohen, Wilson, Stiles, J Charlton, Moore, Ball, Hunt, Baker, Eastham, R Charlton and substitute, Hunter) defeats Spain 0-2 in a friendly match at the Bernabeu Stadium ▪ 21-year-old Peter Rodrigues transfers from Second Division Cardiff City to First Division Leicester City for £40,000 ▪ 29-year-old Gordon Honeycombe reads the news for ITN ▪ The Labour government's Race Relations Act comes into force - making racial discrimination in public places a civil offence ▪ People queue for tickets to see *The Black and White Minstrels* performing on stage at the Victoria Palace in London ▪ Ian Brady and Myra Hindley are charged with the Moors murders and committed for trial ▪ Celebrated broadcaster Richard Dimbleby dies aged 52 in London ▪ *Rubber Soul* - the new LP from The Beatles is number one in the album chart at Christmas. Tracks include: ***Drive My Car***, ***Norwegian Wood (This Bird Has Flown)***, ***Nowhere Man***, ***Michelle***, ***Girl*** and ***In My Life*** ▪ The double A sided single ***Day Tripper / We Can Work It Out*** by The Beatles climbs to number one in the weekly pop chart - and stays at the top for five weeks! ▪ The 'Fab Four' tour the UK in December - playing at Glasgow (Odeon), Newcastle (City Hall), Liverpool (Empire), Manchester (Apollo), Sheffield (City Hall), Birmingham (Odeon), Hammersmith (Odeon), Finsbury Park (Astoria) and Cardiff (Capitol) ▪ 32-year-old MJK Smith leads England's cricketers on a tour of Australia. 25-year-old Geoffrey Boycott scores 63 not out in the opening Test Match at Brisbane ▪ "I think he got the point" - 35-year-old Sean Connery returns as James Bond (aka 007) in *Thunderball* - and kills Vargas (an evil henchman) with a speargun. 24-year-old Claudine Auger plays Bond-girl Domino. 43-year-old Adolfo Celi plays Largo - Bond's criminal adversary from SPECTRE ▪ 55-year-old Mrs. Mary Whitehouse (from rural Worcestershire) forms the National Viewers and Listeners Association - with the aim of stepping up efforts to 'clean up' television and radio ▪ 54-year-old Sir Hugh Greene (Director General of the BBC) commissions Johnny Speight to write scripts for a full series of *Till Death Us Do Part* ▪ Miss Marple features in *At Bertram's Hotel* - the latest 'whodunit' novel from 75-year-old crime-writer Agatha Christie ▪ 52-year-old Bill Shankly's Liverpool football team is top of Division One ▪ Harry Potts' Burnley are second, with strikers - 22-year-old Willie Irvine and 24-year-old Andy Lochhead both in fine goal scoring form ▪ Birmingham City appoint 49-year-old Stan Cullis as manager ▪ 25-year-old Denis Law scores twice as Matt Busby's Manchester Utd beat Bill Nicholson's Tottenham Hotspur 5-1 in front of 39,511 at Old Trafford ▪ 24-year-old Tony Hateley scores twice as Dick

Taylor's Aston Villa beat Harry Catterick's Everton 3-2 in front of 18,826 at Villa Park ▪ "Let's hang on to what we've got. Don't let go girl, we've got a lot" - ***Let's Hang On*** by The Four Seasons with the sound of Frankie Valli is number four in the pop chart ▪ ***The Spanish Flea*** by Herb Alpert is number three ▪ Families (wearing paper party hats) sit around small Formica dining tables devouring turkey and home-made mince pies ▪ Silver sixpenny bits are hidden inside Christmas puddings ▪ 53-year-old Chancellor of the Exchequer Jim Callaghan speaks on the radio ▪ The economy is in a poor state ▪ There's a deficit of £358 million in the UK's trade balance of payments ▪ The mining industry is shrinking ▪ The National Coal Board operates 504 collieries (41 fewer than last year) ▪ There are 455,000 mine workers (45,000 fewer than last year) ▪ Annual coal production stands at 192 million tonnes (6 million fewer than last year) ▪ 45-year-old Roy Jenkins replaces 63-year-old Frank Soskice as Home Secretary in the Labour government ▪ Expensively suited and all 'tooled up', 32-year-old gangster twins Reginald and Ronald Kray host a number of lavish parties at nightclubs in East London ▪ "When I was seventeen, it was a very good year" - 50-year-old singer Frank Sinatra performs ***It Was A Very Good Year*** ▪ "I'm Jake the Peg, diddle-iddle-iddle-um. With my extra leg, diddle-iddle-iddle-um" - 35-year-old Rolf Harris performs ***Jake The Peg*** ▪ "I'm just a little tin soldier in your hands. I'm good for nothing but to obey your commands" - ***Wind Me Up (Let Me Go)*** by 25-year-old Cliff Richard is number two on the hit parade ▪ Communication technology moves on apace ▪ More and more households are installing telephones ▪ The new GPO trim-phone is in short supply due to strong demand ▪ People celebrate the new year ▪ A 'bumper' beer can of Watney's *Party Four* costs 8s/5d ▪ Food technology moves on apace ▪ New packaging for *Golden Wonder* crisps means they are 'Now Crackle Fresh'.

New Year 1966

Camberwick Green on TV

Monarch:	Queen Elizabeth II (aged 39)
Prime-minister:	Harold Wilson (aged 49)
Chancellor:	James Callaghan (aged 53)
Home Secretary:	Roy Jenkins (aged 45)
Foreign Secretary:	Michael Stewart (aged 59)
Football Manager:	Alf Ramsey (aged 46)
New car reg. suffix:	'D'

▪ 'D' registration cars go on sale ▪ The top selling Morris and Austin *1100s* are now available with a four-speed automatic gearbox ▪ The latest Vauxhall *Cresta* comes in 'Standard', 'Deluxe' or 'Executive' forms ▪ Vauxhall drops the *Velox* from its range ▪ 'Elegant, purposeful, outstandingly equipped' - The sporty and stylish Ford *Corsair V4 GT* costs £928 and has a top speed of 97 mph ▪ The new Minister for Transport, 55-year-old Barbara Castle, infuriates car owners by suggesting that the trial motorway speed limit of 70 mph could be made permanent ▪ Many motorists ignore the limit and continue driving their Ford *Cortinas* and Vauxhall *Vivas* at 80 mph - or even faster ▪ 'Getaway people get Super National' - *National* advertises its brand of petrol ▪ 23-year-old Paul McCartney (from The Beatles) is pictured on the front cover of the latest *Rave* magazine ▪ ***Day Tripper/ We Can Work It Out*** by The Beatles remains at number one on the hit parade ▪ "She's..." ***A Must To Avoid*** ("... a complete impossibility") by Herman's Hermits (with, lead singer, 18-year-old Peter Noone) climbs from number nineteen to number nine ▪ 18-year-old Gerry Rafferty from Paisley in Scotland writes pop songs in his bedroom ▪ 37-year-old Bob Holness presents *Double Spin* (a show for younger listeners) on BBC radio's Light Programme ▪ "Don't some mothers 'ave 'em!" - Jimmy Clitheroe stars as *The Clitheroe Kid* on Mondays at 7.30 p.m. ▪ "How do. How are yer?" - 61-year-old Wilfred Pickles presents *Have A Go!*, on Tuesday evenings ▪ On television, 38-year-old Huw Thomas reads the news for ITN ▪ The bodies of two young girls (aged 5 and 6) are discovered on Cannock Chase in Staffordshire and police begin a manhunt to find the killer ▪ 19-year-old Hayley Mills and 23-year-old Ian McShane star at cinemas in *Sky West and Crooked* ▪ 'Brace Yourself for Greatness' - 40-year-old Richard Burton plays the role of Alec Leamas in *The Spy Who Came in from the Cold* - a movie based on a novel by 34-year-old John Le Carre ▪ Tony Waddington's Stoke City football team (of Division One) suffers a shock FA Cup defeat, losing 0-2 in the third round against Walsall (of Division Three) in front of 32,676 spectators at the Victoria Ground. 19-year-old Allan Clarke scores Walsall's second goal ▪ 16-year-old Joe Royle makes his debut for Everton in a 2-0 defeat against Blackpool ▪ Television police drama *Softly Softly* (a spin-off from *Z Cars*) begins on BBC One - with 40-year-old Stratford Johns playing Detective Chief Superintendent Charlie Barlow ▪ 23-year-old actor Neville Buswell makes his first appearance as Ray Langton in ITV's *Coronation Street* ▪ "Baby, I feel good, from the moment I rise. Feel good from morning..." ***Till The End Of Day*** by The Kinks reaches number eight in the pop chart ▪ "So, still runs the river on its journey to the sea. So, still beats my heart for you're far, so far, away from me" - ***The River*** by 38-year-old Ken Dodd peaks at number three ▪ Harold Wilson's Labour government continues its ambitious programme of building thousands of new council homes ▪ Working-class families move into small, concrete, terraced dwellings on the Brownfield Estate in East London ▪ Children from middle-class families return home from school to watch *Jackanory*, *The Magic Roundabout*, *Vision On* (presented by 39-year-old Pat Keysell and 40-year-old Tony Hart) and *Blue Peter* (presented by 32-year-old Christopher Trace, 31-year-old John Noakes and 28-year-old Valerie Singleton) ▪ 35-year-old Bert Foord forecasts the weather on BBC One ▪ South Wales and the Midlands are hit by snow and freezing rain ▪ Radio Caroline's pirate radio ship runs aground (with 22-year-old DJ Tony Blackburn on board) at Frinton ▪ "Keep on running, keep on hiding. One fine day I'm gonna be the one to make you understand. Oh yeah, I'm gonna be your man" - ***Keep On Running*** by The Spencer Davis Group moves to the top of the pop chart ▪ The 'Space Race' continues ▪ NASA scientists look on enviously as the USSR's *Luna 9* makes a soft landing on the Moon ▪ Back in England - Euston Railway Station is in the middle of a major redevelopment program, as part of a plan to prepare the country's entire rail network for electrification ▪ 'A love caught in the fire of revolution' - *Dr. Zhivago* (with 24-year-old Julie Christie and 33-year-old Omar Sharif) is now showing at cinemas ▪ 50-year-old Norman Wisdom appears in his first colour movie, *The Early Bird* - and it's a hoot! ▪ "Michelle, ma belle. These are words that go together well, my…" ***Michelle*** by The Overlanders is number one in the pop chart ▪ "But I know better now, now that we're worlds apart. Now as the teardrops start…" ***Love's Just A Broken Heart*** by 22-year-old Cilla Black is number five ▪ "Here is a box, a musical box, wound up and ready to play" - television programme *Camberwick Green*, with Windy Miller, Dr. Mopp, Captain Snort and PC McGarry (number 452), keeps young viewers entertained ▪ England's cricketers win the third Test Match in Sydney, with Bob Barber and John Edrich both scoring centuries and Geoffrey Boycott hitting 84. The series ends in a 1-1 draw - which means the Australians retain the Ashes. R W Barber, G Boycott, J H Edrich, K F Barrington, M C Cowdrey, M J K Smith (cpt), J M Parks (wk), F J Titmus, B R Knight, D A Allen, D J Brown, K Higgs, W E Russell and I J Jones are all downcast after failing in yet another Ashes series. Australia have now held the trophy for seven years ▪ Alf Ramsey's England football team is preparing for the FIFA world cup tournament in July ▪ 23-year-old Nobby Stiles scores the winning goal (in a friendly) for the national side in a 1-0 victory over West Germany at the Empire Stadium. England's full line-up for the match is: G Banks, Cohen, K Newton, Moore, J Charlton, Hunter, Ball, Hunt, G Hurst, R Charlton and substitute, Wilson ▪ "I want to go and discuss with them absolutely frankly some of the big world problems: means of reducing tension between East and West; the problems of Vietnam, of course, and also to see what we can do next to discuss measures to stop the spread of nuclear weapons." - 49-year-old prime-minister Harold Wilson flies into Moscow for talks with Soviet leaders: 62-year-old Aleksey Kosygin (prime-minster) and 59-year-old Leonid Brezhnev (Communist Party secretary) ▪ "England swings like a pendulum do. Bobbies on bicycles, two by two" - ***England Swings*** by 30-year-old Roger Miller peaks at number thirteen in the pop chart ▪ "Woke up this morning..." ***You Were On My Mind*** by 26-year-old Crispian St. Peters is number two ▪ 25-year-old pop star Billy Fury from Liverpool features on the front cover of the latest *New Musical Express* paper ▪ 27-year-old footballer Roger Hunt bags a hat-trick for Bill Shankly's Liverpool in a 4-0 win over Sunderland in a First Division match at Anfield ▪ 31-year-old David Herd bags a hat-trick for Matt Busby's Manchester Utd in a 4-2 win over Burnley at Old Trafford ▪ 35-year-old Roy Sproson is on the score-sheet for Fourth Division Port Vale in a 2-0 victory over Halifax Town at Vale Park ▪ 26-year-old Jimmy 'Greavsie' Greaves scores a consolation goal for Tottenham Hotspur as Spurs lose 2-1 against Preston North End in the fifth round of the FA Cup ▪ ***These Boots Are Made For Walkin'*** ("... and that's just what they'll do. One of these days these boots are gonna walk all over you") by 25-year-old Nancy Sinatra climbs to number one on the hit parade ▪ "Here it comes. Here it comes. Here comes your..." ***19th Nervous Breakdown*** by The Rolling Stones (with, lead singer, 22-year-old Mick Jagger) is number two ▪ The Labour government has a majority of just four MPs in the House of Commons ▪ Harold Wilson calls a snap general election - hoping to increase his majority to a much higher number and gain a mandate to finish the job his government has started ▪ The country will go to the polls on Thursday 31st March ▪ Edward Heath (leader of the Conservative opposition) welcomes the prospect of a general election and says "It is really essential to get an honest government at Number 10. A government that will act, not talk." ▪ Mr. Wilson insists that Labour has achieved far more for economic and social advancement after 500 days in power than the Conservatives had done in 5,000. "We have made a start," he says, "and I think the country recognises it." ▪ Life continues ▪ Household technology moves on apace ▪ Housewives crave a new-fangled clothes washer for the kitchen ▪ The Bendix *LA* automatic, front loading washing machine costs £117/5s/6d ▪ Husbands crave the very latest in home entertainment ▪ *Radio Rentals* offer attractive deals on 'colour ready' 23-inch television sets ▪ There's activity on football's transfer market ▪ 25-year-old centre-forward Ian Towers leaves Harry Potts' First Division Burnley and joins Third Division Oldham Athletic for £20,000 ▪ 25-year-old centre-forward Joe Baker leaves Billy Wright's Arsenal and joins Johnny Carey's Nottingham Forest for £65,000 ▪ "Bar-bar-bar, bar..." ***Barbara Ann*** by the Beach Boys (with, lead singer, 23-year-old Brian Wilson) climbs to number three in the pop chart ▪ ***My Love*** ("... is warmer than the warmest sunshine, softer than a sigh") by 33-year-old Petula Clark peaks at number four ▪ 'Bloodthirsty Vampire Lives Again!' - 43-year-old Christopher Lee stars at cinemas in *Dracula: Prince of Darkness* ▪ 19-year-old singer David Jones from Brixton changes his name to David Bowie ▪ 'Just add milk and whisk' - new Bird's *Dream Topping* adds a luxury fresh taste to all your sweets.

Spring 1966

Moors' murderers convicted

Monarch:	Queen Elizabeth II (aged 40)
Prime-minister:	Harold Wilson (aged 50)
Chancellor:	James Callaghan (aged 54)
Home Secretary:	Roy Jenkins (aged 45)
Foreign Secretary:	Michael Stewart (aged 59)
Football Manager:	Alf Ramsey (aged 46)
New car reg. suffix:	'D'

▪ 31-year-old Eddie Richardson and 42-year-old 'Mad' Frankie Fraser are arrested by police after a shootout between rival criminal gangs at Mr. Smith's Club in London ▪ "We've got..." ***A Groovy Kind Of Love*** by The Mindbenders is number two on the hit parade ▪ 32-year-old gangster Ronald Kray shoots and kills George Cornell at the Blind Beggar pub in Whitechapel ▪ *Bang Bang* ("... my baby shot me down") by 19-year-old Cher reaches number three in the pop chart ▪ A fight breaks out in the bar of the Crown Inn at Gorton in Manchester ▪ 11-year-old schoolboy Tim Martin dreams of one day owning a chain of pubs - selling cheap beer to the people of Britain; manned by surly barstaff, possessing just a rudimentary understanding of the concept of customer service ▪ ***The Sun Ain't Gonna Shine Anymore*** ("... the moon ain't gonna rise in the sky") by the Walker Brothers spends four weeks at the top of the pop chart ▪ "I gotta have you, you know, and..." ***I Can't Let Go*** by The Hollies reaches number two ▪ 'The newest and funniest DOCTOR of them all!' - 42-year-old Leslie Phillips, 59-year-old James Robertson Justice and 27-year-old Shirley Anne Field star in *Doctor in Clover* ▪ 36-year-old jockey Pat Taafe rides *Arkle* to victory in the Cheltenham Gold Cup for the third year running ▪ 'England Loses The World Cup' - the solid gold FIFA World Cup trophy is stolen from a display stand in Westminster. Seven days later, it's found under a hedge by a dog called Pickles ▪ "Come tomorrow, will I be older? Come tomorrow, maybe a soldier? Come tomorrow, may I be bolder than today" - ***Shapes Of Things*** by The Yardbirds moves up to number three on the hit parade ▪ A general election takes place ▪ 'You Know Labour Government Works' - 50-year-old Labour leader Harold Wilson (from Huddersfield) defeats 49-year-old Conservative leader Edward Heath (from Broadstairs) by a majority of ninety-eight - and Labour wins another term in office, with an increased majority. (Labour: 364 seats, Conservatives: 253 seats, Liberals: 12 seats) ▪ 45-year-old Home Secretary Roy Jenkins embarks on an ambitious programme to reform police forces and prisons, to end discrimination in the workplace and to establish a fairer and more liberal society as a whole ▪ 25-year-old John Lennon makes a controversial statement claiming The Beatles are more popular than Jesus ▪ 'Glowing with warmth and wonder!! The gay and exciting adventures of Elsa the Lioness' - *Born Free* (starring 34-year-old Virginia McKenna, 44-year-old Bill Travers and Elsa the Lioness) draws crowds to the cinema ▪ "Born free. As free as the wind blows As free as the grass grows" - 35-year-old Matt Monro sings ***Born Free*** ▪ "Somebody help me, yeah ..." ***Somebody Help Me*** ("... now") by the Spencer Davis Group reaches number one in the pop chart ▪ "Picked her up on a Friday night…" ***Sha La La La Lee*** by The Small Faces (19-year-old Ronnie Lane, 17-year-old Kenney Jones, 20-year-old Ian McLagan and 19-year-old, lead singer, Steve Marriott) is number three ▪ All one-hundred and twenty-four people on board a BOAC Boeing *707* are killed when the jet plane crashes in Japan ▪ Back in England - there's a spell of warm weather at the end of April ▪ Families enjoy a weekend by the seaside ▪ Adverts for *Midland Counties* ice-cream say, 'Liberate a lolly from the Counties cooler today!' ▪ "You'll never fall each time you call, hold tight, hold tight..." ***Hold Tight!*** by Dave Dee, Dozy, Beaky, Mick and Tich (a group of five friends from Wiltshire) reaches number four and stays on the chart for seventeen weeks ▪ "I was born with a plastic spoon in my mouth" - ***Substitute*** by The Who (a group comprising of 22-year-old Roger Daltrey, 20-year-old Pete Townshend, 21-year-old John Entwistle and 19-year-old Keith Moon) is number five ▪ 35-year-old Clint Eastwood and 41-year-old Lee Van Cleef star at cinemas in Sergio Leone's 'spaghetti western' *For a Few Dollars More* ▪ 25-year-old actress Julie Christie wins an Oscar for her performance in *Darling* ▪ 21-year-old maverick footballer Rodney Marsh leaves Fulham and joins Third Division Queens Park Rangers ▪ Carnaby Street in London is crammed with fab and groovy clothes boutiques ▪ Kids get stoned and purchase colourful garments at *Granny Takes A Trip* - a brand new 'psychedelic' fashion shop on the King's Road in Chelsea ▪ Women wear 'drop-waist' mini-dresses and white slingback shoes ▪ Men 'gab up' in paisley patterned shirts and pastel coloured slacks ▪ "They seek him here. They seek him there. His clothes are loud, but never square" - ***Dedicated Follower Of Fashion*** by The Kinks peaks at number four in the pop chart ▪ ***You Don't Have To Say You Love Me*** ("... just be close at hand") by 27-year-old Dusty Springfield spends a week at number one ▪ 'This is luxury you can afford by Cyril Lord' - Young married couples dream of wall-to-wall 'fitted' carpets in their home ▪ Cool young men dream of driving fab foreign cars ▪ The Alfa Romeo *Duetto* (soon to be known as the *Spider*) is launched at the Geneva Motor Show ▪ BMW introduces a small two-door saloon called the *1600-2* ▪ 26-year-old Jackie Stewart wins the motor racing Grand Prix at Monaco in a BRM. Stewart's team mate, 37-year-old Graham Hill, is third ▪ Jimmy Hagan's West Bromwich Albion football team loses 2-1 in the first leg of the League Cup final against Ron Greenwood's West Ham Utd, but recovers in the second leg to gain an aggregate 5-3 victory overall ▪ Jimmy 'Greavsie' Greaves and Bobby Charlton score the goals as Alf Ramsey's England team (G

Banks, Armfield, Wilson, Peters, J Charlton, Hunter, Paine, Greaves, R Charlton, G Hurst, Tambling) defeats Yugoslavia 2-0 in a friendly at Wembley ▪ "What a day for a..." ***Daydream*** ("... What a day for a day dreamin' boy") by The Lovin' Spoonful is number two in the pop chart ▪ "Hello darkness my old friend, I've come to talk with you again" - ***Sound Of Silence*** by The Bachelors is number three ▪ 19-year-old striker Allan Clarke transfers from Third Division Walsall to First Division Fulham for £37,500 ▪ 16-year-old goalkeeper Peter Shilton makes his debut for First Division Leicester City and keeps a clean-sheet in a 3-0 victory over Everton ▪ 27-year-old striker Roger Hunt scores twice as Bill Shankly's Liverpool beat Chelsea 2-1 in front of 53,754 at Anfield and 'The Reds' are the new champions of Division One. Tommy Lawrence, Chris Lawler, Gerry Byrne, Ron Yeats, Geoff Strong, Peter Thompson, Willie Stevenson, Gordon Milne, Ian Callaghan, Roger Hunt and 21-year-old uncompromising defender Tommy Smith have all been outstanding ▪ Billy Wright's Arsenal team loses three matches on the trot and narrowly avoids relegation to Division Two ▪ 'It's a grand old team to support!' - Everton win the FA Cup! 26-year-old defender Brian Labone lifts the famous silver trophy as 'The Toffees' come from two-nil down to beat Sheffield Wednesday 3-2 in the final at Wembley. 36-year-old Jack Taylor from Wolverhampton is referee. A ticket for the standing enclosure at the Empire Stadium costs ten shillings ▪ Families flock to the cinema ▪ 41-year-old George Cole is Flash Harry in *The Great St. Trinian's Train Robbery* ▪ Men flock to the cinema ▪ 31-year-old Sophia Loren (38-24-38) stars as *Judith* - 'a woman wronged beyond words' ▪ "When she moves, she walks so fine like a flamingo. Crimson dress that clings so tight. She's out of reach and out of sight" - ***Pretty Flamingo*** by Manfred Mann is new at number one in the pop chart ▪ "What's it all about?..." ***Alfie*** by Cilla Black is number nine ▪ "I don't want no bird's respect. I wouldn't know what to do with it" - 33-year-old actor Michael Caine stars as *Alfie* at the pictures ▪ 41-year-old Kenneth Robinson presents *Points Of View* on BBC One ▪ 26-year-old John Cleese, 36-year-old Ronnie Barker and 35-year-old Ronnie Corbett perform a comedy sketch about the British class system on *The Frost Report* - "I know my place", says working-class Corbett ▪ "HOW!" - *How* (presented by 54-year-old Jack Hargreaves) is a new tea-time show for the kids on ITV ▪ British Railways operate a fully electrified service from London Euston to Birmingham, and then onto Manchester and Liverpool ▪ "I wish I was..." ***Homeward Bound*** by Simon and Garfunkle reaches number nine in the pop chart ▪ "Let me go home, let me go home. I want to go home" - ***Sloop John B*** by The Beach Boys reaches number two ▪ 29-year-old Gordon Honeycombe reads the news for ITN ▪ The trial of 28-year-old Ian Brady and 23-year-old Myra Hindley takes place at Chester Assizes. Both are found guilty of the Moors murders and sentenced to life in prison ▪ Growth in the economy remains slow despite prime-minister Harold Wilson's push for greater productivity ▪ The balance of payments between import and export levels has improved slightly ▪ "I see a red door and I want it painted black" - ***Paint It Black*** by The Rolling Stones (with, lead singer, 22-year-old Mick Jagger) moves to the top of the pop chart - and stays for a week ▪ ***Wild Thing*** ("... you make my heart sing. You make everything groovy") by The Troggs (with, lead singer, 24-year-old Reg Presley) is number two ▪ The Who (with, lead singer, 22-year-old Roger Daltrey) play a gig at the Corn Exchange in Newbury ▪ Youngsters go zonkers at ginchy rave-ups, with many feeling regret the next morning when they have to get up for work ▪ 55-year-old Kenneth Robinson from Warrington is Labour's Minister for Health ▪ Adverts say, 'Drinka Pinta Milka Day' ▪ Rowntree *Jelly Tots* sweets are new.

Summer 1966

Hurst. He could make it three ... he has!

Monarch:	Queen Elizabeth II (aged 40)
Prime-minister:	Harold Wilson (aged 50)
Chancellor:	James Callaghan (aged 54)
Home Secretary:	Roy Jenkins (aged 45)
Foreign Secretary:	George Brown (aged 51)
Football Manager:	Alf Ramsey (aged 46)
New car reg. suffix:	'D'

▪ 26-year-old comic Jimmy Tarbuck appears on stage at the ABC Theatre in Great Yarmouth and is heckled by a bald man in the audience ▪ 'Nothing Can Faze...' *Modesty Blaise*, starring 34-year-old Monica Vitti, 28-year-old Terence Stamp and 45-year-old Dirk Bogarde, is now showing at cinemas ▪ *Kaleidoscope*, starring 29-year-old Warren Beatty and 27-year-old Susannah York, is coming soon ▪ ***Strangers In The Night*** ("... exchanging glances") by 50-year-old Frank Sinatra is number one in the pop chart ▪ ***Monday Monday*** ("... so good to me") by The Mamas and the Papas is number three ▪ Bob Ferris (played by 28-year-old Rodney Bewes) purchases a mod scooter and Terry Collier (played by 31-year-old James Bolam) helps Bob practice emergency stops, in BBC Two's comedy drama *The Likely Lads* ▪ The sun shines ▪ Schoolboys kick leather 'casey' footballs in the park and use jumpers for goal-posts ▪ 11-year-old Jeff Stelling from Hartlepool storms off from his friends 'in a huff' when the goal he's just scored is ruled out for offside ▪ "With your long blonde hair and eyes of blue, the only thing I ever get from you is sorrow..." ***Sorrow*** by The Merseys is number four in the pop chart ▪ "All I wanted was someone. I have him now, it is done..." ***Nothing Comes Easy*** by 19-year-old Sandie Shaw is number fourteen ▪ The sun continues to shine ▪ Families head for the seaside ▪ Bespectacled dads walk along the sea-front with flip-up, clip-on sun glass covers attached to their glasses ▪ Fish and chips wrapped in newspaper costs 1s/9d ▪ *Butlin's* open a new holiday camp at Barry Island ▪

'Come alive! - You're in the *Pepsi* Generation! ▪ Tinned beverage technology moves on apace - some drinks cans now come with a new-fangled 'ring-pull' ▪ "Dear Sir or Madam, will you read my book, it took me years to write, will you take a look?" - ***Paperback Writer*** is the tenth number one hit for The Beatles ▪ ***When A Man Loves A Woman*** ("... can't keep his mind on nothin' else") by 24-year-old Percy Sledge moves up to number four ▪ 25-year-old pop star Cliff Richard appears on stage (at Earls Court) alongside American evangelist Billy Graham - and Richard proclaims his new found faith in Jesus ▪ "You silly old moo!" - 40-year-old Warren Mitchell stars as Alf Garnett in *Till Death Us Do Part* ▪ 56-year-old Mrs. Mary Whitehouse (from rural Worcestershire) is outraged ▪ England's footballers embark on a tour of Scandinavia and then onto Eastern Europe, playing in a number of 'friendly' matches as preparation for the upcoming world cup tournament ▪ Jimmy 'Greavsie' Greaves is in fine fettle. The 26-year-old striker scores four goals in a 1-6 victory over Norway ▪ Cricketer Gary Sobers leads the West Indies to a 3-1 Test series victory over Colin Cowdrey's England ▪ Racing driver Graham Hill finishes third in the British Grand Prix at Brands Hatch. Jim Clark is fourth and Chris Irwin from Wandsworth is seventh ▪ 41-year-old Richard Baker reads the news on BBC One ▪ Harold Wilson's Labour government resists growing pressure to devalue the pound and introduces a six month wage freeze instead ▪ "The taxman's taken all my dough and left me in my stately home, lazing on a..." ***Sunny Afternoon*** by The Kinks climbs to number one on the hit parade ▪ "Don't run away to somebody new..." ***Nobody Needs Your Love*** ("... more than I do") by 26-year-old Gene Pitney is number two ▪ "And do I love you, my oh my. Yeah..." ***River Deep, Mountain High*** by 34-year-old Ike Turner and his wife, 26-year-old Tina, is number three ▪ 42-year-old Billy Wright is sacked as Arsenal manager after four years in charge ▪ 47-year-old physiotherapist Bertie Mee takes over as boss at Highbury ▪ Former Charlton Athletic manager Jimmy Seed dies aged 71 in South London ▪ 46-year-old Hughie Green presents a new series of the popular talent show *Opportunity Knocks*, on ITV ▪ 40-year-old David Jacobs presents *Juke Box Jury* on BBC One ▪ The songs - ***Get Away*** (by 23-year-old Georgie Flame and the Blue Flames) and ***Out Of Time*** (by 25-year-old Chris Farlowe and the Thunderbirds) both spend a week at the top of the pop chart ▪ England's footballers take part in the FIFA World Cup competition ▪ A 0-0 draw against Uruguay is followed by victories over Mexico (2-0, with goals from Charlton and Hunt), France (2-0, Hunt scores both), Argentina (1-0, Hurst) and Portugal (2-1, Charlton scores both) - Alf Ramsey's team is through to the world cup final, where they will face West Germany on the thirtieth of July at Wembley. Star striker Jimmy 'Greavsie' Greaves is set to miss the final due to an injury picked up in the game against France ▪ On the big day, warm sunshine breaks through the clouds and the temperature rises to 73 degrees Fahrenheit ▪ 24-year-old Geoff Hurst scores a hat-trick in a wonderful 4-2 victory. Hurst's third goal comes in the last few seconds of added time and prompts 43-year-old ITV commentator Hugh Johns to say, "Hurst, he could make it three... he has! That's it! That's it!" ▪ Over on BBC One, 46-year-old commentator Kenneth Wolstenholme utters the equally memorable words, "And here comes Hurst. He's got ... some people are on the pitch, they think it's all over. It is now!" ▪ England's footballers have won the world cup! ▪ There are scenes of great joy and jubilation at Wembley ▪ 24-year-old Nobby Stiles dances on the pitch ▪ 31-year-old hardman Jack Charlton is in tears ▪ The whole nation celebrates as never before ▪ The names: Gordon Banks, George Cohen, Ray Wilson, Jack Charlton, Bobby Moore (captain), Nobby Stiles, Alan Ball, Bobby Charlton, Geoff Hurst, Martin Peters and Roger Hunt are etched, forever, into football history ▪ "Well, we're all football crazy and it's plain to see, that we're all so happy, like one big family" -

35-year-old Lonnie Donegan sings ***World Cup Willie*** ▪ 52-year-old Robert Dougal reads the news on BBC One ▪ 30-year-old Harry Roberts shoots dead two policemen, and 38-year-old John Duddy murders a third police officer, at Shepherd's Bush in London. The two men, along with their accomplice Jack Witney, evade arrest and go on the run. A nationwide hunt gets underway to find the three policeman killers ▪ 51-year-old George Brown is appointed Foreign Secretary in Harold Wilson's Labour government ▪ "I want to spend my life, with a girl like you. Ba-ba-ba-ba-baah, ba-ba-ba-ba" - ***With A Girl Like You*** by The Troggs is new at number one on the hit parade ▪ ***Black is Black*** ("... I want my baby back") by Los Bravos is number two ▪ ***Love Letters*** ("... straight from your heart, keep us so near while apart") by 31-year-old Elvis Presley is number six ▪ Men of all ages flick through the pages of motoring magazines and dream of owning a new car ▪ The latest Triumph *Vitesse* has a 1998cc engine giving a top speed of 100 mph ▪ The luxurious Jaguar *MKII* saloon remains popular - seven years after it was first launched. The top-of-the-range 3.8 litre model has a top speed of 125 mph ▪ Stoke City sign 29-year-old inside-forward George Eastham from Arsenal for £35,000 ▪ Everton sign 21-year-old (world cup hero) Alan Ball from Blackpool for a new record transfer fee of £110,000 - Ball scores on his league debut for Everton in a 0-1 away win against Vic Buckingham's Fulham ▪ "Six guineas a day plus expenses" - 48-year-old Alfred Burke stars as Private Investigator Frank Marker in a new series of *Public Eye* on ATV ▪ Graham Parker presents the weather forecast on BBC One ▪ The month of August is mostly wet and cool ▪ "Hot town..." ***Summer In The City*** ("... back of my neck getting dirty and gritty") by The Lovin' Spoonful is number nine on the weekly hit parade ▪ ***Yellow Submarine*** by The Beatles is new at number eight ▪ ***Mama*** by 25-year-old Dave Berry is number five ▪ "Frying tonight!" - *Carry On Screaming!* with smouldering 38-year-old vamp Fenella Fielding is now showing at cinemas ▪ 'You are cordially invited to George and Martha's for an evening of fun and games' - 34-year-old Elizabeth Taylor stars alongside her 40-year-old husband Richard Burton in *Who's Afraid of Virginia Woolf?* ▪ 'The Incredible Revolution of Sex in the Sixties' - *Mayfair* magazine is launched, with a cover price of five shillings ▪ There's widespread furore following John Lennon's statement (from back in March) that The Beatles are more popular than Jesus ▪ 56-year-old Mrs. Mary Whitehouse (from rural Worcestershire) is outraged ▪ The Beatles' new LP, *Revolver*, is number one in the album chart. "Let me tell you how it will be. There's one for you, nineteen for me" - ***Taxman*** is the opening track on side one. ***Good Day Sunshine*** is the opening track on side two ▪ People spend a night in - watching telly ▪ The current series of *The Likely Lads* ends with Terry Collier signing up for a three year stint in the army, leaving Bob Ferris at home in Newcastle with his flat feet ▪ 49-year-old McDonald Hobley presents *It's A Knock Out*, a new 'outside broadcast' of fun events played between teams from northern English towns. 56-year-old Eddie Waring is referee for Heat 2 in Yorkshire, when Otley take on Ilkley and win by fifteen points to three ▪ ***They're Coming To Take Me Away Ha-Haa*** ("... hee-hee") by Napoleon XIV climbs to number four in the pop chart ▪ ***Lovers Of The World Unite*** by David and Jonathan peaks at number seven ▪ 20-year-old footballer 'super' Georgie Best is on the score-sheet for Manchester Utd in a 5-3 victory over West Bromwich Albion in front of 41,543 spectators at Old Trafford ▪ Men of all ages read *Charles Buchan's Football Monthly* magazine ▪ Woman of all ages read *Woman's Realm* ▪ Young couples save up to get married and look forward to a long and happy life together ▪ The average price of a house in the UK is £3,500 ▪ A modern new Ford *Anglia* motorcar costs £503/19s/2d. The *Deluxe* version is £565/8d/4d ▪ A more traditional Morris *Minor 1000* is £516/6d/3d ▪ Everyday life is busy ▪ 'A *Mars* a day helps you work, rest and play' - a *Mars* bar costs ninepence.

Autumn 1966

Disaster at Aberfan

Monarch:	Queen Elizabeth II (aged 40)
Prime-minister:	Harold Wilson (aged 50)
Chancellor:	James Callaghan (aged 54)
Home Secretary:	Roy Jenkins (aged 46)
Foreign Secretary:	George Brown (aged 52)
Football Manager:	Alf Ramsey (aged 46)
New car reg. suffix:	'D'

▪ The summer holidays end and children return to school ▪ *4a - Things we do*, *4b - Fun at the farm, 4c - Say the sound* - youngsters improve their reading skills, using Ladybird's *Key Words* range of books ▪ 66-year-old Queen Elizabeth the Queen Mother is on hand at Barrow-in-Furness to attend the launch of Britain's first Polaris-class nuclear powered ballistic submarine - HMS *Resolution* ▪ "So we sailed up to the sun, till we found a sea of green. And we lived beneath the waves, in our yellow submarine. We all live in a yellow submarine, yellow submarine…" ***Yellow Submarine*** by The Beatles moves up to number one in the pop chart and stays at the top for four weeks ▪ ***God Only Knows*** ("... what I'd be without you") by The Beach Boys is number two ▪ The old electric powered trolley-buses in Newcastle-upon-Tyne are replaced by diesel vehicles ▪ 21-year-old Angela Rippon reads the local news on BBC Plymouth ▪ Police officers continue their nationwide hunt for policeman killers Harry Roberts and John Duddy and their accomplice Jack Witney ▪ 50-year-old Harold Wilson's Labour government increases family allowances ▪ Tins of Heinz *Hot Snack Specials* (with a range comprising of Lamb Garni, Ham Mornay, Beef Italienne and Chicken Noodle Snack) are available in shops, priced between 1s/9d and three shillings ▪ A pack of twenty filtered Player's *No. 6* cigarettes costs 3s/6d ▪ A pint of Watney's *Red Barrel* is 2s/2d ▪ People enjoy an evening at the local *Odeon* ▪ A ticket for a seat in the stalls costs

3s/8d. A ticket in the circle is 4s/9d ▪ 'Alone with the Excitement and Emotions of Tomorrow!' - 26-year-old Julie Christie stars as Linda Montag in *Fahrenheit 451* ▪ 24-year-old Rita Tushingham and 28-year-old Oliver Reed star in *The Trap* ▪ 35-year-old train robber Buster Edwards is caught and arrested after three years on the run ▪ 37-year-old Ronnie Biggs, 34-year-old Charlie Wilson and 34-year-old Bruce Reynolds (suspected ring leader of the gang) remain at large ▪ ***I'm A Boy*** ("... I'm a boy, but my ma won't admit it") by The Who (with, lead singer, 22-year-old Roger Daltry and, lead guitarist, 21-year-old Pete Townshend) reaches number two on the hit parade ▪ ***Too Soon To Know*** by 30-year-old Roy Orbison is number three ▪ Motoring technology moves on apace ▪ Vauxhall launches the all new *Viva HB* motorcar (priced from £626/2s/9d) ▪ Ford launches the incredible new *Cortina MKII* (priced from £610/6s/9d) ▪ Rootes Group introduces the 'up-market' Hillman *Hunter* (priced from £837/11s/-) ▪ Production of Austin and Morris motorcars is brought to a halt when workers go on strike at Longbridge in Birmingham ▪ The Almondsbury motorway interchange opens near Bristol ▪ A road toll bridge over the River Severn is also new ▪ Television viewers tune-in to see the Grand Final of BBC's *It's A Knockout*, with teams from Lytham St. Annes and Bridlington competing in fun events such as Magnetised Boots, Pillows to Billows, Belter Skelter and The Goalkeepers. After a closely fought contest, Bridlington are proclaimed the winners ▪ Circus owner and veteran entertainer Billy Smart dies aged 72 in Ipswich ▪ "Top of the morning" - the dulcet tones of 28-year-old Terry Wogan are heard for the first time on BBC radio's Light Programme ▪ "I thought you'd listen to my reasoning, but now I see you don't hear a thing. Try to make you see, how it's got to be. Yes it's..." ***All Or Nothing*** by The Small Faces (with, lead singer, 19-year-old Steve Marriott) is new at number one ▪ ***Got To Get You Into My Life*** by Cliff Bennett and the Rebel Rousers is number six ▪ 39-year-old Huw Thomas reads the news for ITN ▪ 49-year-old Dr. Helen Davidson is beaten to death near her home at Amersham in Buckinghamshire ▪ 30-year-old rock singer Johnny Kidd is killed in a car crash on the A58 in Lancashire ▪ Millions stay in to watch television ▪ Elsie Tanner (played by 42-year-old Pat Phoenix) is held at knifepoint by a deranged woman in ITV's popular soap-opera *Coronation Street* ▪ Dr. James Kildare (played by 32-year-old Richard Chamberlain) falls out with his colleagues in BBC's popular hospital drama *Dr. Kildare* ▪ 19-year-old Chelsea footballer Peter 'Ossie' Osgood breaks his leg in a match against Blackpool after tackling 19-year-old Emlyn Hughes ▪ 25-year-old striker Tony Hateley transfers from Aston Villa to Chelsea for £100,000 ▪ 21-year-old midfielder George Graham transfers from Chelsea to Arsenal for £50,000 (plus Tommy Baldwin) ▪ 27-year-old half-back Calvin Palmer transfers from Stoke City to Sunderland for £70,000 ▪ "I hear the sound of…" ***Distant Drums*** by the late Jim Reeves spends five weeks at number one in the pop chart ▪ ***You Can't Hurry Love*** ("... No, you'll just have to wait") by The Supremes is number three ▪ 33-year-old Michael Aspel reads the news on BBC One ▪ The entire nation is grief stricken when one hundred and sixteen school children are killed at Aberfan in South Wales. The tragedy is caused by a colliery slag heap collapsing onto a nearby junior school and other buildings. 50-year-old prime-minister Harold Wilson, 45-year-old Prince Philip the Duke of Edinburgh and 40-year-old Queen Elizabeth II each visit the village to pay their respects ▪ 44-year-old traitor and spy George Blake escapes from Wormwood Scrubbs, using a rope ladder thrown over the perimeter wall, and absconds to Moscow ▪ Policeman killers, Harry Roberts and John Duddy and their accomplice Jack Witney are found hiding in a barn near Bishop's Stortford. (The gang have been on the run from the police for three months). The men are charged on three counts of murder and taken into custody ▪ Pop singer Alma Cogan dies of cancer at the age of 34 ▪ Millions of TV viewers watch 23-year-old Carol White in *Cathy Come Home* - the harrowing story a young mother whose children are taken away by social services ▪ ***Reach Out I'll Be There*** ("... to love and comfort you") by The Four Tops spends three weeks at number one in the pop chart ▪ ***Bend It*** ("... bend it, just a little bit") by Dave Dee, Dozy, Beaky, Mick and Tich (a group of five friends from Wiltshire) reaches number two ▪ 62,085 football spectators attend Old Trafford where 26-year-old Denis Law scores the winning goal for Matt Busby's Manchester Utd in a 1-0 victory over Joe Mercer's Manchester City ▪ 36-year-old Roy Sproson scores for Fourth Division Port Vale in a 1-1 draw with Tranmere Rovers ▪ Members of England's victorious world cup football team are presented to 40-year-old Queen Elizabeth at the Royal Variety Show ▪ The economic policies of Harold Wilson's Labour government are criticised by 41-year-old Margaret Thatcher MP ▪ ***No Milk Today*** ("... my love has gone away. The bottle stands forlorn, a symbol of the dawn") by Herman's Hermits is number seven in the pop chart ▪ ***High Times*** by 24-year-old Paul Jones is number four ▪ 'Change Your Partners: The Practice of Wife and Husband Swopping is Growing' - the second edition of *Mayfair* magazine is now on sale at newsagents ▪ 'The Face of 1966' - 16-year-old model Twiggy (with long painted eye-lashes, and wearing a trendy peaked black cap) appears on the front cover of *Honey* magazine ▪ 24-year-old disc jockey Dave Cash sits aboard a ship in the North Sea playing hit pop songs for pirate radio station 'Big L' (Radio London) ▪ Youngsters rush out to buy the latest 7-inch singles at record shops for 7s/2d ▪ "Don't want you goin' round with no one else, 'cause when I'm with you..." ***I Can't Control Myself*** by The Troggs is number two on the hit parade ▪ ***Winchester Cathedral*** ("... you're bringing me down") by The New Vaudeville Band is number four ▪ Construction work continues on the new Victoria underground line in London - it's due to open in

1968 and will have state-of-the-art 'self driving' trains ▪ "Evening, all" - 70-year-old Jack Warner stars in a new series of *Dixon of Dock Green* on BBC One ▪ 46-year-old Patrick Troughton takes over from 58-year-old William Hartnell as *Dr. Who* ▪ "Biff!" "Bang!!" "Ker-powww!!!" - over on ITV, 38-year-old Adam West stars as *Batman* (and 21-year-old Burt Ward is Robin) ▪ "I'm pickin' up good vibrations. She's givin' me excitations" - ***Good Vibrations*** by The Beach Boys moves to the top of the pop chart ▪ ***Stop Stop Stop*** by The Hollies is number two ▪ Nottingham Forest's football manager Johnny Carey signs 21-year-old winger Barry Lyons from Rotherham Utd for £45,000 ▪ Sheffield Wednesday's football manager Alan Brown signs 25-year-old striker John Ritchie from Stoke City for £70,000 ▪ 29-year-old Bobby Charlton scores twice as Matt Busby's high-flying Manchester Utd beat Southampton 1-2 at the Dell ▪ A few days later, 20-year-old 'super' Georgie Best and 26-year-old Denis Law score the goals as Utd beat Leicester City 1-2 at Filbert Street ▪ 26-year-old Jimmy 'Greavsie' Greaves and 23-year-old Terry Venables are among the scorers for Tottenham Hotspur in a 3-4 defeat against West Ham Utd at White Hart Lane ▪ The rate of exports from British industries is low ▪ The 'trade gap' in the balance of payments is increasing and the country needs a new competitive edge ▪ Labour prime-minister Harold Wilson, Chancellor of the Exchequer Jim Callaghan and Foreign Secretary George Brown meet to discuss ways of boosting the economy ▪ "You gotta gimme some lovin'. Gimme..." ***Gimme Some Lovin'*** by The Spencer Davis Group moves up to number two in the pop chart ▪ ***Help Me Girl*** by Eric Burdon and the Animals is number fourteen ▪ 'A racing car disguised as a family saloon' - The latest Ford *Cortina Lotus* motorcar costs £1,068, has a top speed of 108 mph and accelerates from 0-60 mph in 10.4 seconds ▪ "Swingin', pops!' - young 'cats' meet at the pub for a 'zingy' night out ▪ A pint of *Double Diamond* in the Red Lion is two shillings.

Christmas 1966

Twiggy is the Face of 1966

Monarch:	Queen Elizabeth II (aged 40)
Prime-minister:	Harold Wilson (aged 50)
Chancellor:	James Callaghan (aged 54)
Home Secretary:	Roy Jenkins (aged 46)
Foreign Secretary:	George Brown (aged 52)
Football Manager:	Alf Ramsey (aged 46)
New car reg. suffix:	'D'

▪ A sudden drop in temperature brings heavy frosts ▪ The Midlands is badly affected as the icy conditions leads to chaos on the roads ▪ Motorists are forced to abandon their cars in Banbury when treacherous black-ice turns the Oxford, Bloxham, Warwick and Middleton Roads into ice-rinks ▪ Banbury Utd's football match against Margate (in the Southern League) is called off ▪ "No comment. No comment at all." - is the response of 52-year-old Labour Foreign Secretary George Brown when questioned over Britain's possible new application to join the European Common Market. Speculation that Britain will re-apply for membership is rife after Mr. Brown's recent meeting with President de Gaulle in Paris ▪ "Yes, they'll all come to meet me. Arms reaching, smiling sweetly. It's good to touch the…" ***Green Green Grass Of Home*** by 26-year-old Tom Jones from Pontypridd climbs to number one in the pop chart - and stays there for seven weeks! ▪ ***What Would I Be*** ("… without your love? I'll never know") by 38-year-old Val Doonican is number two ▪ Schoolboys ask Santa Claus for a pair of football boots and a *Slazenger Challenge* leather 'casey' football for Christmas ▪ Schoolgirls ask for a *Tiny Tears* doll ▪ Families enjoy turkey for Christmas dinner, with some choosing prawn cocktail as a 'starter' ▪ Later, on Christmas Day, many have fun with a great new game called *Twister* ▪ "So you finally named the day, when wedding bells will chime. I was sorry to hear you say, you're gonna be his not mine" - ***Semi-Detached Sub-***

urban Mr. James by Manfred Mann slides down the pop chart after reaching number two ▪ ***Just One Smile*** by 26-year-old Gene Pitney peaks at number eight ▪ Robert Dougal reads the news on BBC One ▪ Unemployment has risen to 530,000 since Harold Wilson's Labour government took office two years ago ▪ Chancellor of the Exchequer Jim Callaghan has managed to reduce the balance of payments deficit from £358 million to £105 million - but is under pressure to do even better ▪ The coal industry continues to decline ▪ 180 million tonnes of coal have been mined in Britain this year - down by 12 million tonnes compared to 1965. The output level is now the lowest since 1926 ▪ Two new sections of M1 motorway open - and the 'national road' now runs uninterrupted for 113 miles between Harrow and Nottingham ▪ Young people flock to cinemas ▪ 23-year-old Lynn Redgrave stars as Georgina Parkin in *Georgy Girl* ▪ 20-year-old Hayley Mills and 22-year-old Hywel Bennett star in *The Family Way* ▪ 26-year-old Cliff Richard and 20-year-old Viviane Ventura star in *Finders Keepers* ▪ Old people stay indoors watching television ▪ *Man Alive* (presented by 35-year-old Desmond Wilcox) is on BBC Two on Wednesday evenings ▪ US military planes drop bombs on Hanoi ▪ 19-year-old British soldier Leslie Grantham murders a taxi driver in Germany ▪ 33-year-old gangster twins Reginald and Ronald Kray organise the escape of Frank 'Mad Axe Man' Mitchell from Dartmoor Prison - Mitchell is smuggled into London and spends a number of days hiding from the police ▪ "The most heinous crime to have been committed in this country for a generation or more" - Mr. Justice Glyn-Jones sums up at the Old Bailey at the end of the trial of Harry Roberts, John Duddy and Jack Witney. The three men are sentenced to thirty-years in prison for shooting dead three police officers in August ▪ Noisy schoolboys spend Saturday mornings in the stalls at the local *Roxy* cinema ▪ 'All New High Adventure!' - 30-year-old Mike Henry is The King of the Jungle in *Tarzan's Valley of Gold* ▪ England's world cup winning football captain,

25-year-old Bobby Moore, is voted BBC's 'Sports Personality of the Year' ▪ Blackpool's football manager Ron Suart signs 22-year-old midfielder Alan Suddick from Newcastle U for £60,000 ▪ "Hello, good evening and welcome" - 27-year-old David Frost presents *The Frost Programme* on ATV ▪ Pop stars, 23-year-old Mick Jagger and 26-year-old Chris Farlowe are studio guests for the final edition of *Ready, Steady Go!* ▪ 26-year-old John Lennon falls in love with 33-year-old Yoko Ono ▪ Japanese firm Nissan begins importing *Datsun* motorcars to the UK. The small *1000 de Luxe* model has a top speed of 76 mph and accelerates from 0-60 mph in 21.7 seconds ▪ Lotus launches the *S1 Europa* sports car with a top speed of 120 mph and capable of accelerating from 0-60 mph in 10 seconds ▪ The stunning new Jensen *Interceptor* (hand-built at a factory in West Bromwich) has a top speed of 133 mph and hits 60 mph in just 7.3 seconds ▪ *Pippin* comic is new for very young children - it's on sale now in newsagents for 7d ▪ "Train whistle blowing, makes a sleepy noise. Underneath their blankets, go all the girls and boys. Rockin' rollin' ridin', out along the bay. All bound for Morningtown many miles away" - ***Morningtown Ride*** by The Seekers is a smash hit, reaching number two on the hit parade ▪ ***Save Me*** by Dave Dee, Dozy, Beaky, Mick and Tich (a group of five friends from Wiltshire) is number three ▪ ***Pamela Pamela*** ("... remember the days, of inkwells and apples and books and school plays?") by 21-year-old Wayne Fontana from Manchester is number eleven ▪ 32-year-old footballer David Herd scores a hat-trick, and 26-year-old Denis Law adds another, as Matt Busby's Manchester Utd beat West Bromwich Albion 3-4 at the Hawthorns to go top of Division One ▪ Bill Shankly's Liverpool are close behind, after a 2-1 win against Tommy Docherty's Chelsea ▪ 24-year-old centre-forward Ron Davies scores the only goal for Ted Bates' Southampton in a 1-5 defeat against Ron Suart's Blackpool. 'The Saints' are stranded at the foot of Division One ▪ 37-year-old Frank 'Mad Axe Man' Mitchell is driven off into the night by members of the Kray twins' Firm - never to be seen again ▪ Reinforced concrete columns support the bridges and flyovers of a new five-mile section of M1 motorway which is under construction at Edgware in London ▪ Queues form outside picture houses for *The Bible ... In The Beginning* - the latest Hollywood blockbuster. 26-year-old Michael Parks is Adam, 24-year-old Ulla Bergryd is Eve, 60-year-old John Huston is Noah, 36-year-old Richard Harris is Cain, 34-year-old Peter O'Toole plays the Angels and 43-year-old Ava Garner is Sarah ▪ 'You caught the pussycat! Now Chase the Fox! - 41-year-old Peter Sellers stars alongside his wife, 23-year-old Britt Ekland, in *After the Fox* ▪ 'Their first BIG screen adventure in COLOUR!' - Jeff Tracy and his sons (Scott, Virgil, Alan and Gordon) do battle with The Hood in *Thunderbirds are Go* - a wonderful new feature-length movie from Gerry and Sylvia Anderson ▪ Speculation that Britain will re-apply to join the European community is growing ▪ 50-year-old prime-minister Harold Wilson and his Foreign Secretary George Brown plan to visit the capitals of six Common Market countries early in the new year ▪ ***Green Green Grass Of Home*** by Tom Jones remains at number one in the pop chart ▪ ***Sunshine Superman*** by 20-year-old Donovan is number two ▪ "Bomp-bomp-bomp, b-bomp-bomp…" ***I Feel Free*** by Cream climbs to number eleven ▪ 31-year-old writer David Nobbs drinks wine and works on his second novel ▪ 26-year-old footballer Jimmy 'Greavsie' Greaves scores twice as Bill Nicholson's Tottenham Hotspur beat Joe Harvey's Newcastle Utd 4-0 at White Hart Lane ▪ 'Twiggy-Rigs are the Greatest!' - 16-year-old model Twiggy launches her own fashion range ▪ A trouser suit costs 9 guineas ▪ A teen-y tent dress is 8 guineas ▪ 30-year-old actress Una Stubbs purchases the latest 'mod-cons' for her kitchen ▪ A Hotpoint *Supermatic* twin tub washing machine costs 77 guineas ▪ A *Kenwood Chef* food-mixer is 30 guineas.

New Year 1967

The Monkees come to England

Monarch:	Queen Elizabeth II (aged 40)
Prime-minister:	Harold Wilson (aged 50)
Chancellor:	James Callaghan (aged 54)
Home Secretary:	Roy Jenkins (aged 46)
Foreign Secretary:	George Brownt(aged 52)
Football Manager:	Alf Ramsey (aged 47)
New car reg. suffix:	'E'

▪ It's a bright but bitterly cold start to the new year ▪ The old electric powered trolley-buses in Manchester have been replaced by modern diesel vehicles ▪ 'E' registration cars go on sale ▪ The up-market Vauxhall *Cresta De Luxe* is now available as an estate. The versatile and luxurious new car has a 3.3 litre engine, a fold-away rear seat, deep-pile carpeting, an off-side wing mirror as standard and costs £1,507/9s/- including Purchase Tax. Top speed is 110 mph ▪ 56-year-old Minister for Transport Barbara Castle infuriates drivers by making the temporary 70 mph trial motorway speed limit permanent ▪ *Till Death Us Do Part* (starring 40-year-old Warren Mitchell, 59-year-old Dandy Nicholls, 35-year-old Tony Booth and 29-year-old Una Stubbs) pokes fun at the notion of abstaining from sex before marriage ▪ 'From protest to participation' - 56-year-old Mrs. Mary Whitehouse (from rural Worcestershire) publishes a new book - *Cleaning Up TV* ▪ 24-year-old housewife Margaret Lovell completes the ironing and minutes afterwards gives birth to her first son, Andrew, at Ford Way in Armitage ▪ "I can't see anything. Hello, the bow's up. I have gone..." the final words of 'Speed Ace' Donald Campbell are recorded on tape as the 45-year-old is killed during an attempt on the world water speed record in *Bluebird K7* on Lake Coniston ▪ London Airport, with its passenger terminals Europa and Oceanic, is now known simply as 'Heathrow' ▪ 'A unique manhunt across the capitals of Europe' - 34-year-old Peter O'Toole, 34-year-old Omar Sharif, 30-year-old Tom Courtenay and 47-year-old Donald Pleasence star at cinemas in *Night of the Generals* ▪ 42-year-old Marlon Brando and 32-year-old Sophia Loren star in *A Countess from Hong Kong* - a new movie, written and directed by 77-year-old Charlie Chaplin ▪ ***Happy Jack*** ("… wasn't old, but he was a man. He lived in the sand at the Isle of Man") by The Who climbs to number three in the pop chart ▪ "Why should we be in..." ***Dead End Street*** by The Kinks is number six ▪ 37-year-old politician Jeremy Thorpe is the new leader of the Liberal party - taking over from 53-year-old Jo Grimond ▪ The domestic economy remains weak ▪ Unemployment is rising ▪ 50-year-old prime-minister Harold Wilson and 52-year-old Foreign Secretary George Brown visit European leaders to 'test the water' for Britain's possible entry into the Common Market ▪ 67-year-old Arthur K. Chesterton is chairman of the newly formed National Front political movement ▪ "I thought love was only true in fairy tales, meant for someone else but not for me" - ***I'm A Believer*** by The Monkees reaches number one in the pop chart - and stays there for four weeks ▪ Davy Jones, Micky Dolenz, Mike Nesmith and Peter Tork tour Britain - and are greeted by crowds of hysterical teenage boys and girls ▪ ***Night Of Fear*** - the debut single from The Move is number two ▪ Pirate radio station Radio Caroline broadcasts from a ship in the North Sea. 21-year-old disc jockey Dave Lee Travis is on air at 12 noon, followed by 26-year-old Tommy Vance at 3 p.m ▪ ***Hey Joe*** ("… where you goin' with that gun of yours?") by The Jimi Hendrix Experience reaches number six in the pop chart ▪ ***Matthew And Son*** ("… the work's never done. There's always something new") by Cat Stevens is number two ▪ 46-year-old football manager Alf Ramsey receives a knighthood ▪ 19-year-old half-back Emlyn Hughes leaves Blackpool and joins Bill Shankly's Liverpool for £65,000 ▪ Johnny Carey's Nottingham Forest (with Grummitt, Winfield, McKinley, Lyons, Barnwell, Wignall and Storey-Moore) gain a 1-0 victory over Don Revie's hard-tackling Leeds Utd (with Sprake, Cooper, Bremner, Charlton, Hunter, Lorimer and

Giles) and move up to third in Division One ▪ "You're gonna find me, out..." ***In The Country*** by Cliff Richard and the Shadows is number six in the pop chart ▪ ***Standing In The Shadows Of Love*** by The Four Tops is new at number ten ▪ "Here is the clock, the Trumpton clock. Telling the time steadily, sensibly, never too quickly, never too slowly. Telling the time for…" *Trumpton* is new on TV - with firemen Pugh, Pugh, Barney-McGrew, Cuthbert, Dibble and Grub ▪ 62-year-old Jennie Lee is the new Secretary of State for the Arts in Harold Wilson's Labour government ▪ At cinemas, 44-year-old Paul Scofield plays Sir Thomas More and 39-year-old Robert Shaw plays King Henry VIII in *A Man For All Seasons* ▪ 31-year-old Chaim Topol plays the role of Tevye the Dairyman in a stage production of *Fiddler On The Roof* at Her Majesty's Theatre in London ▪ The *Daily Mail* reports four-thousand holes in Blackburn Lancashire - as John Lennon and Paul McCartney write songs for the next Beatles' album ▪ Police raid the Sussex home of 23-year-old Keith Richards - looking for illegal drugs ▪ The double A sided single ***Ruby Tuesday / Let's Spend The Night Together*** ("… now I need you more than ever") by The Rolling Stones is number three in the pop chart ▪ ***Sugar Town*** by 26-year-old Nancy Sinatra is number eight ▪ 'Turn on, tune in, drop dead' - the first edition of *Oz* magazine is published by 25-year-old Richard Neville and 29-year-old Jim Anderson, from a small basement flat in Notting Hill ▪ 'A time when there was no law and man… woman… and beast roamed the Earth untamed!' - 26-year-old Raquel Welch (37-22-35) draws crowds of men to the cinema to see *One Million Years B.C.* ▪ 33-year-old Leslie Crowther presents *Children's Favourites* on BBC radio's Light Programme on Saturday mornings ▪ 47-year-old Jon Pertwee sings ***My Grandfather's Clock*** ("… was too tall for the shelf, so it stood ninety years on the floor") ▪ Matt Busby's Manchester Utd beat Johnny Carey's Nottingham Forest 1-0 in a top-of-the-table Division One clash in front of 62,727 spectators at Old Trafford. 26-year-old Denis Law scores the winning goal ▪ Bottom-of-the-table Blackpool sack manager Ron Suart and appoint 45-year-old Stan Mortensen as boss at Bloomfield Road ▪ 53-year-old Liverpool manager Bill Shankly watches 19-year-old Howard Kendall play for Preston North End - and is impressed with the guile and skill of the talented young left-half ▪ "Love, this is my song. Here is a song, a serenade to you. This world cannot be wrong, if in this world there is you" - ***This Is My Song*** by 34-year-old Petula Clark is number one in the pop chart ▪ ***Edelweiss*** ("… Edelweiss, every morning you greet me. Small and white, clean and bright, you look happy to meet me") by 32-year-old Vince Hill is number two ▪ The Small Faces appear 'for one night only' at the Locarno in Swindon ▪ The Troggs appear 'for one night only' at the ABC in Chester ▪ 'Go Ahead: Tell the End (It's Too Hilarious to Keep Secret) But Please Don't Tell the Beginning!' - *Gambit*, starring 32-year-old Shirley MacLaine and 33-year-old Michael Caine, is at cinemas ▪ 54-year-old Gordon Wilkins presents *Wheelbase* - a motoring programme on BBC Two television ▪ Wealthy middle-aged men purchase sleek, fast, luxurious cars ▪ The stunning new Jensen *Interceptor* costs £3,742/11s/2d (including Purchase Tax) and has a top speed of 133 mph ▪ Confirmed bachelors purchase two seater sports cars ▪ The new Triumph *Spitfire MKIII* costs £717 (including Purchase Tax) and has a top speed of 100 mph ▪ Family men purchase sensible cars ▪ The *Austin 1800* costs £832/17s/11d (including Purchase Tax) ▪ The *1800 de Luxe* is £872/15s/5d (including Purchase Tax) ▪ Millions watch on television as Rita Rawlins (played by 29-year-old Una Stubbs) burns a copy of Mary Whitehouse's book, *Cleaning Up TV*, in an episode of *Till Death Us Do Part* ▪ Trendy home-owners paint the interior walls of their houses with a gloss, or emulsion, or eggshell finish ▪ 'Jasmine Yellow', 'Pastel Green', 'Dawn Pink' and 'Begonia' are popular colours ▪ Adverts say, 'For the paint that lasts longer say *Dulux* to your decorator'.

Spring 1967

Barefoot Sandie Shaw wins Eurovision

Monarch:	Queen Elizabeth II (aged 41)
Prime-minister:	Harold Wilson (aged 51)
Chancellor:	James Callaghan (aged 55)
Home Secretary:	Roy Jenkins (aged 46)
Foreign Secretary:	George Brown (aged 52)
Football Manager:	Alf Ramsey (aged 47)
New car reg. suffix:	'E'

▪ The economy is slow and unemployment is rising ▪ Prime-minister Harold Wilson and Chancellor of the Exchequer Jim Callaghan work late into the night at Downing Street - devising ways to improve things ▪ The possibility of Britain applying to join the European Common Market is being considered ▪ Elsewhere, life continues as normal ▪ Television viewers are transfixed on Saturday evenings when BBC Two broadcasts a new drama set in Victorian times. "London 1879: In England today there is no more charming and instructive site than an upper-middle-class family in full plumage. This particular family is called Forsyte" - *The Forsyte Saga* (with 52-year-old Kenneth More, 38-year-old Eric Porter, 30-year-old Nyree Dawn Porter and 29-year-old Susan Hampshire) is a huge success ▪ ITV broadcasts *Coronation Street* on Monday and Wednesday evenings. Viewers watch spellbound as a train crashes into the terraced houses in Weatherfield and Jack Walker, Elsie Tanner and miserable Ena Sharples are all lucky to survive ▪ BBC begins broadcasting the popular police drama *Z Cars* on Monday and Tuesday evenings - every week ▪ 'Carry On Laughing until you have hysterics … But -' *Don't Lose Your Head* is at cinemas - starring Sid 'Ha-ak-ak' James, Kenneth Williams, Jim Dale, Charles Hawtrey, Joan Sims and with 52-year-old Peter Butterworth as Citizen Bidet ▪ ***I Was Kaiser Bill's Batman*** by 40-year-old Whistling Jack Smith is number five on the hit parade ▪ "Oh, who would think a boy and bear could be well accepted everywhere? It's just amazing how fair people can be" - ***Simon Smith And The Amazing Dancing Bear*** by The Alan Price Set is number four ▪ "Love..." ***This Is My Song*** ("... Here is a song, a serenade to you") by 45-year-old Harry Secombe is number two ▪ 24-year-old model Anita Pallenberg breaks off her relationship with 25-year-old Brian Jones of the Rolling Stones, and begins dating Jones' bandmate 23-year-old Keith Richards ▪ 22-year-old maverick footballer Rodney Marsh scores a goal as Third Division Queens Park Rangers beat First Division West Bromwich Albion 3-2 in the first League Cup final to be played at Wembley ▪ In Division One, 16-year-old Ian 'Chico' Hamilton scores on his debut for Tommy Docherty's Chelsea in a 1-1 draw against Tottenham Hotspur, before 27-year-old Jimmy 'Greavsie' Greaves equalizes for Spurs ▪ Matt Busby's high-flying Manchester Utd defeat West Ham Utd 3-0 - and the names 'Best, Charlton, Law' feature together on the score-sheet ▪ "Please release me, let me go. For I don't love you anymore" - ***Release Me*** by 31-year-old Engelbert Humperdinck is a million selling smash hit - the record reaches number one in the pop chart - and stays there for six weeks! ▪ "In Penny Lane there is a barber showing photographs" - ***Penny Lane / Strawberry Fields Forever*** by The Beatles stalls at number two ▪ At the pictures, 57-year-old David Niven stars as Sir James Bond in *Casino Royale*. 41-year-old Peter Sellers is Evelyn Tremble and 31-year-old Ursula Andress (38-25-35) is Vespa Lynd ▪ 32-year-old Elsa Martinelli and 43-year-old Leslie Phillips star in Gerry O'Hara's new thriller, *Maroc 7* ▪ The record ***Maroc 7*** by The Shadows reaches number twenty-four on the hit parade ▪ 63-year-old Bob Hope hosts the Academy Awards Show in Santa Monica ▪ 35-year-old Elizabeth Taylor wins an Oscar for her performance as Martha in *Who's Afraid of Virginia Woolf?* ▪ 45-year-old Paul Scofield wins an Oscar for his performance as Sir Thomas More in *A Man For All Seasons* ▪ Crowds flock to the West End of London to see 31-year-old Topol starring in the stage production of *Fiddler On the Roof* ▪ 31-year-old Rod Hull plays the role of Caretaker Clot in *The Super Flying Fun Show* on children's television in Australia ▪ ***Ha! Ha! Said The Clown*** ("... has the king lost his crown?") by Manfred Mann reaches number six in the pop chart ▪ ***Purple Haze*** ("... all in my brain. Lately things, they don't seem the same") by The Jimi Hendrix Experience peaks at number three ▪ 42-year-old Kenneth Kendall reads the news on BBC One television ▪ Unemployment rises to 631,000 ▪ Labour prime-minister Harold Wilson is under pressure to improve the country's economy, and to do so, quickly ▪ Britain applies for membership of the European Common Market ▪ "And then I go and spoil it all by saying..." ***Something Stupid*** ("... like, I love you") by 26-year-old Nancy Sinatra and 51-year-old Frank Sinatra reaches number one in the pop chart ▪ "Walk out. Girl don't you walk out, we've got things to say" - ***A Little Bit Me A Little Bit You*** by The Monkees is number four ▪ 12-year-old Keith Lyon is stabbed to death near Brighton. A manhunt gets underway - but the killer cannot be found ▪ The *Torrey Canyon* supertanker runs aground in the sea off Land's End and RAF planes are sent to bomb the wreckage to minimise any damage from the oil spillage ▪ 32-year-old singer Elvis Presley marries 21-year-old Priscilla Wagner in Las Vegas ▪ 28-year-old daredevil Evel Knievel jumps over sixteen cars on his motorbike at the Ascot Speedway in California ▪ Back in England - 24-year-old Jimi Hendrix sets fire to his guitar on stage at the Astoria ▪ 'The dazzle and madness of London today' - young lovers rush to the cinema to see Michelangelo Antonioni's film, *Blow-Up*. 29-year-old Vanessa Redgrave, 25-year-old Sarah Miles, 20-year-old Jane Birkin and 25-year-old David Hemmings are the stars ▪ 'Far out' and 'weird, man' - 'Tripping' young people dance and swirl in colourful gowns as 'happenings' take place in fields and parks all around the country ▪ "I wonder if one day that, you'll say that you care. If you say you love me madly, I'll gladly be there" -

Puppet On A String by 20-year-old barefoot singer Sandie Shaw wins the Eurovision Song Contest in Vienna - and the song becomes a number one hit in Britain ▪ "They call me..." ***Mellow Yellow*** by 20-year-old Donovan is number eight ▪ 16-year-old schoolboy Gordon Brown from Kirkcaldy is blinded in his left eye after receiving a blow to the head during a rugby match ▪ 29-year-old footballer Derek Dougan transfers from Matt Gillies' First Division Leicester City to Ronnie Allen's Second Division Wolverhampton Wanderers and scores a hat-trick against Hull City on his home debut at the Molineux ▪ 20-year-old Howard Kendall transfers from Jimmy Milne's Second Division Preston North End to Harry Catterick's First Division Everton for £80,000. Liverpool manager Bill Shankly has missed his chance to sign Kendall - a highly rated young left-half ▪ Scottish football supporters celebrate as Denis Law, Bobby Lennox and Jim McCalliog score the goals that give their team a 3-2 victory over Sir Alf Ramsey's world champions ▪ ***There's A Kind Of Hush*** ("... all over the world") by Herman's Hermits is number seven in the pop chart ▪ ***Jimmy Mack*** ("... when are you comin' back?") by Martha and the Vandellas reaches number twenty-one ▪ Hundred to one long-shot *Foinavon* wins the Grand National ▪ Oxford win the Boat Race for the third consecutive year ▪ 20-year-old soldier Leslie Grantham is sentenced to life imprisonment for the murder of a taxi driver in Germany ▪ Back in Britain - the road network continues to develop and grow ▪ The M1 motorway is extended from Nottingham to Mansfield ▪ The M4 motorway tunnel at Newport in South Wales is completed ▪ 58-year-old James Mason stars at cinemas in *The Deadly Affair* - a spy film based on a novel by 35-year-old John Le Carre ▪ 46-year-old Yul Brynner and 24-year-old Britt Ekland star in *The Double Man* ▪ Matt Busby's high-flying Manchester Utd thrash West Ham 1-6 at Upton Park (goal scorers: Charlton, Law 2, Crerand, Best, Foulkes) and Utd are the new champions of Division One. Alex Stepney, Tony Dunne, Bill Foulkes, Bobby Noble, David Sadler, Nobby Stiles, John Aston, Bobby Charlton, Paddy Crerand, David Herd, Denis Law and 20-year-old 'super' Georgie Best have all been outstanding for Utd ▪ "Ahh, you're drunk, your drunk, you silly ol' fool, as drunk as drunk can be" - ***Seven Drunken Nights*** by The Dubliners climbs to number seven in the pop chart ▪ "Hey there..." ***Georgy Girl*** ("... swinging down the street, so fancy free") by The Seekers is number three ▪ Johnny Carey's Nottingham Forest are runners-up - finishing four points behind Utd ▪ Spurs are third ▪ 25-year-old Ron Davies of Southampton is Division One's top scorer with thirty-seven goals ▪ Jimmy Hill's Coventry City (with John Tudor, Ernie Machin and 20-year-old Bobby Gould) are promoted to the First Division as champions of Division Two ▪ Ronnie Allen's Wolverhampton Wanderers (with Peter Knowles, Derek Dougan and 24-year-old Ernie Hunt) also gain promotion to the top division ▪ Dick Taylor's Aston Villa and Stan Mortensen's Blackpool are relegated to Division Two ▪ 29-year-old England goalkeeper Gordon Banks leaves Leicester City and joins Tony Waddington's Stoke City for £52,000 ▪ 23-year-old half-back Ian Moir transfers from Blackpool to Chester City for £10,000 ▪ ***I Can Hear The Grass Grow*** ("... I can hear the grass grow. I see rainbows in the evening") by The Move is number five on the weekly hit parade ▪ ***Pictures Of Lily*** ("... Lily, oh Lily") by The Who climbs to number four ▪ 48-year-old Bill Nicholson leads out the Tottenham Hotspur team and 39-year-old Tommy Docherty leads out the Chelsea team for the FA Cup final at Wembley. Spurs gain a 2-1 victory with goals from Jimmy Robertson and Frank Saul. A standing ticket for the east enclosure at the Empire Stadium costs ten shillings ▪ Jock Stein's Celtic FC defeat Inter Milan 2-1 in Lisbon and become the first British team to win the European Cup ▪ 34-year-old striker Dennis Viollet plays his final game for Stoke

City ▪ "Words, words. They're all we have to go on" - 29-year-old Tom Stoppard's new play, *Rosencrantz and Guildenstern Are Dead*, opens at the National Theatre ▪ The controversial *Son of Man* (written by Dennis Potter) is transmitted as part of BBC One's 'The Wednesday Play' series ▪ 57-year-old Mrs. Mary Whitehouse (from rural Worcestershire) sends a stern letter of complaint to Sir Hugh Greene, Director General of the corporation ▪ 39-year-old actor Roger Moore drives a white Volvo *P1800* motorcar in *The Saint* on ITV - 27-year-old Kate O'Mara features in a couple of episodes of the popular series ▪ 36-year-old comedian Les Dawson from Manchester appears on ITV's weekly talent contest, *Opportunity Knocks* ▪ 'The Motion Picture They Were Made For!' - 35-year-old Elizabeth Taylor stars alongside her husband, 41-year-old Richard Burton, at cinemas in *The Taming of the Shrew* ▪ "Each night before you go to bed, my baby, whisper a little prayer for me, my baby, and tell all the stars above, this is…" ***Dedicated To The One I Love*** by The Mamas and the Papas is number two in the pop chart ▪ ***Silence Is Golden*** ("… but my eyes still see") by The Tremeloes is new at number one ▪ 50-year-old McDonald Hobley and 32-year-old David Vine introduce a new series of *It's a Knockout* on BBC One. Teams from Llandudno and Colwyn Bay compete against one another in a closely fought contest on Sunday the twenty-first of May ▪ Thomas and Peggy Gallagher of Longsight, Manchester are proud parents of a newborn son, Noel ▪ The Jimi Hendrix Experience, Cream, Pink Floyd and The Move are all on the bill at 'Barbeque 67' - a Spring Bank Holiday festival at Spalding in Lincolnshire ▪ 25-year-old Brian Jones of the Rolling Stones is arrested and charged with possession of marijuana, methamphetamine and cocaine ▪ 'Look, there's the land of wheat and honey' - A new TV commercial proclaims, '*Sugar Puffs* are so crisp and good. That's why the kiddies all love them.'

Summer 1967 ❀

Flowers in Your Hair

Monarch:	Queen Elizabeth II (aged 41)
Prime-minister:	Harold Wilson (aged 51)
Chancellor:	James Callaghan (aged 55)
Home Secretary:	Roy Jenkins (aged 46)
Foreign Secretary:	George Brown (aged 52)
Football Manager:	Alf Ramsey (aged 47)
New car reg. suffix:	'F'

▪ 'Way out, man' - it's a summer of love, peace, drugs and hippies ▪ 33-year-old gangster twins Reginald and Ronald Kray expand their business empire - setting up a supply network for the mass distribution of purple hearts ▪ 51-year-old Labour prime-minister Harold Wilson flies to Canada for talks with Lester Pearson (Canadian prime-minister) in Ottawa. Mr. Wilson then visits *Expo '67* before moving onto Washington for talks with US president Lyndon B. Johnson ▪ Back in Britain - 11-year-old schoolboy John Lydon from Holloway in London smokes cigarettes behind the bicycle shed and feels bored with everything ▪ "Picture yourself in a boat on a river, with tangerine trees and marmalade skies" - The Beatles release their much awaited LP, *Sgt. Pepper's Lonely Hearts Club Band* ▪ Tracks on side one include: ***Lucy In The Sky With Diamonds***, ***Fixing A Hole*** and ***Being For The Benefit Of Mr. Kite!*** Tracks on side two include: ***When I'm Sixty-Four***, ***Lovely Rita*** and ***A Day In The Life*** ▪ The 'Fab Four' from Liverpool perform ***All You Need Is Love*** ("... Love is all you need") to 350 million viewers in the first ever worldwide 'live' television link ▪ Beautiful people travel to San Francisco - take hallucinogenic drugs, promote world peace and indulge in free love ▪ 28-year-old Scott McKenzie features on the front cover of the latest *New Musical Express* paper - advertising his new pop single, ***San Francisco (Be Sure To Wear Some Flowers In Your Hair)***. The song enters the hit parade at number thirteen ▪ BBC

Two broadcasts tennis from Wimbledon - and it's in colour! ▪ 28-year-old Ann Jones from Birmingham makes it through to the final - but loses (3-6, 4-6) to 23-year-old Billie Jean King on Centre Court ▪ The liberalisation programme of Labour's 46-year-old Home Secretary Roy Jenkins gathers momentum ▪ Homosexuality is decriminalised ▪ 'Sexual intercourse began - in nineteen sixty-three' - 44-year-old Philip Larkin from Coventry writes the first lines of a new poem called *Annus Mirabilis* ▪ Adults enjoy an evening at the cinema ▪ *The Long Duel* (with 47-year-old Yul Brynner, 53-year-old Trevor Howard and 21-year-old Charlotte Rampling) is now showing ▪ Schoolboys spend Saturday mornings in the stalls ▪ *Jule's Verne's Rocket to the Moon* (starring 58-year-old Burl Ives, 56-year-old Terry-Thomas and 41-year-old Lionel Jeffries) is on general release ▪ "Hi, hello, how are you?" - 22-year-old disc jockey Roger 'Twiggy' Day from Cheltenham spins discs for pirate radio station Caroline - broadcasting from a ship in the North Sea ▪ "We skipped the light fandango, turned cartwheels 'cross the floor. I was feeling kinda seasick, but the crowd called out for more" - ***A Whiter Shade Of Pale*** by Procol Harum (with, lead singer, 22-year-old Gary Brooker - formerly of The Paramounts) climbs to number one in the pop chart - and stays there for six weeks! ▪ "Dirty old river, must you keep rolling? Flowing into the night" - ***Waterloo Sunset*** by The Kinks (with, lead singer, 23-year-old Ray Davies) reaches number two ▪ Keith Richards (aged 23) is sentenced to a year in prison and Mick Jagger (aged 23) is sentenced to three-months - both on drug charges. The two men spend a night in jail, before being released on bail. The custodial sentences are then overturned at an appeal hearing ▪ 'Monkee Exclusive!' - 21-year-old Micky Dolenz and 21-year-old Davy Jones feature in the latest edition of *Rave* magazine ▪ 'FAB! It's cool' - Lyons Maid introduce the *FAB* ice-lolly ▪ Cricketers, John Edrich and Geoffrey Boycott stride out together to open the batting for England against India at Headingley. Boycott scores 246 not out, and Brian Close's team wins the match by six wickets ▪ 21-year-old wicket-keeper Alan Knott makes his Test Match debut at Trent Bridge ▪ 11-year-old schoolboy cricketer Ian Botham from Yeovil listens to commentary on a transistor radio ▪ "Here we come, walking down the street. We get the funniest looks from, everyone we meet. Hey! Hey! We're…" The Monkees play a concert at the Empire Pool in Wembley - and it's a sell-out ▪ ***Okay!*** by Dave Dee, Dozy, Beaky, Mick and Tich (a group of five friends from Wiltshire) is number four on the hit parade ▪ "Hey..." ***Carrie-Anne*** ("... what's your game now? Can anybody play?) by The Hollies is number three ▪ 34-year-old Andrew Gardner and 39-year-old Alastair Burnet present ITN's new *News at Ten* programme ▪ Seventy-two people are killed and twelve are seriously injured when a British Midlands' Argonaut passenger plane crashes at Stockport near Manchester. The aircraft was on its way back from Majorca when engine failure bought it down six miles short of the airport ▪ In other news, 51-year-old prime-minister Harold Wilson is a guest at the Llangollen International Music Eisteddfod, where he addresses a crowd of 30,000 people before taking lunch at a hotel in the town ▪ 38-year-old Liberal leader Jeremy Thorpe visits Aberystwyth as a guest of the newly formed Welsh Liberal party ▪ 41-year-old Queen Elizabeth II welcomes 61-year-old King Faisal of Saudi Arabia on an official state visit to Britain ▪ ***If I Were A Rich Man*** ("… Ya-da deedle-deedle, bubba-bubba deedle-deedle dum") by 31-year-old Topol climbs to number nine in the pop chart ▪ ***See Emily Play*** by Pink Floyd is number six ▪ "HOW!" - children rush home after school to watch *How* on ITV (presented by Jack Hargreaves, Jon Miller, Bunty James and 24-year-old Fred Dinenage) ▪ Town planners get creative - London Street in Norwich is the first shopping street in the country to be 'pedestrianised' ▪ "There goes my only possession…" ***There Goes My Everything*** by 31-year-old Engelbert Humperdinck spends twenty-nine weeks in the pop chart, peaking at number two ▪ ***All You Need Is Love*** ("… love. Love is all you need") by The Beatles spends three weeks at number one ▪ "The four kings of EMI are sitting stately on the floor. There are birds out on the sidewalk and a valet at the door" - ***Alternate Title*** by The Monkees climbs to number two ▪ 56-year-old Transport Minister Barbara Castle announces a new national speed limit on roads - it's set at 60 mph for single carriageways and 70 mph for dual carriageways ▪ A new elevated section of M1 motorway opens near Sheffield ▪ 'F' reg cars go on sale ▪ Four star leaded petrol is 5s/6d a gallon ▪ The latest Ford *Cortina MkII* 1300cc achieves 33 mpg and has a top speed of 82 mph ▪ The sun shines at Silverstone, where 31-year-old Jim Clark wins the British Grand Prix in a dark green and yellow Lotus racing car (number 5). 33-year-old John Surtees is sixth in a white and red Honda (number 7). 38-year-old Graham Hill is forced to retire from the race ▪ Long-haired hippies dance, trip and annoy narrow minded middle-aged people ▪ "If you're going to…" ***San Francisco (Be Sure To Wear Some Flowers In Your Hair)*** - by 28-year-old Scott McKenzie moves to number one on the hit parade - and stays at the top for four weeks ▪ "What did you do there? I got high-ie. What did you feel there? Well, I cr-i-ied. But why the tears there? I'll tell you why-ie-ie. It's all too beautiful" - ***Itchycoo Park*** by The Small Faces is number three ▪ Pink Floyd (21-year-old Syd Barrett, 23-year-old Roger Walters, 24-year-old Richard Wright and 23-year-old Nick Mason) release their first album, *Piper at the Gates of Dawn*, containing the tracks: ***Astronomy Domine***, ***Flaming***, ***Interstellar Overdrive*** and ***The Gnome*** ▪ 24-year-old guitarist Jimi Hendrix appears on the front cover of *Rave* magazine ▪ 34-year-old playwright Joe Orton is bludgeoned to death by his partner, Kenneth Halliwell. 41-year-old Halliwell then commits suicide, overdosing on sleeping tablets ▪ 36-year-old England cricketer Ken Barrington scores a century in each of the three Test Matches against Pakistan - and England win the series ▪ The Labour government's Marine Broadcasting Offences Act comes into effect - banning pirate radio stations ▪ The 'Big L' (Radio London) transmits ***A Day In The Life*** by The Beatles - and goes off air ▪ Radio Caroline changes its name to Radio Caroline International - and continues broadcasting ▪ "Let it please be him. Oh, dear God..." ***It Must Be Him*** ("... It must be him, or I shall die") by 27-year-old Vikki Carr reaches number two in the pop chart ▪ ***She'd Rather Be With Me*** by The Turtles peaks at number four ▪ "The things I do for England" - People flock to the cinema to see the new James Bond film, *You Only Live Twice.* 36-year-old Sean Connery is 007. 59-year-old Bernard Lee is M. 52-year-old Desmond Llewelyn is Q. 40-year-old Lois Maxwell is Miss Moneypenny. 47-year-old Donald Pleasance is Ernst Stavro Blofeld - a master criminal with a secret base inside a volcano ▪ ***You Only Live Twice*** ("... or so it seems. One life for yourself, and one for your dreams") - the theme song from the movie is performed by 27-year-old Nancy Sinatra ▪ 79-year-old Edith Evans stars at cinemas in *The Whisperers* - a film from 41-year-old director Bryan Forbes ▪ 34-year-old movie star Jayne Mansfield dies in a car crash in Louisiana ▪ Back in England - 25-year-old Fred West murders 18-year-old Anne McFall (who is pregnant with his child) and buries her body in a field at Much Marcle in Herefordshire ▪ In a separate incident, the body of a 7-year-old girl is discovered on Cannock Chase in Staffordshire. Police link this murder with last year's discovery of two other bodies at a nearby location and a major search operation gets underway to find the killer ▪ 41-year-old David Coleman presents *Grandstand* on BBC television ▪ American athlete Jim Ryun sets a new world record time of 3 minutes 51.1 seconds for running the mile ▪ 10-year-old schoolboy Sebastian Coe from Stratford-on-Avon puts on a vest and a pair of shorts and goes out for a run ▪ 11-year-old Steve Ovett from

Brighton does likewise ▪ "And it looks like I'm never gonna fall in love again" - ***I'll Never Fall In Love Again*** by 27-year-old Tom Jones is number four in the pop chart ▪ "My make-up is dry and it clags on my chin. I'm drowning my sorrows in whisky and gin" - ***Death Of A Clown*** by 20-year-old Dave Davies is number three ▪ *Soccer Star* - the weekly football magazine (now with a full-colour cover) is on sale at newsagents for 1s/3d ▪ 38-year-old Tommy Cummings is appointed manager of Second Division Aston Villa - and boosts his team's forward line by signing two strikers: 20-year-old Brian Greenhalgh and 27-year-old Brian Godfrey from Preston North End for a combined fee of £35,000 ▪ 32-year-old Brian Clough is appointed manager of Second Division Derby County - and signs 19-year-old centre-half Roy McFarland from Tranmere Rovers for £25,000 ▪ 26-year-old centre-forward Tony Hateley leaves Chelsea and joins Bill Shankly's Liverpool for £96,000 ▪ 21-year-old Keith Weller leaves Tottenham Hotspur and joins Millwall for £18,000 ▪ The new season gets underway ▪ 22-year-old goalkeeper Pat Jennings scores direct from a clearance kick in the Charity Shield, as Tottenham Hotspur draw 3-3 with Matt Busby's Manchester Utd in front of 54,106 at Old Trafford ▪ 21-year-old Colin Bell and 23-year-old Neil Young both score twice as Joe Mercer's Manchester City beat Southampton 4-2 in a Division One match in front of 22,002 at Maine Road ▪ Development work gets underway to build a brand new town at Milton Keynes in Buckinghamshire ▪ Families enjoy a night in, watching telly ▪ Elsie Tanner (played by 43-year-old Pat Phoenix) prepares for her wedding in *Coronation Street* ▪ Meg Richardson (played by 47-year-old Noele Gordon) takes a well earned holiday in *Crossroads* ▪ "Up, up and away. My beautiful, my beautiful balloon?" - ***Up, Up And Away*** by The Johnny Mann Singers climbs to number six in the pop chart ▪ "I could spend my life..." ***Just Loving You*** by 25-year-old Anita Harris also reaches number six ▪ 32-year-old Brian Epstein (manager of The Beatles) dies from an accidental drugs overdose in London - the tragedy is front-page headline news in the daily papers ▪ 18-year-old footballer Trevor Brooking makes his debut for Ron Greenwood's West Ham Utd in a 3-3 draw against Burnley in Division One ▪ Bill McGarry's Ipswich Town thrash Bristol City 5-0 in Division Two ▪ Arthur Turner's Oxford Utd beat Bury 5-4 in Division Three ▪ Allan Brown's Luton Town beat Barnsley 2-0 in Division Four ▪ 51-year-old Labour prime-minister Harold Wilson and his 46-year-old Home Secretary Roy Jenkins continue their programme of modernising Britain ▪ A controversial Private Member's Bill (from 29-year-old Liberal MP David Steel) calling for abortions to be legalised is debated in the House of Commons ▪ The economy remains weak ▪ The balance of payments figure has taken a turn for the worst ▪ The level of exports is considerably lower than the level of imports, and the main priority of Harold Wilson's Labour government is to turn this around and close the 'trade gap' ▪ "Another..." ***Pleasant Valley Sunday*** ("... here in status symbol land") by The Monkees is number eleven on the hit parade ▪ "And no-one's getting fat, except Mama Cass" - ***Creeque Alley*** by The Mamas and the Papas (John Phillips, Denny Doherty, Michelle Phillips and 25-year-old Mama Cass Elliot) is number nine ▪ A *Mini Cooper* belonging to pop singer Anita Harris is stolen from a street outside her flat in Kensington ▪ Bars and restaurants in Hastings are packed with 'groovy young cats' for the Bank Holiday Monday Festival of Music - The Kinks, The Crazy World of Arthur Brown, Geno Washington and Dave Dee, Dozy, Beaky, Mick & Tich are all on the bill ▪ *Barclays* bank installs the world's first cash dispensing machine at its branch in Enfield ▪ Schoolboys run errands for their fathers ▪ A pack of twenty *Guards* cigarettes costs 4s/3d ▪ A pack of twenty Player's *No. 6* is 3s/6d.

Autumn 1967

Captain Scarlet. Indestructible.

Monarch:	Queen Elizabeth II (aged 41)
Prime-minister:	Harold Wilson (aged 51)
Chancellor:	Roy Jenkins (aged 47)
Home Secretary:	James Callaghan (aged 55)
Foreign Secretary:	George Brown (aged 53)
Football Manager:	Alf Ramsey (aged 47)
New car reg. suffix:	'F'

▪ "I had..." ***The Last Waltz*** ("... with you. Two lonely people together") by Engelbert Humperdinck climbs to number one - and stays there for five weeks! ▪ The summer holidays end and children return to school ▪ *5a - Where we go, 5b - Out in the sun, 5c - More sounds to say* - youngsters improve their reading skills, using Ladybird's *Key Words* range of books ▪ Big boys play conkers on the playground ▪ "Grocer Jack, grocer Jack, get off your back, go into town, don't let them down. Oh no, no" - ***Excerpt From A Teenage Opera*** by 23-year-old Keith West from Dagenham is number two in the pop chart ▪ ***Heroes And Villians*** ("... just see what you've done") by The Beach Boys is number eight ▪ 63-year-old Joan Crawford, 36-year-old Diana Dors and 19-year-old Judy Geeson star at cinemas in *Berserk!* - a horror-thriller ▪ 'If what happens in 'The Penthouse' happened to you ... you wouldn't want to talk about it either!' - 45-year-old Terence Morgan and 30-year-old Suzy Kendall star in *The Penthouse* ▪ 18-year-old model Twiggy (with boyishly short hair and black painted eye-lashes) appears on the front cover of *Vogue* magazine ▪ Cases of foot and mouth disease are reported at farms in Shropshire and hundreds of animals are slaughtered ▪ Six small 'flying-saucers' are discovered in southern England ▪ 45-year-old Raymond Baxter presents *Tomorrow's World* on BBC One ▪ "This is the voice of the Mysterons. We know that you can hear us Earth" - Schoolboys are enthralled by *Captain Scarlet and the Mys-*

terons - a new programme on ITV ▪ "I am not a number! I am a free man!" - Adults are confused by *The Prisoner*, with 39-year-old Patrick McGoohan in the title role ▪ The weather turns cold ▪ People stay indoors, watching television ▪ The popular police drama *Z Cars* is broadcast twice weekly ▪ "Evening, all" - 71-year-old Jack Warner stars in a new series of *Dixon of Dock Green* ▪ Over on ITV - Elsie Tanner (played by 43-year-old Pat Phoenix) marries her old wartime sweetheart, Steve Tanner, in *Coronation Street* ▪ ***Reflections*** ("... of, the way life used to be") by Diana Ross and the Supremes is number seven in the pop chart ▪ ***Let's Go To San Francisco*** by The Flowerpot Men is number four ▪ 44-year-old Eamonn Andrews introduces ITV's *World of Sport* on Saturday afternoons ▪ 47-year-old wrestler Mick McManus deploys a forearm smash in a televised bout with 41-year-old Jackie Pallo ▪ 'Two, forty-seven. Music Power!' - 24-year-old Tony Blackburn welcomes listeners to the fab new sound of Radio One (on 247 medium wave) ▪ "I'm just sitting watching..." ***Flowers In The Rain*** by The Move is the first record played - the song reaches number two on the hit parade ▪ "And the lights all went out in..." ***Massachusetts*** by The Bee Gees is the second record played on the new radio station - the song reaches number one ▪ Radio One's team of disc jockeys keeps the pop music coming all day long - Jimmy Young, Kenny Everett, Simon Dee, Dave Cash, Pete Brady, Pete Murray and David Symonds play the most popular '45s' ▪ "Weeee love you. Of course we do" - the psychedelic sound of ***We Love You*** by the Rolling Stones (with, lead singer, 24-year-old Mick Jagger) is number eight in the pop chart ▪ "Don't turn around now" - ***From The Underworld*** by The Herd (with, lead singer, 17-year-old Peter Frampton) is number six ▪ "I looked to the sky where an elephant's eye was looking at me, from a bubblegum tree" - ***Hole In My Shoe*** by Traffic (with, lead singer, 19-year-old Steve Winwood) climbs to number two ▪ Crazy cats in purple trousers and paisley patterned shirts gather together to score mind bending drugs ▪ 'Blowing in the mind' - the cover design of the latest edition of *Oz* magazine is, like, far out, man ▪ 22-year-old Sheffield Utd striker Mick Jones transfers to Leeds Utd for £100,000 ▪ 18-year-old goalkeeper Peter Shilton scores a goal (direct from a clearance kick) as his Leicester City team beats Southampton 1-5 at The Dell ▪ 20-year-old striker John Radford bags a hat-trick as his Arsenal team beats Fulham 5-3 at Highbury ▪ Food technology moves on apace ▪ People devour exciting new 'salt 'n' vinegar' flavoured crisps from *Smiths* ▪ ***Baby Now That I've Found You*** ("... I can't let you go") by The Foundations is new at number one in the pop chart ▪ ***Zabadak!*** ("... Kara kakora ka karakak") by Dave Dee, Dozy, Beaky, Mick and Tich (a group of five friends from Wiltshire) is number three ▪ 33-year-old gangster Reginald Kray stabs Jack 'The Hat' McVitie to death in London - and members of the Kray Firm throw the body into the sea off Newhaven ▪ Britain's entry into the European Common Market is blocked for a second time - by France ▪ With the economy in such a poor state, and with a multi-million pound 'trade gap' in the balance of payments between imports and exports, prime-minister Harold Wilson is forced to devalue the pound against the dollar. The 51-year-old goes on TV to explain why - he says his decision will tackle the root cause of Britain's economic problems and will not affect the "pound in your pocket" ▪ 41-year-old Margaret Thatcher MP is promoted to Edward Heath's shadow Cabinet ▪ *The Dirty Dozen* with Lee Marvin, Charles Bronson and Telly Savalas is now showing at cinemas ▪ 'Bilko joins the 'Carry On' Legion!' - 56-year-old Phil Silvers appears alongside 25-year-old Anita Harris and the rest of the Carry On team in *Carry On Follow That Camel* ▪ Mickey the Monkey features on the front cover of the *Topper* comic - on sale at newsagents every Thursday for 5d ▪ "In and out of the..." ***Red Balloon*** ("...

Marry the farmer's daughter") by The Dave Clark Five soars to number seven in the pop chart ▪ "I've missed you..." ***You've Not Changed*** ("... at all") by 20-year-old Sandie Shaw stalls at number eighteen ▪ 21-year-old footballer 'super' Georgie Best scores twice as Manchester Utd beat Tottenham Hotspur 3-1 at Old Trafford ▪ Goalkeeper Gary Sprake keeps a clean sheet as hard-tackling Leeds Utd thrash Chelsea 7-0 at Elland Road ▪ "I let my heart fall into careless hands..." ***Careless Hands*** ("... they broke my heart in two") by 35-year-old Des O'Connor climbs to number six in the pop chart ▪ "So..." ***Let The Heartaches Begin*** ("... I can't help it, I can't win") by 26-year-old Long John Baldry is new at number one ▪ 41-year-old Queen Elizabeth II launches the luxury *QE2* liner at Clydebank ▪ Former prime-minister Clement Attlee dies aged 84 in London ▪ Housewives seek value for money in their weekly grocery shopping ▪ *Kwik Save* has a chain of thirteen supermarket stores and is still expanding ▪ Car drivers expect a little 'extra' from their motorcar ▪ Ford introduces the *Cortina 1600E* with *Rostyle* wheels, vinyl roof, burr walnut woodgrain-trimmed dash, bucket seats and a sports steering wheel - top speed is 98 mph and acceleration from 0-60 mph takes 12.5 seconds ▪ Jaguar *MKII* saloons are rebadged as *240* and *340* - the top-of-the-range 3.8 litre model is discontinued ▪ The Triumph *Herald* gets a face-lift and now has a bigger engine and improved performance ▪ People buy the latest 7-inch singles at *HMV* for 7s/3d ▪ "I know you've deceived me, now here's a surprise. I know that you have, 'cause there's magic in my eyes" - ***I Can See For Miles*** ("... and miles") by The Who is number ten on the hit parade ▪ "I feel it in my fingers, I feel it in my toes" - ***Love Is All Around*** by The Troggs is number five ▪ 2-year-old Mark McLachlan from Scotland has an afternoon nap, falling swiftly to sleep as a nearby transistor radio plays pop tunes ▪ Footballers, 30-year-old Bobby Charlton and 21-year-old 'super' Georgie Best are on the score-sheet for Matt Busby's Manchester Utd in a 4-0 victory over Noel Cantwell's Coventry City in front of 54,253 spectators at Old Trafford ▪ Three days later Utd lose 3-1 to Johnny Carey's Nottingham Forest in front of 49,946 at the City Ground ▪ The new film *Two for the Road* (with 37-year-old Audrey Hepburn and 31-year-old Albert Finney) is at cinemas ▪ 'There are two kinds of women … all the others and Raquel Welch as Fathom' - 27-year-old Raquel Welch (37-22-35) stars in spy comedy *Fathom* ▪ Hippies with painted faces preach peace and love, man ▪ "On a warm San Franciscan night. Old child, young child, feel alright. On a warm San Franciscan night" - ***San Franciscan Nights*** by 26-year-old Eric Burdon and the Animals is number seven in the pop chart ▪ "First..." ***There Is A Mountain*** ("... then there is no mountain, then there is") by 21-year-old Donovan is number eight ▪ BBC One TV programmes on a Saturday night include: *Tom and Jerry* - a cartoon from Hanna and Barbera; *Dr. Who* - starring 47-year-old Patrick Troughton; *The News and The Weatherman*; *Dee Time* - with 32-year-old Simon Dee; *The Monkees* - featuring 25-year-old Peter Tork, 24-year-old Mike Nesmith, 22-year-old Micky Dolenz and 21-year-old Davy Jones; *Dixon of Dock Green* - starring 72-year-old Jack Warner; *The Val Doonican Show* - with the popular 40-year-old singer from Ireland; *The Saturday Thriller*; and *Match of the Day* - presented by 47-year-old Kenneth Wolstenholme ▪ 29-year-old footballer Johnny Quinn transfers from Sheffield Wednesday to Rotherham Utd for £27,000 ▪ Joe Mercer's Manchester City move up to third in Division One after thrashing Sheffield Utd 5-2 in front of 31,922 spectators at Maine Road. Neil Young, Mike Summerbee, Colin Bell and Stan Bowles (2) score the goals for City ▪ 53-year-old Mercer signs 23-year-old Franny Lee from Bolton Wanderers for £60,000, to boost City's chances of winning their first league title in thirty-one years ▪ 27-year-old Jimmy 'Greavsie' Greaves is on the score-sheet for Bill Nicholson's Tottenham Hotspur in a 1-1 draw against Johnny Carey's Nottingham Forest ▪ At Westminster, MP's vote in favour of the Private Member's Bill introduced by 29-year-old David Steel and the Abortion Act gains royal assent - making it legal for pregnancies to be terminated in certain carefully defined circumstances ▪ 'A willful passionate girl and ... the three men who want her!' - 27-year-old actress Julie Christie stars alongside 29-year-old Terence Stamp, 50-year-old Peter Finch and 33-year-old Alan Bates in *Far from the Madding Crowd* ▪ 41-year-old Richard Burton and 35-year-old Elizabeth Taylor star in *Dr. Faustus* ▪ The Beatles release the double EP ***Magical Mystery Tour*** - tracks include: *The Fool On The Hill*, *Your Mother Should Know* and *I Am The Walrus* ("... goo goo, ga-joob") ▪ The Adams Singers perform beautiful songs on *Sing Something Simple* on Radio Two ▪ Men drive home from the pub after a pleasant evening drinking with friends in 'the Snug' at the Red Lion ▪ It's estimated that approximately 2,000 deaths a year are caused by drunken drivers, and the figure is increasing ▪ "Unless the rise is checked, we could have something like a million casualties a year by 1980" - 57-year-old Barbara Castle (Transport Mininster in Harold Wilson's Labour government) launches a new-fangled device called the 'breathalyzer' - a new 'blow-in-the-bag' contraption for police officers to use when testing a driver's blood alcohol concentration ▪ A brand new *TR5* sports car costs £1,260 (including taxes) and has a top speed of 117 mph ▪ The latest Hillman *Hunter* four-door saloon costs £862 (including taxes) and has a top speed of 90 mph ▪ The wonderful new Triumph *Herald 13/60* costs £727/17s/3d (including taxes) and has a top speed of 85 mph ▪ A pint of mild in the Red Lion is 1s/7d ▪ A whisky chaser is two shillings ▪ Drivers are wary of the new breathalyzer ▪ "Muraymints, Murraymints - the too good to hurry mints!" - a pack of *Murraymints* is 4d.

Christmas 1967

Colour TV is here

Monarch:	Queen Elizabeth II (aged 41)
Prime-minister:	Harold Wilson (aged 51)
Chancellor:	Roy Jenkins (aged 47)
Home Secretary:	James Callaghan (aged 55)
Foreign Secretary:	George Brown (aged 53)
Football Manager:	Alf Ramsey (aged 47)

▪ Cold air and freezing rain sweep in from the North ▪ People stay indoors ▪ 'Cheers!' - *Davenports* deliver beer at home ▪ A four-pint can of bitter costs 8s/6d ▪ A seven-pint can of bitter is 14s/3d ▪ Police stop suspected drunken drivers at the side of the road and ask them to blow into a breathalyzer ▪ ***If The Whole World Stopped Loving*** ("...the way you stopped loving me") by 40-year-old Val Doonican is number three on the weekly hit parade ▪ ***All My Love*** ("... came to nothing at all, my love") by 27-year-old Cliff Richard is number eight ▪ Noisy schoolboys spend Saturday mornings in the stalls at the local cinema ▪ 'Tarzan battles a madman's lust for power!' - 29-year-old Ron Ely is The King of the Jungle, and 12-year-old Manuel Padilla Jr. is Jai, in *Tarzan's Jungle Rebellion* ▪ 'The Jungle is JUMPIN'!' - Walt Disney's *The Jungle Book* is also now showing ▪ Thousands of animals are slaughtered as foot and mouth disease spreads across farms in the Midlands and in Wales. ▪ The economy is in a poor shape ▪ The bank lending rate is 8% ▪ The balance of payments deficit has grown to a whopping £495 million ▪ The number of coal miners in the UK has fallen to 390,000 and the level of coal production has fallen to 178 million tonnes ▪ Labour prime-minister Harold Wilson makes a change in his Cabinet ▪ 47-year-old Roy Jenkins moves from the Home Office to the Treasury to become the new Chancellor of the Exchequer ▪ 55-year-old Jim Callaghan moves in the opposite direction - vacating the Treasury to take up the role of Home Secretary ▪ Five secretarial employees (Joan Southwell, Brenda Mumford, Carol Ann Fry, Valerie White and Christine French) at Colt Ventilation and Heating in Surbiton offer to work an additional half hour each week - without pay ▪ "You say yes, I say no. You say stop and I say go, go, go. (Oh no). You say goodbye, and I say hello" - ***Hello Goodbye*** is The Beatles' thirteenth number one hit single - and the record remains in top spot for seven weeks! ▪ ***Everybody Knows*** ("... you're tired of me. Everybody knows we're through") by The Dave Clark Five is number two ▪ 24-year-old Carol White and 29-year-old Terence Stamp star at cinemas in *Poor Cow* - a film directed by 31-year-old Ken Loach and based on a novel by 31-year-old Nell Dunn ▪ 37-year-old Richard Harris, 30-year-old Vanessa Redgrave and 27-year-old David Hemmings star in *Camelot* - 'the musical' ▪ 10-year-old schoolboy Nigel Kennedy from Brighton practices the violin ▪ Aston Villa gain a 0-2 away victory over Rotherham Utd in Division Two of the Football League ▪ A new section of M1 motorway opens - and the 'national road' now runs uninterrupted for 147 miles between London and Rotherham ▪ Commercial television is thriving ▪ Ground breaking series *The Prisoner* continues, with viewers hoping to discover the true identify of Number 1; and to see if Number 6 will ever escape from The Village ▪ *The Golden Shot* airs on Sunday afternoons in the (ATV) Midland region, hosted by 39-year-old Bob Monkhouse and with 29-year-old 'Bernie the Bolt' - and his crossbow ▪ Over on BBC Two, a small number of programmes are now being broadcast in full-colour ▪ "Oh I could hide beneath the wings of the bluebird as she sings, the six o'clock alarm would never ring. But it rings and I rise, wipe the sleep out of my eyes, the shavin' razor's cold and it stings" - ***Daydream Believer*** by The Monkees climbs to number five in the pop chart ▪ "Just..." ***Walk Away Renee*** by The Four Tops reaches number three ▪ Soul singer Otis Redding dies aged 26 in a plane crash in Wisconsin, USA ▪ "You may not realise it but I was once a weak man / Once a week is enough for any man" - *Carry On Doctor*, starring 41-year-old Kenneth Williams as Doctor Tinkle and 44-year-old Hattie Jacques as Matron, draws crowds to the cinema. The obligatory sexy nurses are played by 30-year-old Barbara Windsor (36-24-34) and 25-year-old Anita Harris (34-23-34) ▪ 'A story as fresh as the girls in their minis ...' *To Sir, With Love*, starring 40-year-old Sidney Poitier, 19-year-old Judy Geeson, 23-year-old Christian Roberts and 30-year-old Suzy Kendall, goes on general release at picture houses ▪ 'They lie, they cheat, they destroy... they even try to love' - *The Comedians*, starring 53-year-old Alec Guinness, 46-year-old Peter Ustinov, 42-year-old Richard Burton and 35-year-old Elizabeth Taylor, is also now showing ▪ Popular British boxing champion 33-year-old Henry Cooper (aka Our 'Enry) is BBC's 'Sports Personality of the Year' ▪ Two heavy falls of snow leave the country white over ▪ Roads become blocked and many motorists are forced to abandon their cars ▪ A Riley *4/72* ('C' reg, in two-tone - green and beige) is stranded on the A52 near Sandiacre ▪ A Singer *Vogue* ('E' reg, in Regency Grey) is stuck on the B581 at Sutton in the Elms ▪ 21-year-old footballer Colin Bell scores (with an orange ball) as Joe Mercer's high-flying Manchester City play sublimely to beat Bill Nicholson's Tottenham Hotspur 4-1 in snowy conditions at Maine Road - the match will later come to be known as the 'Ballet on Ice' ▪ 22-year-old Leeds Utd goalkeeper Gary Sprake throws the ball into his own net by mistake and helps Liverpool to a 2-0 victory at Anfield ▪ 21-year-old 'super' Georgie Best scores twice as Matt Busby's Manchester Utd beat Wolverhampton Wanderers 4-0 in front of 63,450 people at Old Trafford ▪ 37-year-old Roy Sproson is on the score-sheet as Fourth Division Port Vale beat Halifax Town 2-1 in front of 6,946 at Vale Park ▪ Christmas Day arrives ▪ The 'must-have' toy for schoolboys on Christmas morning is *Action Man* from Palitoy ▪ The 'must-have' toy for girls is a *Sindy* doll from Pedigree Toys ▪ "I hope and pray that with God's help, this Christmas spirit of family unity will spread and grow among our Commonwealth family of nations" - the TV Christmas message from 41-year-old Queen Elizabeth II is broadcast in colour for the first time ▪ 'They're young... they're in love' - the movie *Bonnie and Clyde* (starring 30-year-old Warren Beattie and 26-year-old Faye Dunaway) is a huge box office hit ▪ *Just a Minute* is chaired by 44-year-old Nicholas Parsons on BBC radio ▪ ***Hello Goodbye*** by The Beatles' remains at number one in the pop chart ▪ ***Here We Go Round The Mulberry Bush*** by Traffic is number eight ▪ ***Thank U Very Much*** ("... for the Aintree Iron. Thank you very much. Thank you very, very, very much") by The Scaffold is number four ▪ 19-year-old footballer Trevor Brooking scores his first league goal for West Ham Utd in a 4-2 victory over Leicester City at Upton Park ▪ "Roll-up. Roll-up for the Mystery Tour" - The Beatles leave television viewers bemused on Boxing Day evening when the weird and confusing new film *Magical Mystery Tour* is broadcast on BBC One ▪ *Do Not Adjust Your Set* is new on ITV - featuring Eric Idle, Michael Palin, Terry Jones and with 27-year-old David Jason as super-hero 'Captain Fantastic' ▪ *Bedazzled!* is at cinemas - with 30-year-old Peter Cook as the Devil and with 32-year-old Dudley Moore as Stanley Moon ▪ 'I'm Backing Britain' - a patriotic campaign to boost the economy is underway as more employees at Colt Ventilation and Heating in Surbiton begin working extra hours - without pay! ▪ Staff at hundreds of other companies across the country follow suit ▪ 27-year-old pop star Tom Jones is number two on the hit parade with ***I'm Coming Home*** ("... to your loving heart") ▪ Young footballer Trevor Brooking scores his second league goal for West Ham Utd in another 2-4 victory over Leicester City - this time, at Filbert Street in the return league fixture between the two clubs ▪ The average price of a house in the UK is £3,800 ▪ Men enjoy an hour or two in the pub ▪ A pint of Watney's *Red Barrel* is 2s/3d ▪ Women finish the washing-up and other household chores, before sitting down to relax for just a few minutes ▪ Adverts say, 'Now hands that do dishes can feel soft as your face, with mild green *Fairy Liquid*' ▪ The *Twix* chocolate bar is new.

New Year 1968

The all new Ford Escort

Monarch:	Queen Elizabeth II (aged 41)
Prime-minister:	Harold Wilson (aged 51)
Chancellor:	Roy Jenkins (aged 47)
Home Secretary:	James Callaghan (aged 55)
Foreign Secretary:	George Brown (aged 53)
Football Manager:	Alf Ramsey (aged 48)
New car reg. suffix:	'F'

▪ Snow ploughs and gritting lorries get stuck as heavy flurries of snow spread rapidly over much of the country ▪ Construction work on a new section of the M1 motorway near Barnsley comes to a temporary halt ▪ Eleven people are killed when a train collides with a lorry on a level crossing at Hixon in Staffordshire ▪ "I am a little..." ***Tin Soldier*** ("... that wants to jump into your fire") by The Small Faces is number fourteen in the pop chart ▪ "I'd sing the song that I sang then about the time they called me..." ***Jackie*** by 25-year-old Scott Walker is number twenty-four ▪ 20-year-old Peter Noone (from Herman's Hermits) and 77-year-old Stanley Holloway star at cinemas in *Mrs. Brown, You've Got a Lovely Daughter* ▪ 31-year-old Tommy Steele and 24-year-old Julia Foster star in the musical *Half A Sixpence* ▪ 'Nobody knows what he does … just that he has 100 girls to do it with!' - 46-year-old Dirk Bogarde and 29-year-old Susannah York star in spy film *Sebastian* ▪ Severe storms at sea lead to the sinking of three fishing trawlers from Hull ▪ The *St Romanus* goes down in the North Sea; and the *Kingston Peridot* and *Ross Cleveland* both perish off the coast of Iceland ▪ A total of fifty-eight fishermen lose their lives ▪ Families of the victims begin a campaign to improve the safety practices of the British fishing industry ▪ 37-year-old Peter Woods reads the news on BBC One ▪ A test Polaris nuclear missile is fired from HMS *Resolution* - Britain's state-of-the-art ballistic submarine ▪ Police officers at Scotland Yard have cause to celebrate when 35-year-old train robber Charlie Wilson is caught after nearly four years on the run. Wilson is sent back to prison to resume his thirty year sentence ▪ Bruce Reynolds and Ronnie Biggs remain at large ▪ "Bonnie and Clyde advanced their reputation, and made the graduation into the banking business" - ***The Ballad Of Bonnie And Clyde*** by 24-year-old Georgie Fame is number one on the hit parade ▪ "Guess I could find somebody too, but I don't want no one but you. How could you leave without regret…" ***Am I That Easy To Forget*** by 31-year-old Engelbert Humperdinck is number three ▪ 22-year-old footballer Martin Chivers transfers from Southampton to Tottenham Hotspur for £125,000 and scores on his debut for Spurs in a 1-2 victory over Sheffield Wednesday. (27-year-old Jimmy 'Greavsie' Greaves is also on the score-sheet) ▪ ***Bend Me Shape Me*** ("… any way you want me. Long as you love me, it's alright") by Amen Corner is new at number three in the pop chart ▪ ***Nights In White Satin*** ("… never reaching the end") by The Moody Blues is number nineteen ▪ Some people hold high aspirations ▪ A new colour TV license costs £10 a year - that's double the price of a black and white license ▪ A repeat of *The Virginian* (starring James Drury) is on BBC One ▪ Over on ITV, the final episode of *The Prisoner* sees Number 6 (played by 39-year-old Patrick McGoohan) being set free. Or does it? - it's all rather confusing ▪ Elsie Tanner's marriage breaks down after just three months - and the popular character returns to *Coronation Street* where she's comforted by her old friend Len Fairclough ▪ 57-year-old Mrs. Mary Whitehouse (from rural Worcestershire) is outraged ▪ "Open up your eyes, then you'll realise, here I stand with my..." ***Everlasting Love*** by Love Affair is number one in the pop chart ▪ ***She Wears My Ring*** ("... to show the world that she belongs to me") by Solomon King climbs to number three ▪ 27-year-old 'pin-up' Raquel Welch (37-22-35) appears on the front cover of *Parade* - the weekly paper on sale at newsagents every Wednesday for a shilling ▪ Matt Gillies' Leicester City football team beats high-flying Manchester City 4-3 in the Fourth Round of the FA Cup in front of 41,892 at Filbert Street. (8-year-old Roy Lavery from Leicester attends the match with his dad) ▪ 17-year-old Richard Branson launches a magazine for students ▪ ***Judy In Disguise (With Glasses)*** by John Fred and the Playboy Band is number three in the pop chart ▪ "Give me pennies, I'll take anything. Now listen while I play, my..." ***Green Tambourine*** by The Lemon Pipers climbs to number seven ▪ The economy remains sluggish ▪ 47-year-old Chancellor of the Exchequer Roy Jenkins works hard at Number 11 Downing Street - trying to turn the country's fortunes around ▪ 51-year-old Labour prime-minister Harold Wilson endorses the 'I'm Backing Britain' campaign - and encourages people to work extra hours without additional pay ▪ Housewives redeem their *Green Shield Stamps* at *Green Shield Stamps* shops ▪ A *Moulinex* electric foodmixer (complete with plastic bowl) is 7 books ▪ An electric blanket for a double-bed is 7¾ books ▪ A *Bex Bissell* carpet sweeper is 5 books ▪ Hippies smoke marijuana and ponder the meaning of life ▪ The Beatles travel to India to study transcendental meditation ▪ "When I look up to the sky, I see your eyes, a funny kind of yellow" - ***Pictures Of Matchstick Men***, the debut single from Status Quo, reaches number seven in the pop chart ▪ "Come all without. Come all within. You'll not see nothing like the..." ***Mighty Quinn*** by Manfred Mann is number one for two weeks ▪ 'It's rough, raw and randy' - 19-year-old Dennis Waterman, 30-year-old Suzy Kendall and 21-year-old Maureen Lipman star at cinemas in *Up the Junction* ▪ *The Herbs* is a new TV programme for children and features Parsley the Lion and Dill the Dog ▪ The US intensifies its bombing campaign in Vietnam ▪ Banners say, 'Make Love Not War' ▪ 23-year-old footballer Franny Lee scores four goals in four games for Joe Mercer's high-flying Manchester City ▪ 21-year-old 'super'

Georgie Best sores six goals in five games for Matt Busby's Manchester Utd ▪ 25-year-old Ron Davies and 19-year-old Mick Channon score for Ted Bates' Southampton in a 2-2 draw against Johnny Carey's Nottingham Forest ▪ There's a flurry of activity on the transfer market ▪ 21-year-old striker Bobby Gould leaves Noel Cantwell's Coventry City and joins Bertie Mee's Arsenal for £90,000 ▪ 20-year-old full-back Derek Parkin leaves Tom Johnston's Huddersfield Town and joins Ronnie Allen's Wolverhampton Wanderers for £80,000 ▪ 21-year-old defender David Webb leaves Ted Bates' Southampton and joins Dave Sexton's Chelsea for £60,000 ▪ 23-year-old winger Mike Trebilcock leaves Harry Catterick's Everton and joins George Smith's Portsmouth for £40,000 ▪ 25-year-old centre-forward Frank Clarke transfers from Arthur Rowley's Shrewsbury Town to Alec Stock's Queens Park Rangers for £34,000 ▪ "You're the lady, you're the lady that I love / I'm the lady, the lady, who?" - ***Cinderella Rockefella*** by 26-year-old Esther Ofarim and her husband, 30-year-old Abi Ofarim, spends three weeks at number one on the hit parade ▪ "I-ah, could have built a world around her" - ***Little Girl*** by The Troggs enters the chart at number fifty ▪ Ron Greenwood's West Ham Utd football team thrashes Vic Buckingham's Fulham 7-2 in front of 31,248 spectators at Upton Park. 19-year-old Trevor Brooking and 26-year-old Geoff Hurst both score twice. 26-year-old (captain) Bobby Moore, 24-year-old Martin Peters and 24-year-old Brian Dear are also on the score-sheet for 'The Hammers' ▪ Actors: Eric Sykes, Tommy Cooper, Jimmy Edwards and Roy Castle appear in the silent comedy *The Plank* ▪ Saturday evening television programmes on ATV include: *Time for Blackburn* - with 25-year-old Tony Blackburn; *Doddy's Music Box* - with 40-year-old Ken Dodd; and a brand new series of *Life with Cooper* - starring 46-year-old Tommy Cooper ▪ Motoring technology moves on apace ▪ The ageing Ford *Anglia 105E* is replaced by the all new Ford *Escort* - the *1100 Deluxe* model costs £687, comes with two wing mirrors, a top speed of 80 mph and the capability to accelerate from 0-60 mph in 21.5 seconds ▪ The new Vauxhall *Victor* has bucket seats in the front, instead of the usual bench seat ▪ The latest Ford *Cortina Super* has the option of fully reclining front seats ▪ 'I spy with my little eye, something beginning with SEX … and I mean to put a stop to it' - 59-year-old Bette Davis and 34-year-old Sheila Hancock star at cinemas in *The Anniversary* ▪ 36-year-old Stephen Boyd, 24-year-old Camilla Sparv and 47-year-old Leo McKern star in *Assignment K* - a thriller from 56-year-old director Val Guest ▪ "Six guineas a day plus expenses" - 49-year-old Alfred Burke stars as Private Investigator Frank Marker in a new series of *Public Eye* on ATV ▪ Alf Garnett (played by 42-year-old Warren Mitchell) shouts the words "bloody God" on BBC One's *Till Death Us Do Part* ▪ 57-year-old Mrs. Mary Whitehouse (from rural Worcestershire) writes to the Director of Public Prosecutions asking for action to be taken against the BBC for blasphemy ▪ Young people groove and gyrate to the latest pop sounds ▪ *Defiant* transistor radios, radiograms and record players (with four-speed auto-changers) are on sale now at *Co-Op* stores ▪ "Run and get the fire brigade, get the fire brigade, see the buildings really start to burn! Ooh" - ***Fire Brigade*** by The Move (with, lead singer, 21-year-old Roy Wood, and, drummer, 23-year-old Bev Bevan) climbs to number three in the pop chart ▪ "My, my, my, Delilah. Why, why, why…" ***Delilah*** by 27-year-old Tom Jones peaks at number two ▪ Stoke City beat West Ham Utd 2-0 at the Victoria Ground, and then lose their next seven football matches in Division One ▪ 23-year-old striker Peter Noble leaves Joe Harvey's Newcastle Utd and joins Danny Williams' Swindon Town for £8,000 ▪ 53-year-old Alan Brown returns to Roker Park for a second stint as manager of Sunderland ▪ Adverts say, 'Beanz Meanz Heinz'.

Spring 1968

Pan's People on Top of the Pops

Monarch:	Queen Elizabeth II (aged 42)
Prime-minister:	Harold Wilson (aged 52)
Chancellor:	Roy Jenkins (aged 47)
Home Secretary:	James Callaghan (aged 56)
Foreign Secretary:	Michael Stewart (aged 61)
Football Manager:	Alf Ramsey (aged 48)
New car reg. suffix:	'F'

▪ 47-year-old Chancellor of Exchequer Roy Jenkins delivers his first Budget for Harold Wilson's Labour government ▪ Large tax increases are announced on petrol, alcohol and tobacco ▪ Road tax goes up from £19/5s/- a year to £25/- ▪ Jenkins says the country is in for two years of 'hard slog' ▪ 57-year-old Barbara Castle moves from the Department of Transport to become the new Secretary of State for Employment and Productivity ▪ The 'I'm Backing Britain' campaign continues ▪ People pin union jack badges to their lapels ▪ Tens of thousands of workers put in extra hours without pay ▪ "I'm backing Britain, yes I'm backing Britain, we're all backing Britain today. The feeling is growing, so let's keep it going, the good times are blowing our way" - 40-year-old Bruce Forsyth sings ***I'm Backing Britain*** ▪ On Thursday the twenty-eighth of March, the Labour government suffers defeats in three by-elections - with all seats falling to Conservative opposition ▪ 33-year-old Kenneth Baker takes Acton ▪ 34-year-old Keith Speed takes Meriden ▪ 48-year-old Donald Williams is triumphant in Dudley ▪ 39-year-old Tony Richardson's new movie, *The Charge of the Light Brigade*, draws crowds to the cinema. 54-year-old Trevor Howard, 64-year-old Sir John Gielgud, 31-year-old Vanessa Redgrave and 26-year-old David Hemmings are the stars ▪ Five people die when a BOAC Boeing *707* passenger jet catches fire during take-off from Heathrow ▪ 22-year-old footballer Martin Chivers is on the score-sheet for Tottenham Hotspur in a 6-1 victory over his old club, Southampton ▪ A group of five friends from Wiltshire reach number one in the pop chart - ***The Legend Of Xanadu*** by Dave Dee, Dozy, Beaky, Mick and Tich is top of the hit parade ▪ ***(Sittin' On) The Dock Of The Bay*** ("… watchin' the tide roll away") by the late Otis Redding is number three ▪ Thousands of people gather in Grosvenor Square to protest against the war in Vietnam ▪ Banners say, 'End British Support for US Imperialist War' ▪ "Jennifer Juniper lives upon the hill. Jennifer Juniper sitting very still" - ***Jennifer Juniper*** by 22-year-old Donovan climbs to number five in the pop chart ▪ 'Would you give a home to a girl like Luci?' - 15-year-old Linda Hayden, 36-year-old Diana Dors, 33-year-old Keith Barron and 34-year-old Ann Lynn star at cinemas in *Baby Love* ▪ 'The Race is On!' - 24-year-old Barry Evans and 19-year-old Judy Geeson star in Clive Donner's *Here We Go Round the Mulberry Bush* ▪ 47-year-old Richard 'Dicky' Attenborough and 26-year-old David Hemmings star in *Only When I Larf* - a film from 57-year-old director Basil Dearden ▪ 39-year-old Dr. Martin Luther King is shot and killed in Memphis, Tennessee. Murderer James Earl Ray flees to London where he's apprehended and extradited back the US ▪ 55-year-old Enoch Powell MP makes a speech in Birmingham predicting, 'Rivers of Blood.' Powell is promptly sacked from Edward Heath's shadow Cabinet ▪ British Motor Holdings (with the Morris, Austin and Jaguar marques) merges with Leyland Motor Corp (with Standard, Triumph and Rover marques) to form The British Leyland Motor Corporation. 54-year-old Sir Donald Stokes is chairman of the new organisation ▪ A *MKII* version of the popular Morris and Austin *1100* motorcar is now available - with a 1300cc engine also added to the range ▪ The latest MG *Midget* (two-seater, soft-top) has a 1275cc engine, producing a top speed of 93 mph and an acceleration time of 13.1 seconds from 0-60 mph ▪ Four star leaded petrol is six shillings a gallon ▪ Construction work is underway on the new M62 motorway. The new road will be the

UK's highest motorway, carrying vehicles across the Pennines between Lancashire and Yorkshire ▪ Progressive middle-class men purchase cars designed for comfort and speed ▪ A stylish, new ('F' reg) Sunbeam *Rapier Fastback* costs £1,340/4s/9d, has a top speed of 103 mph and accelerates from 0-60 mph in 12.8 seconds ▪ A Ford *Corsair 2000E* costs £1,107/18s/4d, has a top speed of 97 mph and accelerates from 0-60 mph in 13.5 seconds ▪ Rakish, divorced men, with an eye for the ladies, purchase sports cars ▪ A Triumph *Spitfire MKIII* costs £745/15s/-, has a top speed of 100 mph and can reach 60 mph in 12.5 seconds ▪ Bearded university lecturers purchase affordable, practical cars ▪ A new Wartburg *Knight* costs £639/13s/1-, has a two-stroke engine, a top speed of 81 mph and comes complete with mudflaps ▪ Spring sunshine arrives ▪ The clocks go forward by one hour ▪ 42-year-old Detective Chief Superintendent Leonard 'Nipper' Read and his police team conduct an early morning raid on suspected London criminals ▪ 34-year-old gangster twins Reginald and Ronald Kray are among the eighteen men arrested ▪ *Red Alligator* wins the Grand National, at odds of one-hundred to seven ▪ "On white horses, let me ride away, to my world of dreams so far away" - the theme tune from children's TV programme ***The White Horses*** is a hit song for Jacky ▪ 23-year-old footballer Terry Cooper scores the only goal as Don Revie's hard-tackling Leeds Utd defeat Bertie Mee's Arsenal 1-0 in the League Cup final at Wembley ▪ 25-year-old Ernie Hunt transfers from Harry Catterick's Everton to Noel Cantwell's Coventry City for £65,000 ▪ 24-year-old centre-forward Willie Irvine transfers from Harry Pott's Burnley to Second Division Preston North End for £45,000 ▪ Dads watch excitedly as sexy dance troupe Pan's People (with Louise, Flick, Babs, Ruth, Andi and Dee Dee) makes its TV debut on *Top of the Pops* ▪ 18-year-old singer Mary Hopkin appears on *Opportunity Knocks!* ▪ 11-year-old Mark E. Smith from Prestwich in Manchester plays records in his bedroom ▪ The avant-garde rock/pop music on Velvet Underground's new album, *White Light/White Heat*, piques the interest of a small number of people - the LP fails to make it into the British pop chart ▪ "Oh no Mrs. Robinson, I find you very desirable" - *The Graduate*, starring 30-year-old Dustin Hoffman, 36-year-old Anne Bancroft and a red Alfa Romeo *Spider* motorcar, is now showing at cinemas ▪ 'Mother, I'm not a child' - 46-year-old Deborah Kerr and 58-year-old David Niven star in *Prudence and the Pill* ▪ The Abortion Act 1967 comes into force and the termination of pregnancies is now lawful in certain circumstances ▪ ***Lady Madonna*** ("… children at your feet, wonder how you manage to make ends meet") by The Beatles enters the Top 50 at number eleven and climbs to number one the following week ▪ "She flies like a bird, oh me, oh my-ie" - ***I Can't Let Maggie Go*** by The Honeybus soars to number eight ▪ The current television series of *Public Eye* comes to an end. Popular fictional Private Investigator Frank Marker (played by 50-year-old Alfred Burke) is sentenced to two and half years in prison for receiving stolen goods ▪ A new silver one shilling coin (embossed with the wording '5 new pence') and a new silver two shilling coin (embossed with the wording '10 new pence') are introduced - in preparation for decimalisation in three years' time ▪ The country's motorway network continues to expand ▪ The government announces plans to build a further 166 miles of carriageway over the next twelve months ▪ Additions will be made to the M5, M6 and M56 motorways ▪ Rover introduces a V8 3500cc version of the popular *P6* luxury motorcar. Top speed is 114 mph and acceleration from 0-60 mph takes 10.5 seconds ▪ 32-year-old champion racing driver Jim Clark is killed in a Formula Two race in Germany after crashing his Lotus into trees at Hockenheim. Fellow racing drivers are devastated by the death ▪ Clark's close friends Graham Hill and Jackie Stewart call for greater safety measures in motor sport - and a campaign gets underway to force race operators to take action ▪ "They call her..." ***Valleri*** by The Monkees is new at number nineteen on the hit parade ▪ ***If I Were A Carpenter*** ("... and you were a lady. Now, would you marry me anyway? Would you have my baby?") by The Four Tops is number seven ▪ 42-year-old David Coleman and 35-year-old Frank Bough take turns presenting *Grandstand* on BBC One on Saturday afternoons ▪ On the final day of the Division One football season - Joe Mercer's high-flying Manchester City win 3-4 away at Newcastle Utd to pip Matt Busby's Manchester Utd to the League title. Ken Mulhearn, Tony Book, Mike Doyle, George Heslop, Glyn Pardoe, Alan Oakes, Colin Bell, Tony Coleman, Franny Lee, Neil Young and 25-year-old Mike Summerbee have all been outstanding for City. The blue side of Manchester celebrates late into the night! ▪ The Small Faces feature on the front cover of the latest *New Musical Express* paper ▪ 'The Station of the Stars!' - 19-year-old DJ Noel Edmonds spins discs on Radio Luxembourg ▪ "Put your hands in the air. Simple Simon says, shake them all about" - ***Simon Says*** by the1910 Fruitgum Company is number two in the pop chart ▪ "I love..." ***Jennifer Eccles*** ("... I know that she loves me") by The Hollies is number seven ▪ The FA Cup final takes place at Wembley on Saturday the eighteenth of May. 26-year-old centre-forward Jeff Astle scores the only goal as Alan Ashman's West Bromwich Albion beat Harry Catterick's Everton 1-0 (after extra-time). 30-year-old captain Graham Williams lifts the famous silver trophy for West Brom. A ticket for the standing enclosure at the Empire Stadium costs ten shillings ▪ ***Congratulations*** ("... and jubilations, I want the world to know I'm happy as can be") by 27-year-old Cliff Richard is number one in the pop chart ▪ ***Step Inside Love*** ("... Step inside love! Step inside love! I want you to stay") by 25-year-old Cilla Black is number eight ▪ 35-year-old Yoko Ono attends Abbey Road studios as The Beatles record their new album ▪ Tensions grow between John Lennon, Paul McCartney, Ringo Starr and George Harrison ▪ 26-year-old Brian Jones of the Rolling Stones is arrested and charged with possession of cannabis. Jones avoids a prison sentence and is fined £50 plus £105 costs ▪ Four people are killed in a gas explosion at Ronan Point 'hi-rise' tower block in Canning Town ▪ "And I think to myself..." ***What A Wonderful World*** by 67-year-old Louis Armstrong moves to the top of the pop chart - and stays there for four weeks ▪ ***Lazy Sunday Afternoon*** ("... I've got no mind to worry. I close my eyes and drift away") by The Small Faces (21-year-old Steve Marriott, 19-year-old Kenny Jones, 22-year-old Ian McLagan and 22-year-old Ronnie Lane) is number two ▪ *Ostrich Country*, the second novel from 33-year-old writer David Nobbs, is published ▪ People enjoy a night in, watching the TV 'box' ▪ Grumpy Albert Tatlock's house is burgled on ITV's *Coronation Street* ▪ 37-year-old Jimmy Ellis plays Sgt Bert Lynch in 'The Guilty Ones' - the latest episode from BBC's *Z Cars* ▪ 41-year-old Katie Boyle and 33-year-old David Vine present *It's A Knockout* on BBC One. A team representing the town of Worthing outwits a team representing Cheltenham, winning by ten points to eight, after competing in events such as: Swinging Words, Wall Game, Self Service and Flower Pot Tennis. (The victorious team from Worthing now qualifies for the Jeux Sans Frontieres competition, which will be held in France later this year) ▪ 41-year-old disc jockey Jimmy Savile takes his turn to present *Top of the Pops* on Thursday evenings ▪ "Young girl, get out of my mind. My love for you is way out of line, better run girl. You're much too..." ***Young Girl*** by Union Gap featuring Gary Puckett moves to the top of the hit parade ▪ "Everyday I wake up, then I start to break up. Lonely is..." ***A Man Without Love*** by 32-year-old Engelbert Humperdinck reaches number two ▪ "It's just too good to be true..." ***Can't Take My Eyes Off You*** by 40-year-old Andy Williams is number eight ▪ Loving couples canoodle in the back row at cinemas ▪ A ticket in the stalls costs 4s/9d ▪ 16-year-old Olivia Hussey and 17-year-old Leonard Whiting star in *Romeo and Juliet* ▪ 45-year-old Derek Aylward and 18-year-old Francoise Pascal star in *School for Sex* ▪ Celebrity couple and Hollywood film stars, 42-year-old Richard Burton and his wife, 36-year-old Elizabeth Taylor, are pictured together on the front cover of the latest edition of *TV Times* - available now at newsagents for eightpence ▪ ***I Don't Want Our Loving To Die*** by The Herd (with, lead singer, 18-year-old Peter Frampton - aka 'The Face of 1968') is number five in the pop chart ▪ 'Peace Not War' - Forty students brandishing placards gather together to demonstrate against the war in Vietnam as 52-year-old prime-minister Harold Wilson and his wife, Mary, pay a visit to Edinburgh ▪ The economy is in a poor shape ▪ The Labour government imposes new lending restrictions on banks ▪ Share prices plummet and the pound falls to a new all-time low ▪ 49-year-old merchant banker Major Jocelyn Hambro donates £11,000 to the Conservative party and describes Mr. Wilson as "the worst prime-minister since Lord North." ▪ "So much to do..." ***If I Only Had Time*** by 21-year-old John Rowles from New Zealand moves down the weekly pop chart, after peaking at number three ▪ ***Sleepy Joe*** by Herman's Hermits is number twelve ▪ Matt Busby's Manchester Utd football team makes it through to the final of the European Cup after beating Hibernians of Malta, Sarajevo, Gornik Zabrze and Real Madrid ▪ The final is played-out on a warm Wednesday evening at Wembley, where 30-year-old Bobby Charlton (2), 22-year-old 'super' Georgie Best and 19-year-old Brian Kidd score the goals to give Utd a 4-1 victory over Benfica (after extra-time). The red side of Manchester celebrates late into the night! ▪ "The sun always shines down in my…" ***Rainbow Valley*** by Love Affair climbs to number five on the hit parade ▪ Adverts proclaim, 'Happiness is a cigar called *Hamlet*'.

Summer 1968

Jumpin' Jack Flash, it's a gas, gas, gas

Monarch:	Queen Elizabeth II (aged 42)
Prime-minister:	Harold Wilson (aged 52)
Chancellor:	Roy Jenkins (aged 47)
Home Secretary:	James Callaghan (aged 56)
Foreign Secretary:	Michael Stewart (aged 61)
Football Manager:	Alf Ramsey (aged 48)
New car reg. suffix:	'G'

▪ The weather is mostly dull and wet ▪ 37-year-old Lionel Tutt wins a beer drinking competition at Bilton near Hull - downing seventeen pints of Younger's *Tartan* keg beer in just one hour ▪ Schools put on sports days and jamborees ▪ 7-year-old Sean O'Meara from Rugeley comes second from last in the egg and spoon race ▪ "How tickled I am!" - 40-year-old entertainer Ken Dodd appears in summer season at Blackpool ▪ 44-year-old comedian Tony Hancock commits suicide in Australia ▪ *Witchfinder General* (with 57-year-old Vincent Price) is now showing at cinemas ▪ 25-year-old Cilla Black stars in *Work is a Four Lettered Word* ▪ 9-year-old schoolboy Steven Patrick Morrissey listens to a transistor radio at home in Manchester ▪ 4-year-old Johnny Maher peers longingly at a toy wooden guitar hanging in the window at Emily's corner shop ▪ ***Do You Know The Way To San Jose*** ("...I've been away so long, I may go wrong and lose my way") by 27-year-old Dionne Warwick is number eight in the pop chart ▪ "Wheel's on fire. Rolling down the road" - ***This Wheel's On Fire*** by Julie Driscoll and the Brian Auger Trinity is number ten ▪ 39-year-old racing driver Graham Hill wins the Grand Prix at Monaco in a red and white *Gold Leaf* sponsored Lotus (number 9) ▪ 22-year-old footballer 'super' Georgie Best is banned from driving for six months after crashing his Jaguar into another car ▪ 26-year-old footballer Alan Mullery is the first player to be sent off for England, as Sir Alf Ramsey's team (G Banks, K Newton, Wilson, Mullery, Labone, Moore, Ball, Peters, R Charlton, Hunt, Hunter) loses 1-0 to Yugoslavia at the European Championships in Italy ▪ Back in Britain - 32-year-old jockey Lester Piggott rides *Sir Ivor* to victory in the Epsom Derby ▪ 26-year-old Fred West murders 15-year-old Mary Bastholm and buries her body in a field near Bishop's Cleeve ▪ "She was always young at heart, kinda dumb and kinda smart. And I loved her so" - ***Honey*** by 27-year-old Bobby Goldsboro is number two in the pop chart ▪ ***Yummy Yummy Yummy*** ("... I got love in my tummy") by Ohio Express is number five ▪ 43-year-old Jack Lemon and 46-year-old Walter Matthau star at cinemas in *The Odd Couple* ▪ 'Together they devour life' - 42-year-old Richard Burton stars alongside his wife, 36-year-old Elizabeth Taylor, in Tennessee Williams' latest movie, *Boom!* ▪ The 'hard slog' to get the economy moving (as outlined by Chancellor of the Exchequer Roy Jenkins) is underway ▪ NHS prescription charges are reintroduced at a rate of 2s/6d per item ▪ There's widespread industrial unrest throughout the country ▪ Railway workers go on strike demanding a nine percent pay increase ▪ Female workers at Ford in Dagenham go on strike demanding equal pay with men ▪ White collar workers go on strike at British Leyland causing thousands of production workers to be laid-off ▪ Austin *Mini* and Austin *1800* assembly lines grind to a halt ▪ Retail prices are rising ▪ The *J. Lyons & Co* Corner House restaurant on Coventry Street in London closes down after a sharp downturn in trade ▪ "But it's all right now, in fact it's a gas. But it's all right, I'm jumpin' Jack Flash, it's a gas, gas, gas" - ***Jumpin' Jack Flash*** by The Rolling Stones (24-year-old Mick Jagger, 24-year-old Keith Richards, 27-year-old Charlie Watts, 30-year-old Bill Wyman and 26-year-old Brian Jones) is number one on the hit parade ▪ "Hurdy gurdy, hurdy gurdy, hurdy gurdy gurdy he sang" - ***Hurdy Gurdy Man*** by 22-year-old Donovan is number four ▪ Hallmark Records release a budget priced, cover-version pop compilation LP called *Top of the Pops* - with a pretty girl pictured on the sleeve ▪ 16-year-old Ritchie Cole from Shepherd's Bush replaces Steve

Crutchley as drummer in The Stray - a teenage rock band ▪ 11-year-old Danny Baker from Bermondsey listens to a transistor radio in his bedroom ▪ 'Music lovin', on 2-4-7 Radio One!' - disc jockeys: Tony Brandon, Dave Cash and Pete Murray play the latest pop tunes on Radio One ▪ The songs: ***Baby Come Back*** by The Equals, ***I Pretend*** by 36-year-old Des O'Connor and ("Here she comes now, sayin'…") ***Mony Mony*** by Tommy James and the Shondells are smash hits - all three spending time at number one in the pop chart ▪ ***Son Of Hickory Holler's Tramp*** by 36-year-old O.C. Smith reaches number two ▪ ***Last Night In Soho*** by Dave Dee, Dozy, Beaky, Mick and Tich (a group of five friends from Wiltshire) peaks at number eight ▪ Sea transport technology moves on apace ▪ The *Seaspeed SRN4* hovercraft car passenger service to France is launched. 37-year-old Princess Margaret marks the occasion by paying a royal visit to the hoverport at Dover ▪ 'Thundering into your sights. Staggering the imagination. Brains' greatest inspiration!' - schoolboys flock to cinemas to see Gerry Anderson's *Thunderbird 6* ▪ 'It's all in the mind y'know!' - *Yellow Submarine*, an animated film from The Beatles is also now showing, with 24-year-old Geoffrey Hughes providing the voice of Paul McCartney ▪ 28-year-old James Caan stars in *Submarine X-1* ▪ ***MacArthur Park*** ("… is melting in the dark") by 37-year-old Richard Harris remains in the pop chart for twelve weeks, peaking at number four ▪ "Yesterday has just departed and tomorrow hasn't started, all that really matters is right now" - ***Yesterday Has Gone*** by Cupid's Inspiration also reaches number four and stays in the chart for eleven weeks ▪ Cricketers, 27-year-old Geoffrey Boycott and 30-year-old John Edrich stride out together to open the batting for England against Australia at Old Trafford, with England hoping to achieve their first series victory against the Aussies since 1956. Boycott hits 35 runs, Edrich scores 49 and 36-year-old Basil D'Oliveira makes 87 - but England lose by 159 runs. The next three matches at Lord's, Edgbaston and Headingley, end in draws. England gain a victory at the Oval in the final Test, with batsmen Edrich and D'Oliveira making centuries and with 23-year-old bowler Derek Underwood taking 7 wickets for 50 runs. The series is tied at one match apiece, which means Bill Lawry's Australians retain the Ashes. England players - J H Edrich, G Boycott, C Milburn, M C Cowdrey (cpt), T W Graveney, D L Amiss, R M Prideaux, K F Barrington, R W Barber, B L D'Oliveira, E R Dexter, B R Knight, A P E Knott (wk), K W R Fletcher, R Illingworth, J A Snow, K Higgs, P I Pocock, D J Brown and D L Underwood are all downcast after failing to win back the Ashes ▪ 29-year-old tennis player Rod Laver (from Australia) beats 23-year-old Tony Roche (also from Australia) 6-3, 6-4, 6-2 in the men's singles final at Wimbledon ▪ 25-year-old Billie Jean King (from America) beats 30-year-old Judy Tegart (from Australia) 9-7, 7-5 in the women's final ▪ American athlete Jim Hines sets a new world record by running the 100 metre sprint in 9.99 seconds ▪ "I am the god of hell fire and I bring you..." ***Fire*** ("... I'll take you to burn") by The Crazy World of Arthur Brown is number one for a week ▪ "Well, I'm so tired of cryin', but I'm out..." ***On The Road Again*** by Canned Heat is number eight ▪ British Rail's last ever steam train service runs from Liverpool to Carlisle ▪ 32-year-old Swiss racing driver Jo Siffert wins the British Grand Prix at Brands Hatch. 34-year-old John Surtees is fifth in a Honda. 29-year-old Jackie Stewart is sixth in a Matra-Ford ▪ 'G' reg cars go on sale ▪ Ford *Cortina MkII*, Morris *1100*, Austin *Mini* and the new Ford *Escort* are the most popular models on the road ▪ A tiny, fab and groovy Italian Fiat *500* costs just £446/15s/- and comes complete with a sunroof ▪ 34-year-old gangster twins Reginald and Ronald Kray appear in court at Bow Street for preliminary hearings on charges of conspiracy to murder ▪ 'Enlist in the 'Carry On' Army and see the World of Laughter!' - *Carry On Up the Khyber* (featuring 55-year-old Sid 'Ha-ak-ak' James as Sir Sidney Ruff-Diamond, 42-year-old Kenneth Williams as The Khasi of Kalabar and 34-year-old Bernard Bresslaw as Bungdit Din) is now showing at picture houses. The film closes with the legend, 'I'm Backing Britain' written on a union jack ▪ 'An unusual and important motion picture from the author of 'the Bridge on the River Kwai'!' - 45-year-old Charlton Heston and 23-year-old Linda Harrison star in *Planet of the Apes* ▪ "Who do you think you are kidding Mr. Hitler, if you think old England's done?" - *Dad's Army* debuts on TV, with 52-year-old Arthur Lowe as Captain Mainwaring, 56-year-old John Le Mesurier as Sergeant Wilson, 48-year-old Clive Dunn as Lance-Corporal Jones, 72-year-old Arnold Ridley as Private Godfrey and 22-year-old Ian Lavender as Private 'stupid boy' Pike ▪ The 'hard slog' to get the economy moving appears to be getting even harder. Ten months after Harold Wilson's decision to devalue the pound, the 'trade gap' in the balance of payments between imports and exports remains high - currently standing at £30 million ▪ "We'll fly… ***High In The Sky*** ("… where rainbows go by, leave troubles behind") by Amen Corner climbs to number six in the pop chart ▪ ***I Say A Little Prayer*** ("… for you") by 26-year-old Aretha Franklin reaches number four ▪ Tyrannosaurus Rex (featuring 20-year-old Marc Bolan) perform at a hippie pop festival on the Isle of Wight ▪ "Outtasight, man!" - youngsters wear tie-dyed T shirts and faded blue jeans ▪ Tensions remain high between the four members of The Beatles as they put the finishing touches to their new LP (which will come to be known as the 'White Album') ▪ "One for sorrow, two for joy, three for a girl and four for a boy" - 29-year-old Susan Stranks presents *Magpie* on ATV ▪ "And here's to you..." ***Mrs. Robinson*** ("… Jesus loves you more than you will know") by Simon and Garfunkle is number four in the pop chart ▪ ***Dance To The Music*** by Sly and the Family Stone is number seven ▪ Five years after the Great Train Robbery, 36-year-old (ring leader) Bruce Reynolds is still in hiding from the police, 'lying low' and living under an alias in Torquay ▪ There's more activity on football's transfer market ▪ 22-year-old striker Allan Clarke leaves relegated Fulham and joins First Division Leicester City for £150,000 ▪ 22-year-old striker Jimmy Greenhoff leaves First Division Leeds Utd and joins Second Division Birmingham City for £75,000 ▪ 33-year-old centre-half Dave Mackay leaves First Division Tottenham Hotspur and joins Second Division Derby County for £5,000 ▪ 42-year-old former striker Arthur 'dead shot' Rowley takes over from John Harris as manager of relegated Sheffield Utd ▪ 46-year-old Christopher Lee stars at cinemas as an evil villain in *The Blood of Fu Manchu* ▪ 35-year-old TV presenter Dickie Davies takes over as host on *World of Sport*. The regular Saturday show includes a twenty-five minute feature called *On the Ball* - hosted by 36-year-old Brian Moore and 40-year-old Jimmy Hill ▪ The new football season gets underway ▪ The names, 'Best, Charlton, Law' feature together on the score-sheet for Manchester Utd as Matt Busby's team loses 5-4 against Jack Marshall's Sheffield Wednesday ▪ Ron Greenwood's West Ham Utd thrashes Harry Potts' Burnley 5-0 at Upton Park with 19-year-old Trevor Brooking (2), 26-year-old Geoff Hurst (2) and 24-year-old Martin Peters on the score-sheet ▪ Don Revie's hard-tackling Leeds Utd record a 1-0 victory over Liverpool, with a goal from 23-year-old Mick Jones - and Leeds are the early leaders in Division One ▪ "Let's get together and..." ***Do It Again*** by The Beach Boys (with, lead singer, 26-year-old Brian Wilson) is number one in the pop chart for a week ▪ "Thank you for the days, those endless days, those sacred days you gave me" - ***Days*** by The Kinks (with, lead singer, 24-year-old Ray Davies) reaches number twelve ▪ 77-year-old veteran entertainer Stanley Holloway is pictured on the front cover of the latest edition of *TV Times* ▪ 29-year-old David Frost hosts a weekend chat show on ITV ▪ Working men pop out the house on Saturday evenings ▪ *Augustus Barnett* off-license stores offer a wide range of wines, beers and spirits ▪ The new Watney's *Party Seven* 'bumper' sized can of beer costs fifteen shillings.

Autumn 1968

Hair

Monarch:	Queen Elizabeth II (aged 42)
Prime-minister:	Harold Wilson (aged 52)
Chancellor:	Roy Jenkins (aged 48)
Home Secretary:	James Callaghan (aged 56)
Foreign Secretary:	Michael Stewart (aged 62)
Football Manager:	Alf Ramsey (aged 48)
New car reg. suffix:	'G'

▪ Retail prices are rising ▪ Inflation has jumped to 6% ▪ The 'trade gap' in the balance of payments has increased to £66 million ▪ Industrial disputes continue at British Leyland car factories ▪ Workers at Cowley and Longbridge are on a go-slow ▪ The 'I'm Backing Britain' campaign has fizzled out ▪ Harold Wilson's Labour government is under intense pressure ▪ Chancellor of the Exchequer Roy Jenkins and Minister for Productivity Barbara Castle defend the government's faltering Incomes Policy ▪ Edward Heath's opposition Conservative Party is making gains in the opinion polls ▪ 15-year-old public schoolboy Tony Blair bunks off an economics class at Fettes College in Edinburgh ▪ 11-year-old schoolboy Alistair Campbell from Yorkshire reads books at home in his bedroom ▪ 21-year-old entrepreneur Alan Sugar sets up a new limited company called A. M. S. Trading (General Importers) ▪ 'Five of the West's fastest guns say Come and Get It!' - *The Good, the Bad and the Ugly* (a 'spaghetti western' film), starring 38-year-old Clint Eastwood, 52-year-old Eli Wallach and 43-year-old Lee Van Cleef, is now showing at cinemas ▪ 'So you don't believe in glory, and heroes are out of style' - *The Green Berets* (with 61-year-old John Wayne, 37-year-old David Janssen and 34-year-old Jim Hutton) goes on general release ▪ "Evening, all" - 72-year-old Jack Warner stars on BBC television in a new series of *Dixon of Dock Green* ▪ "I've just gotta get a message to you. Hold on, hold on" - ***I've Gotta Get A***

Message To You by The Bee Gees spends a week at number one in the pop chart ▪ ***Hello I Love You*** ("...won't you tell me your name") by The Doors (with, lead singer, 24-year-old Jim Morrison) reaches number fifteen ▪ Nottingham Forest are forced to switch their home football matches to nearby Meadow Lane after a fire at the City Ground destroys the main stand ▪ 28-year-old Tottenham Hotspur footballer Jimmy 'Greavsie' Greaves scores a hat-trick as the Spurs thrash Burnley 7-0 at White Hart Lane ▪ 20-year-old goalkeeper Ray Clemence keeps a clean sheet on his debut for Liverpool in a 2-0 victory over Swansea Town in a mid-week League Cup tie at Anfield ▪ "Nah, nah, nah, na-na-na-na. Na-na-na-na..." ***Hey Jude*** by The Beatles (27-year-old John Lennon, 26-year-old Paul McCartney, 25-year-old George Harrison and 28-year-old Ringo Starr) spends two weeks at number one ▪ "While I'm alone and blue as can be..." ***Dream A Little Dream Of Me*** by 27-year-old Mama Cass reaches number eleven ▪ 'Who says piracy is obsolete entertainment?' - 40-year-old James Coburn, 59-year-old James Mason, 29-year-old James Fox and 29-year-old Susannah York star in *Duffy* - the latest blockbuster from Columbia Pictures ▪ 'The most delightful fugitives Scotland Yard never caught!' - 47-year-old Peter Ustinov, 33-year-old Maggie Smith and 55-year-old Karl Malden star in *Hot Millions* - a new movie from MGM ▪ Robert Dougall reads the news on BBC One ▪ 39-year-old Raymond Morris from Walsall is arrested by police after attempting to abduct a young girl ▪ The new Terminal 1 building at Heathrow airport is now operational ▪ 42-year-old Queen Elizabeth II performs the official opening of the redeveloped Euston Railway Station ▪ Thousands of happy commuters wait patiently in the cavernous departure hall at the new £15 million state-of-the-art transport hub, checking train information on the large overhead display panel ▪ The new Victoria underground tube line opens between Walthamstow and Highbury & Islington ▪

A new section of M1 motorway opens near Rotherham - and the 'national road' now runs uninterrupted for 174 miles between London and Wakefield ▪ Construction work continues on the new M62 motorway across the Pennines ▪ The eastbound and westbound carriageways separate from each other on a high point near Windy Hill, and Stott Hall Farm is now encircled by six lanes of asphalt ▪ 'Well off' young men drive their cars, fast, on the country's ever expanding network of motorways ▪ The latest Marcos *GT* sports car (with three litre engine) has a top speed of 125 mph and accelerates from 0-60 mph in just 6.8 seconds ▪ A Gilbern *Genie* (manufactured in Wales) has a top speed of 116 mph and accelerates from 0-60 mph in 10.7 seconds ▪ The latest Austin *Mini Cooper S* has a top speed of 98 mph and accelerates from 0-60 mph in 10.3 seconds ▪ 34-year-old John Bromley presents the sports news on ITV ▪ 35-year-old Donald Crowhurst sets sail in the Golden Globe solo round-the-world yacht race ▪ 34-year-old boxer Henry Cooper (aka Our 'Enry) defeats Karl Mildenberger at Wembley ▪ 22-year-old Manchester Utd footballer 'super' Georgie Best is sent off for fighting in a World Club Championship game against Estudiantes of Argentina. Utd lose 2-1 on aggregate over two matches ▪ At the weekend, young men take their girlfriends for a night out at the cinema ▪ 21-year-old Marianne Faithfull stars as Rebecca in the weird and erotic *Girl on a Motorcycle* ▪ 23-year-old Mia Farrow stars in *Rosemary's Baby* - a terrifying psychological horror film from 34-year-old director Roman Polanski ▪ 24-year-old Veronica Carlson stars alongside 46-year-old Christopher Lee in *Dracula Has Risen from the Grave* ▪ Hot blooded, working men stay home on weekday evenings - watching TV ▪ 22-year-old Alexandra Bastedo stars as Sharron Macready in *The Champions* ▪ 24-year-old Gabrielle Drake features in an episode of *The Saint*, alongside 40-year-old Roger Moore ▪ The dark nights begin to draw in ▪ An experiment is under way to see if it's beneficial to maximise daylight hours in the afternoons - at the expense of darker mornings ▪ The clocks do not get 'put back' an hour this year ▪ ***Those Were The Days*** ("... my friend. We thought they'd never end. We'd sing and dance forever and a day") by 18-year-old Mary Hopkin climbs to number one - and stays there for six weeks! ▪ "What am I supposed to do with a girl like..." ***Jesamine*** by The Casuals (with, lead singer, 22-year-old John Tebb) reaches number two ▪ 23-year-old footballer Mick Jones scores the only goal as Don Revie's hard-tackling Leeds Utd beat Ferencvaros 1-0 on aggregate over two legs to win the Inter Cities Fairs Cup ▪ 22-year-old Paul Nicholas, 21-year-old Oliver Tobias and 19-year-old Floella Benjamin star in *Hair* - a raunchy new musical in London's West End ▪ "I ain't got no home, ain't got no shoes. Ain't got no money, ain't got no class. Ain't got no skirts, ain't got no sweater. Ain't got no perfume, ain't got no bed, ain't got no man. Ain't got no mother, ain't got no culture. Ain't got no friends, ain't got no schoolin'. Ain't got no love, ain't got no name. Ain't got no ticket, ain't got no token, ain't got no god" - ***Ain't Got No - I Got Life*** by 35-year-old Nina Simone (from North Carolina) climbs to number two in the pop chart ▪ 'An epic drama of adventure and exploration' - Stanley Kubrick's *2001: A Space Odyssey* goes on general release at cinemas ▪ *Funny Girl* (starring 26-year-old Barbra Streisand and 36-year-old Omar Sharif) is also now showing ▪ 27-year-old Ed 'stewpot' Stewart presents *Junior Choice* on Radio One ▪ "Puff the magic dragon, lived by the sea. He frolicked in the autumn mist in a land called Honah Lee" - Peter, Paul and Mary sing ***Puff, The Magic Dragon*** ▪ Children are issued with orange reflective armbands - to wear on their way to school on dark, dreary mornings ▪ First class postage stamps are introduced costing 5d each ▪ Second class stamps are 4d ▪ ***Little Arrows*** ("... in your clothing, little arrows in your hair. When you're in love, you'll find those little arrows everywhere") by 29-year-old Leapy Lee from Eastbourne is number two in the pop chart ▪ "I don't wanna hear it. No more fussin' an a fightin', baby..." ***Hold Me Tight*** by 28-year-old Johnny Nash from Houston in Texas is number five ▪ The Olympic Games get underway at the Estadio Olimpico Universitario stadium in Mexico ▪ American athlete Dick Fosbury uses a revolutionary new 'flopping' technique in the high-jump event and clears a height of 2.4 metres - it's a new world record! ▪ Great Britain wins five gold medals, including one for 24-year-old David Hemery in the 400m hurdles - who sets a new world record time of 48.12 seconds ▪ Back in England - crowds flock to the cinema for an evening of entertainment ▪ 32-year-old Albert Finney directs and stars in *Charlie Bubbles* - a wonderful comedy drama set in Manchester. 36-year-old Billie Whitelaw, 35-year-old Colin Blakely and 22-year-old Liza Minnelli all co-star in the film ▪ 35-year-old Michael Caine and 34-year-old Nanette Newman star in *Deadfall* - a movie directed by Newman's husband, 42-year-old Bryan Forbes ▪ 26-year-old footballer Geoff Hurst bags six goals in one match as Ron Greenwood's West Ham Utd thrash Alan Brown's Sunderland 8-0 at Upton Park. (27-year-old Bobby Moore and 20-year-old Trevor Brooking are also on the score-sheet for 'The Hammers') ▪ 33-year-old Jack Charlton scores a header as hard-tackling Leeds Utd defeat Bertie Mee's Arsenal 2-0 in a top-of-the-table clash at Elland Road ▪ 21-year-old defender Jim Thomson transfers from Chelsea to Harry Potts' Burnley for £40,000 ▪ 19-year-old striker Alun Evans transfers from Wolverhampton Wanderers to Bill Shankly's Liverpool for £100,000 ▪ "Turning and turning the world goes on. We can't change it my friend" - ***Les Bicyclettes De Belsize*** by 32-year-old Engelbert Humperdinck is number five in the pop chart ▪ "Take a load off Fanny. Take a load for free" - ***The Weight*** by The Band is number twenty-one ▪ 28-year-old John Lennon divorces Cynthia, his wife of six years ▪ 41-year-old football manager Bill McGarry takes over from Ronnie Allen at Wolverhampton Wanderers ▪ Wolves sign promising midfielder 17-year-old Kenny Hibbitt from Bradford Park Avenue ▪ 27-year-old centre-forward Andy Lochhead leaves Burnley and transfers to Matt Gillies' Leicester City ▪ *Match of the Day* is broadcast in colour for the first time ▪ Highlights are shown of Chelsea beating Manchester City 2-0 at Stamford Bridge with Tommy Baldwin and Peter 'Ossie' Osgood scoring the goals for Chelsea ▪ The London Motor Show opens at Earls Court ▪ Jaguar replaces the ageing *MKII 240* and *340* models with the sleek new *XJ6* motorcar - power assisted steering is standard on all new models and air-conditioning is an optional extra on the 4.2 litre car ▪ Reliant launches the fibreglass bodied *Scimitar GTE* with a top speed of 117 mph and capable of accelerating from 0-60 mph in 10.7 seconds ▪ 39-year-old racing driver Graham Hill wins the Formula One world championship and dedicates it to his late team mate, Jim Clark ▪ "There must be some kinda way out of here, said the joker to the thief" - ***All Along The Watchtower*** by The Jimi Hendrix Experience is number five in the pop chart ▪ "What would you do if I sang out of tune? Would you stand up and walk out on me?" - ***With A Little Help From My Friends*** by 24-year-old Joe Cocker moves to number one ▪ The Beatles' new 'double' LP (known as the 'White Album') is top of the album chart - tracks include: ***Back In The USSR***, ***Dear Prudence***, ***Ob-La-Di, Ob-La-Da***, ***The Continuing Story Of Bungalow Bill***, ***While My Guitar Gently Weeps***, ***Blackbird***, ***Piggies*** and ***Rocky Raccoon*** ▪ Footballers, 22-year-old 'super' Georgie Best and 28-year-old Denis Law score the goals as Matt Busby's mid-table Manchester Utd beat Wolverhampton Wanderers 2-0 at Old Trafford in Division One ▪ Veteran entertainer Bud Flanagan dies aged 72 - just a few weeks after recording the theme song for new TV comedy *Dad's Army* ▪ 41-year-old disc jockey Alan 'Fluff' Freeman presents

Pick of the Pops on Radio One ▪ "And every night I'm there, I break my heart to please..." ***Eloise*** by 20-year-old Barry Ryan climbs to number two on the hit parade ▪ ***Elenore*** ("... gee, I think you're swell and you really do me well. You're my pride and joy, et cetera") by The Turtles is number seven ▪ 36-year-old Peter O'Toole stars at cinemas as Henry II in *The Lion in Winter*. 61-year-old Katharine Hepburn is Eleanor of Aquitaine. 30-year-old Anthony Hopkins is Richard the Lionheart ▪ 56-year-old Chief Superintendent Tommy Butler and his team of Scotland Yard detectives track down 37-year-old train robber Bruce Reynolds to an address in Torquay. Reynolds is arrested, charged and sentenced to twenty-five years in prison ▪ 39-year-old Ronnie Biggs remains at large ▪ Households throughout the country embrace new technology ▪ Owning a telephone is now more affordable than ever ▪ There's high demand for GPO's exciting new trimphone - waiting time for an installation is around eight weeks ▪ 18-year-old DJ David 'Kid' Jensen joins Radio Luxembourg ▪ "He'll seek you here, he'll seek you there. The devil will seek you everywhere" - ***Race With The Devil*** by Gun climbs to number eight in the pop chart ▪ Times are changing ▪ Carnaby Street is now crammed with tourists - eager to purchase hippy merchandise ▪ The King's Road in Chelsea is where the 'cool cats' hang out ▪ Women wear corduroy jump-suits, and coat their eye-lashes in thick black mascara ▪ Men wear their hair long, and favour bushy sideburns ▪ The Who, The Small Faces and The Mindbenders are on the bill for an 'all-nighter' at the Roundhouse in Chalk Farm ▪ 26-year-old Brian Jones of the Rolling Stones purchases Cotchford Farm near Hartfield in East Sussex. The fine property (once owned by author A. A. Milne) comes complete with an outdoor swimming pool ▪ Schoolboys stay up late, eating snacks and watching television ▪ ITV broadcasts fifteen seconds of the infamous nude scene from the hit musical *Hair* ▪ 'You get a lovely lot of Quavers in a bag' - *Quavers* cheese-flavoured crisps are new.

Christmas 1968

Lily the Pink and Spiro-Graph

Monarch:	Queen Elizabeth II (aged 42)
Prime-minister:	Harold Wilson (aged 52)
Chancellor:	Roy Jenkins (aged 48)
Home Secretary:	James Callaghan (aged 56)
Foreign Secretary:	Michael Stewart (aged 62)
Football Manager:	Alf Ramsey (aged 48)
New car reg. suffix:	'G'

▪ The weather turns chilly - leading to widespread frost and ice ▪ Strike action by union members continues to blight the declining UK car industry ▪ Five thousand workers at Ford's factory in Dagenham are laid-off because of a shortage of disc brake components ▪ Despite industrial unrest and an increasing number of unofficial strikes, prime-minister Harold Wilson and Chancellor of the Exchequer Roy Jenkins are cheered by some good news ▪ The 'trade gap' in the balance of payments has fallen to £17 miilion - the lowest level since Mr. Wilson devalued the pound in 1967 ▪ 10-year-old schoolboy Julian 'Jools' Holland from Blackheath plays piano for his friends ▪ ***This Old Heart Of Mine*** ("... been broke a thousand times") by The Isley Brothers is number three on the hit parade ▪ The theme tune from ***The Good The Bad And The Ugly*** by Hugo Montenegro is number one on the hit parade ▪ 'They Won't Stay Dead! They keep coming back in a blood thirsty lust for HUMAN FLESH!' - *The Night of the Living Dead* terrifies cinema goers ▪ 38-year-old Steve McQueen and his Ford *Mustang* car star in the action movie *Bullitt* ▪ 'Get Rich Quick ... Get Dead Quicker!' - 41-year-old Richard Johnson and 43-year-old Honor Blackman star in *A Twist of Sand* ▪ 'This is to certify that JOE 90 is an authorised agent for World Intelligence Network' - schoolboys watch excitedly as *Joe 90* appears on TV for the first time ▪ Children's author Enid Blyton dies aged 71 at a nursing home in London ▪ *Coronation Street* stars, 33-year-old Anne Reid (Valerie Barlow) and 36-year-old Bill Roache (Ken Barlow) are pictured together on the front cover of the latest edition of *TV Times* ▪ "Pleased to meet you. Hope you guess my name" - ***Sympathy For The Devil*** is the opening track on *Beggars Banquet*, a new LP from The Rolling Stones, which is number three in the album chart ▪ 31-year-old footballer Jimmy Melia transfers from Southampton to Aldershot for £9,000 ▪ 22-year-old David Webb of Chelsea is pictured on the front cover of the latest *Goal* magazine ▪ 24-year-old champion Olympic hurdler David Hemery is BBC television's 'Sports Personality of the Year' ▪ Motoring technology moves on apace ▪ The new Triumph *2.5 PI* motorcar has a petrol injected engine - there's no carburettor ▪ BMW adds a two litre engine to its small, two-door saloon and launches the *2002* ▪ 'And all because… the lady loves *Milk Tray*' - Cadbury's use a mysterious 'man of action' to advertise their chocolates ▪ "My girl goes wild for Dairy Box, she's a Dairy Box girl" - Rowntrees use 32-year-old Una Stubbs to advertise *Dairy Box* ▪ Middle class men treat their ladies to an evening out at the cinema ▪ 'Which side will you be on…' *if...* (starring Malcolm McDowell, Mick Travis and 23-year-old Christine Noonan) is now showing ▪ Working class men treat their ladies to a night out at the pub ▪ A 'snowball' at Christmas goes down a treat ▪ Newspaper adverts claim, 'All the women in your life love *Warnink's* advocaat' ▪ Parents in Birmingham take their children to see Santa in his grotto at the Beehive department store on Albert Street ▪ 38-year-old Bert Foord presents the weather forecast on BBC One ▪ Temperatures drop and thick snow descends across Britain on Christmas Eve ▪ The Midlands is worst affected, with Birmingham getting up to six-inches ▪ A Morris *Minor* ('D' reg, in Rose Taupe) is stranded on the A458 at Halesowen ▪ A Vauxhall *Viva* ('F' reg, in Eclipse Blue) is stuck on the B4181 near Walsall ▪ 'A simple and fascinating way to DRAW a million marvellous patterns' - children have hours of fun with new *Spiro-Graph* ▪ Young schoolboys receive a *Lego* set on Christmas morning ▪ Older boys get a *Meccano* construction set ▪ Faberge introduces *Brut 33* - a budget priced cologne for men ▪ ***1-2-3 O'Leary*** ("… games I played with Mary, way back in the wildwood, of our careless childhood. Then we both discovered, how friends turn to lovers") by 36-year-old Des O'Connor is number four on the hit parade ▪ ***I'm A Tiger*** ("… I'm a ti-ger. I'm a tiger, I'm a ti-ger") by 20-year-old Lulu moves down the chart to number twelve ▪ The cold weather snap continues and the snow lies deep ▪ Families stay in and watch television together ▪ On the twenty-fifth of December, ITV broadcasts: *The Courage of Lassie*, with a young Elizabeth Taylor; followed by *Opportunity Knocks*, presented by 48-year-old Hughie Green; and then comes a thrilling episode of *Coronation Street* in which Elsie Tanner's estranged husband is murdered ▪ BBC One broadcasts: *Christmas Night with the Stars*, featuring comedy duo Morecambe and Wise, the cast from Dad's Army, Harry Worth and Marty Feldman; next comes *Doddy for Christmas*, with 41-year-old Ken Dodd; followed by the film *Some Like It Hot*, starring Marilyn Monroe and Tony Curtis ▪ "Please sir, I want some more" - *Oliver!* (starring 10-year-old Mark Lester) is at the pictures ▪ 19-year-old centre-forward Joe Royle scores a hat-trick past 19-year-old goalkeeper Peter Shilton, as Harry Catterick's Everton thrash Matt Gillies' Leicester City 7-1 in front of 42,492 spectators at Goodison Park. Gillies is promptly sacked and Frank O'Farrell takes over as Leicester manager ▪ 38-year-old Roy Sproson scores the winning goal as Fourth Division Port Vale beat Wrexham 1-0 in front of 5,421 spectators at Vale Park ▪ Labour prime-minister Harold Wilson and his Chancellor of the Exchequer, Roy Jenkins, remain under pressure from rising prices and the ongoing battle to reduce the large deficit in the balance of payments ▪ 58-year-old Barbara Castle (Minister for Productivity) devises a plan to arrest the decline in British industry ▪ For people in working-class communities, times remain hard ▪ The number of NCB collieries has been reduced in the past year from 406 to 330 ▪ The number of miners has fallen again (it's now just 330,000) and production of coal has also fallen (to 170 million tonnes) ▪ 11-year-old schoolboy Billy Bragg from Barking writes poetry at home in his bedroom ▪ An evening out at the cinema is a rare treat ▪ 38-year-old Sean Connery and 34-year-old Brigitte Bardot (36-20-35) star in *Shalako* - a 'Western' movie from Edward Dmytryk ▪ 43-year-old Richard Burton, 38-year-old Clint Eastwood and 35-year-old Mary Ure star in *Where Eagles Dare* - a wartime thriller from Brian G. Hutton ▪ "We'll drink (a drink - a drink) to Lily the pink (the pink - the pink). Saviour of our human race" - ***Lily The Pink*** by The Scaffold (with 24-year-old Mike McGear - aka Mike McCartney, 31-year-old Roger McGough and 32-year-old John Gorman) is number one on the Top 50 hit parade ▪ ***I'm The Urban Spaceman*** ("... baby, I've got speed. I've got everything I need") by The Bonzo Dog Doo-Dah Band (with 25-year-old Vivian Stanshall and 25-year-old Neil Innes) is number five ▪ 36-year-old sailor Donald Crowhurst reports a false position in the Golden Globe solo round-the-world yacht race ▪ 11-year-old Mary Bell is sent to a secure unit in St. Helens after being convicted of the manslaughter of two boys aged just 3 and 4 in Newcastle earlier this year ▪ The 'Space Race' continues ▪ *Apollo 8* (with astronauts Frank Borman, Jim Lovell and Bill Anders) orbits the Moon ▪ "Barbarella's psychedelia!" - Men flock to the cinema to see 31-year-old Jane Fonda in the futuristic film *Barbarella* ▪ Families rush to see *Chitty Chitty Bang Bang*, with 42-year-old Dick Van Dyke, 38-year-old Sally Ann Howes and 42-year-old Lionel Jeffries. "Ice-cream, lollipops; all free today" - 59-year-old Robert Helpmann is the Child Catcher ▪ Prime-minister Harold Wilson and his Home Secretary, Jim Callaghan, watch anxiously as tensions grow in Northern Ireland between Loyalists and Nationalists ▪ The guitar instrumental ***Sabre Dance*** by Love Sculpture is number five in the pop chart ▪ ***May I Have The Next Dream With You*** ("... dear? Just a dream between us two") by 24-year-old Malcolm Roberts from Manchester is number eight ▪ 43-year-old Nat Lofthouse takes over as football manager of Second Division Bolton Wanderers ▪ First Division Nottingham Forest sack 49-year-old Johnny Carey after a poor run of form ▪ 21-year-old Emlyn Hughes scores the winning goal as Bill Shankly's top-of-the-table Liverpool beat Tottenham Hotspur 1-0 ▪ Don Revie's hard-tackling Leeds Utd are in second place, with 26-year-old Billy Bremner and 22-year-old Peter Lorimer in fine form ▪ "Why do you..." ***Build Me Up Buttercup*** ("... baby, just to let me down") by The Foundations climbs to number two in the pop chart ▪ ***Love Child*** ("... never meant to be. Love child, born in poverty. Love child, never meant to be. Love child, take a look at me") by 24-year-old Diana Ross and the Supremes reaches number fifteen ▪ Footballers, 25-year-old Martin Peters, 27-year-old Alan Mullery and 22-year-old Colin Bell are England's midfield trio in a 1-1 draw against Bulgaria at Wembley. 27-year-old centre-forward Geoff Hurst scores the goal for 48-year-old Sir Alf Ramsey's team ▪ 40-year-old Tommy Docherty is the new manager of Second Division Aston Villa ▪ More than four-hundred-thousand houses have been built in Britain this year - it's the highest annual figure, ever ▪ The average price of a property is £4,000 ▪ Families strive to improve their lives ▪ A GEC *Albany 3* electric cooker (with three super-speed radiant rings) costs £39/19s/6d ▪ A Baird twenty-inch television set is available from *Radio Rentals* for the payment of just 9s/8d a week ▪ A new-fangled Bush nineteen-inch 'colour' set is also available - even though the two main TV channels (BBC One and ITV) are still only transmitting programmes in black and white! ▪ Barbara Castle (Minister for Productivity) meets with George Woodcock, General Secretary of the TUC, to discuss ways of getting greater output from the workforces in manufacturing industries ▪ Some people get up slightly earlier for work ▪ Adverts say, 'Take *Bournvita* tonight - Take tomorrow in your stride'.

New Year 1969

The Beatles perform on a London rooftop

Monarch:	Queen Elizabeth II (aged 42)
Prime-minister:	Harold Wilson (aged 52)
Chancellor:	Roy Jenkins (aged 48)
Home Secretary:	James Callaghan (aged 56)
Foreign Secretary:	Michael Stewart (aged 62)
Football Manager:	Alf Ramsey (aged 49)
New car reg. suffix:	'G'

▪ It's a mild start to the new year, turning colder in February ▪ There's much unrest in the country ▪ Students protest in London ▪ Rioting breaks out in the Bogside area of Derry ▪ ***Something's Happening*** ("... and it started happening when you walked by-ie-ie") by Herman's Hermits climbs to number six on the hit parade ▪ "The only one who could ever reach me, was the..." ***Son Of A Preacher Man*** by 29-year-old Dusty Springfield peaks at number nine ▪ 31-year-old Vanessa Redgrave and 29-year-old James Fox star at cinemas in *Isadora* - a movie dramatisation of the life of American dancer Isadora Duncan ▪ 22-year-old Hayley Mills, 24-year-old Hywel Bennett and 36-year-old Billie Whitelaw star in *Twisted Nerve* - a psychological thriller from director Roy Boulting ▪ 'The hostess with the mostess' - 21-year-old Annie Aston joins 41-year-old Bob Monkhouse on ATV's popular game-show *The Golden Shot* ▪ A wildcat strike at Jaguar's factory in Coventry halts production of the brand new *XJ6* motorcar ▪ 58-year-old Barbara Castle MP angers trade unions with her White Paper, 'In Place of Strife', which proposes government intervention in industrial disputes ▪ 60-year-old Vic Feather succeeds 64-year-old George Woodcock as General Secretary of the Trades Union Congress ▪ 55-year-old Jack Jones (General Secretary of the Transport and General Workers' Union) is unimpressed with the new government initiative ▪ 52-year-old Labour prime-minister Harold Wilson seeks to reassure the unions that the country is still heading in the right direction ▪ The 'hard slog' predicted by 48-year-old Chancellor of the Exchequer Roy Jenkins continues. The main priority is to reduce the 'trade gap' in the balance of payments. The second priority is to achieve a sustained level of growth ▪ The annual license fee for a black and white television set goes up from £5 to £6 ▪ It's rumoured that car road tax is about to rise from £25 to £35 - it turns out to be untrue ▪ 37-year-old Rupert Murdoch buys the *News of the World* ▪ "Desmond has a barrow in the marketplace. Molly is the singer in a band" - ***Ob-La-Di, Ob-La-Da*** by The Marmalade spends three weeks at number one in the pop chart ▪ The Beatles (28-year-old John Lennon, 26-year-old Paul McCartney, 25-year-old George Harrison and 28-year-old Ringo Starr) make their final public appearance - performing on the rooftop of the Apple Corps building at number 3 Savile Row in London. 22-year-old keyboard player Billy Field joins the 'Fab Four' in performances of the songs: ***Get Back***, ***Don't Let Me Down***, ***I've Got A Feeling***, ***One After 909***, ***Dig A Pony*** and ***God Save The Queen*** before police officers arrive to break up the impromptu concert ▪ *Hostile Witness* (starring 35-year-old Sylvia Syms) goes on general release at cinemas ▪ *Subterfuge* (starring 35-year-old Joan Collins) is also now showing ▪ 56-year-old Richard Nixon is the new president of the USA - Nixon travels to London in late February for a meeting with Harold Wilson ▪ 36-year-old Donald Crowhurst continues to send false radio reports claiming to be sailing his yacht around the world, whilst actually hiding in the South Atlantic ▪ ***Albatross*** by Fleetwood Mac (comprising of: 20-year-old Jeremy Spencer, 22-year-old Peter Green, 18-year-old Danny Kirwan, 23-year-old John McVie and 21-year-old Mick Fleetwood) spends a week at number one in the pop chart ▪ "Callin' out around the world, are you ready for a brand new beat?" - ***Dancing In The Street*** by 27-year-old Martha Reeves and the Vandellas is number four ▪ "It's what's happening!' - 26-year-old Dave Cash presents the afternoon show on Radio One ▪ 29-year-old John Peel is an occasional presenter of the midnight show, *Night Ride* ▪ 24-year-old Diana Ross and the Supremes perform their new song, ***I'm Gonna Make You Love Me*** ("... Oh, yes I will. Yes I will") ▪ "I am a lineman for the county" - 32-year-old Glen Campbell sings ***Wichita Lineman*** ▪ 28-year-old striker Jimmy 'Greavsie' Greaves scores a goal (and 23-year-old goalkeeper Pat Jennings keeps a clean sheet) as Bill Nicholson's Tottenham Hotspur defeat Walsall 0-1 in the third round of the FA Cup ▪ 22-year-old winger Roger Morgan transfers from Les Allen's Queens Park Rangers to Spurs for £100,000 ▪ Crowd trouble breaks out and missiles are thrown at Elland Road during a Division One match between Don Revie's hard-tackling Leeds Utd and Sir Matt Busby's Manchester Utd. A late, winning goal from 26-year-old Mike O'Grady ensures a 2-1 victory to Leeds ▪ 'Forget the medals, throw away the rule book. If you want to survive PLAY DIRTY' - *Play Dirty* (starring 35-year-old Michael Caine) is on general release at cinemas ▪ 'Unbelievable!' - 11-year-old schoolboy Chris Kamara from Middlesbrough plays football with his friends in the park - and scores an own goal ▪ The final episode of *The Saint* (starring 41-year-old Roger Moore as Simon Templar) is broadcast on ITV ▪ The first episode of a bright new comedy called *On the Buses* (with 52-year-old Reg Varney as driver Stan Butler and with 42-year-old Stephen Lewis as Inspector Blake) cheers the hearts of the nation ▪ Ford launches the stunning new *Capri* - it's 'The Car You Always Promised Yourself'. The entry level *1300* model costs £890 and has a top speed of 84 mph. The *1600GT* costs £1,042 and has a top speed of 96 mph. The *2000GT* costs £1,088 and has a top speed of 106 mph ▪ 'Remember: Mirror - Signal - Manoeuvre when overtaking' - A copy of the latest *Highway Code* costs 1s/6d ▪ Led Zeppelin (25-year-old Jimmy Page, 20-year-old John Bonham, 23-year-old John Paul Jones and 20-year-old Robert Plant) release their eponymous debut LP, which reaches number six in the album chart ▪ "Goodbye Blackberry Way. I can't see you, I don't need you" - ***Blackberry Way*** by The Move (with, lead singer, 22-year-old Roy Wood) is new at number one in the pop chart ▪ ***For Once In My Life*** ("… I have someone who needs me") by 18-year-old Stevie Wonder is number three ▪ The murder trial of 35-year-old twins Reginald and Ronald Kray gets underway at the Old Bailey - with a host of previously loyal associates now giving evidence against the brothers ▪ In a separate trial at Stafford Crown Court, evil 39-year-old Raymond Morris from Walsall is sentenced to life imprisonment for the rape and murder of a girl on Cannock Chase ▪ Tens of thousands of working-class families feed two-shilling coins into the payment slot at the back of their rented TV sets ▪ BBC One programmes on a Saturday night include: *Dr. Who* - starring 48-year-old Patrick Troughton; *The News and The Weatherman* - with Graham Parker; *Tom and Jerry* - a ten-minute cartoon from Hanna and Barbera; *Here's Lucy* - starring Lucille Ball; *Lulu* - a programme of music and laughter with 20-year-old singer Lulu; *The Morecambe and Wise Show* - with 42-year-old Eric Morecambe and 43-year-old Ernie Wise; *The Rolf Harris Show* - featuring 38-year-old Rolf Harris; *The Saturday Thriller*; *The News* - read by 55-year-old Robert Dougal; *Match of the Day* - introduced by 42-year-old David Coleman; and *Braden's Week* - presented by 52-year-old Bernard Braden ▪ A full scale search for missing disc jockey Jimmy Savile is called off when the 42-year-old turns up at a hotel, after getting lost on a hike to the top of Ben Nevis ▪ "One road leads to sadness, one road leads to pain. One road shows you, life is a game" - ***One Road*** by Love Affair enters the pop chart at number forty-eight ▪ ***Love Is Love*** by 20-year-old Barry Ryan is new at number thirty-seven ▪ 47-year-old Matt Gillies is the new football manager at Nottingham Forest ▪ 35-year-old Bobby Robson is the new manager at Ipswich Town ▪ 26-year-old Billy Bremner scores twice as Don Revie's hard-tackling Leeds Utd beat Coventry City 3-0 to move up to second place in Division One ▪ There's a major shock in the FA Cup when Ron Greenwood's First Division West Ham Utd (with Geoff Hurst, Billy Bonds, Martin Peters, Bobby Moore, Trevor Brooking and 21-year-old Harry Redknapp) lose 3-0 to Tommy Eggleston's Third Division Mansfield Town in the fifth round ▪ Crowds flock to the cinema ▪ 'Yer never saw Alf like this before!' - 43-year-old Warren Mitchell stars as Alf Garnett in a film version of *Till Death Us Do Part.* 61-year-old Dandy Nicholls, 37-year-old Tony Booth and 31-year-old Una Stubbs also feature in the popular new movie ▪ The manufacturing industry is struggling to improve efficiency and increase levels of output - as demanded by Labour's 58-year-old Productivity Minister Barbara Castle ▪ Vic Feather of the TUC criticises the measures set out in the government's latest bill, aimed at reducing the number of strikes ▪ Working life is hard for many people ▪ A new night-shift is introduced at Jaguar's car factory in Coventry - with the aim of increasing production numbers of the new *XJ6* model ▪ Sixteen-hundred workers at Rover in Solihull are laid-off because of a shortage of gearboxes ▪ 52-year-old Labour prime-minister Harold Wilson travels to West Berlin to pledge his continued support for the freedom of the city. Mr. Wilson's trip comes at a time when the Communist East German Government has just restricted free movement for West German MPs, civil servants and members of the armed forces - all of whom can no longer travel by road or rail across East Germany to Berlin ▪ ***(If Paradise Is) Half As Nice*** ("... as heaven that you take me to") by Amen Corner is number one on the hit parade ▪ ***Please Don't Go*** ("... I beg you, don't go, for I need you here with me") by 60-year-old Donald Peers is number three ▪ Families enjoy toast and marmalade at breakfast time ▪ Adverts for *Nimble* bread declare, 'Slice for slice it's lighter than ordinary bread' ▪ Adverts for Robertson's *Golden Shred* marmalade say, 'Look for the golly on the jar.'

Spring 1969

Ronnie and Reggie Kray convicted

Monarch:	Queen Elizabeth II (aged 43)
Prime-minister:	Harold Wilson (aged 53)
Chancellor:	Roy Jenkins (aged 48)
Home Secretary:	James Callaghan (aged 57)
Foreign Secretary:	Michael Stewart (aged 62)
Football Manager:	Alf Ramsey (aged 49)
New car reg. suffix:	'G'

▪ The economy is weak ▪ Prices continue to rise ▪ 53-year-old prime-minister Harold Wilson and his Labour government push for economic growth in the fields of science and technology ▪ The British built Concorde passenger airplane makes its maiden flight - piloted by 45-year-old Brian Trubshaw. The sleek new 'supersonic' jet embarks on a short trip from Filton near Bristol, to RAF Fairford in Gloucestershire ▪ Queen Elizabeth II opens (officially) the brand new Victoria underground railway line in London - riding as a passenger in the cab of a shiny new tube train on the seventh of March ▪ A few weeks later, the 42-year-old monarch opens the new Terminal 1 building at Heathrow ▪ 34-year-old Maggie Smith stars at cinemas in *The Prime of Miss Jean Brodie* ▪ 45-year-old Richard 'Dicky' Attenborough leads an all-star cast in *Oh! What a Lovely War* ▪ 34-year-old Billy Smart Jr. opens a new safari park at Windsor and families travel from all around to see the monkeys ▪ "Forget about tomorrow…" ***Surround Yourself With Sorrow*** by 26-year-old Cilla Black climbs to number three on the hit parade ▪ ***Monsieur Dupont*** ("… La-la-la-lah") by 22-year-old Sandie Shaw peaks at number six ▪ ***I Spy (For The FBI)*** by Jamo Thomas stalls at number forty-four ▪ *B&Q* opens its first large store, in Southampton ▪ 'Fast new electric Flymo - the airborne mower' - blue and white *Flymo* 'hover' lawn mowers are exciting and new and are in huge demand ▪ 39-year-old Leonard Parkin reads the news for ITN ▪ 'Brotherhood of Evil' - 35-year-old twins Reginald and Ronald Kray are found guilty of murder, after a trial lasting thirty-nine days at the Old Bailey. Mr. Justice Melford Stevenson imposes a life sentence on both men "... which I would recommend should not be less than thirty years" ▪ *The Assassination Bureau* (with 31-year-old Oliver Reed, 47-year-old Telly Savalas and 30-year-old Diana Rigg) draws crowds to the cinema ▪ 'It's a Mad, Mad Flick - Gangsters - Fun - Dames!' - *Crooks and Coronets* (with 81-year-old Edith Evans) is also now showing ▪ 48-year-old Chancellor of the Exchequer Roy Jenkins presents his Budget on behalf of Harold Wilson's Labour government ▪ Petrol goes up by 2d a gallon ▪ "A dead end Budget by a fag end Government" - is the opinion of 52-year-old Edward Heath (leader of the Conservative opposition) ▪ "But where do you go to my lovely, when you're alone in your bed? Tell me the thoughts that surround you, I want to look inside your head, yes I do" - ***Where Do You Go To, My Lovely*** by 27-year-old Peter Sarstedt spends four weeks at the top of the pop chart ▪ ***The Way It Used To Be*** by 33-year-old Engelbert Humperdinck is number three ▪ 'The sound of today!' - Radio One's weekday schedule is - Tony Blackburn (7 a.m. to 9 a.m.), Family Choice (9 a.m. to 10 a.m.), Jimmy Young (10 a.m. to 12 noon), Radio One Club (12 noon to 2 p.m.), Dave Cash (2 p.m. to 4.15 p.m.) and Tony Brandon (4.15 p.m. to 6.30 p.m.) ▪ People buy the latest 7-inch singles at *Woolworths* for 8s/6d ▪ 26-year-old 'Beatle' Paul McCartney marries 27-year-old photographer Linda Eastman at Marylebone Register Office in London ▪ Miserable Ena Sharples (played by 70-year-old Violet Carson) is arrested in ITV's *Coronation Street* for demonstrating against the closure of the pensioners' clubhouse ▪ There's a spell of rainy weather ▪ Damp school children (with packed lunches) trudge around Chester Zoo, looking at the monkeys ▪ *Princes* salmon paste sandwiches taste great ▪ 13-year-old April Fabb goes missing from her home in Norfolk ▪ 20-year-old Lulu is joint winner in the Eurovision song contest singing ***Boom Bang-A-Bang***. The song reaches number two on the hit parade ▪ "Talking 'bout you and me and the..." ***Games People Play*** by 29-year-old Joe South peaks at number six ▪ 31-year-old Dustin Hoffman and 30-year-old Jon Voight star at cinemas in *Midnight Cowboy* ▪ 39-year-old Christopher Plummer, 45-year-old Glynis Johns and 30-year-old Susannah York star in *Lock Up Your Daughters!* ▪ 16-year-old Jenny Agutter appears in BBC TV's soap-opera *The Newcomers* ▪ 34-year-old David Vine introduces a new series of *It's a Knockout* on BBC One - and he's joined by former football referee Arthur Ellis (aged 52) and former Rugby League coach Eddie Waring (aged 59) ▪ 38-year-old comedian (and former *Opportunity Knocks* contestant) Les Dawson from Manchester appears in his own ITV show, *Sez Les* ▪ 24-year-old footballer Franny Lee scores his first goal for Sir Alf Ramsey's England team (G Banks, K Newton, Cooper, Mullery, J Charlton, Moore, F Lee, Bell, G Hurst, Peters, O'Grady) in a 5-0 victory over France at Wembley. (27-year-old Geoff Hurst scores a hat-trick in the same match) ▪ Third Division Swindon Town stun Bertie Mee's First Division Arsenal in the League Cup final at Wembley with a 3-1 victory after extra time. 23-year-old Don Rogers scores twice for 'The Robins' and 22-year-old Bobby Gould scores for 'The Gunners' ▪ 22-year-old 'super' Georgie Best scores twice, and 24-year-old Willie Morgan bags a hat-trick, as Sir Matt Busby's Manchester Utd thrash Queens Park Rangers 8-1 in Division One ▪ 22-year-old Peter Lorimer comes on as a substitute for Don Revie's hard-tackling Leeds Utd in a 0-0 draw against Wolverhampton Wanderers. (Leeds are now six points clear of Liverpool at the top of Division One) ▪ The 'Space Race' continues ▪ The lunar module from *Apollo 10* flies close to the Moon's surface ▪ "I bet you're wonderin' how I knew, about your plans to make me blue" - ***I Heard It Through The Grapevine*** by 29-year-old Marvin Gaye is number one on the hit parade ▪ "And for hours, you're just..." ***Gentle On My Mind*** by 51-year-old Dean Martin is number two ▪ Rumours of Paul

McCartney's death begin to spread - they're false! ▪ 'Hair Peace. Bed Peace' - 28-year-old John Lennon and 36-year-old Yoko Ono stage a 'bed-in' in Amsterdam ▪ The Who play a concert at the Pavilion Ballrooms in Bournemouth - tickets are 12s/6d ▪ 36-year-old Donald Crowhurst turns his yacht around and sails for home - after cheating in the Golden Globe solo round-the-world race ▪ The new *QE2* ocean liner sails from Southampton to New York on her maiden voyage across the Atlantic - the crossing takes 4 days, 16 hours, 35 minutes ▪ 49-year-old Cliff Michelmore presents *Holiday 69* on BBC One - and viewers find out about a golfing break in Estoril and a wine-tasting tour of the Cote de Beaune ▪ "Get up in the morning, slaving for bread, sir, so that every mouth can be fed. Poor, poor, me …" ***Israelites*** by Desmond Dekker and the Aces climbs to the top of the pop chart ▪ "Ever since I was a young boy, I've played the silver ball. From Soho down to Brighton, I must've played 'em all" - ***Pinball Wizard*** by The Who (with, lead singer, 25-year-old Roger Daltrey) is number four ▪ A second series of *Dad's Army* begins on Saturday evenings on BBC television - the six episodes to be broadcast include, 'The Battle of Godfrey's Cottage', 'Sgt. Wilson's Little Secret' and 'A Stripe for Frazer' ▪ 58-year-old Sir Hugh Greene steps down from his role as Director General of the BBC ▪ 58-year-old Mrs. Mary Whitehouse enjoys a nice cup of tea at her home in rural Worcestershire ▪ Adverts on ITV are enhanced with catchy jingles ▪ 'When you haven't got time to eat, Unzip a Banana!' ▪ 'Trebor mints are a minty bit stronger!' ▪ 61-year-old Vic Feather of the TUC continues to oppose Barbara Castle's plan to restrict workers from taking industrial action ▪ Shop stewards at British Leyland's factory in Birmingham call for production staff to go on strike ▪ The exciting Austin *Maxi* motorcar is launched, with prices starting at £979. The new *Maxi* comes with a large boot area for luggage, folding rear seats, five forward gears and a top speed of 88 mph ▪ 40-year-old racing driver Graham Hill wins the Monaco Grand Prix for a fifth time ▪ 33-year-old John Spencer wins the Player's *No.6* World Snooker Championship - defeating Gary Owen from Wales by 37 frames to 24 in the final ▪ 55-year-old Liverpool football manager Bill Shankly makes additions to his squad at Anfield. 'Shanks' signs 21-year-old full-back Alec Lindsay from Bury for £68,000 and 20-year-old centre-half Larry Lloyd from Bristol Rovers for £60,000 ▪ 22-year-old Manchester Utd star 'super' Georgie Best is voted European Footballer of the Year ▪ "Jojo was a man who thought he was a loner, but he knew it wouldn't last" - ***Get Back*** by The Beatles with Billy Preston enters the hit parade at number one - and stays there for six weeks! ▪ ***Goodbye*** ("… goodbye my love, goodbye") by 19-year-old Mary Hopkin peaks at number two ▪ 19-year-old goalkeeper Peter Shilton is on the losing team in the FA Cup final as Frank O'Farrell's Leicester City go down 1-0 to Joe Mercer's Manchester City. (25-year-old Neil Young scores the only goal of the game). A ticket for the standing enclosure at the Empire Stadium in Wembley costs 12s/6d ▪ 17-year-old goalkeeper John 'Budgie' Burridge makes his league debut for Workington Town in Division Four in a 3-2 victory over Newport County. A season ticket at Workington's Borough Park ground costs £8 ▪ "My sleeves are all torn, my buttons are loose, my make-up's starting to fail me. The sparkle you put in my dolly eye is gone since that cloudy bye-bye day" - ***Come Back And Shake Me*** by 22-year-old Clodagh Rodgers is number three in the pop chart ▪ "Hey, Mr..." ***Ragamuffin Man*** ("... just look at you now, I wonder how you can be satisfied") by Manfred Mann is number ten ▪ 41-year-old Don Revie's hard-tackling Leeds Utd are the new champions of Division One. In their all-white jerseys, shorts and stockings, Gary Sprake, Paul Reaney, Paul Madeley, Terry Cooper, Billy Bremner, Johnny Giles, Eddie Gray, Norman Hunter, Mick Jones, Peter Lorimer and 33-year-old Jack Charlton have all been outstanding ▪ 34-year-old Brian Clough's Derby County (with Les Green, Ron Webster, John Robson, Dave

Mackay, Roy McFarland, Willie Carlin, Alan Durban, John O'Hare, Alan Hinton and Kevin Hector) are champions of Division Two ▪ Disagreements between Harold Wilson's Labour government and Vic Feather of the TUC lead to divisions in the Cabinet. Speculation in the media suggests that 57-year-old Home Secretary Jim Callaghan is ready to seize power ▪ Mr. Wilson is resolute and determined to stay at Number 10 Downing Street ▪ "I shall always worry about Jim" - popular radio serial *The Dales* (featuring 62-year-old Jessie Matthews as doctor's wife Mrs. Mary Dale) comes to an end after running for twenty-one years ▪ "I kept sneaking looks at those heavenly black stockings under the table. I promised myself that she would be my bird. Whether she liked it or not." - A*ll Neat in Black Stockings* (starring 18-year-old Susan George) goes on general release at cinemas ▪ 54-year-old Norman Wisdom and 18-year-old Sally Geeson star in *What's Good for the Goose* - the story of a middle-aged assistant bank manager having a fling with a young woman ▪ "Get that bus out!" - a new TV series of *On the Buses* begins, with 42-year-old Stephen Lewis as Blakey, 52-year-old Reg Varney as Stan, 37-year-old Bob Grant as Jack, 38-year-old Michael Robbins as Arthur and 32-year-old Anna Karen as Olive ▪ "I'd like to say thank you on behalf of the group and ourselves and I hope we've passed the audition" - 28-year-old Ringo Starr makes a quip at the end of the recording of ***Get Back*** by The Beatles with Billy Preston - the song remains at number one in the pop chart ▪ "A sentimental song for..." ***My Sentimental Friend*** ("... over there") by Herman's Hermits moves up to number two ▪ "Oh, we won't give in. Let's go..." ***Living In The Past*** by Jethro Tull (with, lead singer, 21-year-old Ian Anderson) reaches number three ▪ Bathroom equipment manufacturer Armitage Ware merges with Shanks Holdings Ltd, and 'Armitage Shanks' is the new name soon to be seen on toilets, urinals and wash-basins all around the world ▪ The 'trade gap' figure in the balance of payments is reducing and Chancellor of the Exchequer Roy Jenkins predicts that there will be a surplus by the end of the year ▪ After recent criticsm of the Labour goverment, prime-minister Harold Wilson reassures the country, saying "I know what is going on. I am going on. Your government is going on." ▪ A deal is struck with the TUC and Mr. Wilson strengthens his position as prime-minister - after recent speculation that Jim Callaghan was about to move into Number 10 Downing Street ▪ Almost immediately, thousands of British Leyland workers come out on strike ▪ Production of the new Austin *Maxi* slows to a halt ▪ Men pop out to the local off-licence ▪ A can of lager costs 1s/4d ▪ Adverts say, 'I'd lager have a *Skol*' ▪ 57-year-old Home Secretary Jim Callaghan addresses the annual meeting of the County Councils' Association in London and makes no mention of his differences with prime-minister Harold Wilson ▪ 52-year-old Leader of the Opposition Edward Heath addresses a conference of Conservatives in London and tells delegates that the Labour Government is rapidly losing control of the Commons. "Its members do not bother to come up and vote and when they are there they are tearing themselves apart." says Mr. Heath ▪ ***Get Back*** ("... Jojo. Go home") by The Beatles with Billy Preston is still number one in the pop chart ▪ "Shall I tell you about my life? They say I'm a..." ***Man Of The World*** by Fleetwood Mac is number two ▪ ***Road Runner*** by Junior Walker and the All Stars is number twelve ▪ ***Time Is Tight*** by Booker T & The MGs is number fifteen ▪ 27-year-old Brian Jones of the Rolling Stones receives medical treatment in hospital after crashing his motorbike through a shop window ▪ Mods and rockers fight on the seafront at Folkestone ▪ A men's *Terylene* single-breasted suit costs £6/6s/- ▪ A men's *Bri Nylon* shirt (with button-down collar) is 25/- ▪ A can of *Cossack* hairspray is 5s/10d ▪ Lambrettas are advertised as motor scooters with 'Real Poke' ▪ A new *Lambretta SX150* costs £200.

Summer 1969

Barbara Windsor's boobs

Monarch:	Queen Elizabeth II (aged 43)
Prime-minister:	Harold Wilson (aged 53)
Chancellor:	Roy Jenkins (aged 48)
Home Secretary:	James Callaghan (aged 57)
Foreign Secretary:	Michael Stewart (aged 62)
Football Manager:	Alf Ramsey (aged 49)
New car reg. suffix:	'H'

▪ The sun shines ▪ Prime-minister Harold Wilson (a keen pipe smoker) takes a holiday in the Isles of Scilly ▪ Opposition leader Edward Heath (a keen sailor) wins a trophy at the Royal Temple Yacht Club's annual regatta in Ramsgate ▪ Schoolboys drink *Top Deck* shandy and pretend to be drunk ▪ Factories shut down for two weeks as workers go on holiday ▪ "Oh, go on, Dick. The further you're in the nicer it feels" - saucy postcards continue to sell well at seaside resorts ▪ 23-year-old footballer 'super' Georgie Best takes a holiday in Majorca with his actress girlfriend, 18-year-old Susan George ▪ 27-year-old Brian Jones of the Rolling Stones is unable to obtain a work permit for a planned tour of the USA - due to his recent drug convictions ▪ "This is the dawning of the age of…" ***Aquarius*** by 5th Dimension reaches number eleven in the pop chart ▪ "I've gotta go to Piccadilly, got a Piccadilly of a day to do it on" - ***Dick-A-Dum-Dum*** by 37-year-old Des O'Connor peaks at number fourteen ▪ 'Everybody loves Otley … Well, almost everybody' - *Otley* (with 32-year-old Tom Courtenay, 30-year-old Romy Schneider, 42-year-old Leonard Rossiter and 34-year-old James Bolam) is at cinemas ▪ 'Hey, big spender!' - 35-year-old Shirley Maclaine stars in *Sweet Charity* (an arty new musical) featuring fab and groovy dance routines choreographed by Bob Fosse. 25-year-old Suzanne Charny mesmerizes audiences, dancing the 'The Aloof' ▪ 19-year-old model Twiggy appears on the front cover of *Fashion* magazine ▪ Women wear halter-neck tops, cropped trousers and sandals ▪ Men wear fringed suede jackets, bell-bottom jeans and buckle-strap ankle boots with a Cuban heel ▪ "Dizzy, I'm so dizzy my head is spinning. Like a whirlpool it never ends, and it's you girl making it spin" - ***Dizzy*** by 27-year-old Tommy Roe climbs to number one in the pop chart ▪ Brian Jones is sacked from the Rolling Stones. Band members, Mick Jagger, Keith Richards and Charlie Watts inform the 27-year-old that his services are no longer required ▪ *The Liver Birds* is a fab new comedy on BBC One, starring 27-year-old Polly James as Beryl and 28-year-old Pauline Collins as Dawn ▪ A new series of *Public Eye* begins on ITV, with popular fictional Private Investigator Frank Marker (played by 51-year-old Alfred Burke) now out of jail and living in Brighton ▪ "Flash cleans floors fast and no messing"- 59-year-old Molly Weir advertises *Flash* powder ▪ There's a flurry of activity on football's transfer market ▪ First Division Sheffield Wednesday sign 18-year-old midfielder Tommy Craig from Aberdeen for £100,000 ▪ Second Division Aston Villa sign 22-year-old midfielder Bruce Rioch from Luton Town for £100,000 ▪ Second Division Queens Park Rangers sign 26-year-old midfielder Terry Venables from Tottenham Hotspur for £70,000 ▪ 29-year-old centre-half Ian Ure leaves Bertie Mee's Arsenal and joins Manchester Utd for £80,000 ▪ 20-year-old Prince Charles is invested at Caernarfon. The ceremony draws a few boos and hisses from the gathered crowd, as the young Prince's cavalcade passes through the streets ▪ ***Oh, Happy Day*** by Edwin Hawkins Singers reaches number two in the pop chart ▪ ***Snake In The Grass*** by Dave Dee, Dozy, Beaky, Mick and Tich (a group of five friends from Wiltshire) stalls at number twenty-three ▪ 53-year-old Gregory Peck and 37-year-old Anne Heywood star at cinemas in *The Chairman* - a thrilling new spy film ▪ 30-year-old Ann Jones from Birmingham wins the ladies' tennis championship at Wimbledon - after coming from behind to beat 25-year-old Billie Jean King 3-6, 6-3, 6-2 in the final on centre-court ▪ 30-year-old Rod Laver from Australia wins the men's title for the second year running ▪ 25-year-old golfer Tony Jacklin from Scunthorpe wins the British Open at Royal Lytham & St. Annes ▪ Cricketers, 28-year-old Geoffrey Boycott and 31-year-old John Edrich stride out together to open the batting for England against the West Indies at Old Trafford. Boycott scores 128. Edrich makes 58 (before being run out) and England win by ten wickets ▪ 60-year-old Sir Matt Busby stands down as Manchester Utd manager (after twenty-four years in charge) and is succeeded by 31-year-old Wilf McGuinness ▪ "I've lived a life that's full, I've travelled each and every highway. And more, much more than this, I did it..." ***My Way*** by 53-year-old Frank Sinatra reaches number five on the hit parade and stays in the pop charts for more than two years! ▪ "People say I'm the life of the party 'cause I tell a joke or two. Although I might be laughin' loud and hearty, deep inside I'm blue" - ***Tracks Of My Tears*** by Smokey Robinson and the Miracles is number nine ▪ Parents take their children to see matinee films at the local cinema during the summer holiday ▪ 'They'll stop at nothing ... to stop each other!' - 44-year-old Tony Curtis, 58-year-old Terry-Thomas, 31-year-old Peter Cook, 34-year-old Dudley Moore and 32-year-old Susan Hampshire star in *Monte Carlo or Bust!* ▪ Walt Disney's *Herbie the Love Bug* is also now showing ▪ 49-year-old actress Betty Driver from Leicester makes her first appearance as Betty Turpin on ITV's *Coronation Street* ▪ 29-year-old Ian Cullen plays PC Joe Skinner in BBC's popular police drama *Z Cars* ▪ *A Piece of the Sky is Missing*, the third novel from 34-year-old writer David Nobbs, is published ▪ "It is finished. It is finished. IT IS THE MERCY" - 36-year-old sailor Donald Crowhurst makes his final log-book entry before jumping overboard and drowning - after cheating in the Golden Globe round-the-world yacht race ▪ "Standing in the dock at Southampton. Trying to get to Holland or France. The man in the mac' said 'You've gotta go back.' You know, they didn't even give us a chance" - ***The Ballad Of John And Yoko*** by The Beatles is new at number one in the pop chart ▪ "On a cold and grey Chicago mornin', a poor little baby child is born..." ***In The Ghetto*** by 34-year-old Elvis Presley is number two ▪ Actress and singer Judy Garland dies aged 47 in London from an accidental drugs overdose ▪ The 'Space Race' is over ▪ *Apollo 11* (with astronauts: Neil Armstrong, Michael Collins and Edwin 'Buzz' Aldrin) lands successfully on the Moon ▪ Millions of television viewers watch as 38-year-old Armstrong walks on the lunar surface and says, "That's one small step for man, one giant leap for mankind" ▪ In Los Angeles, California, three members of the Manson Family (an evil hippy cult) brutally murder actress Sharon Tate and four other people ▪ The following night, seven members of the Manson Family brutally murder Leno and Rosemary LaBianca, at the couple's home in the Los Feliz district of L.A. ▪ Back in England - around twenty-thousand car workers (from both Ford and British Leyland) are currently laid-off due to industrial action by component suppliers ▪ 'H' reg cars go on sale but, because of recent strikes, there's a shortage in showrooms of Ford, Rover, Austin and Morris models ▪ Footballer 'super' Georgie Best takes delivery of a brand new, bright yellow Lotus *Europa* sports car. Top speed is 120 mph and acceleration time from 0-60 mph is 9 seconds ▪ Aston Martin announces the arrival of a *DB6 MkII* (with power steering fitted as standard). Top speed is 144 mph and acceleration time for 0-60 mph is 7.5 seconds ▪ "Call out the instigators, because there's..." ***Something In The Air*** by Thunderclap Newman (with, lead singer, 24-year-old Speedy Keen) is number one on the hit parade ▪ "Lie-la-lie. Lie-la-la, lie-la, lie-lie, la-la-lie. Lie-la-la-la-la-lie, la-la, la-la-lie" - ***The Boxer*** by Simon and Garfunkle (27-year-old Paul Simon and 27-year-old Art Garfunkle) is number six ▪ "Now, really let's see those chests come out!" - 31-year-old Barbara Windsor (36-24-34) loses her bikini top in *Carry On Camping* ▪ 27-year-old Brian Jones (formerly) of the Rolling Stones is found dead at the bottom of a swimming pool in the grounds of his home at Cotchford Farm, East Sussex ▪ John Timpson and Peter Woods present *Newsroom* on BBC Two television on weekday evenings at 7.30 pm ▪ Nationalists and Loyalists clash in the Battle of the Bogside in Derry ▪ Mods and rockers fight on the beach at Brighton ▪ Adverts for motor scooters claim, 'Vespa... puts you ahead of the crowd' ▪ A new *Vespa 125* costs £149 ▪ The Who appear 'for one night only' on stage at the Pavilion in Bath ▪ The Rolling Stones (with, lead singer, 26-year-old Mick Jagger and, guitarist, 25-year-old Keith Richards) play a free concert in Hyde Park. Jagger dedicates the performance to former band member Brian Jones, who died two days earlier ▪ "I met a gin-soaked, bar-room queen in Memphis. She tried to take me upstairs for a ride. She had to heave me right across her shoulder, 'cause I just can't seem to drink ya off my mind. It's the..." ***Honky Tonk Women*** is a smash hit - the song reaches number one in the pop chart - and stays there for five weeks! ▪ (Like), long haired hippies follow their own inner compasses and gather together at music festivals (man) ▪ 26-year-old Jimi Hendrix plays at Woodstock ▪ 28-year-old Bob Dylan plays the Isle of White ▪ Blodwyn Pig perform a night-time session for 29-year-old Radio One disc jockey John Peel ▪ 42-year-old Alan 'Fluff' Freeman presents *Pick of the Pops* on Sunday afternoons ▪ "All we are saying, is..." ***Give Peace A Chance*** by The Plastic Ono Band is number two in the pop chart ▪ ***My Cherie Amour*** ("... lovely as a summer day") by 19-year-old Stevie Wonder is number four ▪ Bathroom manufacturer Armitage Shanks introduces a trendy new colour called Avocado to its range of water closets, wash-basins and baths ▪ Tens of thousands of people are shocked and controversy ensues when the latest issue of *Oz* magazine is published with a front cover showing two naked men (one black, one white) embracing each other ▪ 59-year-old Mrs. Mary Whitehouse (from rural Worcestershire) is outraged ▪ MPs gather in the chamber at the House of Commons ▪ 48-year-old Chancellor of the Exchequer Roy

Jenkins is questioned over the balance of payments. It's thought by some that the economy is not performing quite as well as the Labour government claims ▪ Thousands of British Leyland car workers are on a go-slow ▪ Construction work continues on the M62 motorway across the Pennines ▪ The impressive new bridge at Scammonden Dam (with a span of 410 feet) is almost complete ▪ 30-year-old racing driver Jackie Stewart wins the British Grand Prix at Silverstone in a pale blue Matra-Ford (number 3) ▪ "You're only supposed to blow the bloody doors off!" - *The Italian Job* (starring 36-year-old Michael Caine and 69-year-old Noel Coward) goes on general release at cinemas. "Get your skates on, mate. Get your skates on, mate" - the cast perform the song ***Get A Bloomin' Move On (The Self Preservation Society)*** ▪ 38-year-old Matt Monro sings ***On Days Like These*** ("... when skies are blue and fields are green, I look around and think about what might have been") ▪ "I cried for you, I cried for you" - ***Saved By The Bell*** by 19-year-old Robin Gibb climbs to number two in the weekly pop chart ▪ "Lie down gal, let me push it up, push it up. Lie down" - ***Wet Dream*** by 24-year-old reggae singer Max Romeo is number ten ▪ *Shoot!* football magazine is launched, with 'League Ladders' free inside. 28-year-old Bobby Moore of West Ham and England is pictured on the front cover of the first edition ▪ 31-year-old Bobby Charlton of Manchester Utd and England is pictured on the front cover of the latest *Goal* magazine ▪ 24-year-old Bobby Moncur scores three goals as Joe Harvey's Newcastle Utd beat Ujpesti Dozsa 6-2 on aggregate to win the Inter Cities Fairs Cup ▪ 22-year-old striker Allan Clarke leaves Leicester City and joins champions Leeds Utd for £165,000. Clarke scores his first goal for Leeds on his league debut in a 3-1 victory over Tottenham Hotspur at Elland Road ▪ 23-year-old 'super' Georgie Best scores for Manchester Utd in a 3-1 win against Sunderland in front of 50,570 at Old Trafford ▪ 53-year-old Labour prime-minister Harold Wilson meets with his 48-year-old Chancellor of the Exchequer

Roy Jenkins. The two men decide to re-structure the country's finances ▪ The International Monetry Fund agrees to lend Britain £417 million, but the arrangement comes with strict conditions which will mean greater economic and financial austerity for everyone ▪ "Who governs Britain? The IMF or the TUC?" - 55-year-old Iain MacLeod (Conservative Shadow Chancellor) is highly critical of Mr. Wilson and Mr. Jenkins and the Labour government as a whole ▪ "In the year 2525, if man is still alive, if woman can survive" - ***In The Year 2525 (Exordium And Terminus)*** by Zager and Evans climbs to the top of the hit parade ▪ Times are changing ▪ Close male friends enjoy an evening at the cinema ▪ *Staircase* - 'a sad gay story', starring 43-year-old Richard Burton and 61-year-old Rex Harrison as two middle-aged hairdressers in London, goes on general release ▪ 30-year-old Patrick Mower, 21-year-old Dennis Waterman and 20-year-old Madeleine Hinde star in the dark and disturbing *The Smashing Bird I Used to Know* ▪ The halfpenny coin is no longer legal tender ▪ 28-year-old Ed 'stewpot' Stewart presents *Junior Choice* on Radio One ▪ "I saw a mouse. (Where?) There on the stair. (Where on the stair?) Right there. A little mouse with clogs on. (Well, I declare) Going clip-clippety-clop on the stair. Oh yeah" - Ronnie Hilton sings ***A Windmill In Old Amsterdam*** ▪ Schoolboys run errands for their mothers ▪ A pint of milk costs 10d ▪ 'Well-to-do' young men zip along English dual-carriageways in open-top sports cars ▪ A new Triumph *TR6* costs £1,333/19s/2d, has a top speed of 120 mph and accelerates from 0-60 mph in 8.2 seconds ▪ A new Triumph *Vitesse Convertible* costs £1,020/12s/6d, has a top speed of 103 mph and accelerates from 0-60 mph in 11.3 seconds ▪ A new MG *Midget* costs £838, has a top speed of 94 mph and can reach 60 mph in 12.9 seconds ▪ The late summer sun beats down ▪ Drivers take a break at the Blue Boar services at Watford Gap - many enjoy a thirst quenching, cool, fizzy drink ▪ Adverts say, '*Coca-Cola* - It's the Real Thing'.

Autumn 1969

Monty Python's Flying Circus

Monarch:	Queen Elizabeth II (aged 43)
Prime-minister:	Harold Wilson (aged 53)
Chancellor:	Roy Jenkins (aged 49)
Home Secretary:	James Callaghan (aged 57)
Foreign Secretary:	Michael Stewart (aged 63)
Football Manager:	Alf Ramsey (aged 49)
New car reg. suffix:	'H'

▪ Leader of the Conservative opposition Edward Heath and Shadow Chancellor Iain MacLeod continue to criticise the Labour government's economic record ▪ 48-year-old Chancellor of the Exchequer Roy Jenkins returns from a meeting in Washington with the IMF and says "This is the moment to press on with our strategy, and not to falter" ▪ "Now he's waving. Coo-eee" - Cartoon couple Joe and Petunia star in public information films on TV ▪ "Evening, all" - 73-year-old Jack Warner stars in a new series of *Dixon of Dock Green* ▪ BBC One begins broadcasting TV programmes in full colour ▪ Five of the franchised commercial television companies (ATV, Granada, Yorkshire, LWT and Thames) also begin colour broadcasts ▪ "Every one that little bit sweeter, because we pick 'em younger" - *Birds Eye Peas* is the first colour advert to be shown ▪ Popular soap-opera *Coronation Street* is transmitted in colour ▪ Jack Walker, Annie Walker, Ray Langton, Emily Nugent, Minnie Caldwell and miserable Ena Sharples are recovering after being involved in a horrific coach crash ▪ 44-year-old Richard Baker reads the news on BBC One ▪ Tensions continue to run high between Loyalist and Nationalist communities in Northern Ireland ▪ Harold Wilson's Labour government sends British troops across the Irish Sea ▪ The Troubles begin ▪ "I see a…" ***Bad Moon Rising*** ("… I see trouble on the way") by Creedence Clearwater Revival tops the hit parade ▪ "She's a natural born woman" - ***Natural Born Bugie*** by Humble Pie (with 19-year-old Peter Frampton and 22-year-old Steve Marriott) is number four ▪ The mornings are cold and frosty ▪ Hippies wear tan brown Afghan coats and smoke grass, man ▪ *Student* magazine (produced by 19-year-old publisher Richard Branson) is on sale for 2s/6d ▪ 22-year-old footballer Bruce Rioch (a recent £100,000 signing from Luton Town) scores a consolation goal for Aston Villa in a 2-1 defeat against Nat Lofthouse's Bolton Wanderers in Division Two ▪ 23-year-old Steve Earle scores five goals as Fulham thrash Halifax Town 0-8 at The Shay in Division Three ▪ "And believe it or not, now there's something groovy and good 'bout whatever we got. And..." ***It's Getting Better*** by 28-year-old Mama Cass climbs to number nine in the pop chart ▪ 43-year-old Queen Elizabeth II attends the film premiere of *Battle of Britain* in London. The movie's 'all star' cast includes: 62-year-old Sir Laurence Olivier (as Air Chief Marshal Sir Hugh Dowding), 36-year-old Michael Caine (as Squadron Leader Canfield) and 30-year-old Susannah York (as Section Officer Maggie Harvey) ▪ 'Unchanged men in a changing land' - *The Wild Bunch*, a gripping 'Western' from 44-year-old director Sam Peckinpah, goes on general release ▪ ***Too Busy Thinking 'Bout My Baby*** ("... Oh, I ain't got time for nothin' else") by 30-year-old Marvin Gaye is number five in the pop chart ▪ ***Don't Forget To Remember*** ("... me, and the love that used to be. I still remember you. I love you") by The Bee Gees is number two ▪ Harry Catterick's Everton football team leads the way in Division One - 24-year-old Alan Ball and 21-year-old Jimmy Husband score the goals as 'The Toffees' beat West Ham Utd 2-0 at Goodison Park ▪ 18-year-old Kevin Keegan scores twice for Scunthorpe Utd - as the 'The Iron' lose 3-2 to York City in Division Four ▪ Pop music fans queue outside record shops on Friday the twenty-sixth of September ▪ The new Beatles' LP *Abbey Road* (with its front cover depicting the four Beatles walking on a zebra crossing) sells out fast - the record enters the album chart at number one and stays there for eleven weeks!

Come Together ("... right now, over me") is the opening track on side one. ***Here Comes The Sun*** ("... and I say, it's all right") is the opening track on side two ▪ 31-year-old Arthur Scargill of the Yorkshire NUM calls for miners to go on strike ▪ Industrial action spreads to pits and collieries in other regions of the UK - the strike lasts for two weeks ▪ Walk-outs and go-slows continue at British Leyland factories ▪ Leyland's chairman Sir Donald Stokes warns that industrial action will kill the British car industry - and allow foreign car manufacturers to steal market share ▪ A British built Austin *1100 Super de Luxe* costs £792 including purchase tax ▪ An Italian Fiat *128* costs £825 including purchase tax ▪ A Japanese Datsun *1000 de Luxe* costs £766 including purchase tax ▪ A Czechoslovakian Skoda *1100MB de Luxe* costs £698 including purchase tax ▪ For a second year running the clocks do not get 'put back', as the government assesses the benefits of moving to a new 'British Standard Time' ▪ Children wear orange reflective armbands on their way to school - as the mornings stay darker for longer ▪ 11-year-old schoolboy Lenny Henry from Dudley in Worcestershire tells jokes and makes his friends laugh ▪ 44-year-old Margaret Thatcher MP moves to Education in Edward Heath's Conservative shadow Cabinet ▪ "Je t'aime, je t'aime. Oh, oui, je t'aime!" - ***Je T'Aime... Moi Non Plus*** by Jane Birkin and Serge Gainsbourg spends a week at number one in the pop chart ▪ 34-year-old writer David Nobbs pens humorous scripts and one-line gags for the hit ITV show *Sez Les* - starring 38-year-old comedian Les Dawson ▪ A third series of *Dad's Army* begins on BBC One ▪ 'Poking their diag'noses' into other peoples business!' - *Carry On Again Doctor* is at cinemas, and features 32-year-old Barbara Windsor (36-24-34) in a tiny pink heart shaped bikini ▪ "What do you get when you fall in love? A guy with a pin to burst your bubble" - ***I'll Never Fall In Love Again*** by 27-year-old Bobbie Gentry is new at number one in the pop chart ▪ "Now, I don't blame him 'cause he run and hid, but the meanest thing that he ever did was before he left, he went and named me Sue" - ***A Boy Named Sue*** by 37-year-old Johnny Cash is number four ▪ 31-year-old Terry Wogan presents the afternoon show on Radio One ▪ "And now for something completely different!" - Graham Chapman, John Cleese, Eric Idle, Terry Jones and 26-year-old Michael Palin appear in a new TV comedy called *Monty Python's Flying Circus* ▪ School children watch *The Flaxton Boys*, a gripping drama set in Yorkshire in the year 1854, with 15-year-old Peter Firth as Archie Weekes and 16-year-old David Smith as Jonathan Flaxton ▪ 40-year-old racing driver Graham Hill breaks both legs in a Formula One car crash in the United States ▪ 30-year-old Jackie Stewart wins at Monza in his blue Matra-Ford (number 20) and is crowned world motor racing champion, with three races still to go ▪ ***Sugar Sugar*** ("... you are my candy girl, and you got me wanting you") by The Archies climbs to number one - and stays at the top of the chart for eight weeks! ▪ "Baby..." ***I'm Gonna Make You Mine*** by 26-year-old Lou Christie is number two ▪ 41,826 football spectators turn out at the Baseball Ground to watch a league match between Brian Clough's Derby County and Bill Nicholson's Tottenham Hotspur. Derby win 5-0 with 28-year-old Alan Durban scoring twice ▪ 58,579 spectators turn out at Old Trafford to see Wilf McGuinness' Manchester Utd thrash Ron Greenwood's West Ham Utd 5-2 with 'super' Georgie Best scoring twice and with 31-year-old Bobby Charlton also on the score-sheet ▪ 25-year-old Graham Taylor plays full-back for Lincoln City in Division Four ▪ 30-year-old Big Ron Atkinson plays wing-half for Oxford Utd in Division Two ▪ ***He Ain't Heavy He's My Brother*** by The Hollies is number three in the pop chart ▪ "Ground Control to Major Tom. Take your protein pills and put your helmet on" - ***Space Oddity*** by 22-year-old David Bowie is number five ▪ 26-year-old Tony Blackburn presents the breakfast show on Radio One every weekday from 7 a.m ▪ 44-year-old disc jockey Pete Murray presents *Pete Murray's Open House* (which is broadcast on both Radio One and Radio Two) every weekday at 9 a.m ▪ The double A sided instrumental ***Return Of Django / Dollar In The Teeth*** by The Upsetters is number five in the pop chart ▪ "Get up, get up in the first race, and them pull up the pace"- ***Long Shot Kick De Bucket*** by The Pioneers is number twenty-one ▪ A new seven sided fifty-pence coin is introduced as a replacement for the ten shilling note. (Money will be decimalised in just over a year) ▪ 41-year-old Michael Barratt presents a new tea-time TV show called *Nationwide* ▪ 47-year-old Raymond Baxter presents *Tomorrow's World* ▪ American spacecraft *Apollo 12* (with astronauts: Charles 'Pete' Conrad, Richard Gordon and Alan Bean) lands on the Moon and stays there for twenty-four hours. Millions of television viewers watch as 39-year-old (five-foot-six) Pete Conrad walks on the lunar surface and says, "Whoop-ie! Man. That may have been a small one for Neil, but that was a long one for me" ▪ Back in England - Harold Wilson's Labour government faces more criticism after agreeing to the early prison release of two Soviet spies: Lona Cohen and her husband, Morris. The two are released after serving just eight years of their twenty-plus year sentences in exchange for the release of 31-year-old Gerald Brooke - a British school teacher being held captive in the Soviet Union ▪ Popular fictional detective Hercule Poirot features in *Hallowe'en Party* - the latest 'whodunit' novel from 79-year-old crime-writer Agatha Christie ▪ Children watch TV at home ▪ "There are a lot of people in a town. Do you live in a town? Mary, Mungo and Midge live in this town" - *Mary, Mungo and Midge* is a wonderful new programme ▪ Freda the tortoise (from BBC's *Blue Peter*) is prepared for her winter hibernation ▪ 32-year-old footballer Bobby Charlton appears on ITV's *This Is Your Life* ▪ 17-year-old footballer Steve Perryman makes his debut for Tottenham Hotspur in a 0-1 home defeat to Sunderland ▪ 21-year-old Trevor Brooking opens the scoring for West Ham Utd, before 20-year-old Mick Channon equalizes for Southampton, in a 1-1 draw at The Dell ▪ 22-year-old Peter Lorimer bags a hat-trick as reigning champions Leeds Utd thrash Nottingham Forest 6-1 ▪ In Division Two, 19-year-old Tony Currie scores a goal for Sheffield Utd in a 4-0 victory over Blackburn Rovers ▪ 25-year-old Rodney Marsh scores for Queens Park Rangers in a 1-1 draw against Aston Villa ▪ "I can't help about the shape I'm in. I can't sing, I ain't pretty and my legs are thin" - ***Oh Well*** by Fleetwood Mac is number two in the pop chart ▪ ***Lay Lady Lay*** ("... Lay across my big brass bed") by 28-year-old Bob Dylan reaches number five ▪ Long, grey army overcoats (from *Millets*) are de rigueur for earnest young 'cats' with a serious outlook on life ▪ *The Sun* newspaper changes from a broadsheet to a tabloid ▪ 29-year-old John Lennon returns his MBE to the Queen - as a protest against Britain's support for the war in Vietnam ▪ Private Godfrey (played by 73-year-old Arnold Ridley) is ostracised by the rest of Captain Mainwaring's platoon in *Dad's Army* when it comes to light that Godfrey was a conscientious objector during the First World War ▪ 'What are you afraid of Private Brigg - the jungle or the tarts?' - 25-year-old Hywel Bennett plays the role of Private Brigg in *Virgin Soldiers* - now on general release at cinemas across the country ▪ "In the shower lad!" - *Kes* (a film by Ken Loach), starring 16-year-old David Bradley as bullied schoolboy Billy Casper, is shown at the London Film Festival ▪ Controversial MP Enoch Powell shows celebrity disc-jockey Jimmy Savile around the Houses of Parliament ▪ ***Sugar Sugar*** by The Archies remains at number one in the pop chart ▪ "Places I dream about, I will be getting out then I can follow the sun" - ***(Call Me) Number One*** by The Tremeloes is new at number two ▪ Young women go shopping ▪ *New Look* fashion store opens in Taunton ▪ Young men go to the pub ▪ A pint of Watney's *Red Barrel* is 2s/4d ▪ A pack of twenty *Senior Service* cigarettes costs 3s/9d ▪ Adverts declare, 'Golden Wonder Peanuts - Jungle Fresh!'

Christmas 1969

Morecambe & Wise TV Christmas special

Monarch:	Queen Elizabeth II (aged 43)
Prime-minister:	Harold Wilson (aged 53)
Chancellor:	Roy Jenkins (aged 49)
Home Secretary:	James Callaghan (aged 57)
Foreign Secretary:	Michael Stewart (aged 63)
Football Manager:	Alf Ramsey (aged 49)
New car reg. suffix:	'H'

▪ The nation prepares itself for Christmas ▪ The *TV Times* costs 1s/6d, has a fourteen day schedule showing ITV television programmes and features 37-year-old Des O'Connor (in a red Santa hat and white beard) on the front cover ▪ The *Radio Times* costs 1s/6d, has a fourteen day schedule showing BBC programmes and features an artful yule-tide collage (which includes images of Tommy Steele, Jimmy Tarbuck, Elvis Presley, Rolf Harris, three of the seven dwarfs, a wild stag, Eric Morcambe, Ernie Wise and 43-year-old Jimmy Savile) on the front cover ▪ There's thick fog across much of the country ▪ Three people are killed and dozens more injured in multiple crashes on the M6 motorway ▪ 53-year-old Labour prime-minister Harold Wilson chairs a Cabinet meeting at Number 10 Downing Street, with 59-year-old Barbara Castle (Secretary of State for Employment and Productivity) and 39-year-old Shirley Williams (Minister of State for Home Affairs) in attendance ▪ 44-year-old Conservative MP (and Shadow Education Secretary) Margaret Thatcher tells her Finchley constituents, "No woman in my time will be prime-minister or foreign secretary - not the top jobs. Anyway, I wouldn't want to be prime-minister" ▪ "Something in the way she moves, attracts me like no other lover" - The double A sided single ***Something / Come Together*** by The Beatles moves down the hit parade to number eight ▪ 38-year-old Bert Foord presents the weather forecast on BBC One ▪ Dense fog gives way to brisk winds and sharp, clear skies ▪ Mao 'flu sweeps the South East of England, with tens of thousands of people suffering headaches, pain behind the eyes and violent coughing ▪ 'It's groovy, baby' - 42-year-old Roger Moore and 25-year-old Claudie Lange star at cinemas in *Crossplot* - a film with a story based around a modelling agency in Swinging London ▪ 29-year-old Robin Phillips plays the title role in *David Copperfield.* The all-star supporting cast includes: 46-year-old Richard Attenborough, 32-year-old Susan Hampshire, 45-year-old Ron Moody, 62-year-old Sir Laurence Olivier, 61-year-old Michael Redgrave and 66-year-old Sir Ralph Richardson ▪ "You've painted up your lips and rolled and curled your tinted hair. Ruby, are you contemplating going out somewhere?" - ***Ruby Don't Take Your Love To Town*** by 31-year-old Kenny Rogers and the First Edition climbs to number two in the pop chart and stays there for six weeks ▪ ***Sugar Sugar*** ("… you are my candy girl, and you got me wanting you") by The Archies remains at number one for one more week before being replaced by ***Two Little Boys*** by 39-year-old Rolf Harris ▪ Children are excited - Christmas is coming! ▪ Schoolboys crave a die-cast model of the *Batmobile* (manufactured by *Corgi Toys*) for 13s/6d ▪ Schoolgirls crave a *Sindy* doll (manufactured by *Pedigree*) for 25s/3d ▪ Housewives crave a seasonal tipple ▪ A bottle of *Harvey's Bristol Cream* sherry is 24s/11d ▪ A bottle of *Warnink's* advocaat is 32s/- ▪ The Smith family from Chigwell hires a new-fangled colour TV set from *Radio Rentals* ▪ Two more commercial television companies begin broadcasting in full colour and viewers in the Southern TV region and in Scotland can now watch their favourite programmes in colour ▪ "We are the Diddymen, itsy-bitsy Diddymen" - *Ken Dodd and the Diddymen* is hugely popular with younger viewers ▪ Teenagers enjoy listening to music on portable HMV record players ▪ *Abbey Road* by The Beatles is top of the album chart ▪ Hallmark Records release *The Best of Top of the*

Pops "69" - a budget priced, cover-version pop compilation LP with pretty girls on the sleeve ▪ ***Wonderful World Beautiful People*** ("... you and your girl, things could be pretty") by 25-year-old Jimmy Cliff is number six in the pop chart ▪ ***The Liquidator*** by The Harry J Allstars is number nine ▪ In an act of frustration, 23-year-old footballer 'super' Georgie Best knocks the ball from the hands of referee Jack Taylor after a League Cup semi-final defeat to Manchester City. Best will now face FA disciplinary action for his petulance ▪ 36-year-old Frank Bough introduces *Grandstand* on BBC One on Saturday afternoons ▪ 42-year-old Sam Leitch previews the football ▪ 25-year-old Franny Lee (of Manchester City) misses a penalty and 34-year-old Jack Charlton (of Leeds Utd) heads a goal from his brother's corner kick, as Sir Alf Ramsey's England team (Bonetti, Reaney, E Hughes, Mullery, J Charlton, Moore, F Lee, Bell, Astle, R Charlton, Ball and substitute, Peters) beats Portugal 1-0 on a rain sodden Wembley pitch ▪ In Division One, 19-year-old Alan Whittle scores for top-of-the-table Everton in a 0-1 victory over West Ham Utd at Upton Park ▪ 31-year-old Wimbledon tennis champion Ann Jones is voted BBC's 'Sports Personality of the Year' ▪ 33-year-old Gordon Honeycombe reads the news for ITN ▪ The Troubles prevail in Northern Ireland ▪ Sectarian violence is commonplace as skirmishes continue between Loyalists, Nationalists and the Royal Ulster Constabulary ▪ The Provisional Irish Republican Army (a splinter group of the IRA) is formed ▪ Back in England - people enjoy an evening at the cinema ▪ 30-year-old George Lazenby is the new James Bond (aka 007) in *On Her Majesty's Secret Service*. 31-year-old Diana Rigg captures Bond's heart and becomes his screen wife - but with tragic consequences. 45-year-old Telly Savalas plays master criminal Ernst Stavro Blofeld. 61-year-old Bernard Lee is M. 55-year-old Desmond Llewelyn is Q. 42-year-old Lois Maxwell is Miss Moneypenny ▪ 35-year-old Alan Bates and

31-year-old Oliver Reed wrestle naked in front of the fire in *Women In Love* ▪ "If you're looking for trouble, I'll accommodate ya" - 62-year-old John Wayne stars in *True Grit* ▪ The abolition of the death penalty is made permanent by 57-year-old Home Secretary Jim Callaghan ▪ "I have been a rover, I have walked alone. Hiked a hundred highways, never found a home" - ***Love's Been Good To Me*** by 54-year-old Frank Sinatra from New Jersey is number eight on the hit parade ▪ ***Without Love (There Is Nothing)*** by 29-year-old Tom Jones from Pontypridd is number ten ▪ A fire at the Rose and Crown in Saffron Walden kills eleven people ▪ The outbreak of Mao 'flu spreads from the South East to other areas of the country. People take to their beds with extra blankets and hot water bottles ▪ An eighteen mile stretch of dual carriageway opens between Horwich and Preston in Lancashire ▪ 'Well off' young men drive their cars, hard and fast, on the country's ever-expanding network of motorways ▪ A brand new 'H' reg Ford *Escort Twin Cam* costs £1,242, has a 1600cc engine (manufactured by Lotus), a top speed of 113 mph and accelerates from 0-60 mph in 9.9 seconds ▪ The latest *Mini 1275GT* costs £834, has a redesigned front end and 'go-fast' stripes, a top speed of 91 mph and accelerates from 0-60 mph in 14.5 seconds ▪ A Singer *Chamois Sport* costs £779, has twin headlights, a top speed of 90 mph and accelerates from 0-60 mph in 16.3 seconds ▪ 'Here we go! Morning ray-dee-oh!' - 26-year-old Tony Blackburn presents the breakfast show on Radio One ▪ ***Two Little Boys*** ("... had two little toys. Each had a wooden horse") by 39-year-old Rolf Harris from Australia stays at the top of the pop chart for six weeks ▪ "The world is just a great big onion" - ***The Onion Song*** by 30-year-old Marvin Gaye and 24-year-old Tammi Terrell reaches number nine ▪ ***Green River*** by Creedence Clearwater Revival peaks at number nineteen ▪ Schoolboys read comics ▪ The Christmas edition of *Whizzer and Chips* (with 'Sid's Snake' and 'Me and My Shadow') is on sale at newsagents for 6d ▪ 53-year-old prime-minister Harold Wilson and 49-year-old Chancellor of the Exchequer Roy Jenkins are relieved to see significant improvement in Britain's economy ▪ The balance of payments has moved into a surplus of £100 million - it's the first time in ten years that the value of exports has been greater than the value of imports ▪ More than 300,000 men are employed in the coal industry - many working long, hard shifts in dangerous conditions. 156 million tonnes of coal have been produced in 1969 - that's 54 million tonnes fewer than ten years ago ▪ Working-class families gather around black and white television sets ▪ Affluent, middle-class families gather around colour TV sets ▪ Just under 100,000 colour TV licenses have been issued this year, compared to over 15 million black and white licenses ▪ Morecambe & Wise feature in their first ever Christmas Day TV 'special' - Frankie Vaughan, Nina, Sacha Distel and 42-year-old Fenella Fielding are the guest stars ▪ 20-year-old model Twiggy appears on ITV's *This Is Your Life* ▪ "All my sorrow, sad tomorrow. Take me back to my old home" - ***Reflections Of My Life*** by The Marmalade climbs to number three in the pop chart ▪ 44-year-old Pete Murray and 48-year-old Jimmy Young spin records and chat to their devoted listeners on Radio One on weekday mornings ▪ 11-year-old Simon Mayo from Southgate in Middlesex dreams of one day becoming a famous DJ ▪ 18-year-old footballer Steve Perryman scores his first league goal for Tottenham Hotspur in a 2-0 victory over Crystal Palace ▪ 23-year-old 'super' Georgie Best plays for Manchester Utd on Boxing Day (in front of 52,732 spectators at Old Trafford) in a 0-0 draw against Wolverhampton Wanderers in Division One ▪ 18-year-old Kevin Keegan plays for Scunthorpe Utd (in front of 7,796 spectators at London Road) in a 2-2 draw against Peterborough Utd in Division Four ▪ Schoolboys update their football 'League Ladders' each week ▪ Just one point separates Harry Catterick's Everton (with

West, Labone, Kendall, Ball, Morrissey and Royle) from Don Revie's hard-tackling Leeds Utd (with Sprake, Charlton, Bremner, Giles, Lorimer and Clarke) at the top of Division One ▪ 22-year-old Peter 'Ossie' Osgood scores four goals as third placed Chelsea thrash Crystal Palace 1-5 at Selhurst Park ▪ ***Yester-Me, Yester-You, Yesterday*** by 19-year-old Stevie Wonder is number two in the pop chart ▪ "Take a pinch of white man, wrap it up in black skin, add a touch of blue blood, and a little bitty bit of Red Indian boy" - ***Melting Pot*** by Blue Mink is number three ▪ Motoring technology moves on apace ▪ More and more cars are being fitted with an electronically heated rear window ▪ Middle-class men visit car showrooms ▪ A fabulous new Saab *99* has a top speed of 102 mph and costs £1,295 from the Gunner & Allen dealership at Lee-on-Solent ▪ A wonderful new Volvo *144* has a top speed of 88 mph and costs £1,515 from Swanswell Garage in Coventry ▪ Working-class men stand together on football terraces and cheer on their local team ▪ 19-year-old centre-forward Malcolm Macdonald bags a hat-trick as Luton Town thrash Bradford City 5-0 in front of 11,857 spectators at Kenilworth Road in Division Three ▪ 32-year-old Bobby Charlton is on the score-sheet as Manchester Utd beat Liverpool 1-4 in front of 47,682 spectators at Anfield in Division One ▪ Bill Shankly sells 31-year-old striker Roger Hunt to Bolton Wanderers for £30,000 ▪ "I wish to complain about this parrot what I purchased not half an hour ago from this very boutique" - 30-year-old John Cleese and 26-year-old Michael Palin perform the 'dead parrot sketch' on *Monty Python's Flying Circus* ▪ "This is the planet Earth. Our planet. It is a small planet, wrapped in clouds" - The *Clangers* is new on TV for children ▪ Families listen to music on Ferguson *Solid State* radiograms ▪ "We can't go on together, with..." ***Suspicious Minds*** by 34-year-old Elvis Presley climbs to number two in the pop chart ▪ "I've got to leave old Durham Town, and that leaving's gonna get me down"

- ***Durham Town (The Leavin')*** by 33-year-old Roger Whittaker is number twelve ▪ The Kinks play gigs in Canada ▪ The Rolling Stones play to three hundred-thousand people in California - with Hells Angels providing security around the stage ▪ 18-year-old Meredith Hunter is stabbed and killed ▪ Back in England - The Who play non-stop, two-hour concerts at Liverpool (Empire), London (Coliseum) and Newcastle-upon-Tyne (City Hall) ▪ Construction work is nearing completion on the new Strensham to Tewkesbury section of the M5 motorway ▪ The weather turns cold and frosty ▪ Families huddle together in small living rooms - watching TV ▪ *The Rolf Harris Show* - starring 39-year-old Rolf and featuring dance troupe The Young Generation (which includes 23-year-old Lesley Judd) is enjoyed by millions ▪ 43-year-old Jimmy Savile introduces *Pop Goes The 60s* - a look back at the music of the last decade. The programme features music from: The Bachelors, Kenny Ball and his Jazzmen, The Beatles, Cilla Black, Adam Faith, The Hollies, Horst Jankowski, The Kinks, Lulu, Cliff Richard, The Rolling Stones, The Shadows, Helen Shapiro, Sandie Shaw, Dusty Springfield, The Tremeloes and The Who ▪ 53-year-old Labour prime-minister Harold Wilson sits in an armchair, studying official papers and smoking his pipe ▪ At midnight on the thirty-first of December, crowds of people in clubs and pubs all across the country celebrate the new year - and the dawning of the 1970s ▪ Millions of men enjoy a beer and a smoke ▪ A pint of bitter is 2s/2d ▪ A pack of five Castella cigars is 9s/8d ▪ Adverts say, 'Castella. The man-sized cigar for the man who likes his pint.'

-- o --

Books by the same author:

- LIFE IN ENGLAND non-stop through the 1940s (ISBN 978-1-840-41035-8)
- LIFE IN ENGLAND non-stop through the 1950s (ISBN 978-1-840-41036-5)
- LIFE IN ENGLAND non-stop through the 1970s (ISBN 978-1-840-41038-9)
- LIFE IN ENGLAND non-stop through the 1980s (ISBN 978-1-840-41039-6)

Coming soon:

- LIFE IN ENGLAND non-stop through the 1990s (ISBN 978-1-840-41040-2)

Printed in Great Britain
by Amazon

50617298R00162